T0305369

PHYSICS OF FINANCE

OTHER TITLES IN THE WILEY FINANCE SERIES

PHYSICS OF FINANCE

Gauge modelling in non-equilibrium pricing

KIRILL ILINSKI

JOHN WILEY & SONS, LTD

Chichester • New York • Weinheim • Brisbane • Singapore • Toronto

Other Wiley Editorial Offices

John Wiley & Sons, Inc., 605 Third Avenue,
New York, NY 10158-0012, USA

WILEY-VCH Verlag GmbH, Pappelallee 3,
D-69469 Weinheim, Germany

Jacaranda Wiley Ltd, 33 Park Road, Milton,
Queensland 4064, Australia

John Wiley & Sons (Asia) Pte Ltd, 2 Clementi Loop #02-01,
Jin Xing Distripark, Singapore 129809

John Wiley & Sons (Canada) Ltd, 22 Worcester Road,
Rexdale, Ontario M9W 1Ll, Canada

Library of Congress Cataloging-in-Publication Data

Ilinski, Kirill.
    Physics of finance : gauge modelling in non-equilibrium pricing / Kirill Ilinski.
        p. cm. — (Wiley frontiers in finance)
    Includes bibliographical references and index.
    ISBN 0-471-87738-7 (cloth : alk. paper)
        1. Finance–Mathematical models. 2. Stocks—Prices—Mathematical models. 3. Gauge invariance. 4. Fiber bundles (Mathematics). 5. Quantum theory. 6. Mathematical physics. 7. Equilibrium (Economics). 8. Paradigms (Social sciences). I. Title. II. Series.
HG220.5.I45 2000
332.63'222—dc21
        00-043548

British Library Cataloguing in Publication Data

A catalogue record for this book is available from the British Library

ISBN 0-471-87738-7

Typeset in 10/12pt Times by Techset Composition Ltd, Salisbury, Wiltshire.
Printed and bound by CPI Antony Rowe, Eastbourne
This book is printed on acid-free paper responsibly manufactured from sustainable forestation, for which at least two trees are planted for each one used for paper production.

To my parents

Contents

Preface

THIS book is based on a very appealing observation that the underlying symmetry of financial markets and fundamental theories in physics, namely the gauge symmetry, is the same. This opens the way to using some well-developed physical and geometrical methods in the theory of financial markets and, in particular, to attack the non-equilibrium market dynamics issue. The observation is so simple and unexpected that the usual first reaction is a disbelief. Give it a try. Even if it sounds crazy. One friend of mine, a physicist, after reading the manuscript said that this is science fiction. It is all right with me: any book on mathematical finance is science fiction anyway.

This book is about some new ways to look at old problems, namely non-equilibrium aspects of asset pricing. One might think that the dynamics is not, in fact, that important. Indeed, most of the time, equilibrium and non-equilibrium models give almost the same results, and superficially it is not obvious why one has to worry about additional dynamical complications. The point is that there are periods when the deviations from the equilibrium models are significant and fateful. The large market events are not as uncommon as we would like to think (see Chapter 9 for a sketch), and if they come, they can wipe a player out just because of inappropriate modelling. If you want to learn how to think about the modelling in such cases, this book is for you. It does not matter whether you are an academic, a quant, or a trader – in every case, there will be something you can get from the book: how to construct models, how to criticize, or simply to ignore them. You will learn about the limitations of standard equilibrium pricing models and ways to overcome them. You will read about virtual arbitrage from theoretical and empirical point of views – a subject that, as far as I know, has never seriously been addressed in textbooks. You will see how ignorance about these issues can bring losses of billions and how knowledge can improve your profitability and risk-awareness. And, as a byproduct, you will learn methods that are particularly suitable for dynamical models but can be equally productive used in the equilibrium framework.

However, as the reader already appreciates, this book is not about how to make money. There are a huge number of books that teach how to buy low and sell high. I suppose they do not need my help. In every place where, I think, it is possible to construct a concrete winning trading strategy, I carefully avoid the discussion. Your money is your business. I am talking about principles and models, but it is up to you to work out details for yourself. At the end of the day, if you trade, you are paid for it!

Nor will this book help the reader to sell his/her theoretical physics background in the next interview in the City. If this is your goal, then it is better to read Nasim Taleb's *Dynamical Hedging*[1] and brush up your C++. You will not find here the Greeks for two-barrier options,

P&L diagrams, or other undoubtedly useful stuff, while the differential geometry will not do the trick (at least not yet).

It was very difficult to decide the level of technicality. Shall I explain differential geometry, functional integrals? How many formulae does one need per page to be frightened into respect? Any author knows that whatever level is chosen, it will be wrong for most readers – too easy or too difficult. That is why the level is very inhomogeneous across this book. It is written in such a way that anyone can go through and get a more or less accurate impression of what is going on. Every chapter starts with an introduction explaining what the chapter is about, its objectives, and methods. Then gradually the exposition becomes more and more mathematically demanding. If, at some point, you are fed up with the maths and details, just skip the rest of that section, or even the chapter. Reading like this, you can scan the book in one or two evenings and then return to places that interest you most (I hope there will be some).

Acknowledgements

I want to thank my wife Alexandra for constant friendly support and collaboration, as well as many painful discussions of the text, which nearly ruined our happy family life. I am indebted to David Wilson (at that time at John Wiley & Sons), who first persuaded me to write this book and then was very supportive and patient with me during the process. I am grateful to my editor Samantha Whittaker and all the people at Wiley who made the whole thing possible. I cannot even express how grateful I am to all the postgraduate students in the theoretical physics group at Birmingham University who helped me with the manuscript – I can only imagine how annoying I was sometimes. Supportive remarks and comments of Nasir Afaf, Felipe Aparicio Acosta, Emanuel Derman, Ivar Ekeland, John Juer, Sergey Kiselev, Ely Klepfish, Rodney Morgan, and Michael Theobald were very important to me. My special thanks are due to Gleb Kalinin, who has been my friend and collaborator for many years. The material of some chapters simply would not appear without him and his critical mind. I cannot mention here all the people who have influenced my views on both economic theory and trading: even if you do not see your name, please be sure I remember and I am grateful to all of you.

KIRILL ILINSKI
Birmingham

---

[1]N. Taleb (1999), *Dynamical Hedging*. New York: Wiley.

Introduction

'Fate always wins. Most of the gods throw dice but Fate plays chess … '

Terry Pratchett, *Interesting Times*

T HIS preliminary chapter explains what this book is about and why the reader will find it useful to read it. We start with a comparison of equilibrium and dynamical market models and describe the conflict between them, which has a hundred years' history. A historical review is given in Section 1 to make it easier for non-financial readers to get a feeling for the subject. We then describe some particular dynamical features of financial markets that it would be desirable to include in the picture, together with ways to incorporate these features into market models. In the final section of this chapter (as with later chapters), contents of the chapter are briefly summarized.

1   DYNAMICS VERSUS EQUILIBRIUM

Looking back on the development of the theory of the financial market during the last hundred years, one finds a permanent struggle between two polar views on market behaviour, which are more or less defined by an answer to the following principal question: 'Can the market actually be predicted?' For any market participant, the answer to this question defines her investment strategy and, as a result, her income. If the market is forecastable, then it is worthwhile spending time and money to analyse the price history and the fundamentals. If it is not, then spreading the risk across a group of stocks and following the buy-and-hold strategy would be the best approach. It is not surprising that both schools have their own champions and opponents.

Clearly, the opinion that the market is predictable is much more appealing. This is not just because it would help to make money – at least for some limited period of time before knowledge changes the market – but even more because of the common belief that eventually anything can be understood, explained, and then predicted. It may well take some time, but it is possible in principle: at the end of the day, the financial market is not as complicated as the universe! There is a subtle difference between 'to be predicted' and 'to be explained', but people do not usually pay much attention to this. At the same time, the belief in the general importance of human cognitive functions has deep roots in Western intellectual culture, and has allowed the successful evolution of exact sciences. If the exact sciences flourished on this philosophical ground, then why cannot the social sciences, and economics and finance in particular, do the same?

The boom in the US stock market at the beginning of the 20th century made investment in stocks a profitable and apparently easy way of making money. This led a growing demand for market information, analysis, and, clearly, predictions. Analysing the previous price history, the most accessible market information, became one of the popular approaches to market predictions. Although some simple empirical observations had been known before, such as patterns for points and figures charting, real charting[1] – charting as a science – started here with the Dow theory, which is now commonly recognized as an ancestor of most principles of modern technical analysis, the theory of predicting future prices by analysing the previous price history. It was originated by Charles Dow, one of the founders of Dow, Jones & Co., and the first Editor of *The Wall Street Journal*, in a series of editorial articles published between 1900 and 1902 and developed later by William Peter Hamilton, who took over as Editor in 1903. Originally the Dow theory was not created to forecast stock prices but to quantify general business conditions using stock market trends. At that time, it was not even called 'The Dow theory', the name that was given after Dow's death in 1902. However, almost immediately, it was realized that the principles of the Dow theory can actually be used to predict prices rather than to describe something else.

Let us have a closer look at the main aspects of the Dow theory. First of all, Dow was probably the first to emphasize the importance of price charting. Believing in fundamental analysis for stocks, Dow wanted, however, to characterize in a visual form general market behaviour. To accomplish this task, he used two market averages, now known as the Dow Jones Averages, which were introduced in 1897. The first Dow assumption was that the Averages discount everything, i.e. reflect everything known by all market participants, and hence, give a general picture of the market. Charting the Averages led to the next advance in the theory – an introduction of market trends, or 'tides' as Dow called them. Dow himself distinguished three types of trends: the Primary trends, main trends of the market, which can be bullish (rising) or bearish (falling); the Secondary trends, or corrections to the Primary trends; and short-lived Minor trends, which are subject to manipulations and are unimportant (Fig. 1.1). The Primary trends get the most attention from market participants, since they feature an overall state and last for more than a year.

To identify the trends, it was essential to use both of the Dow Jones Averages and to wait until both confirmed the trend. The principle of mutual confirmation of indicators is still alive in technical analysis. Further confirmation comes from trading volume. Although the Dow theory focuses on the price action, the volume was considered as an important ingredient of the analysis to clarify uncertain situations. The main observation was that the volume grows in the direction of the Primary trend. For example, if the Primary trend is bullish, the volume increases when the market rises and decreases when price falls. Eventually, technical analysis invented many different volume indicators, but the original observation of the Dow theory is still a basis for all of them. Later, the theory was enriched already by Hamilton with notions of technical support and resistance. These are levels on price charts that 'support' the price movements or, correspondingly, 'resist' them. Together with the concept of trends, the support and resistance are the three central points of technical analysis, which were introduced almost a hundred years ago with the Dow theory, and are still widely used today. What is important for us here is to point out that the Dow theory began the view that market dynamics are

---

[1] Technical analysts believe that drawing price charts, i.e. price charting, can help in the prediction of future price movements.

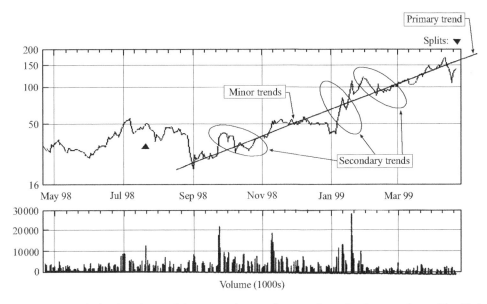

Figure 1.1 Typical price zigzag. Primary trend, secondary trends, and minor trends are identified. Trading volume increases for market advances and decreases during corrections.

reflected in price charts and can be analysed by studying them. The insights obtained during this study can be used later to forecast future market prices.

The Dow theory had a happy life. It was noticed and recognized in its time. Public investors used and still use it. At almost the same time, the French mathematician Louis Bachelier suggested a theory of market behaviour that hosted a very different set of ideas and had a very different life too.

In 1900, Bachelier submitted his dissertation 'The Theory of Speculation' for his degree in Doctor of Mathematical Sciences at the Sorbonne. The class was not impressive, and led to many years of searching for an academic position. Even Henri Poincaré, Bachelier's supervisor, expressed displeasure, saying that 'the topic is somewhat remote from those our candidates are in the habit of treating'. It is clear that in those days, in contrast to what we have now, the subject of the financial market as a complex system was less than unpopular in faculties of the exact sciences. For more than fifty years, Bachelier's work was forgotten, and was discovered only when the mainstream of academic economic thought came to similar conclusions.

What was so arguable about the dissertation except for its unusual subject? The central point of Bachelier's work was a statement that the fluctuations of the stock market are unpredictable and the stock market itself should be considered in terms of probabilities. The probabilistic description alone does not rule out a certain predictability. Indeed, if the probability of a rising market is 70% while the probability of a price fall is only 30%, then one already has a probabilistic prediction and can construct an investment strategy to exploit this information. Bachelier's claim was much stronger. He insisted that the probabilities of rising and falling prices are equal to 50% and the mathematical expectation of the speculator is strictly zero. This effectively precludes any profitable opportunity of making money in the long run, or 'on average'.

The 'fifty–fifty' statement has a powerful but simple rationale. For each deal, there is a buyer and a seller. The buyer believes in the rising market while the seller expects the price to fall. This means that, on average, a speculator anticipates the price to neither rise nor fall! Moreover, any particular investor generally has equal chances of being right or wrong. This picture resulted in the pioneering concept of random price movements, where the price evolves, changing step by step according a random number chosen independently of the previous history. Bachelier also derived a formula for the characteristic uncertainty in price ΔS as a function of time span t:

$$\Delta S = \sigma\sqrt{t}, \tag{1}$$

with the coefficient σ now known as a price volatility. For times t of the order of years, the stock market follows the rule (1) with astonishing precision, which was considered as a confirmation of the original Bachelier assumptions.

A typical price chart created by such random walk is very rough, and indeed resembles real stock market charts (Fig. 1.2). Needless to say, such a market model makes any prediction by technicians meaningless: what is the point of scrupulously studying the price history if new price increments are stochastic and independent of what happened earlier! Bachelier's conjecture, which eventually matured into the Efficient Market Theory, dug a deep trench separating two polar views on the market dynamics.

At this point, the paths of physics and finance crossed for the first time. In 1905, Albert Einstein, famous for his Theory of Relativity, wrote a seminal paper on the statistics of colloidal particles that are small enough to be influenced by thermal fluctuations but large

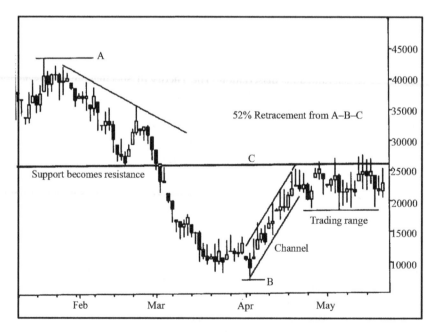

Figure 1.2 A typical price chart created by Brownian motion is very rough, and indeed resembles real stock market charts. From *The New Technical Trader*, by T.S. Chande and S. Kroll, Copyright © John Wiley & Sons, Inc. Reprinted by permission of John Wiley & Sons, Inc.

enough to be observed in a microscope (Fig. 1.3). Such particles are called Brownian particles and their motion is called Brownian motion after the English physicist Robert Brown, who first discovered the phenomenon of their erratic motion. Among other results, Einstein derived the following equation for the dispersion of the particle coordinate Δx as a function of time t:

$$\Delta x = D\sqrt{t}. \tag{2}$$

Here the coefficient D is the so-called diffusion coefficient, for which Einstein also obtained an expression known as the Einstein formula. It is striking how similar the formulae (1) and (2) are. We can add that the underlying mathematics is similar too, if not identical. The fact that the mathematical description of the diffusion process was initially (five years earlier!) developed to describe a stock market is very dear now to physicists converted to financiers.

If one had the means to reliably forecast the market, the wisest investment strategy would be to put money in the most profitable asset and wait until the tide changed to get money back, i.e. 'Put your eggs in the same basket and watch the basket'. Since the stochastic picture of price walks expelled market predictions from the agenda, it had to suggest a new type of question on how to get more rather than less from investment in this random market. The question and the first answer came in 1952 in the paper 'Portfolio selection' by Harry Markowitz, at that time a graduate student at the University of Chicago. Instead of trying to predict the future, a prudent investor can rather consider an *optimal structure* of her portfolio under the uncertainty about the future outcome. If one gives up the desire to foresee the future and embarks on a wild random world, one faces a dilemma between minimizing the risk of possible losses and maximizing the expected return. Dealing with random prices, the risk can be associated with a characteristic fluctuation, or volatility σ, while the return will be a mathematical expectation of the return on one's portfolio μ.

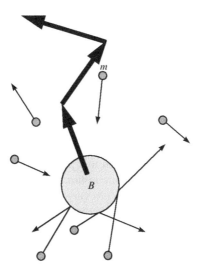

Figure 1.3 Brownian particle B is surrounded by molecules m which move randomly with a thermal kinetic energy and occasionally hit the particle. This causes a change in the particle movement and produces its random (Brownian) motion.

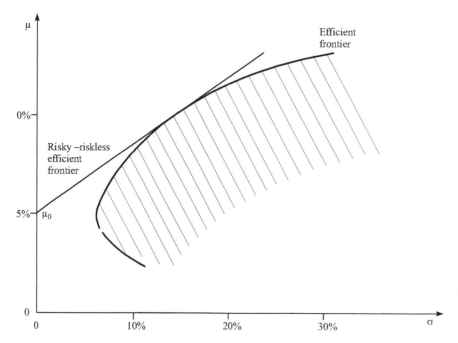

Figure 1.4 The Markovitz–Tobin construction. Efficient frontier and the super-efficient portfolio.

The assumption that the volatility can be identified with risk is arguable. Indeed, one has a risk of losing money only in the face of drawdowns – drawups are welcome. Moreover, the notion of risk is something obscure and intuitive, and depends very much on an investor's perceptions. Some people would disagree with the statement 'The risk is twice as large because the volatility is doubled', while everybody would agree that the risk is actually higher. However, it is very common to use the volatility as a measure of risk, because it simplifies the calculations.[2]

Minimizing the risk σ while keeping the return μ fixed at some constant μ_0 will give a system of linear equations for the components of the optimal portfolio (Fig. 1.4). The optimal portfolio is not unique, because of the existence of the free parameter μ_0. By varying this parameter, one obtains a complete set of optimal portfolios, the so-called optimal frontier. A particular positioning of the investor's portfolio on this frontier is a matter of the investor's choice, which will define how risk-aversive she is. However, any optimal investment should lie on the optimal frontier: if it does not, then it is possible to get either a higher return with the same risk or a smaller risk with the same return.

The dependence on investor's preferences is a very uneasy thing for an economist to put up with. First of all, this risk aversion is difficult to define, especially after what has already been said about risk in general. No-one, as a matter of fact, can determine how risk aversive she is and express it in term of a number. Secondly, decision-making under uncertainty is a tricky business, and has underwater rocks that are studied by experimental economics. Thirdly, the

---

[2] In fact, Markowitz also considered the downside/semistandard deviation as a measure of risk to lose money. The standard deviation is commonly used in calculations because of its greater analytical simplicity. Provided that return distributions are symmetric, semivariance optimizations will be equivalent to standard-deviation-based optimizations.

preferences dependence makes the construction of a pricing model quite a task, which will involve, for example, a poll on public risk-aversion. Fortunately, the difficulties can be reduced by using Tobin's separation theorem, published in 1958. Tobin found that the existence of a riskless asset, such as US Treasury bills, changes the situation dramatically and allows one to match risk preferences with a single super-effective portfolio of risky stocks and some position in the riskless asset. The construction of the super-effective risky portfolio does not depend then on risk preferences, and is unique for all investors. Instead of wondering about a particular point on the Markowitz efficient frontier, an investor has to decide what part of her money will be invested in riskless assets and put the other part in the super-efficient portfolio. Since all rational investors will do the same, the super-efficient portfolio will be a market portfolio, i.e. the portfolio consists of all risky stocks, with shares defined by a ratio of their market capitalization to the capitalization of the entire market.[3] This idea is due to William Sharpe, who took the next step by introducing the Capital Asset Pricing Model (CAPM).

Markowitz's recipe requires a large number of calculations. To find an efficient portfolio among the 500 main stocks comprising the S&P500 stock market index, one has to solve a system of 500 coupled equations subject to the constraint $\mu = \mu_0$. At that time, it was an almost impossible task. And that is not the end of story. The Markowitz–Tobin procedure requires accurate knowledge of all 500 expected returns on the individual stocks, 500 volatilities, and $500 \cdot 499/2 = 124,750$ covariances. Unless they are accurate and reliable, the result is worth nothing. One has to simplify the consideration in order to obtain a manageable model. This was done by William Sharpe. In his paper published in 1963, Sharpe suggested that the essential part of variability of stocks can be explained by their reaction to a common factor, which was chosen to be the performance of the market portfolio. This assumption considerably simplified the calculations, and led to the development of the CAPM in 1964.

The main equation of the CAPM looks simple enough. To put it in one line: the average return r on a security is the sum of a return r_0 on the riskless asset and the risk premium, which is proportional to the difference between the average return r_m on the market portfolio and the return on the riskless asset:

$$r = r_0 + \beta(r_m - r_0). \tag{3}$$

The coefficient β is the covariance of r_m and r scaled by the variance of the market return. As well as being a nice and neat mathematical equation, the expression (3) can, in principle, serve as a basis for an investment strategy: if the return on a stock is lower than predicted by CAPM, buy it and postpone selling until the market corrects the mispricing. In this form, the strategy could be considered as a pure money-making strategy. It is still not what is called an *arbitrage*[4] with abnormal (higher than riskless interest rate) return earned without any risk, because buying a stock and keeping it is a risky operation that may result in capital losses. But if there exists only one, or maybe a few, parameters that govern the prices, then it might be possible to create a portfolio that will both be riskless and abnormally profitable. Basically, if one knows that the market obeys three parameters and can buy a portfolio with shares in five hundred stocks, it is easy to construct riskless portfolios, and it would be rational to search among these portfolios for those with abnormal return. Since everybody will try to do the

---

[3] All investors will only hold the market portfolio when the CAPM conditions hold – in particular, the homogeneous expectations of investors.
[4] An arbitrage is a situation when abnormal return can be earned without any risk.

same, the supply–demand mechanism should make returns on all these riskless portfolios equal to the riskless interest rate. This idea is the essence of the Arbitrage Pricing Theory invented by Stephen Ross in 1976.

At this point, one faces a paradoxical conclusion. The theory started with Bachelier's statement that the market cannot be predicted and follows a random walk, but ends up with forecasting price movements in anticipation of a market correction when there is a discrepancy between the actual market prices and their theoretical predictions. The apparent paradox stems from the main theoretical assumption of market equilibrium. All market models that we have mentioned are models of equilibrium markets. All relevant information is known to all market participants, who are rational enough to absorb it and to react in response to it. Moreover, they do it infinitely quickly, even for the smallest situation. This makes the market as a system reach its equilibrium state momentarily after the news hits it. Unfortunately, nothing is infinitely fast in this world. This includes the market. There are many factors that slow down the reaction, such as transaction costs and bid–ask spread, taxation, and limited available funds. All investors are different, and the influence of these factors on them is different too. This makes the system more and more complex.

The previous consideration prompts the introduction of a characteristic time of market reaction,[5] which we denote by τ_m, and the corresponding average time between arriving news, τ_n. When τ_m is much smaller than τ_n, the system reaches equilibrium quickly, and one can apply equilibrium pricing models. However, when the average time between arriving news or any external impact is comparable to τ_m, the situation should change dramatically. The market has not had enough time to reach equilibrium, and it starts to evolve in a very complicated, maybe even chaotic, way. Market participants notice this, and eventually change their strategies and behavioral models. This makes the equilibrium unstable and, as a matter of fact, irrelevant.

To quantify the market reaction, the most natural thing is to study the previous market behaviour. It would be very logical to assume that if the market reacted in a certain way before and nothing important in the environment has changed since that time, then the market will behave in a similar manner now. But this is essentially the point of view of technical analysis! We have come full circle and returned to the counterposing of the technical approach and standard market theories as dynamics versus equilibrium.[6]

2 NATURAL SCIENCE VERSUS SOCIAL SCIENCE

Theorists are generally never happy about how practitioners run their business. In finance, the pattern started with Alfred Cowles, who in 1933 published an article analysing the performance of various financial advisors. He demonstrated statistically an absence of predictive power in professional market forecasts. Practitioners are never happy with the theory either. George Soros, one of the most prominent practitioners of our times, in his admirable book *Alchemy of Finance* (Soros, 1987), rules out standard economic theory as irrelevant and based on a set of unrealistic axioms. And the equilibrium nature of the theory is

---

[5] Economists use the terms 'price adjustment' and 'speed of price adjustment' for the market reaction and the price equilibration. In what follows, we use the terms interchangeably.
[6] For a review of empirical research into predictability and non-stationarity see Fama (1991).

not the only point to attack. It is rather a consequence of other basic assumptions hidden deep in the theoretical profundity.

Economics was designed to describe a human activity. Soros argues that the very human origin of the subject gradually disappeared from the theory and was substituted by postulates of rationality of participants and their perfect knowledge. In a dynamical market where the prices depend on investors' forecasts, perfect knowledge would include information about the forecasts of all market participants. The impossibility for an investor to get this information leads to its replacement by her own beliefs of what these forecasts are. This poses a principal difficulty: an investor's beliefs about the future are based on some surmised beliefs of others, which in turn will depend on her own beliefs. This places an investor in a situation of imperfect knowledge about the market, and forces her to make decisions under uncertainty. The decision-making strategy is characteristic of a particular investor, and is definitely not unique across the market. Moreover, the strategies are potentially faulty, and lead to market volatility. Soros emphasized that all these factors are neglected in contemporary financial models under the disguise of perfect information and uniform investor's rationality. Although this conclusion is not quite fair, since behavioural finance, research into the influence of so-called noise traders, and inductive reasoning on price dynamics have become more popular during the last decade,[7] one does have to admit that the accepted pricing theory and methods of portfolio selection are still essentially equilibrium approaches and ignore these subtleties.

In his critique, Soros went further, and questioned the very possibility of developing economics as a natural-type science. The construction of pricing models and the corresponding investment strategies is an act of thinking. This thinking changes the object of the study, because the expectations define the price quotes. This leads to further changes in expectations, and so on (Fig. 1.5). Hence one cannot separate the thinking about the object from the

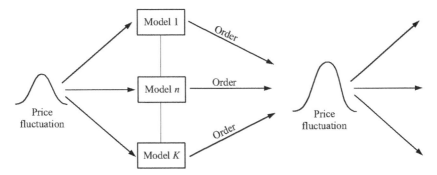

Figure 1.5 Market cycle. This starts with a fluctuation, which can be due to, for example, arrival of a new information about a stock, or can be caused by an unexpected large 'buy' or 'sell'. This fluctuation changes expectations of any given market participant about other investors' beliefs of future, and hence changes the expectations of the future price. Absence of a general rule of beliefs adjustment leads to a diversity of opinions and further price fluctuations.

---

[7] See Brian (1992, 1994) with further development in Brian et al (1996) and LeBaron et al (1999), on market models with behavioural aspects, learning, and inductive reasoning. The papers on this subject are mainly computational. For the most recent review of agent-based computational finance, see LeBaron (2000). This is quite similar to what was advocated by Soros (1987).

object itself. This is the borderline that separates the social sciences from the natural sciences, where the object and a researcher belong to different 'universes'.

Together with internal fallibility of expectations, the impossibility of neglecting the influence of a researcher on the object of her study leads to unavoidable uncertainty immanent to the social sciences. Soros mentioned that in the natural science of physics, there exists a famous example where the object and the researcher cannot be separated. In quantum mechanics, an act of measurement interferes with the effect one wants to measure and leads to an uncertainty in the result of the experiment. This poses a limitation on the accuracy of the measurement, a statement that is formalized by Heisenberg's uncertainty principle. For example, if one aims to measure the coordinate x and the momentum p of an electron, these quantities can only be measured with some errors. The standard deviations of these errors, Δx and Δp, obey the equation

$$\Delta x \, \Delta p = \frac{h}{2\pi},$$

with a single fundamental constant h, called Planck's constant, whatever the method of measurement that was chosen. The measurement device is part of the physical system that it is designed to measure. This resembles the situation that one faces in the social sciences, when the reflection about a system cannot be parted from the system itself.

In spite of the appealing features of the comparison, Soros argues, however, that the analogy is only superficial. First of all, the measurement device is not quite the same as the theory of measurements as a product of human thinking. However, one can reply that human thoughts interfere with the object via a device constructed according to them. Soros replies with the reasoning that in the case of economics the uncertainty is internal and caused by the participants, whereas in physics it results from an attempt to make measurements by some external means. This is also a very arguable point. According to the philosophy prevailing among physicists, quantum uncertainty is a fundamental law of nature. The laws of the microworld are fundamentally different from what we observe in our everyday life and describe in common terms. The peculiarities of quantum physics are just the price that we pay for our inability to think in a 'quantum' manner. This view suggests that the uncertainty cannot be removed or reduced by any improvement in measurement technique or any technological means, including even the use of currently unknown 'fine' fields. This statement is much stronger than just the technological impossibility of accurate measurements, and gave birth to the language of non-commutative operators in the theory of quantum phenomena. Thus the uncertainties in the social and natural sciences can both be considered as endogenous, as long as one bears in mind the existence of some distinctive features.

The conclusion of the last paragraph carries a certain positive message. To understand quantum laws and give a description of them, physicists needed to change paradigm and find an appropriate mathematics. Returning to the example of the electron, physicists were forced to accept a counterintuitive wave–particle dualism, a probabilistic picture, and the corresponding machinery of non-commutative operators to accommodate experimental results. The mathematics was not only a way to describe the microworld. It became a means of study replacing human feelings when the theory outlawed an application of human intuition. It well may happen that the social sciences are waiting for new mathematical tools to be applied to accommodate the peculiarities of thinking systems. The complexity of these systems is not on its own an obstacle in principle to doing so.

3 'FAIR GAME' AND THE FRACTAL MARKET HYPOTHESIS

As mentioned earlier, Bachelier logically arrived at the conclusion that at any arbitrary instant of time, the mathematical expectation of return for an investor is equal to zero: if buyers gain, sellers lose. This is known as a 'fair game' condition. We have deliberately inserted here the word 'return', which implies a certain time interval, or, as we call it, an investment horizon. Nobody said that the horizons have to be the same for all investors. Indeed, in the real market, there are participants with very different investment periods, spanning from one minute to several months. Investors with different time horizons see the market differently and play different strategies. This allows a situation where both a buyer and a seller can gain. Let us consider the example of the price of a security that is in the uptrend but has just gone down several intraday standard deviations owing to a fluctuation. The reaction of an intraday trader is to sell the security in order to buy it lower later in the day in anticipation of an upswing. At the same time, a fund manager who trades weekly can consider the fluctuation as a profitable opportunity to buy low, expecting a continuation of the primary trend. Both the intraday trader and the fund manager enter the profitable, since both of them deal having very different pictures in mind. This example demonstrates another feature of the market that was dropped in standard market models, namely a multilevel structure of the market.

Edgar Peters, who suggested the above example in his book *Fractal Market Analysis* (Peters, 1994), went further and introduced the Fractal Market Hypothesis, which views a market as a system of traders with continuously distributed investment horizons as an alternative to the 'fair game' market. He wrote: 'Except for the securities regulation to protect investors from fraud, there has been no attempt to make the trades "fair"', and proceeds with: 'The technology is in place to ensure that a trader will find a buyer . . . but there is no agreed-on mechanism for determining what the "fair price" should be.'

Peters describes his market as a liquid and stable one. Indeed, the market with many investment horizons is more stable than the market with a single horizon in the sense that a small price fluctuation causes a large price fluctuation less often: when short-time traders panic and sell, the long-time investors step in and support the price. As we discuss in Chapter 6, it is quite realistic (and very convenient) to assume that up to a certain cut-off time, the strategies of investors with different time horizons are similar and differ only in values of parameters. In the example above, the stop-loss is, say, three standard deviations for all investors, but the standard deviations for intraday traders and weekly traders are different. Thus we will use the notion of Fractal Market Hypothesis to say that the market consists of traders with different continuously distributed investment horizons (up to some cut-off) but similar decision-making strategies. The self-similar market structure resembles fractals, geometrical objects composed of pieces that are similar to the whole object and, in turn, consist of smaller components with the same general structure (Fig. 1.6). Fractals were publicized by Benoit Mandelbrot, who discovered their ubiquitousness in nature. This analogy with fractals as self-similar objects prompted Peters to call his model the fractal market.

One can say that the fractal market is less susceptible to the external perturbations unless the market loses its multilevel structure. Loss of structure is a special event when the market goes into a 'free fall'. It can happen when, owing to long-time uncertainty, the long-time investors become myopic and play as short-time traders or temporarily leave the market. According to Peters, these events can be identified as market crashes and treated as special

Figure 1.6 Fractals are self-similar geometrical objects. They consist of parts that are, up to a change of scale, equivalent to the object as a whole. Fractals owe their name to the fact that their dimension, according to some reasonable definition, is not integer but fractal. Intuitively, it is clear that the fractal presented in this figure, called the Sierpinski gasket, is denser than a segment but less dense than a square. The actual fractal dimension of the Sierpinski gasket is equal to $\ln 3/\ln 2 \approx 1.59$.

singular points. To model the singularities, one has to develop a model for a crossover process that governs a crossover between the multilevel structure and the uniform investment horizon.

4   DYNAMICS, VOLUMES, AND MONEY FLOWS

When a market columnist says 'the market gained considerably during the morning session', this is definitely a statement concerning the market dynamics. The price of the market portfolio went up, characterizing the overall market behaviour that morning. However, the prices are just one of the components of the market. Their changes are caused by money flows, which leave less profitable assets for those expected to be more profitable. Without considering the time evolution of the money flows, the picture of the market dynamics is incomplete. We have seen already in discussion of the Dow theory that the trading volume may distinguish a market correction from a turn of the primary trend. Growing volume indicates the strength of the market movement. That is why, when the columnist adds that 'the market rose on a heavy volume', it contributes to the optimistic outlook of investors.

The equilibrium market theory does not need volumes. All that is important is the relative positioning of assets, whatever trades are required to reach this position. The only assumption here is that the market has the possibility to make all these necessary trades instantly. Volumes, as turnovers of assets per unit time, do not appear, because there is no time in the equilibrium world. All relevant events have either already happened, as an infinitely fast market response, or have not yet happened, such as arrival of new information. Everything is different for a dynamical market. The volumes essentially characterize the speed of exchange, and are undoubtedly important. This is why trading volumes are sometimes used to rescale physical times to get the so-called trading time employed in technical indicators. For a dynamical market, the volumes bring in the time evolution that is missed in the equilibrium framework. One can say that money flows are the essence of the dynamical theory.

Following the above picture, the dynamical market consists of prices and money flows. The prices are defined by the money flows according to the demand–supply mechanism. The money flows, in turn, are defined by expectations of market participants, and hence partially by the prices themselves. The money flows and prices form a complete set of variables to describe the system when questions of market reaction to an incoming information or a washing out of a mispricing are concerned.

What type of equations have to be written in order to analyse a market? What kind of theory does it have to be? Let us concentrate for a while on the theory of small market fluctuations around an equilibrium state. In mathematical terms, this means that the time of market reaction τ_m is smaller than the characteristic fluctuation time τ_n but cannot be neglected completely. The market corrects itself in the case of a mispricing that might appear owing to a fluctuation. If the mispricing is realized in the market, speculators expect the correction, and initiate money flows that pour wealth into more profitable securities from less profitable ones. This reduces the mispricing and eventually eliminates it. It is obvious that the equations designed to describe the situation have to be some kind of transfer equations similar to the equations of gasodynamics or thermophysics. This general observation helps, but does not yet define the theory. Indeed, there are many options to develop the theory if the only criterion is to fit the above scheme. Which one should be chosen?

To resolve the situation, we will follow the methodology of the exact sciences. It is often the case that a phenomenon can be described by a number of phenomenological models. If an experiment is inconclusive on the issue of correct model choice, scientists have to come up with something else. Physicists are probably the most experienced at this because they face this situation all the time. How can one develop a theory of nuclear interactions if experiments cannot see deep enough inside the nucleus? How does one choose a model for the grand unification of fundamental forces if the relevant energy scale is out of experimental reach and will be so for many years to come? The solution lies in studying a theory that is based on a set of very plausible assumptions called first principles, and deriving this or that phenomenological model from it as a consequence. We will follow this line and start with a set of first principles that are intuitively clear and experimentally verifiable, to formulate a general theory. After some approximations, this gives rise to various phenomenological models that are less general but better suited to particular applications.

The project sounds impressive, but now the question is how to select the first principles. It is obvious that the first principles for constructing a macroeconomic theory or a theory of long-term market movements will be different from those for the fast market reaction. In the first case, one has to deal with long-term prospects, market fundamentals, risk, and decision-making under uncertainty, government policy and the like. For the fast dynamics, all the issues listed above are irrelevant. For short-time horizons, an investor accepts a small risk. This puts her in the vicinity of certainty and hence makes her marginally risk-neutral. The short-term traders primarily analyse price charts and follow technical analysis. This defines their short-term expectations. Frequent trading in the same market environment allows them to play on statistics using their 'buy–sell' signals and ignoring the marginal risk. It should be clear now that the formulation of the first principles for fast dynamics will be easier and less arguable than for the long-term one. Even so, this still leaves plenty of space for many possible models.

To take the next step, one has to find a symmetry that the theory will obey. The existence of the symmetry reduces the freedom to choose among theoretical approaches and gives an idea about the proper language to use when talking about the theory. The more complicated the symmetry, the fewer options are left for the researcher. It might be that the symmetry is so powerful that it practically fixes the structure of the theory and the corresponding language. Then the only way left for a researcher is to follow the stream. In the next chapter, we will see that this is the case for the fast market dynamics. The financial market possesses an infinite-dimensional symmetry group, the gauge group, which essentially means that for *any arbitrary* moment of time, a simultaneous change of *any* asset units, such as currency units and trading lots, together with the corresponding changes in their prices, leave the dynamics unchanged. This results in the fact that prices and asset units are not the best variables, and one has to use variables that are either invariant with respect to the symmetry or change in a nice simple way. This brings a pretty geometrical picture together with a powerful new language that can be not just a means of description but also an instrument of the study. As a byproduct, it gives an example of how fruitful mutual penetrations of social and natural sciences can be if one dismisses one's prejudices.

5   WHAT IS THIS BOOK ABOUT?

Generally speaking, this book is about market mispricing and the corresponding corrections to the equilibrium market theory. Except for the final section of the final chapter, which is devoted to the consideration of a market that is far from equilibrium, most of the time we will be interested in a quasi-equilibrium market where a virtual mispricing does disappear, though not immediately. Clearly, this is not quite what practitioners such as George Soros would like to see, but it is still, at least theoretically, better than the standard equilibrium market models. To accomplish this task, we apply a mathematical formalism that is new in the financial setting, namely the geometry of fibre bundles.

Fibre bundles are very popular in theoretical physics. All fundamental physical theories describe an evolution on fibre bundles. The origin of the ubiquitousness of the fibre bundles lies in the fact that they are best suited to accommodate a fundamental local symmetry of a theory that is taken as one of the first principles. Later in this book, we will see that the symmetry with respect to the choice of asset units or, to put it another way, to changes of numeraires, leads to a fibre bundle formulation in precise analogy with fundamental physical theories. This geometrical formulation provides useful mathematical objects that can be used in the theory, and also gives a general, but at the same time almost unique, scenario for the theory construction. Chapter 2 introduces fibre bundles to the reader and illustrates the concept with financial examples. At this stage, no complicated mathematical tools are utilized, and the exposition is completely descriptive. We will see that the financial market, as well as any exchange system, has a hidden structure, 'parallel transport', which represents an exchange process. In terms of this 'parallel transport', many financial notions, such as Net Present Value, discounting, and arbitrage, can be reformulated in purely geometrical terms. This unexpected connection covered by Chapter 2 is the basis for all other material in the book.

Chapter 3 sketches the fascinating mathematics of fibre bundles. It is more formal than the preceding chapter, but contains many figures to help a reader to get used to the new concepts. Here we show that many geometrical objects and things from everyday life are actually fibre bundles. This makes the formal definitions easier to digest and makes the discovery of the same objects in the context of the financial market even more surprising and exciting.

Chapter 4 describes applications of fibre bundles in theoretical physics. Starting with a history of electrodynamics, passing through the famous Maxwell's equations and the first gauge symmetry, we follow the path that led eventually to the establishment of Quantum Electrodynamics, currently the most reliable physical theory. The reader will see that the first gauge theory, invented by Hermann Weyl in 1919 to explain electrodynamics and then later rejected, returns as a theory of the financial market.

Starting with Chapter 5, we concentrate on finance. Here the financial fibre bundle will be formally constructed. We will see that in this geometrical framework, prices and money flows are exactly complementary entities, as they should be. Price dynamics in the absence of money flows will be introduced. This is done in such a way that the standard results of mathematical finance appear naturally when one can neglect the fast market dynamics.

Chapters 6 and 7 analyse a simple gauge market model that is designed to give a theoretical description of technical and statistical properties of a single actively traded asset. The first principles for money flow dynamics will be formulated and 'dressed' in geometrical terms. Traders are assumed to maximize a profit from their expectations of market corrections, but these expectations are formulated in a stochastic way, giving rise to a discrepancy of opinions and accommodating Soros' statement of an intrinsic fallibility of market participants. This fallibility actually makes the market more stable compared with the classical deterministic description. Further stability comes from the fractal structure of the market, which is assumed following the Fractal Market Hypothesis. Since we are interested in fast dynamics, the only relevant time frames are short enough to consider the participants with all investment horizons having the same dynamical rules with rescaled values of governing parameters. In this form, the model inherits all the benefits of the equilibrium market models and incorporates the principal features of a dynamical market.

As an example, we consider the S&P500 market index. Starting with a review of empirical results, we constuct a model for the dynamics incorporating first principles as well as the empirical data. The reader will see that the gauge model is able to describe the statistical properties of the index as well as explaining some technical tools used by chartists. This illustrates a connection between technical analysis and market efficiency, which is commented on in Chapter 7 in more general terms. The underlying mathematics for these two chapters is quite complicated, but can be passed over without much harm to general understanding.

After the formulation of the gauge principles of market modelling, we come to asset pricing. Corrections to the equilibrium pricing models are studied in Chapter 8. To make our consideration self-contained, we first derive the Capital Asset Pricing Model and the relations of the Arbitrage Pricing theory, and then show how they can be obtained in the gauge framework. After a discussion of some general properties of this gauge pricing model, we make an approximation to extract the simplest correction to price dynamics due to the presence of money flows. This produces a novel effective model for price evolution. The model is then solved, and the corrections to the pricing equations are obtained.

Virtual arbitrage corrections to the derivative pricing are covered in Chapter 9. A derivative is a special kind of security, the price of which is defined by the price of one or more assets or quantities. These second assets are known as underlying assets. The statistics of the underlying assets, market expectations, and money flow dynamics are the key ingredients of derivatives pricing. Being a particular kind of traded assets, derivatives can be priced using the same principles as were introduced in Chapter 8 for general asset pricing. The fact that to price a derivative one has only to be concerned with a few assets rather than with the whole market allows several simplifications and makes the derivative theory the most developed and dominant part of mathematical finance. It explains why the longest chapter in this book is devoted to derivative pricing. In Chapter 9, we start with an exposition of the main results of the theory of derivatives, including the derivation of the Black–Scholes equation for the derivative price. The chapter continues with a discussion of the results of empirical studies on non-equilibrium dynamics of arbitrage return. Then we derive a gauge model for derivative pricing and show how the results of the standard derivative pricing theory emerge from the gauge model in the limiting case of an infinitely fast market. This also allows us to obtain a general form of corrections, which include corrections due to virtual arbitrage, speculative non-Brownian underlying price dynamics, and the influence of hedging. The corrections to the pricing equation are due to the presence of money flows in both derivatives and the underlying asset market, and reflect the influence of markets on one other. From the general expression for the corrections, we derive a simplified model of the system using the results of Chapter 6. This latter model is discussed in some detail using partial differential equations and stochastic calculus. Exact solutions for the price of the vanilla derivatives under virtual arbitrage are obtained, and the influence of market imperfections such as a bid–ask spread and transaction costs are quantified. A section on derivative pricing for non-equilibrium markets concludes the chapter. In contrast to previous considerations, here we do not assume the quasi-equilibrium nature of the market dynamics, and develop a phenomenological framework based on empirical studies reviewed earlier in the chapter.

This book employs methods of contemporary theoretical physics as well as methods of stochastic calculus that are already widely accepted and popular in finance. However, the reader is not expected to be a physicist or to be familiar with the machinery of quantum field theory. To give the reader command of field-theoretical methods, the book contains a mathematical appendix with a concise description of the methods that we use in the main text. The material is put after the main part so as not to interrupt the logic of the exposition, but it is an essential part of the book. It assumes no initial knowledge of quantum field theory, and is suitable for students with basic mathematical culture. The topics of the appendix include the formalism of creation–annihilation operators, functional integration and approximate methods of calculation of functional integrals, as well as some useful tricks. As a matter of fact, the appendix can be considered and read as a separate entity aiming to introduce methods of quantum field theory to the financial community and to illustrate them with some applications to finance. The methods are illustrated with derivation of exact solutions for two popular interest rate derivative pricing problems. The last section of the appendix is devoted to the derivation of the Itô stochastic calculus in the framework of functional integrals.

6   SUMMARY

- There is empirical evidence that there exists a certain predictability of future returns from publicly available public information, and this predictability is connected with non-stationarity.

- Equilibrium pricing models exclude non-equilibrium dynamics.

- To model non-equilibrium dynamics, one has to include, besides prices, money flows, which both influence prices and are affected by them.

- In the construction of dynamical models for money flows/prices, one can follow a pattern established in physics and formulate some symmetries that the dynamical rules must obey. This will restrict the variety of the models.

7 FURTHER READING

1. A thoughtful and entertaining account of the history of the field can be found in the excellent book by Bernstein (1992).
2. A brief description of the Dow theory as well as a simple introduction to technical analysis can be found in Achelis (1995).
3. For a modern look at the classic Dow theory see an interview with Michael Sheimo by Thom Hartle published in *Technical Analysis of Stocks & Commodities* (Hartle, 1998).
4. An account of George Soros' theory can be found in Soros (1987), with further development to global policy making in Soros (1998).
5. The Fractal Market Hypothesis, its rationale and applications can be found in Peters (1994).

2

Fibre Bundles in Finance: First Contact

I N this chapter, fibre bundles will be informally introduced and some intuitive financial examples will be given. Our intention here is to demonstrate that fibre budle language is indeed a very natural way in which to speak about financial market symmetries.

Experts say that people rest when they contemplate symmetrical figures. One of the ways to explain this phenomenon is that a symmetrical picture is easy to grasp with the eye. This gives the impression that it is comprehensible and easy to control, because it can be decomposed into a small number of simpler ideal figures that are well known and have been recognizable since one's childhood. This argument can be applied to the cognition process in general: in cognizing new things, we try to find a symmetry, to decompose objects into fundamental components or blocks, and to establish links between them.

Symmetry and decomposition into simple fragments are two sides of the same coin. Symmetry allows one to reduce a complex object to a number of simple components. At the same time, simple fundamental elements are a basis for formulating the symmetry. One can say that the symmetry and its related geometry come together. This was a guiding idea for Felix Klein, a famous mathematician of the early 20th century, who defined a geometry by its underlying symmetry. In the next chapters, we postulate a particular symmetry, gauge symmetry, as one of first principles to construct financial models. This symmetry is ultimately connected with a particular type of geometry, the geometry of fibre bundles.

Decomposing the picture, one finds oneself in a position where many elements look similar but differ in minor details that are unimportant for the purpose of the study. It requires a certain idealization to identify them and to deal with them, since they are identical. There are not many ideal shapes in nature. The Earth's surface is not a perfect sphere, but this does not stop people using spherical coordinates to draw maps. Crystal lattices have defects, but often these do not change the main properties of the solid. Idealization allows us to simplify the classification of objects and their interconnections. At this point, mathematics comes to our aid. It classifies objects and their properties and defines possible operations on them. Different objects can produce identical idealized mathematical images, which can therefore be subject to the same mathematical procedures. This creates an important source of investigative tools. A method developed to study one phenomenon can then be applied to a whole range of phenomena with the same general mathematical structure, so that advances in one field are transformed into advances in other fields.

In this chapter, we will see that the financial market has the same underlying geometrical structure as many other natural phenomena. Fundamental forces are just one kind of example. Living systems provide another illustration. Gerhard Mack, a physicist at Hamburg University, argues in his paper 'Gauge theory of things alive and universal dynamics' (Mack, 1994) that the framework is general enough to embrace a basis of biological life on Earth and organizations of human societies. All of these phenomena with little in common are different reincarnations of the same mathematical essence called gauge-invariant dynamics on fibre bundles. Leaving dynamics for the following chapters, we concentrate now on the arena of the action, the fibre bundles.

1 DIFFERENTIAL GEOMETRY ON FIBRE BUNDLES

1.1 Fibre Bundles

We know about geometrical spaces from our school mathematics lessons. Spaces are all around us, and we encounter many examples in our everyday lives. We live in three-dimensional space, we use two-dimensional maps, and we drive along (almost) one-dimensional roads. Generally we understand a space as a volume, area, or distance that can be used or filled by objects. For many purposes, it is important to characterize the position of an object in the space, and this is done by means of coordinates. The smallest number of coordinates that is sufficient to give a position in a space is known as the spatial dimension. By this definition, the dimension is an integer number, so that fractional dimensions are not allowed. There exists a way to generalize the notion of dimension to the case of fractals, i.e. objects with fractional dimension (see Fig. 1.6 in Chapter 1), but this is beyond the scope of this book.

Fibre bundles allow a more general look at spaces. Intuitively and informally, each fibre bundle consists of identical subspaces that are collected or 'glued' together to give the whole space. Let us consider as an example a two-dimensional plane (see Fig. 2.1). On the one hand, the space is the plane we are all used to. But the plane can also be realized as a collection of one-dimensional lines that are put on the surface and then 'nailed' together with the axis X. Each of the one-dimensional lines is identical to the others from a geometrical point of view, and yet they differ in their position on the axis X. The identical subspaces are called the *fibres* and the subspace that 'glues' them together is called the *base*. In general, any fibre bundle E consists of a base B and identical fibres F that are fastened to each point of the base (Fig. 2.2)

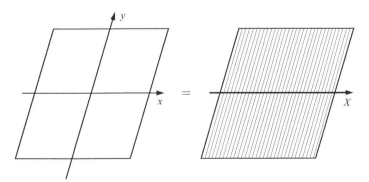

Figure 2.1   A two-dimensional plane can be taken as a first simple example of a fibre bundle. Here the axis is the base, and the lines orthogonal to it are the fibres.

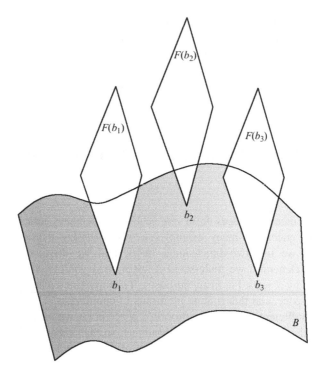

Figure 2.2   A general fibre bundle consists of a base B and fibres F stuck to each point of B.

to make a bundle, which accounts for the generic name. Since to define a position one needs now to define a position on the base and then in the fibre, the dimension of the fibre bundle E is equal to the sum of the dimensions of the base and the fibres:

$$\dim E = \dim B + \dim F.$$

For the plane, this statement equates the dimension of the plane, 2, with the sum of the two 1s that came from the two 1-dimensional axes. In general, a position on the fibre bundle is defined by a pair of coordinates (b, f), where f gives the position in the fibre and b gives the location of the fibre.

What we have done in the case of Fig. 2.1 is that we have actually introduced an additional structure in the space. Why and when do we need it? It happens sometimes that the base and the fibres are of a different nature and it is convenient to separate them in the description. For example, in place of a plane, we can consider a tube (Fig. 2.3), and we see that although the fibres are still the same one-dimensional lines, the base is a circle. The coordinates are then quite different: a coordinate on the line runs from minus infinity to plus infinity, while a coordinate on the circle goes from 0 to 2π, and the point 2π is identified with 0.

The separation is often dictated by the particular features of the problem. If one deals with a system that possesses internal as well as external degrees of freedom, the fibre bundle description appears naturally. Let us consider a perfect city (Fig. 2.4). Identical blocks of flats are built at the nodes of a square lattice on the plane, and each block has five floors with a single flat on every floor. Writing an address on an envelope, one puts something like 'corner of 6th Street and 48th Avenue' and then adds 'Apartment 5'. This apartment is hidden in the

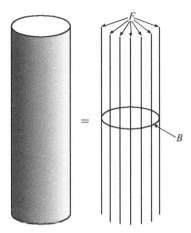

Figure 2.3 A tube can be considered as a fibre bundle with a circular base B and line fibres F. Alternatively, it can be also seen as a fibre bundle with a line base and circular fibres.

block, and plays the role of the internal degree of freedom. The whole collection of flats create a three-dimensional structure, but we prefer to separate the geographical coordinates from the internal one.

All of the examples that we have met so far are very simple in the following sense. They all allow us to use global coordinates to identify a position in the space. If it is possible to find a global coordinate system the corresponding fibre bundle is called *trivial*. Not all fibre bundles

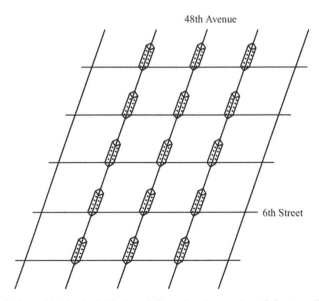

Figure 2.4 Ideal city with identical blocks of flats placed at nodes of the two-dimensional square lattice.

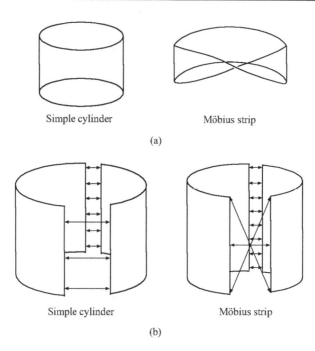

Figure 2.5 (a) Simple cylinder versus the Möbius strip as a trivial fibre bundle versus a non-trivial one. (b) Shows how the strips can be covered by two trivial pieces provided with rules telling one how to 'glue' them together.

are trivial. Figure 2.5(a) presents the so-called Möbius strip in comparison with a simple cylinder. They are both fibre bundles, but the simple cylinder is a trivial one while the Möbius strip is not. It cannot be covered with a single global coordinate system – try yourself. This is where the mathematics comes in. Even if it is impossible to find a global coordinate system for the whole space, it is definitely possible to cover it with several local coordinate systems, provided that we have a rule telling us how to convert one system to another in the region where the coordinate systems overlap. Figure 2.5(b) shows how this works for the Möbius strip. Non-trivial fibre bundles are the source of many interesting effects in physics and mathematics.

More examples of simple fibre bundles are collected in Fig. 2.6.

1.2   Parallel Transport

So far, we have only considered fibre bundles as global geometric constructions. If one is interested in analysing local quantities and comparing things with each other, one needs a 'connection', which plays an essential role in local differential geometry.

Let us imagine that we are watching a particle moving in a fibre bundle E. The particle can move inside the fibre as well as between fibres, so that its position can be described by two sets of numbers, b and f. The set b refers to the particle coordinates on the base B, while the

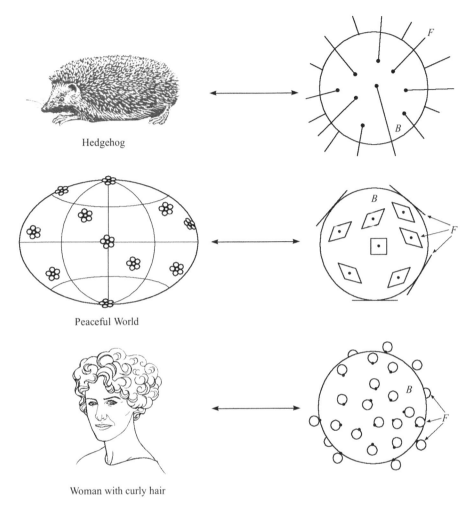

Hedgehog

Peaceful World

Woman with curly hair

Figure 2.6 Further examples of fibre bundles: hedgehog (normal bundle); Peaceful World (tangent bundle); woman with curly hair ($S^2 \times S^1$).

set f denotes the particle coordinates in the fibre $F(b)$ corresponding to point b. Putting aside the issue of coordinates on the base, we will now ask the question: 'What if coordinates in different fibres are not adjusted to each other?' In this case, changing coordinates does not say anything about the real change of the particle's position, which is characterized by a change in the 'real' coordinates.

To get some flavour of this, we return to our perfect city depicted in Fig. 2.4. We can imagine a freak landlady who owns a block on the corner of 6th Street and 48th Avenue and who orders the floors to be numbered from sixth to tenth because she is obsessed with the idea of having the highest building in the city. Obviously this does not make the building any higher, but to her the tenth floor sounds better than the fifth. Nobody can stop her doing this, and it will undoubtedly cause problems for a postman who delivers mail addressed to

'Apartment 5' unless he realizes that this means the tenth floor.[1] He then adjusts the local coordinate system and the commonly accepted one. Without this adjustment, nobody can compare whether the third floor of one building or the fourth floor of another building is higher. The fact that the number 4 is bigger than the number 3 does not say yet that this first apartment is actually located higher. The question 'How much higher?' is meaningless until we define a rule for the comparison. This rule of comparison is called the *connection*. More precisely, it says what apparent change associated with zero 'real' change we have to subtract from the total change in the coordinates to get the 'real' difference. The apparent change is determined purely by the coordinate disagreement in different fibres.

A particle cannot jump from one point to another. It actually moves through the space, making a series of infinitesimal steps. This means that it is sufficient to define the rule of comparison for close points and then sum the differences if distant points have to be considered (see Fig. 2.7). Another reason for defining local objects rather than dealing with global ones is that we always have an intuition for small local changes, while the global constructions are much more obscure. This leaves us with the local connection field.[2] This connection field, also known as the *gauge field*, is defined for all points of the base, and gives the amplitude of the apparent disagreement between the coordinate systems of fibres 'glued' to infinitesimally close points of the base.

The gauge field is a vector field,[3] and has as many components as the number of independent coordinates in the base. Indeed, for each independent direction in the base, one has to provide an independent rule of comparison for the coordinate systems of two nearby points along that direction. Since we want to compare coordinate frames of different fibres at very close points, the frame adjustment can be considered as a composition of frame adjustments along principal independent directions (Fig. 2.7b). If the directions are labeled by $i = 1, \ldots, \dim B$ and the points on the base are parametrized by coordinates b^i, we say that the transition from the point b to the point $b + db$ can be accomplished by a series of transitions along the independent directions: the shift along the first direction db^1 followed by the shift along the second direction on db^2, and so on.

To put things briefly, to find the adjustment $\Delta F(b)$ between the coordinate systems of the fibres $F(b)$ and $F(b + db)$, one has to calculate the scalar product of the difference between the points of the base, db, and the gauge field A:

$$\Delta F(b) = db \cdot AF \equiv \sum_{i=1}^{\dim B} A^i F(b) \cdot db^i.$$

The last equality defines the result in terms of the components. Here the component A^i is a *transformation* of the coordinate system that makes the coordinate systems of $F(b)$ and $F(b + db^i)$ adjusted. In the case of our crazy landlady, the transformation will be the addition of the number 5, so that $\Delta F(b) = 5$.

As is clear from Fig. 2.7, the comparison of two distant objects depends on the route taken between them in the base B. A curve and the connection field along the curve together produce *parallel transport* along the curve. If one considers the coordinates of two elements of the fibres stuck to two distant points, compares them using the connection field and some

---

[1] The example with the landlady is not so unrealistic. The Melbourne office of the Australia and New Zealand Bank does not have a 13th floor: the 14th floor comes straight after the 12th. This is not surprising if one takes into account that the 14th floor is occupied by trading desks!

[2] The word 'field' means just that the connection is a function of coordinates in the base.

[3] That is, a function with values in some vector space.

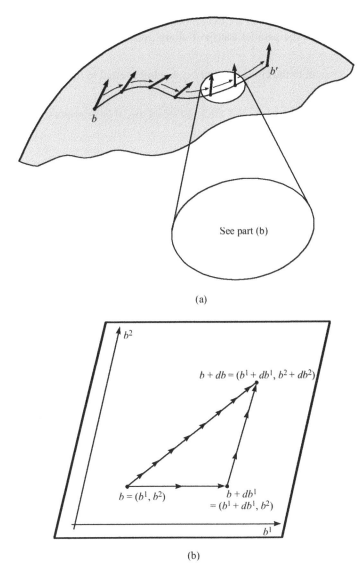

(a)

(b)

Figure 2.7 (a) Any global parallel transport is constructed from a series of local ones. (b) Each of the local parallel transports is approximately a result of the parallel transports along principal directions in the base.

curve, and does not find a difference, then one says that the second element is a result of the parallel transport of the first element along that curve. This means that the difference in the coordinates is purely a result of disadjustment of the coordinate frames, and the *covariant difference along the curve* is zero. If, however, the objects are not connected by parallel transport along a curve, there is a non-zero covariant difference along the curve.

It is time to consider another example. We take the Peaceful World (Fig. 2.6) as the fibre bundle and define the following rules of parallel transport. The fibre bundle consists of the spherical base and the fibres, which are two-dimensional tangent planes stuck to each point of the sphere. The rules of the parallel transport along great circles are as follows (Fig. 2.8):

1. If vector f_1 is tangent to the circle at point b_1, it is transported to the vector f_2 tangent to the circle at the point b_2.

2. If a vector f_3 is orthogonal to the circle at point b_1, it is transported to the vector f_4 orthogonal to the circle at the point b_2.

Any path on the sphere can be decomposed into a series of very small pieces of great circles, and hence parallel transport along great circles defines the parallel transport along all possible curves. If the original vector is not exactly parallel or orthogonal to the circle, it has to be first presented as a sum of parallel and orthogonal components, so that the final result will be a sum of the components after parallel transport.

An example of parallel transport along a closed loop composed of three segments of great circles is presented on Fig. 2.9. We can see that parallel transport of a vector along the loop rotates the vector by 90°. This might be seen as a miracle: step by step, we have adjusted the coordinate frames along the segments, and at the end we forget what we started with! However miraculous this seems, it is the strict result of our definition of parallel transport. As a matter of fact, this is a consequence of the definition of parallel transport and the underlying fibre bundle geometry. We will see in the next subsection that the same rules applied to the case where the base is a plane rather than a sphere will not give any rotation. Since the plane is a sphere with infinite radius and hence zero curvature, we can conjecture that the curvature has something to do with the surprising behaviour. Let us look at this issue more closely.

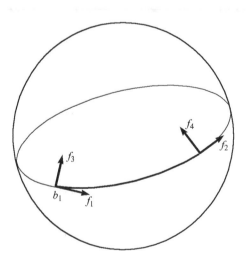

Figure 2.8 Rules for the parallel transport on the sphere. The connection defined by these rules is a special one: it is consistent with the metric on the sphere, induced from the embedding in three-dimensional space.

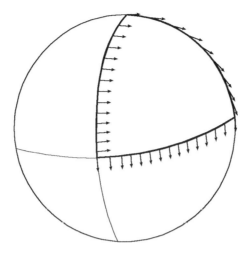

Figure 2.9 Parallel transport along the edges of the spherical triangle enclosed by segments of the great spherical circles. The result of the parallel transport is rotated by an angle of $\pi/2$ compared with the initial vector.

1.3 Curvature

When we defined the general rules for parallel transport, we did not care whether the results of parallel transport along two different curves with the same endpoints are different. Moreover, even if we do care about this and try to find a smooth connection such that the parallel transports along the two curves give the same result, it is often an impossible task. And the origin of this impossibility lies in the geometry of the fibre bundle.

Let us proceed with the example of parallel transport across the Peaceful World fibre bundle (see Fig. 2.8). Instead of drawing a large spherical triangle as was done in Fig. 2.9, we draw a spherical rectangle formed from four great circles (Fig. 2.10). Our aim is to compare the results of parallel transport along the curve $ABCD$ and along the curve AD. It is easy to see from the figure that the results are different. To understand the origin of the difference, we also show the results of parallel transport for the case of a planar base. It is easy to grasp by eye that it is the curved edges of the spherical rectangle that are responsible for the non-zero covariant difference. The covariant difference will become smaller and smaller as the radius R of the sphere tends to infinity. More precisely, the covariant difference will decrease as R^{-2} multiplied by the surface area of the rectangle or, in general, the surface area limited by the two curves. This explains our previous observation about Fig. 2.9: the surface of the spherical triangle is equal to $4\pi R^2/8$, which gives a covariant difference of

$$(4\pi R^2/8)R^{-2} = \pi/2,$$

which we found earlier using a graphical approach. In geometry, R^{-2} is known as the Gaussian curvature $\mathcal{R}$ of the sphere.

Historically, the modern concept of a connection arose from the attempt to find an intrinsic definition of differentiation on a curved two-dimensional space that is embedded in the three-dimensional space of our physical existence. It started with particular examples like the one we have just considered on a sphere. The observation that for two-dimensional surfaces, the

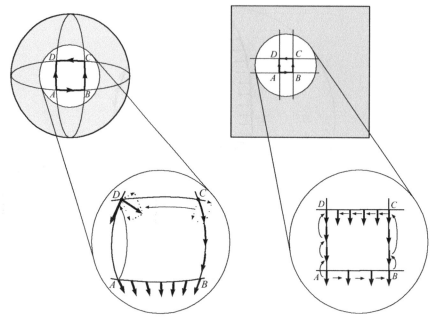

Figure 2.10   Spherical curvature is responsible for non-trivial parallel transport. The same rules of parallel transport applied to the case of the plane do not produce any rotation.

difference between the results of two parallel transports along the edges of a very small surface is equal to the product of the Gaussian curvature and the enclosed surface area gives rise to the terminology that is now commonly used. According to this, the difference Δ between two parallel transports along two curves with the same ends on a base of some fibre bundle with some connection is defined to be equal to the product of the area S enclosed by the curves and the *curvature* $\mathcal{R}$ of the fibre bundle associated with the connection:[4]

$$\Delta = S\mathcal{R}.$$

The curvature of a fibre bundle characterizes its geometry, and hence is a very useful object for study and applications.

2   FINANCIAL EXAMPLES

In this section, we will see that the nice but rather abstract constructions that we learned earlier are directly related to the subject of this book. It will be shown that the notions of fibre bundles, connection, and the corresponding curvature find their place in a financial setting as if they had been specially prepared for it.

   Is this surprising? Not really. It was mentioned above how the fibre bundles are very well suited to describing systems with two sets of coordinates with considerably different

---

[4] Please note that, in general, the curvature of the fibre bundle, $\mathcal{R}$, is not the curvature of the base space, as it is in our example with the sphere. I know this sounds crazy – but just carry on.

meanings. If one wants to characterize a financial portfolio, the dollar value of the portfolio will be a coordinate additional to the set of coordinates that give its composition in terms of shares of the wealth in each portfolio component. This means that the space of portfolios can be considered as a fibre bundle with the base composed of all possible structures of a portfolio that costs one dollar, and the semi-line fibres being all possible money values of the portfolio.

The connection is also in place. The phrase 'The return today is higher than ten years ago' does not say much until the inflation has been specified and the real rate of return calculated using the Fisher formula. We know another name for this action: it is the coordinate systems adjustment. Another example comes from the Foreign Exchange. It is not very clever to compare one dollar and one pound directly. One needs an exchange rate, which says how they are actually to be compared. As we know, to say how to compare means to introduce a connection. In the previous example, the connection is completely defined by the exchange rate, but it is possible to find more complicated financial examples. Since we do not want to try to run before we can walk, we shall start with the Foreign Exchange example and study it in some detail first.

2.1   Foreign Exchange

Let us suppose that we are made an offer: if we pay 10 pounds now, we can immediately receive 20 German marks or 200 French francs or 2000 Japanese yen. How will we decide whether the offer is worthwhile? What one certainly would not do is to say: I have to give up 10 pieces of paper and, in return, I will get 20 (or 200 or even 2000) pieces of paper, and as I end up with at least 10 more pieces of paper, the deal is worthwhile! Instead, one would recognize that in order to evaluate the offer, it is important to convert all the different currencies to a common currency, say dollars, and then undertake the comparison.

This basic example should immediately conjure up thoughts of fibre bundles and the connection concept we discussed earlier. We cannot compare the amounts of money nominated in different currencies directly – first we have to convert them. This is exactly how it was with the two vectors stuck to two different points of the sphere in Fig. 2.8: first one has to bring them to one point, and only then can one compare them. If we use these fibre bundle analogies, we should make them precise. Let us define the base as five points labelled as GBP, USD, DM, FF, and JY (Fig. 2.11) and the fibre as a semi-line with a coordinate f ranging from zero to infinity, $0 \leq f < \infty$. Any amount of money is then characterized by its currency and the number of banknotes. This fibre bundle is the money space. In the present setting, any currency can be exchanged with any other currency, and hence 'curves' in the base consist of all possible jumps from one point of the base to another. The parallel transport associated with each of these curves is simply the currency exchange. The exchange rates constitute the connection on this strange discrete base.

Since all points in the base are equal in rights, we can consider any two points and then generalize the consideration to all other pairs. Assume we have two currencies, dollars and pounds, and want to compare four dollars and three pounds, i.e. we want to compare the numbers 3 and 4 in the coordinate systems of fibres corresponding to the points 'dollar' and 'pound' on the base. Once again, at first glance, four notes seem more attractive than three. However, anyone would prefer to have three pounds, because, at an exchange rate of 1.67 dollars to the pound, one can get five dollars for these three pounds, which is much better than

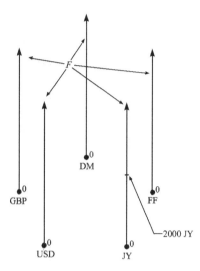

Figure 2.11 The fibre bundle space for the Foreign Exchange. Points on the plane are the base and the semi-lines are the fibres.

to have only four. We see that when assets are transformed from four dollars into three pounds, the real change was equal to $+1$ dollar instead of the initial apparent value -1:

$$3 \text{ pounds} - 4 \text{ dollars} = 3 \times 1.67 \text{ dollars} - 4 \text{ dollars} \simeq 1 \text{ dollar.}$$

Putting it more mathematically, the covariant difference between 3 pounds and 4 dollars along the curve of direct exchange is equal to $+1$, although the naive calculation gives -1.

In this case, the real value of four dollars was $4/1.67 \simeq 2.40$ pounds. For a mathematician, all this would mean that 2.40 pounds are the result of the parallel transport of 4 dollars along the direct link connecting dollars and pounds in the base.

2.2 Net Present Value and Discounting as Parallel Transport

First of all, let us recall what the Net Present Value (NPV) is.[5] The NPV investment method works on the simple, but fundamental, principle that money has a time value. This time value has to be taken into account through the so-called discounting process.

In the same way as money in different currencies cannot be compared directly, but first has to be converted to a common currency, money in the same currency, but coming at different points in time cannot be compared directly, but must first be converted to a common point in time. This reflects the time value of money.

Intuitively it is clear that, given the choice between 100 pounds now or 100 pounds in one year's time, most people would take the 100 now since the money could be placed in a risk-free deposit at some interest rate r and so generate some additional income. Then, in one

---

[5] The Net Present Value method in investment appraisal is explained in detail in many financial textbooks. I like most Lumby (1994).

year's time, 100 pounds would turn into $(1 + r)100$ pounds instead of keeping the initial 100 pounds only. Therefore r represents the time value of money.

Passing over the differences between different operational definitions of interest rates,[6] we are now ready to formulate what the NPV is: if an amount of money F is to be received in T years' time, the Present Value of that amount, $NPV(F)$, is the sum of money P (principal) that, if invested today, would generate the compound amount F in T years' time:

$$NPV(F) \equiv P = \frac{F}{(1 + r)^T}.$$

The interest rate involved in this calculation is known as the discount rate and the term $(1 + r)^{-T}$ is known as the T-year discount factor D_T:

$$D_T = (1 + r)^{-T}. \tag{1}$$

In a similar way, to calculate the present value of a stream of payments, the above formula is applied to each individual payment and the resulting individual present values are then summed. The NPV investment appraisal method states that if the NPV of an investment project is positive, the company should invest in the project; if it is negative, it should not invest. The same NPV principle can be applied to comparative analysis of several projects: one should invest in the project with the highest NPV.

Net Present Value gives us another financial example of parallel transport. Assume that we can choose between 100 pounds now or 103 pounds a year later. At first glance, 103 banknotes seem more attractive than 100. However, the reader is likely to choose 100 now because at an interest rate of 5% it will become 105 pounds in a year's time, which is definitely better than 103. Instead of counting all the pounds in a year later, we can count them now. Then, we will be able to compare 100 pounds with the discounted value of 103 pounds, that is the Net Present Value is equal to $103/(1 + 0.05) = 98.10$ pounds. Again one can see that as the assets move in time from pounds at present to pounds a year later, the real change is -2 pounds instead of the initial $+3$:

$$103 \text{ pounds in a year' s time} - 100 \text{ pounds now}$$
$$= (103 - 100 \times 1.05) \text{ pounds in a year' s time}$$
$$= -2 \text{ pounds in a year's time}.$$

The parallel transport of 100 pounds amounts to 105 pounds, and the covariant (real) difference is -2 pounds.

What is important here for our goals is the following geometrical interpretation: the discounting procedure plays the role of a 'parallel transport' in the fibre bundle that consists of the time axis as the base and, as before, semi-lines as the fibres (Fig. 2.12). The multiplication by the discounting factor in (1) is then the adjustment of the coordinate systems at different moments in time, and the discount rate coincides with the connection vector field.

---

[6] There exist many different definitions of interest rates and the corresponding discount factors, such as simple and compound interest rate, continuous compounding, flat and effective interest rates, and the like. The differences can be found in the textbook by Blake (1990).

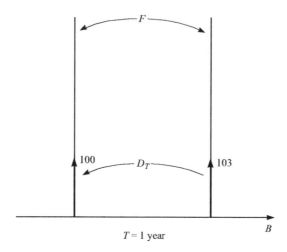

Figure 2.12   The fibre bundle space for Net Present Value calculations. The time axis is the base and the semi-lines are the fibres.

2.3   Two Generalizations: Many Assets and Time

To start with, currency exchange is no more than the buying and selling of currencies. It is clear that the picture can then be generalized to the trade of generic assets. For our purposes, the nature of the assets, the currencies, does not matter that much. All that we needed to define the parallel transport rules was the fact that the assets can be exchanged. This means that we can construct a fibre bundle for any market dealing with any kind of assets. To this end, we have to label the assets, put points with these labels on a plane, connect points that represent directly exchangeable assets, and stick semi-lines to each point. An example of the construction for the case of German marks, IBM shares, dollars, and US Treasury bills is depicted in Fig. 2.13. One can exchange German marks with dollars, but not with IBM shares directly, since the price of shares is nominated in dollars. This is why there is a direct link between USD and GM but there is no such link between DM and IBM shares or US Treasury bills. All the rest is similar to what we have done in the Foreign Exchange example.

The next step is to 'marry' space and time and to create a fibre bundle suitable for the description of a dynamical environment. To do this, we have to take a product of bases invented to describe the movements of money across the market and the movement in time staying in the same asset. The new base then consists of time axes piercing plane at points labelled by the names of assets existing in the market. Figure 2.14 shows how to enrich Fig. 2.13 to include time. The new fibre bundle is given by semi-line fibres stuck to each point of the new base. The coordinates in the semi-lines account for the number of banknotes in the corresponding currencies at the corresponding time. This fibre bundle already allows one to compare money in different assets and different moments of time. For example, one can compare 10 pounds now and 30 dollars in three years time, or 5 IBM shares and 60 French francs. Knowing how to compare assets we actually know how to calculate covariant differences and hence to characterize dynamics of income. This is what we need to formulate a mathematical model for the dynamics.

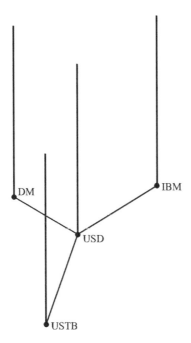

Figure 2.13 An example of the fibre bundle space for a general financial market. Points on the plane are the base and the semi-lines are the fibres.

To sum up, we can say that when financiers buy and sell securities, exchange currency, or calculate NPV, they make parallel transports in fibre bundles. Any exchange market possesses the structure of a fibre bundle provided with rules of parallel transport within it. This statement is perfectly general, and does not depend on the nature of the exchangeable assets, the preferences of market participants, or any other market details.

3 FINANCIAL ELECTRODYNAMICS

The section has two goals. The first is to demonstrate what kind of theory one can construct using elements of the fibre bundle geometry as building blocks and hence to justify the time spent in learning these new elements. The second goal is to give a flavour of what we are going to achieve and to prepare the intuitive ground for further chapters where the dynamics is studied in detail.

Once again, we start with a simple example. Let us denote the spot exchange rate of dollars to pounds by $F(t)$ at time t and their respective interest rates by r_1 and r_2. Assuming that all relevant information that can effect the exchange rates between t and $t + dt$ is known[7] and is

---

[7] There is no stochasticity in the problem, and the rates are known with certainty. If uncertainty is considered then $F(t + dt)$ has to be viewed as the corresponding forward price, as in the case of Covered Interest Parity.

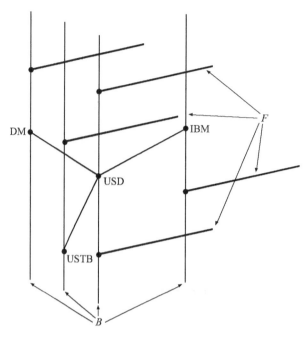

Figure 2.14   Generalization of Fig. 2.13 to include time. The base consists of time axes piercing a plane at points labelled by the names of assets. The fibre bundle is given by semi-line fibres stuck to the each point of the base.

reflected in these rates, we ask how $F(t)$ and $F(t+dt)$ are interrelated. It is easy to find that this interrelation can be expressed by a simple equation:[8]

$$F(t)(1+r_2) = F(t+dt)(1+r_1).$$ (2)

Let us explain why. What happens if for some reason the right-hand side of the relation is greater than the left-hand side? This will immediately result in a response from 'smart money', who will borrow pounds at time t, exchange them immediately into dollars, deposit the dollars until time $t+dt$ at the interest rate r_1, and then exchange them back to pounds. The situation when the right-hand side of (2) is greater than the left-hand side will ensure a riskless profit from the arbitrage transaction described above. This situation will not last for long: since few sellers will choose to sell dollars at time t and few buyers will choose to buy dollars at time $t+dt$ at initial prices, the exchange rates will change until the equality (2) is redeemed. It is also easy to make certain that the left-hand side of (2) cannot stay greater than the right-hand side for a long time. Therefore the equation expresses the condition of absence of arbitrage. However, we are more interested here in the restoration process rather than in the equation (2) itself.

The process of restoration or, as we are going to refer to it, relaxation will take some time, the length of which is determined by the market liquidity as well as market imperfections such as transaction costs and the bid–ask spread. The same factors will define the speed of the

---

[8] For example, if the difference of the annual interest rates $r_2 - r_1$ is 1%, the exchange rate in one year's time will be approximately 1% higher than today.

price adjustment. For instance, the relaxation is faster when the deviation from a balanced price is great (which attracts a large number of arbitrageurs despite transaction costs) compared with cases where deviations are small and transaction costs make transactions profitable only for big arbitrageurs.[9] The closer the market is to perfection, the less time that relaxation takes and the higher its speed is.

Using this example, we can identify two issues that will play a very important role in further studies.

3.1   Arbitrage as Curvature

Arbitrage returns gained from mispricing are always associated with the flow of assets along two different routes having a common beginning and end. In the previous example, we have compared route (a_1), i.e. pounds at time $t \rightarrow$ dollars at time $t \rightarrow$ dollars at time $t + dt \rightarrow$ pounds at time $t + dt$, with route (a_2), i.e. pounds at time $t \rightarrow$ pounds at time $t + dt$ (Fig. 2.15). Returns gained from these two routes of transactions are expressed by (2), assuming there is no arbitrage. Similarly, a pair of routes (b_1) and (b_2) can be introduced that begin and end in dollars.

Instead of two routes, a closed path of the asset flow can be studied. It follows the first route from the starting point to the end, and then the second route from the end to the starting point. In our case, it will be a cyclic path (c), i.e. pounds at time $t \rightarrow$ dollars at time $t \rightarrow$ dollars at time $t + dt \rightarrow$ pounds at time $t + dt \rightarrow$ pounds at time t. Having assigned to each segment of this path a respective exchange or interest factor to adjust coordinate

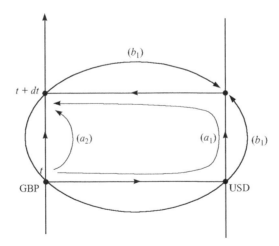

Figure 2.15   Two ways from pounds at time t to pounds at time $t + dt$. Different results of the parallel transport along the curves give rise to arbitrage opportunities.

---

[9] Theobald and Yallup (1999) found also that the speed of adjustment depends on the stock capitalization, and is smaller for smaller-capitalization stocks. See Chapter 7 for more details.

systems,[10] and having multiplied these factors along the path and subtracted one, we will get the quantity

$$R(c) = F^{-1}(t)(1 + r_2)^{-1}F(t + dt)(1 + r_1) - 1, \qquad (3)$$

which is equal to the discounted profit from an arbitrage transaction when 'cash' follows route (a_1) and 'debts' follow route (a_2). Further, we will use the term 'excess return on the arbitrage operation' to define this value. It is obvious from our previous discussion of the curvature that *the value R(c) of the excess return on the arbitrage operation actually represents the curvature* associated with the connection defined by the exchange rates and the interest rates. This is a very important observation, and it will play a central role below.

Besides a cyclic path (c), there is another cyclic path $(-c)$, which is derived from (c) by changing the flow direction. This path can also be described by an equation:

$$R(-c) = F(t)(1 + r_2)F^{-1}(t + dt)(1 + r_1)^{-1} - 1, \qquad (4)$$

which is equal to the discounted return on an arbitrage operation when 'cash' follows route (b_1), and 'debts' follow route (b_2). Combining (3) and (4), one can obtain the following value:

$$R = R(c) + R(-c), \qquad (5)$$

defining an opportunity to carry out a (certain) profitable arbitrage operation. The quantity R is non-negative, and is equal to zero only if there is no arbitrage. In this case, (2) is equivalent to the equation $R = 0$. It is more convenient to use the quantity R rather than (3) and (4) separately, especially when we do not want to specify which particular operation is profitable. Indeed, it does not matter which particular operation is profitable: if one operation generates losses then the opposite operation generates a profit. Therefore the quantity R characterizes the existence of arbitrage without specifying a particular arbitrage operation. The introduction of the notation R in (5) is not accidental. The quantity R is directly related to the curvature of the financial fibre bundle. In the case of electrodynamics, R is equal to the energy of the electromagnetic field. This moves us closer to the electrodynamical analogy.

3.2   Charges, Forces, and Gauge Symmetry

Let us go back to the mechanism of establishing balance described in the paragraph after (2). Speaking in general terms, we can conclude that 'cash' flows to undervalued assets from overpriced assets and 'debts' flow backwards, so if 'cash' flows like charged particles experiencing a force then 'debts' behave like particles with opposite charge. What is more, assets flowing in such a way make this force change, diminishing its value and reducing the mispricing. In physics, this effect is referred to as screening (Fig. 2.16). Thus we may conclude that a financial system behaves in the same way as a system of charges in a force field that is created and changed by these charges. Using physical notation, we can determine that a financial system that consists of 'cash', 'debts', and an arbitrage field looks apparently like classical electrodynamics, which deals with positive charges, negative charges, and the electromagnetic field. However, there are two differences. The first has something to do with the underlying base geometry. The financial 'electrodynamics' lives not in conventional three-dimensional space (four-dimensional space–time) but in a strange discrete space (quasi-one-

---

[10] Assuming that each segment that flows backwards has an inverse factor.

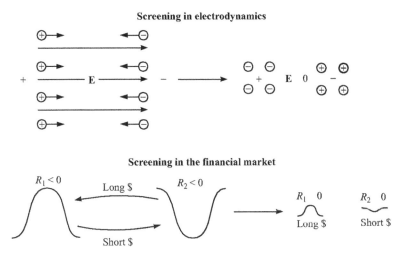

Figure 2.16 Screening in electrodynamics and in finance. In electrodynamics, charges move to diminish the field and to minimize the overall energy of the system. In finance, 'cash' and 'debts' flow to profit from a mispricing. The flows lead to changes in prices that effectively reduce mispricing.

dimensional space–time). In the example with dollars and pounds, this new financial space consists of two points only – a point 'dollars' and a point 'pounds' where assets 'jump' from one point to another. The second difference is less obvious, and is related to a structural symmetry hidden in the fibre bundle formulation of the theories. Let us look more closely at this issue.

At first glance, the analogy with electrodynamics may seem purely superficial to economists as well as physicists. Frankly speaking, the experience of presenting the subject at different seminars with audiences varying from high-energy physicists to financial quantitative analysts shows that at this point people stop listening and start to pack their bags: they believe it is the end of the story, the connection with electrodynamics is unjustified, and there are a huge number of models giving the same picture. Usually it takes another half an hour to formalize the consideration and convince them to drop these charges. Indeed, as has already been mentioned, there are several ways of writing equations describing migration and screening, electrodynamics being just one of the options. That is why, without additional arguments, favouring electrodynamics seems artificial and unjustified. Such additional arguments are provided in the form of a general powerful symmetry that singles out 'electrodynamics' from a great number of other competitive theories.

Let us study equations (3) and (4) in more detail. It is easy to see that they have certain remarkable properties: they do not change when currency units and their respective exchange and interest rates are changed. For instance, suppose that between time t and $t + dt$, we decide to use pence instead of pounds. This decision will not affect the dollar's interest rate and exchange rate at time t, but it will diminish the exchange rate 100 times at time $t + dt$ (when a pound will cost 100 new units, i.e. pence) and increase the interest factor 100 times – having deposited one pound, one will get $100(1 + r_2)$ pence. The factor of 100 will vanish, and (3) and (4) will remain unchanged. We could have applied this argument to a simultaneous change of both dollars and pounds, which would not alter the result – (3) and (4), based on closed paths, do not change. Going further and applying this approach to any tradeable (exchangeable) asset, one can see that equations such as (3)–(5) remain unchanged when the scale of the assets's units changes, irrespective of whether it is currency, bonds, or stocks. In the first case, the change in scale would mean denomination; in other cases, the change of the traded lot or merge and split.

Suppose now that we are trying to construct a theory that has the property of not changing when the units of measurements are arbitrarily chosen, that is, it does not depend on the choice of the financial assets' units, the currency nominal values, the lot size, etc.[11] There is no doubt that the real world has this property – at least to a certain extent: agents do not start behaving in a different way because they are dealing just with 100 pence instead of one pound or if there are only 50 shares in the lot instead of 100 (we will see some empirical discussion of this in the last section of Chapter 5). In building this theory one can only use those mathematical objects that remain unchanged when the units of measurement are changed, for instance, quantities defined by (3)–(5). We will prove in Chapters 5 and 6 that in this case, the simplest non-trivial theory will be almost equivalent to electrodynamics! It is this very property that distinguishes electrodynamics from a great number of other competitive theories. It is simply impossible to do it in another way.

In building a model, it is not chance that we started by looking at the symmetries of the theory. We were aided by the methodology of physics. All contemporary physical theories are based on the symmetry inherent in them. The General Theory of Relativity is built on the assumption that the choice of coordinates is not essential for the statement of the law governing the motion of bodies.[12] Quantum electrodynamics can be built on the assumption that the wave function's phase cannot be physically seen and its selection is arbitrary. Theories of weak and strong interactions also have fundamental symmetries of selection of physically equivalent objects. Physicists refer to such symmetries as *gauge symmetries*. The theory of the financial market described in this book can be also called a gauge one – the Gauge Theory of Arbitrage (GTA). The word 'gauge' in the name is explained by the fact that, from a geometrical point of view, as we will see in Chapter 4, a force field appears in the gauge theory to preserve its gauge symmetry. The word 'arbitrage' appears in order to emphasize that the role of the force moving money flows is played by the excess return on arbitrage operation in exactly the same way that the electromagnetic field is a force field in electrodynamics. From a mathematical point of view, the financial theory looks very much like electrodynamics, with this additional difference between them: *instead of a gauge group of quantum phase rotation, a gauge group of dilatations of financial assets units has to be used.*

3.3   Uncertainty and Quantization

Up to this point, information capable of affecting prices has been known in advance, which means that there was no uncertainty. The real financial world is clearly far from this picture. Any financial operation is associated with risk. That is why we have to generalize the theory to the case of uncertain or random prices.

---

[11] That is, nothing depends on the choice of a *numeraire* for any asset at any moment of time.
[12] This looks rather like our freedom to choose the units in (3)–(5).

Describing random characteristics, such as the exchange rate, for example, in a month's time, we are not able to predict their exact value. All that is possible to do is to predict the probability with which we can expect a certain value of the exchange rate. According to its definition, the probability is equal to the number of times a certain result is expected to be achieved under identical experimental conditions divided by number of experiments. This means that, applying a probabilistic description, we expect that the experiment will be repeated in exactly the same way many times. It is evident that this condition cannot be met in the example with the exchange rate: there is only one April and only one May in 1998. Trying to repeat the experiment in May–June, we will encounter different conditions in the market, and consequently we will have to change the conditions of the experiment. Moreover, the result of the experiment in April–May may affect the outcome of the experiment in May–June. This shows that the very concept of probability in this case can be difficult to define. We will try to overcome these difficulties by looking at short periods of time, when it can be assumed that all external factors remain unchanged.

Like random values, the random paths that prices follow are also described by probabilities, in this case the probability of covering the whole path.[13] Such a probability is referred to as the path weight. The weight fully defines a statistical model, and the choice of the weight is a key step in building a theory. Here again we are faced with the problem of choice. To make our choice, we will use the following considerations: the weight must keep the symmetry of the theory constructed before stochasticity entered it, that is, the weight must be based on gauge-invariant quantities such as (3)–(5). In the situation where the world becomes less and less arbitrary, the weight must identify paths with minimum mispricing opportunities; that is, the weight must identify the paths on which the quantity (5) has a minimum value. In the approximation where the speed of money flows is infinite and they do not effectively participate in the description, the theory must reproduce the results of financial mathematics. It turns out that the theory developed from these assumptions technically looks similar to quantum electrodynamics (in imaginary time), just as a theory without stochasticity is similar to classical electrodynamics.

Why 'quantum'? In quantum mechanics, the complete set of classical coordinates of a system in phase space cannot be determined precisely, and one has to allow for a stochastic error that cannot be predicted. In other words, quantum mechanics is a probabilistic theory by its very nature. This is why many convenient and powerful methods have been developed in the framework of quantum field theory, one of which is the calculus of random trajectories. In this language, the theory of the random financial market and quantum electrodynamics in imaginary time almost coincide.

The last remark of this chapter again concerns the words that we use to describe the theory. Many discussions of the subject show that at this stage the following misunderstanding sometimes emerges, and we would like to clarify it. The arbitrage itself implies the possibility of performing an operation with a risk-free rate of return that is higher than, say, a bank deposit interest rate. In this sense, after the uncertainty has been introduced into the theory, buying shares cannot be considered as such an operation because of the assumed random walk of the share price and the corresponding risk. What do we mean then by using the word 'arbitrage'? If the randomness of the price is similar to quantization, the rate of return on an arbitrage operation is now a 'quantum' variable that does not have a well-defined value and cannot be taken as a real number. This exactly resembles the situation with the electro-

---

[13] Strictly speaking, one has to work with probability weights on a space of random trajectories.

magnetic field, which, after quantization, is not a number but a quantum variable, an operator. However, this does not stop physicists using the same name for the variable, imagining virtual quantum fluctuations, and describing the influence of these fluctuations on electric charges, keeping in mind the calculation of the corresponding matrix elements. In the same way, we understand the arbitrage rate of return in the financial setting. It causes money flows, it is virtual, it fluctuates. For us, the word 'arbitrage' is just a matter of convenient agreement. It might be seen as misleading, but we keep using it because of the analogy with electro-dynamics and because in some cases (see Chapters 8 and 9) it does indeed give the correct image common in financial mathematics.

4 SUMMARY

- Fibre bundles are spaces with two different sets of coordinates. They are suitable for describing systems with internal as well as external degrees of freedom.

- A fibre bundle consists of a base and fibres that are stuck to each point of the base.

- To compare coordinates in different fibres, one has to introduce the connection, which is a rule for adjustment of coordinate systems in different fibres.

- The connection defines parallel transport along curves in the base. Different curves with the same endpoints can give different results. The difference defines the curvature of the fibre bundle.

- The financial market can be considered as a fibre bundle. The corresponding connection is given by prices and discount factors.

- The curvature of the financial fibre bundle gives the excess return on an arbitrage operation.

- Gauge invariant financial dynamics, i.e. dynamics that obey a symmetry with respect to change of asset units, resemble electrodynamics. Here 'cash' plays the role of positive charges, 'debts' play the role of negative charges, and the excess return on an arbitrage operation is an analogue of the electromagnetic field.

5 FURTHER READING

1. An interesting application of gauge ideas to biological systems was suggested by Gerhard Mack (1994). Further developments of the idea of generalized dynamics can be found in Mack (1996).
2. The fibre bundle structure of the financial market was first suggested in Ilinski (1997) and independently and almost simultaneously by Young (1999).
3. Early criticism of the Gauge Theory of Arbitrage can be found in Sornette (1998).

3

Fibre Bundles: Mathematics

A FTER 'hand-waving' in Chapter 2, this chapter is more mathematical. We give formal definitions of manifolds, fibre bundles, connections, and the corresponding curvatures, and spend some time discussing transformation laws and lattice modifications. All of these subjects are relevant for our purpose of a geometrical description of financial markets, which starts with Chapter 5. Section 8 of this chapter does not have a direct connection with other material in this book; it is labelled 'for the curious', and can be omitted without affecting the understanding of the the main text. It is included to give a feeling of why fibre bundles are so popular in pure mathematics and to demonstrate the beauty of this geometry that sometimes reveals itself in an unexpected way.

The mathematics behind fibre bundles is quite complicated, and there are many texts that cover the subject with different levels of complexity. We give some references at the end of the chapter. Although the pleasure of contemplation of the numerous successes of this branch of contemporary mathematics repays the work needed for its study, it takes a lot of time to become proficient in the subject. This chapter in no way pretends to give a review – even a concise one. It would be fairer to say that we rather introduce expressions that formalize the concepts learned in the previous chapter and substitute figures by formulae.

I MANIFOLDS

To do any kind of calculations in a space, one inevitably has to deal with functions of points in the space. Since the only effective way to describe functions is to introduce coordinates in the space first and then to define a function as a function of the coordinates, one has to be able to introduce a coordinate system in the space. Manifolds are a general class of spaces where it is possible to define coordinate frames without contradictions.

The simplest examples of manifolds are n-dimensional Euclidean spaces such as the one-dimensional line, the two-dimensional plane, and their higher-dimensional analogues. These spaces have natural coordinate systems that represent a point as a set of real numbers $(x_1, x_2, \ldots, x_n)$ where n is the dimension of the space. There is no other way to introduce coordinates in a space except to map this space into a n-dimensional Euclidean space and then use the standard coordinates. It is often the case that it is impossible to map a general space to Euclidean space globally but one can do this locally in a neighbourhood of every point of the space. This is already sufficient to define the local coordinates, and the only problem left is to make the local coordinates consistent with each other. This is the rationale behind the notion of a manifold in geometry.

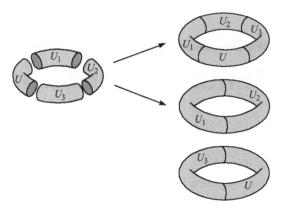

Figure 3.1 With the same neighbourhoods, different rules of identification give different manifolds.

Informally, a real *n-dimensional manifold M* is a space that looks like a Euclidean *n*-dimensional space around each point. More precisely, a manifold is defined by introducing a set of neighbourhoods U_i that cover the space M and have one-to-one correspondence with domains of the Euclidean space. If the neighbourhoods overlap, one has to define a rule for the identification of the coordinates from different neighbourhoods in the overlapping region. These are the rules that define the geometry of the manifold: different rules give different manifolds (see Fig. 3.1). If the rules for the identification are smooth, the manifold is also called smooth. Now let us formalize the above consideration in the following definition.

Definition I   A space M is a *smooth n-dimensional manifold* if the following hold:

1. There exists a set of neighbourhoods $U_i \in M$ such that their union[1] gives the whole space M:

$$\bigcup U_i = M.$$

2. There exist functions ϕ_i that map the neighbourhoods into open domains of n-dimensional Euclidean space and obey the following condition: for any two neighbourhoods U_i and U_j with non-zero intersection $U_i \cap U_j \neq \emptyset$, the map[2]

$$\phi_i \circ \phi_j^{-1} : \phi_j(U_i \cap U_j) \to \phi_i(U_i \cap U_j)$$

is a smooth function on Euclidean space.

The domains $\phi_i(U_i)$ are called *charts*, and the whole set of charts comprises an *atlas*.

In Chapter 2, we met a simple but non-trivial manifold – the two-dimensional sphere. It is defined by the following equation in three-dimensional Euclidean space:

$$x_1^2 + x_2^2 + x_3^2 = 1.$$

---

[1] In what follows we use the notation $\cup$ and $\cap$ for the operations of taking union and intersection.
[2] The notation $\phi_i \circ \phi_j^{-1}(x)$ means $\phi_i(\phi_j^{-1}(x))$.

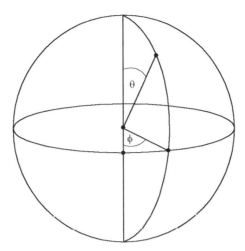

Figure 3.2   Spherical coordinates (θ, ϕ) on a sphere.

We will now show that the sphere cannot be covered by one coordinate system. To see this, let us introduce the spherical coordinates (ϕ, θ) as depicted on Fig. 3.2:

$$x_1 = \cos \phi \sin \theta, \quad x_2 = \sin \phi \sin \theta, \quad x_3 = \cos \theta.$$

The points on the Euclidean plane with coordinates $0 \leq \phi < 2\pi$, $0 < \theta < \pi$ have one counterpart on the sphere. These are hence the proper coordinates. However, there are points with $\theta = 0$ and $\theta = \pi$ that have only one point on the sphere for all values of ϕ. These are singular points of the coordinate system. The point on the sphere is therefore not a single-valued function of the coordinates (ϕ, θ). To cover the sphere with these pole points, one has to use two neighbourhoods and a corresponding coordinate identification rule (see Fig. 3.3).

A natural problem that appears in the geometry of manifolds is the problem of classification. Let us define equivalent manifolds as manifolds that can be smoothly transformed into each other (see Fig. 3.4). This smooth transformation leaves unchanged some characteristics of the manifold, such as its dimension. The characteristics of the manifold that stay the same under any smooth transformation are called *topological invariants*. We can classify the manifolds by a set of invariants that completely define the manifold up to a smooth transformation. Unfortunately, in this general form, the problem cannot be solved for high-dimensional manifolds, but for one- and two-dimensional manifolds the problem allows such a solution.

We start with one-dimensional manifolds. The reader can persuade herself that any compact[3] one-dimensional one-piece manifolds are equivalent to a circle, open manifolds are equivalent to a line, and manifolds with a boundary are equivalent to a segment or a semi-line. The classification of the two-dimensional manifolds is slightly more demanding. We will do it only for the case of compact one-piece manifolds that can be embedded in three-dimensional space without self-intersections.[4]

---

[3] Finite and without boundaries.
[4] These are so-called compact orientable manifolds.

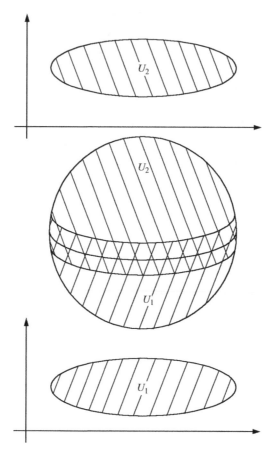

Figure 3.3   To cover a sphere, one has to use at least two neighbourhoods U_1 and U_2 and a rule for their identification.

First of all, the sphere is one such manifold. It consists of one piece, is compact, and can be considered as a surface in the three-dimensional Euclidean space. A torus gives another example. The torus differs from the sphere by the hole 'inside'. One can imagine other surfaces that will have two or more similar holes. The number of holes is called the *genus* of the surface. It turns out that the genus is the only invariant that is needed to classify the surfaces: any compact orientable two-dimensional manifold is equivalent to a surface with some genus g. The reader can construct as many of these manifolds as she wants by 'gluing' handles to the sphere (see Fig. 3.5). Each additional handle increases the genus of the surface by one.

The dimension of the manifold and its genus are the global invariants of the surface. It might then be very surprising to learn that the global characteristics are ultimately connected with local characteristics of the manifold such as the local Gaussian curvature. This connection is a particular case of general statements known under the name of index theorems, which we touch upon in the appendix to this chapter.

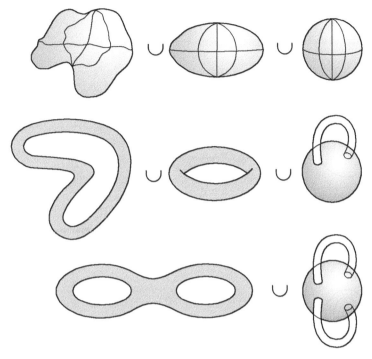

Figure 3.4 Examples of equivalent manifolds.

Not all two-dimensional manifolds can be embedded in three-dimensional space without self-intersections. The Klein bottle is a famous example. It can be constructed from the Möbius strip (Fig. 3.5 in Chapter 2) by identifying the edges of the strip (see Fig. 3.6). One can see that there is no possibility to imagine the Klein bottle in our three-dimensional space without self-intersections. However, even this bizarre manifold will unfold and present a hypersurface in a Euclidean space of high enough dimension. A general fact about embedding is given by the following theorem, known as Whitney's theorem:[5]

Theorem I Any smooth n-dimensional manifold M can be embedded as a hypersurface without intersections in N-dimensional Euclidean space, where $N > 2n$.

This theorem states that an abstract notion of manifolds in principle does not contain objects that are different from hypersurfaces embedded in Euclidean space of an appropriate dimension. In the general case, $N = 2n + 1$, but for particular spaces one can prove the existence of more restrictive estimates. For example, the Klein bottle can be embedded in four-dimensional Euclidean space. But do not try it at home!

---

[5] The theorem is very popular among market chaologists. They believe that markets move along some low-dimensional attractors in multidimensional parameter space. It is technically impossible to construct the attractor. However, as the theorem says, one can map the attractor in some N-dimensional Euclidean space and observe the market dynamics in it. Since the dimension N is supposed to be small, to predict market movements, one can use simple low-dimensional maps. Empirical tests do not support this sort of idea, even for the high-frequency regime (see Part II of Dunis and Zhon, 1998). For a recent review of empirical results on applications of the dynamical systems theory to financial markets, see also Barnett and Serletis (2000).

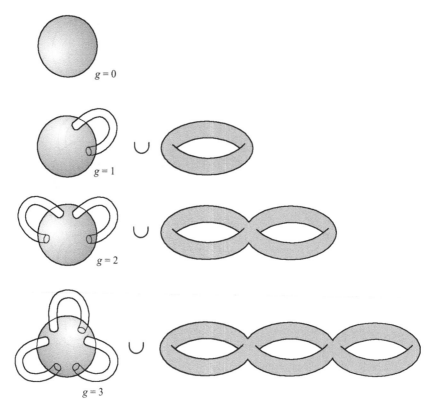

Figure 3.5   Construction of a general two-dimensional compact manifold.

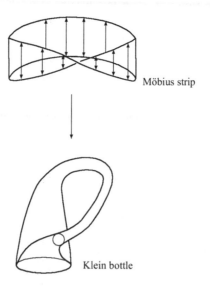

Figure 3.6   Klein bottle.

2   FIBRE BUNDLES

In Chapter 2, we informally introduced the fibre bundle spaces, explained why they appear in mathematics and in applications, and gave several intuitive examples. This section contains some formal definitions that we will use in following chapters.

As introduced before, a fibre bundle consists of a base and the fibres associated with each point on the base. The base and the fibres are manifolds, and their structures induce the manifold structure in the fibre bundle. This means that the fibre bundle is covered by neighbourhoods made from the corresponding neighbourhoods of the base and the fibres. These composite neighbourhoods together with identification rules provide coordinates in the fibre bundle. This construction is formalized by the following definition (Dubrovin et al, 1985):

Definition 2   A *smooth fibre bundle* is a composite object, made up of the following:

1. A smooth manifold E called the *total (bundle) space.*

2. A smooth manifold B called the *base space.*

3. A smooth map $p : E \rightarrow B$ called the *projection*, whose Jacobian is required to have maximal rank $n = \dim B$ at every point.[6]

4. A smooth manifold F called the *fibre.*

5. A group G of smooth transformations of the fibre F (this implies that the action $G \times F \rightarrow F$ is smooth on $G \times F$); this group is called the *structure group* of the fibre bundle.

6. A 'fibre bundle structure' linking the above entities, and defined as follows. The base B comes with a particular system of local coordinate neighbourhoods U_i (called the *coordinate neighbourhoods* or *charts*), above each of which the coordinates of the direct product are introduced via a diffeomorphism[7] $\phi_i : F \times U_i \rightarrow p^{-1}(U_i)$ satisfying $p\phi(f, x) = x$;   the   transformations $\lambda_{ij} = \phi_j^{-1} \circ \phi_i : F \times U_{ij} \rightarrow F \times U_{ij}$,   where $U_{ij} = U_i \cap U_j$, are called the *transition functions* of the fibre bundle. Every transformation λ_{ij} has the form

$$\lambda_{ij}(f, x) = (T^{ij}f, x),$$

where for all i, j, x the transformation $T^{ij}(x)$ is an element of the structure group G.

The definition looks terribly complicated, but actually it just puts in mathematical symbols what we have said in words. Let's see it step by step. Items 1, 2, and 4 are clear. Item 3 states the fact that the base can be obtained from the whole fibre bundle if one neglects degrees of freedom hidden in the fibre. This projects all points of a fibre to a single point, associated with the corresponding point in the base. Doing so, we obtain the whole base and no pieces of it can be missed. Item 5 introduces the structure group of the fibre bundle. This is a group of transformations of the fibres. We need these transformations to identify coordinates in fibres for overlapping neighbourhoods. Item 6 of the definition looks the most threatening.

---

[6] The *Jacobian* of a map is the matrix of its first derivatives. If the rank of this matrix is equal to dim B at every point, the map is indeed a projection.

[7] *Diffeomorphisms* are one-to-one smooth maps.

However, it simply says that the neighbourhoods covering the fibre bundle can be constructed as pairs of neighbourhoods in the base, U_i, and of neighbourhoods of the fibres so that the coordinates in the fibre bundle can also be given by pairs (f, x) where f is a set of coordinates in the fibre and x is a set of coordinates in the base. To identify coordinates in overlapping regions, one has to introduce the transition functions λ_{ij} that transform a pair (f, x) into the pair $(T^{ij}f, x)$, where the transformation T^{ij} is an element of the structure group and maps a coordinate system of the fibre above U_i into the coordinate system in the fibre above U_j.

Using new terms, we can present a fibre bundle as a union of fibres $F_b = p^{-1}(b)$ for any element $b \in B$. This union is parametrized by the base B and 'glued together' by the topology of the space E using the transition functions λ_{ij}. The total space E can be represented as $E = \bigcup_i F \times U_i$. For each of the charts U_i, the coordinate system in the fibre F can be chosen independently. This generates two independent coordinate systems in F for each overlap neighbourhood $U_{ij} = U_i \cap U_j$. To identify equivalent points (to 'glue them together') in different coordinate systems, one uses elements of the structure group G, stating that

$$T^{ij}f|_{U_i} = f|_{U_j}, \quad f \in F.$$

It follows from the definition of the functions T^{ij} that

$$T^{ij}(x) = (T^{ji}(x))^{-1}, \quad T^{ij}(x)T^{jk}(x)T^{ki}(x) = 1,$$

where the second equation is understood as holding on the region of intersection $U_i \cap U_j \cap U_k$.

The simplest example to demonstrate how the definition works is the Möbius strip (Fig. 2.5, Chapter 2). We do it following Definition 2 item by item:

1. The Möbius strip is the total fibre bundle space.

2. The base is the circle S^1 parametrized by the angle θ. The circle is covered by two semicircular neighbourhoods U_1 and U_2 as shown in Fig. 3.7:
$$U_1 = \{\theta : -\epsilon < \theta < \pi + \epsilon\}, \quad U_2 = \{\theta : \pi - \epsilon < \theta < 2\pi + \epsilon\}.$$

3. The projection p is the projection of the strip onto the central circle S^1 of the strip.

4. The fibre F is an interval on the real line with coordinates $x \in [-1, 1]$.

5. The structure group G in this case is the group of multiplications by -1, the so-called Z_2 group. It contains only two elements: -1 and $(-1)^2 = 1$.

6. The set of neighbourhoods of the fibre bundle consists of only two elements, $E_1 \equiv U_1 \times F$, with coordinates (θ, x_1) and $E_2 \equiv U_2 \times F$, with coordinates (θ, x_2). The transition functions relate x_1 and x_2 in the overlapping region $U_1 \cap U_2$:
$$x_1 = 1 \cdot x_2 \quad \text{for} \quad \{\theta : -\epsilon < \theta < \epsilon\},$$

$$x_1 = -1 \cdot x_2 \quad \text{for} \quad \{\theta : \pi - \epsilon < \theta < \pi + \epsilon\}.$$

Identification of x_1 and $-x_2$ in the second case twists the strip and gives it its non-trivial global topology. To get simple cylinder, one has to use the identification $x_1 = x_2$ for both cases.

The simple cylinder is a trivial fibre bundle and the Möbius strip is a non-trivial fibre bundle. Let us formalize this intuitive difference:

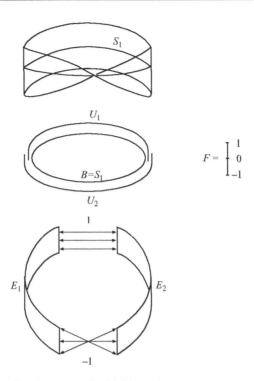

$$F = \begin{cases} 1 \\ 0 \\ -1 \end{cases}$$

Figure 3.7 Two neighbourhoods to cover the Möbius strip.

Definition 3   A fibre bundle E is *trivial with fibre F* if it is globally isomorphic to the fibre bundle $B \times F$ with some base B and fibre F.

The definition says that a fibre bundle is trivial if one can introduce a global coordinate system such that any point of the space will be given by the pair of coordinates (x, f), where f is a set of coordinates in the fibre and x is a set of coordinates on the base. All of the financial examples that we mentioned in Chapter 2 are trivial fibre bundles. There exists a theorem that any fibre bundle over a contractible base is trivial. The word 'contractible' means that the base can be shrunk smoothly to a point. Two-dimensional compact surfaces are not contractible, but the two-dimensional disk is. Thus non-trivial fibre bundles can only be constructed when the global topology of the base is non-trivial.
    We conclude this section with another definition:

Definition 4   A *principal fibre bundle* is defined to be a fibre bundle whose fibre F coincides with the structure group, which acts on the fibre $F = G$ as $g : G \rightarrow G$, $g(x) = gx$ (left translations).

Principal fibre bundles play a very important role in gauge theories. If a fibre bundle with some fibre F is a space of matter fields, like the money spaces with semi-line fibres in the financial examples of Chapter 2, the principal fibre bundle is a space of gauge fields, the fields that carry the interaction. In the financial setting, the principal fibre bundle is the space of prices and discount factors. Trajectories in this space give prices and interest rate paths as functions of time.

3   CONNECTIONS ON FIBRE BUNDLES

Now we make more formal the definition of a connection that was introduced in Chapter 2. As was explained there, a connection allows one to do differential calculus on a fibre bundle, i.e. calculate derivatives, finite differences, integrals, and so on. Being able to do differential calculus is a key aspect in defining and studying dynamics in fibre bundles.

A fibre bundle with connection can be imagined as a family $\{F_b\}$ of fibres (whose union $\bigcup_b F_b$ is the total space E) that is also provided with a rule for 'parallel transport'. Given any path $\gamma \equiv \{\gamma(t)\}_{a \le t \le b}$, in the base B, the connection defines a rule for 'parallel transporting' the fibre F along the path γ from one end to the other.

Definition 5   For any curve γ in the base, a *connection* is a map of the fibre $F_{\gamma(a)}$ associated with the point $\gamma(a)$ of the base to the fibre $F_{\gamma(b)}$ above the point $\gamma(b)$,

$$\phi_\gamma : F_{\gamma(a)} \to F_{\gamma(b)},$$

that satisfies the following natural requirements:

1. $\phi(\gamma)$ depends continuously on the path $\gamma(t)$: a small change in the path cannot lead to a large change as a result of parallel transport.

2. $\phi(\gamma)$ is independent of the parametrization of the path. This means that the parallel transport is actually defined by the path rather than by the function $\gamma(\cdot)$: different functions that give the same curve in the base will cause the same parallel transport.

3. $\phi(\gamma)$ is the identity map if $\gamma(t) = \text{const}$: if there is no path then there is no transport.

4. The following equations hold:

$$\phi(\gamma_1 \gamma_2) = \phi(\gamma_1)\phi(\gamma_2), \quad \phi(\gamma^{-1}) = (\phi(\gamma))^{-1}. \tag{1}$$

The first relation states that parallel transport along two consecutive curves is equivalent to parallel transport along the resulting combined curve. The second says that the parallel transport along the same curve but performed in the opposite direction generates the inverse parallel transport.

This definition of a connection is too general for our goals. In what follows, we will use a more specific connection, the so-called G-connection. A connection is called a G-connection if the map ϕ_γ is an element of the structure group for any curve in the base:

$$\phi_\gamma F_{\gamma(a)} = g(\gamma)F_{\gamma(a)}, \quad g(\gamma) \in G \quad \forall \gamma.$$

The function $g(\gamma)$ inherits the four properties of the map ϕ_γ listed above; one has just changed ϕ to g. Using $g(\gamma)$, we define the parallel transport of an element f of the fibre F along the path γ: the expression $g(\gamma)f \in F_{\gamma(b)}$ is the result of the parallel transport of $f \in F_{\gamma(a)}$.

We know that a connection is the essential ingredient in defining covariant differences and covariant derivatives. But first we need to define the objects of these operations. These are functions on the base with values in the fibre.

Definition 6   A *cross-section* of a fibre bundle is a map $\psi : B \rightarrow E$ such that $p\psi(x) = x$ for any x in B, i.e. $\psi(x)$ is an element of F_x for each x.

For any cross-section, we can now define the *covariant difference* of its values at points $\gamma(a)$ and $\gamma(b)$ connected by the curve γ:

$$\Delta_\gamma \psi \equiv \psi(\gamma(b)) - g(\gamma)\psi(\gamma(a)). \tag{2}$$

The covariant difference depends on the curve, so one will generally have different covariant differences calculated along different curves.

The definition of the connection as a map from curves in the base to the structure group is not particularly convenient in practical applications. It is always easier to study local changes and then sum them to give global ones. Fortunately, the property (1) of the connection allows us to reduce any global problem to a set of local ones where parallel transport along very small curves can be considered. In this case, if γ is an infinitesimal path connecting points x and $x + dx$ in the base and G is a Lie group, the covariant difference transforms to the *covariant derivative* $D\psi$:

$$D\psi(x)\, dx \equiv \sum_{\mu=1}^{\dim B} D_\mu \psi(x)\, dx^\mu = \sum_{\mu=1}^{\dim B} \left(\frac{\partial \psi(x)}{\partial x^\mu} - A_\mu(x)\psi(x) \right) dx^\mu. \tag{3}$$

Here we have used the smoothness of parallel transport to write the element of the structure group g as

$$g(\gamma) \simeq 1 + \sum_{\mu=1}^{\dim B} A_\mu(x + dx/2)\, dx^\mu \simeq 1 + \sum_{\mu=1}^{\dim B} A_\mu(x)\, dx^\mu,$$

with $A_\mu(x)$ being elements of the Lie algebra of the structure group G. Equation (3) expresses in mathematical terms our verbal definitions of Chapter 2 for the apparent and the 'real' changes: the term $A_\mu(x)\psi(x)\, dx^\mu$ stands for the apparent change in the value of the cross-section and is caused by non-adjustment of the coordinate systems in the fibres $F_{\gamma(a)}$ and $F_{\gamma(b)}$. The difference between the nominal change and the apparent change is expressed in the covariant derivative and characterizes the 'real' change.

Starting with the fields $A_\mu(x)$ and the infinitesimal parallel transport, one can get the finite parallel transport by summing the infinitesimal results. There is, however, a more straightforward way to reach the same final results without complicated summations. This method uses the *equation of parallel transport*. This is the equation for the cross-section ψ such that all values of ψ along a curve γ result from parallel transport of its value $\psi(\gamma(a))$. By definition, this means that the value $\psi(\gamma(b))$ will be the solution of the problem of parallel transport of an element $f = \psi(\gamma(a))$ along the curve γ. It is a one-step procedure to find the equation. If the cross-section ψ results from parallel transport, the covariant derivative of ψ has to be zero along all infinitesimal segments of the curve γ:

$$\dot{\gamma} \cdot D\psi(x) \equiv \sum_{\mu=1}^{\dim B} D_\mu \psi(x) \frac{d\gamma^\mu(t)}{dt} = 0,$$

since the infinitesimal curve dx^μ can be written as $\dfrac{d\gamma^\mu(t)}{dt}\, dt$. Taking into account that

$$\sum_{\mu=1}^{\dim B} \frac{d\gamma^\mu(t)}{dt} \cdot \frac{\partial \psi(x)}{\partial x^\mu} = \frac{d\psi(t)}{dt},$$

we rewrite the equation for the cross-section as

$$\frac{d\psi(t)}{dt} = \sum_{\mu=1}^{\dim B} \frac{d\gamma^{\mu}(t)}{dt} \cdot A_{\mu}(x)\big|_{x=\gamma(t)}\psi(t). \tag{4}$$

This is a system of first-order differential equations, which requires only one initial condition $\psi(\gamma(a)) = f$.

For an illustration, we return to the Peaceful World (tangent bundle) example (Fig. 2.6 in Chapter 2). The base is the two-dimensional sphere with local spherical coordinates θ and ϕ. The fibres are the tangent planes, and hence they are also two-dimensional. Since A_{μ} are transformations of the tangent planes, they are two-by-two matrices and have matrix elements $-\Gamma^{j}_{\mu i}$, which are called the Christoffel symbols. Using this notation, (4) can be rewritten as

$$\frac{d\psi^{i}(t)}{dt} + \sum_{\mu,j=1}^{2} \frac{d\gamma^{\mu}(t)}{dt}\Gamma^{i}_{\mu j}\psi^{j} = 0, \quad i = 1, 2.$$

The diligent reader can spend some time checking that the solutions of these equations do indeed give the rules for parallel transport shown in Fig. 2.8 of Chapter 2 if the Christoffel symbols are defined as

$$\Gamma^{2}_{12} = \Gamma^{2}_{21} = \cot\theta, \quad \Gamma^{1}_{22} = -\cos\theta\sin\theta, \quad \Gamma^{i}_{\mu j} = 0 \quad \text{otherwise.}$$

This particular form for the Christoffel symbols is chosen because the corresponding parallel transport does not change the metric on the sphere inherited from the embedding three-dimensional Euclidean space, but we do not stop here to demonstrate this.

4 CURVATURE

Since the curve γ enters directly into the equation for parallel transport (4), the result of the parallel transport depends not only on the endpoints $\gamma(a)$ and $\gamma(b)$ but on the whole path γ. This means that the results of parallel transports with the same endpoints but different paths can be different. The *curvature of a fibre bundle* is a measure of this difference. In physics and in finance, the difference will signal the presence of a force that influences the system in question. The curvature is designed to quantify the force.

To define curvature, we consider parallel transport along an infinitesimal rectangle $ABCD$ in the base (Fig. 3.8). The points A, B, C, and D have corresponding coordinates $x - a/2 - b/2$, $x + a/2 - b/2$, $x + a/2 + b/2$, and $x - a/2 + b/2$. Performing the first parallel transport along the edge AB, the element f_A transforms to f_B:

$$f_B = \left(1 + \sum_{\mu=1}^{\dim B} A_{\mu}(x - b/2)a^{\mu}\right)f_A,$$

so that the covariant difference along the edge is zero. In a similar manner, the result of parallel transport along the second edge BC has the form

$$f_C = \left(1 + \sum_{\mu=1}^{\dim B} A_{\mu}(x + a/2)b^{\mu}\right)f_B.$$

Repeating this procedure for the other two edges, we come to the result of parallel transport along the loop $ABCD$:

$$f'_A = \left(1 - \sum_{\mu=1}^{\dim B} A_\mu(x - a/2)b^\mu\right)\left(1 - \sum_{\mu=1}^{\dim B} A_\mu(x + b/2)a^\mu\right)$$

$$\times \left(1 + \sum_{\mu=1}^{\dim B} A_\mu(x + a/2)b^\mu\right)\left(1 + \sum_{\mu=1}^{\dim B} A_\mu(x - b/2)a^\mu\right)f_A.$$

Expanding $A_\mu(x + dx)$ as

$$A_\mu(x) + \sum_{v=1}^{\dim B} \frac{\partial A_\mu(x)}{\partial x^v} dx^v,$$

one can see that parallel transport results in the following change of the original element f_A:

$$f'_A - f_A = \frac{1}{2}\sum_{\mu, v=1}^{\dim B} (a^v b^\mu - a^\mu b^v) R_{v\mu} f_A.$$

where we have defined the *curvature tensor* $R_{\mu v}$ as

$$R_{v\mu} = \frac{\partial A_\mu(x)}{\partial x^v} - \frac{\partial A_v(x)}{\partial x^\mu} - A_v(x)A_\mu(x) + A_\mu(x)A_v(x). \tag{5}$$

The quantities $\sigma^{v\mu} \equiv a^v b^\mu - a^\mu b^v$ are nothing other than the components of the bivector corresponding to the surface of the rectangle $ABCD$: $\sigma^{v\mu}$ is the area of the projection of the rectangle onto the plane spanned by the axes x^v and x^μ. When considering parallel transport for infinitesimal surfaces, the form of the surface does not really matter: one can cover the surface with rectangles and then sum the results. This means that for any infinitesimal cyclic path γ, the operator of parallel transport can be represented in the form:

$$g(\gamma) = 1 + \frac{1}{2}\sum_{\mu, v=1}^{\dim B} R_{v\mu}\sigma^{v\mu}. \tag{6}$$

This last equation establishes the meaning of the curvature as a measure of non-trivial parallel transport in fibre bundles.

Looking at (5) we would like to make two notes. At first sight, the last two terms on the right hand side of the equation appear to be equal and hence to cancel each other. This is not quite true though – there exist examples where the result of the transformations $A_\mu A_v$ and $A_\mu A_v$ will be different. These correspond to so-called non-commutative structure groups. If, however, the structure group is commutative, i.e. any two transformations performed in different orders give the same result, the last two terms can be dropped and the curvature tensor elements will be simplified:

$$R_{v\mu} = \frac{\partial A_\mu(x)}{\partial x^v} - \frac{\partial A_v(x)}{\partial x^\mu}. \tag{7}$$

The multiplication group is a commutative group: there is no difference between multiplying 5 by 2 or 2 by 5. Since the structure group of both electrodynamics and 'financial' electrodynamics is actually the multiplication group, the curvature tensors for these have the simplified form (7).

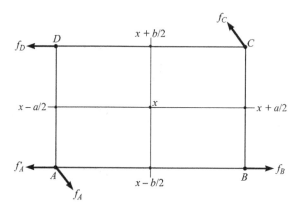

Figure 3.8 Parallel transport along the edges of the infinitesimal rectangle *ABCD*.

The second note connects the curvature tensor and the covariant derivatives. It is easy to check that the curvature tensor element $R_{\nu\mu}$ is equal to the commutator of the covariant derivatives D_ν and D_μ:

$$R_{\nu\mu}(x) = D_\mu D_\nu - D_\nu D_\mu \equiv [D_\mu, D_\nu]. \tag{8}$$

For the covariant derivative, the Jacobi identity

$$[[D_\nu, D_\mu], D_\xi] + [[D_\xi, D_\nu], D_\mu] + [[D_\mu, D_\xi], D_\nu] = 0$$

holds for any indices μ, ν and ξ. This results in the *Bianchi identity* for the elements of the curvature tensor:

$$D_\nu R_{\mu\xi} + D_\xi R_{\nu\mu} + D_\mu R_{\xi\nu} = 0.$$

In the case of commutative structure groups one can drop the nonlinear terms, and the last equality becomes

$$\frac{\partial R_{\mu\xi}}{\partial x^\nu} + \frac{\partial R_{\nu\mu}}{\partial x^\xi} + \frac{\partial R_{\xi\nu}}{\partial x^\mu} = 0. \tag{9}$$

We use the Bianchi identity in this form in the next chapter when we talk about the Maxwell equations in electrodynamics.

5 TRANSFORMATION LAWS

In this section, we introduce gauge transformations in a fibre bundle and consider how the connection and the curvature tensor change under these transformations. It will turn out that some objects are invariant under the transformations and, hence, should be used to construct models that obey the gauge symmetry – the symmetry with respect to gauge transformations.

Definition 7   A *gauge transformation* in a fibre bundle with structure group G is induced by the G-valued function on the base B, $q(x):B \rightarrow G$, and is defined as follows:

$$F_x \rightarrow q(x)F_x,$$

for any point x in the base.

A gauge transformation can be thought of as a point-dependent change of the coordinate system in the fibre for each point of the base. We know already that a connection is a rule for adjustment of the coordinate systems in fibres associated with different points of the base. We should therefore expect that the connection has to change under gauge transformations in order to keep the coordinate systems adjusted. Let us suppose that $g(\gamma)$ was an adjusting transformation of the coordinate frames performed along the path $\gamma(t)$, $a \le t \le b$, before the transformation. After the transformation, the coordinate systems in fibres $F_{\gamma(a)}$ and $F_{\gamma(b)}$ experienced additional 'twist' due to the transformations $q(\gamma(a))$ and $q(\gamma(b))$. This means that to adjust the new coordinate systems, one has to 'untwist' them and then use the initial adjustment $g(\gamma)$. This results in the following simple transformation rule for the connection under gauge transformations:

$$g(\gamma) \rightarrow g^q(\gamma) = q(\gamma(b)) \cdot g(\gamma) \cdot q^{-1}(\gamma(a)) \tag{10}$$

for any path γ and any gauge function q.

Equation (10) immediately leads to the rule for the gauge transformations for the covariant differences and covariant derivatives. By definition, the covariant difference $\Delta_\gamma \psi$ for a cross-section ψ is equal to

$$\Delta_\gamma \psi = \psi(\gamma(b)) - g(\gamma)\psi(\gamma(a)).$$

Under the gauge transformation, $\psi(x)$ transforms to $q(x)\psi(x)$, which, together with the above definition, gives the transformation rule for the covariant difference:

$$\Delta_\gamma^q \psi^q \equiv \psi^q(\gamma(b)) - g^q(\gamma)\psi^q(\gamma(a)) = q(\gamma(b))[\psi(\gamma(b)) - g(\gamma)\psi(\gamma(a))],$$

or, in short form

$$\Delta_\gamma^q \psi^q = q(\gamma(b))\Delta_\gamma \psi. \tag{11}$$

We see that the covariant difference transforms as an element of the fibre.[8]

In a similar way, one can obtain the rules of transformation for the covariant derivative $D\psi$. Taking the infinitesimal curve γ connecting points x and $x + dx^\mu$, we find from (11) that

$$D_\mu^q \psi^q(x) = q(x)D_\mu(x)\psi(x) \tag{12}$$

for any μ and any point x in the base. Here the transformed covariant derivative is defined as

$$D_\mu^q \equiv \frac{\partial}{\partial x^\mu} - A_\mu^q.$$

The formula for the transformed connection field A_μ^q can be found once again from (10) using the definition $A_\mu^q dx \equiv g(\gamma)^q - 1$:

$$A_\mu^q \, dx = q(x + dx^\mu)(1 + A_\mu \, dx)q^{-1}(x) - 1,$$

which, to first order, gives

$$A_\mu^q = q(x)A_\mu q^{-1}(x) + \frac{\partial q(x)}{\partial x^\mu} q^{-1}(x). \tag{13}$$

In the next chapter, we will see that this is exactly the rule of transformation for the electromagnetic vector potential.

---

[8] That is why it has the word 'covariant' in its name.

Finally, we will find the transformation formulae for the elements of the curvature tensor. Since, as (8) shows, the elements of the curvature tensor are the commutators of the covariant derivatives, we can use the gauge transformation rules for the covariant derivatives to find rules for the curvature tensor. Equation (12) states that $D\psi$ is transformed exactly as ψ, i.e. $D^q\psi^q = qD\psi$. The last relation can be rewritten as $D^q\psi^q = qDq^{-1}q\psi$, which means that the covariant derivative operator is changed by the gauge transformation as follows:

$$D^q = qDq^{-1}.$$

One can obtain the same result from (13) by direct calculation. This last equation and (8) allow us easily to derive the gauge-transformed curvature tensor:

$$R^q_{\nu\mu} = D^q_\mu D^q_\nu - D^q_\nu D^q_\mu = q(D_\mu D_\nu - D_\nu D_\mu)q^{-1} = qR_{\nu\mu}q^{-1}. \tag{14}$$

The elements of the curvature tensor transform exactly as operators of covariant differentiation. It is interesting to note, however, that if the covariant derivatives are actually differential operators as well as transformations of the fibre, the elements of the curvature tensor do not contain any differentiations. This note leads us to the following section, which deals with gauge invariance and gauge invariants.

6 INVARIANCE AND INVARIANTS

In physics, a non-trivial parallel transport is treated as a result of the action of some force. Then, if one wants to describe this force, it is important to choose proper dynamical variables. This section is about how to choose the dynamical variables in the case of gauge-invariant dynamics.

The term 'gauge-invariant dynamics' implies that the rules of the dynamics in a fibre bundle do not depend on a particular choice of the coordinate systems in the fibres. *Gauge invariance* means independence of the choice of coordinate systems in the fibres. These coordinate systems can be chosen arbitrarily and independently for any point of the base. This means that any change of coordinate systems – gauge transformations – should not change the dynamical equations. Since the gauge transformations are arbitrary functions on the base, this is a very strong condition on the theory.

For a gauge-invariant theory, the dynamical variables – the observables – should also not depend on the choice of coordinate frame, and should not change under change of frame. In other words, the observables have to be *gauge invariants*. This explains the importance of gauge invariants for construction of the theory.

Let us see if we can already identify some gauge invariants among the objects that we introduced earlier. We would like to have our dynamical variables local. This rules out the possibility of using the operators of parallel transport $g(\gamma)$, which depend on the whole curve γ. The local version of these quantities, the connection vector fields A_μ, also do not suit our goal: the connection vector field transforms as

$$A^q_\mu = q(x)A_\mu q^{-1}(x) + \frac{\partial q(x)}{\partial x^\mu}q^{-1}(x), \tag{15}$$

and is not constant under gauge transformations. Even when the structure group is the group of multiplication, so that $q(x)A_\mu q^{-1}(x) = A_\mu$, the last term on the right-hand side still violates the symmetry.

The situation looks different for the elements of the curvature tensor. The curvature tensor transforms simply as

$$R_{\nu\mu}^q = qR_{\nu\mu}q^{-1},$$

and, at least for the group of multiplications, $R_{\nu\mu}$ is invariant under gauge transformations:

$$R_{\nu\mu}^q = qR_{\nu\mu}q^{-1} = qq^{-1}R_{\nu\mu} = R_{\nu\mu}.$$

We can say that in this case, *the elements of the curvature tensor $R_{\nu\mu}$ are the simplest local gauge-invariant quantities.* In the financial setting, the structure group is the group of multiplication by positive numbers, the dilatation group, and the elements of the curvature tensor are the gauge invariants. We have already seen in Chapter 2 that these correspond to the excess return on an infinitesimal arbitrage operation. These quantities will be employed as the dynamical variables in our gauge financial models.

If the structure group is not commutative, one has to find a way to cancel the factors q and q^{-1} in the last equation. For example, if the fibre is a vector space so that the corresponding structure group is a matrix group, one has to use the trace to get rid of the factors:

$$\text{Tr } qR_{\nu\mu}q^{-1} \equiv \sum_{i,j,k=1}^{\dim B} q_j^i R_{\nu\mu,j}^k (q^{-1})_k^i = \sum_{i,j,k=1}^{\dim B} R_{\nu\mu,j}^k = \text{Tr } R_{\nu\mu}.$$

The last equality shows that in the case of matrix groups, $\text{Tr } R_{\nu\mu}$ is a gauge-invariant quantity. Unfortunately it is equal to zero, since the matrix $R_{\nu\mu}$ is antisymmetric. Then the next simplest combination is $\text{Tr } R_{\nu\mu}R_{\nu\mu}$ which is already symmetric and has non-zero trace. Terms of this type play an essential role in gauge theories with non-commutative structure groups.

7 LATTICE GENERALIZATIONS

Up to now, it has been assumed that the base is a continuous space. However, there is no problem with having the base discrete. Moreover, in many applications, the nature of the problem dictates the discrete character of the base. The crystal lattice in solids gives a physical example. A discrete pointlike base of assets (Fig. 2.13 in Chapter 2) provides an example in a financial setting. Thus it is important to find generalizations of the above constructions to the case of fibre bundles with discrete bases, where we cannot introduce covariant derivatives, define infinitesimal paths, or take continuous limits.

Despite this, the whole concept of connection survives: if there exist fibres with different coordinate systems, there has to be a rule for their adjustment. The adjustments are performed by elements of a structure group that depend upon a path in the base. Exactly as paths on a continuous space are continuous, paths on a discrete space are discrete. They consist of a set of points of the base $\gamma \equiv \{x_1, x_2, \ldots, x_n\}$. The points x_1 and x_n are the endpoints of the path. One can envisage this path as an ordered series of jumps between the points of the set: the first is between x_1 and x_2, the second between x_2 and x_3, and so on until the final jump from x_{n-1} to x_n (see Fig. 3.9). The connection along the path is defined as the product of the structure group elements corresponding to each of the elementary jumps:

$$g_\gamma = g_{x_n, x_{n-1}} \cdots g_{x_3, x_2} g_{x_2, x_1}.$$

Having this definition of a connection along the path γ, one can use (2) for the covariant difference without any other modifications.

The next step is to define the lattice curvature. As before, the curvature is related to parallel transport around closed loops, which in discrete space are N-gons Γ with vertices $x_1, x_2, \ldots, x_N$ joined consecutively by links. We call these N-gons *plaquettes*. It is possible to associate a parallel transport along the loop around every plaquette on the base. The parallel transport operator is defined as

$$g_\Gamma = g_{x_1, x_N} \cdots g_{x_3, x_2} g_{x_2, x_1},$$

which gives rise to the lattice curvature R_Γ:

$$R_\Gamma = g_\Gamma - 1.$$

This definition is motivated by (6) and gives the correct continuous limit when the plaquette shrinks to infinitesimal size. This construction will be used in lattice gauge theories in both physical and financial settings.

8   FOR THE CURIOUS: INDEX THEOREMS

We mentioned in Section 1 that there exist relationships between global and local properties of fibre bundles. These relationships are known as *index theorems*. More precisely, index theorems establish a relationship between the analytical properties of differential operators on a fibre bundle and the global topological properties of the fibre bundles themselves.

The example of an index theorem that we are going to consider is the Gauss–Bonnet theorem for the case of a compact two-dimensional surface M. As we know from Section 1, any compact two-dimensional surface can be smoothly deformed to a sphere with 'handles'

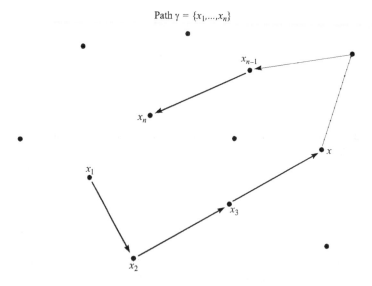

Figure 3.9   A path on a discrete base space. The path consists of a series of jumps between points x_1 and x_2, x_2 and x_3, and so on until the final jump from x_{n-1} to x_n.

glued to it (see Fig. 3.5). The number of 'handles', g, is called the *genus* of the surface M, and it completely characterizes this class of two-dimensional manifolds. The genus g is the topological characteristic that appears in the Gauss–Bonnet theorem.

As differential operator, we consider the covariant derivative on the tangent fibre bundle, where the fibres are the tangent planes associated with each point of the base M. The next step is to provide the surface with a metric, i.e. to define a scalar product of vectors in the fibres. This metric can be inherited from the embedding three-dimensional space or it can be obtained by smooth deformations of the latter. The connection that we choose to define the covariant derivative has to be consistent with the metric, which means that the covariant derivative of two cross-sections ψ_1 and ψ_2 must obey the condition

$$D(\psi_1 \cdot \psi_2) = (D\psi_1 \cdot \psi_2) + (\psi_1 \cdot D\psi_2)$$

at any point of the base. The covariant derivative is a differential operator, and cannot be used directly as an analytical quantity in the theorem. But, as we remember, the elements of the curvature tensor do not contain any differentiations, and are useful ingredients for the theorem. As soon as the covariant derivative has been defined, one can calculate the elements of the curvature tensor R_{ij} as the commutators of the derivatives following (8). By definition, $R_{ij} = -R_{ji}$, which results in the equalities $R_{11} = R_{22} = 0$ and leaves us with the only independent element R_{12}. Furthermore, the fibre is the tangent plane and its dimension is equal to 2. This gives us R_{12} as two-by-two matrix. It turns out that this matrix is also antisymmetric, and is completely defined by one number, which is, up to rescaling, the Gaussian curvature $\mathcal{R}$ of the surface:

$$\mathcal{R}(x) = \frac{1}{R_1 R_2},$$

where R_1 and R_2 are the principal of radii curvature of the surface at the point x (Fig. 3.10). This is the Gaussian curvature, which constitutes the local analytical characteristic in the theorem.

Having prepared all the necessary components, we are ready to formulate the Gauss–Bonnet theorem:

$$\chi(M) = \frac{1}{2\pi} \int_M \mathcal{R} \; ds. \tag{16}$$

Here $\chi(M) \equiv 2 - 2g$ is the so-called *Euler characteristic* of the manifold M. The theorem connects the genus of the surface with the integral of the Gaussian curvature over the surface.

For the case of the sphere, $g = 0$ and $\chi(M) = 2$. The Gaussian curvature is constant on the surface and equal to R^{-2}, where R is the radius of the sphere. Integration of the curvature over

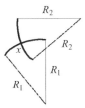

Figure 3.10   Principal radii of curvature at point x.

the surface gives the result 4π, and the right-hand side of (16) is thus equal to 2. This proves the theorem for the case of the sphere.

It is also easy to illustrate the theorem for the case of a torus, which has $g = 1$ and $\chi(M) = 0$. The torus can be imagined as a plane rectangle with opposite edges identified. Since the rectangle was 'cut out' of a plane with zero Gaussian curvature, the Gaussian curvature on the torus and its integral over the surface will be zero too. This equates the left- and right-hand sides of the theorem.

The Gauss–Bonnet theorem is just one of the index theorems. Although the theorems will not play any role in the following consideration of financial gauge models, they do play an important role in physical theories. That is why we decided to touch upon them here – if the physical and financial theories have similar mathematics, one would also expect the emergence at some point of the index theorems. Even if this does not happen, it is fun to understand what mathematicians can do in this fascinating geometry!

9 SUMMARY

- Manifolds are a general type of spaces where one can define coordinates self-consistently.

- Fibre bundles are manifolds with two different sets of coordinates: the first set gives the coordinates in the fibres and the second gives the coordinates on the base. Coordinate systems in the fibres are made consistent with each other using identification performed by elements of the structure group.

- A connection defines adjustment of the coordinate systems in fibres associated with different points of the base. If a connection is a G-connection then the adjustment transformation is an element of the structure group.

- The curvature tensor is connected with parallel transport around an infinitesimal loop, and gives the difference between the initial and transported fibre elements.

- Gauge transformations are point-dependent changes of coordinate systems in fibres. The curvature tensor can be used to construct quantities that are invariant under gauge transformations.

- It is possible to define connections and curvature for fibre bundles with a discrete base.

10 FURTHER READING

1. There exists a vast literature on fibre bundles and their applications. We list here four texts, with different scopes and different levels of abstraction: Husemoller (1994), Dubrovin et al (1985), Schwarz (1994), and Eguchi et al (1980).
2. Lattice connection and curvature are explained in detail in Creutz (1983).

4

Fibre Bundles: Physics

'The axiomatic basis of theoretical physics cannot be extracted from experience but must be freely created ... '

Albert Einstein quoted in Yang, 1980

IN 1998, the International Centre for Theoretical Physics in Trieste, Italy organized a one-month summer school entitled 'Mathematics of Economics: Primer in Economics for Physicists and mathematicians'. There were several prominent economists teaching, and the students were excited and full of expectations. After four weeks of study, finance appeared to be a stochastic calculus, macroeconomics was a word for general equilibrium theory, and microeconomics was a proxy of game theory. Feeling a kind of disappointment, but unable to argue – at the end of the day, the school was on mathematics not on economics – we physicists spent quite a number of hours talking to economists and asking if they really think that economics is about theorems. Or is this just a way to make us – arrogant and formula-addicted – understand it. The honest answer was: 'Look, you do not expect to learn a profession in one month. Can you imagine a primary four-week course in physics for economists?' This was meant to be a joke. But what a challenging joke!

This chapter can be considered as a primary course on gauge theories for economists. It does not assume any residual knowledge of school physics. Everyday experience is just enough. In the case of time limitations or of hard feelings planted in you by physics teachers, this chapter can be omitted without much harm to the understanding of the rest of the book. However, if the reader wants to see the connection between finance and the physics of gauge fields and to fully understand the logic of the later chapters, it would be advisable to get through this part.

We start with a concise history of the theory of electromagnetism, and derive the famous Maxwell's equations. Then it will be shown that the equations actually obey a gauge symmetry. This prompts the idea that the theory of the electromagnetic field can be formulated in purely geometrical terms, starting with some first principles that include gauge invariance. We also touch upon the first gauge theory, proposed by Hermann Weyl to describe electromagnetism, but which was later rejected. Saying a few words about quantum mechanics, we come to Quantum Electrodynamics (QED), the most precise contemporary theory, and other theories of fundamental interactions. We will see that, according to current understanding, all fundamental forces are manifestations of gauge symmetries of nature. This excursion into physics prepares the ground for the surprise of seeing how Weyl's first gauge theory returns as a theory of market dynamics.

The mathematics of this chapter is not very demanding – in contrast to real physical calculations, which are sometimes literally a few metres long! We use material from Chapter 3 extensively. We also refer several times to the Appendix on methods of quantum field theory at the end of the book.

I ELECTROMAGNETISM

From ancient times, it was commonly known that rubbed amber will attract light bodies such as chaff, and that a natural occurring mineral, lodestone, will attract iron. These properties were attributed to divine will, and their natural origin had not been questioned. The first philosopher who expressed an opposing opinion was Thales of Miletus (about 585 BC). He believed that the attraction is a natural property of lodestone and amber.

Although amber did not attract much further interest until the 16th century, the property of lodestone fascinated people in all times. Many philosophers, including Plato (about 427–347 BC), Lucretius (about 98–55 BC) and St Augustine (AD 345–430) made further observations of the properties of lodestone and made contributions to the understanding of their nature.

Lodestone has one property that was recognized very early, and whose application influenced human life and contributed greatly to the progress of civilization. It was observed that a freely suspended or floated lodestone comes to rest in an approximate North–South line. This made possible the invention of the mariner's compass. Greeks, Phoenicians, Chinese, and Arabs claimed credit for it, but there is not sufficient evidence to decide who was the first. In the middle ages, Europeans used the mariner's compass widely and made several improvements to its construction so that it could be used directly for steering instead of merely indicating the direction of the North Star. The most prominent name to be mentioned here is Peter de Maricourt, known as Peter Peregrinus, who described his experiments in a letter sent from the trenches before Lucera in 1259. He discovered and differentiated the poles of a magnet, and showed what effect poles have on each other. Peregrinus also noted that each of the pieces into which a magnet is broken, is itself a complete magnet, so there is no way one can get pure poles by breaking a lodestone into parts.

The next big step was made 300 years later by William Gilbert (1540–1603). Trying to provide a physical basis for Copernicus' heliocentric ideas put forward in 1543, Gilbert discovered the Earth's magnetism. He found that the Earth can be seen as a huge magnet, so that the behaviour of compass needles is a result of the pole–pole interaction discovered by Peregrinus. To demonstrate the Earth's magnetism, he showed that iron can be magnetized by being placed along a meridian. This explained the mysterious magnetism of iron rods taken from churches that had laid in a North–South position for many years. Gilbert then turned his attention to amber attraction, which was thought to be similar to lodestone attraction. He found that in spite of common belief, there are many other materials that exhibit the same properties as amber. Gilbert called them 'electrics'. He also pointed out that the nature of electrics attraction is very different from that of lodestone, and has to be considered separately.

It was Charles Dufay (1698–1739) who realized that electricity is of two kinds. He established that bodies similarly electrified repel while bodies dissimilarly electrified attract each other. The problem was to quantify this interaction. This was accomplished independently and almost simultaneously by Charles Augustin Coulomb (1736–1806) and Henri

Cavendish (1731–1810). In 1785, Coulomb deduced the law of both attraction and repulsion of electric charges and found that the forces varied as the inverse square of the distance between them. In contemporary notation, his result, known now as Coulomb's law, can be written as:

$$\mathbf{F} = q_1 q_2 \frac{\mathbf{r}_1 - \mathbf{r}_2}{|\mathbf{r}_1 - \mathbf{r}_2|^3}. \tag{1}$$

Here $\mathbf{F}$ is the force acting on a point charge q_1, located at $\mathbf{r}_1$, due to another point charge q_2, located at $\mathbf{r}_2$ (see Fig. 4.1). To quantify the force created by the second charge, one can consider the *electric field* $\mathbf{E}(\mathbf{r}_1)$, defined as the force acting on a unit charge placed at point $\mathbf{r}_1$:

$$\mathbf{E}(\mathbf{r}_1) = q_2 \frac{\mathbf{r}_1 - \mathbf{r}_2}{|\mathbf{r}_1 - \mathbf{r}_2|^3}.$$

It was observed experimentally that in the case of many charges, the resulting electric field is the vector sum of the electric fields created by elementary charges. Thus, generally, the electric field is given by the integral

$$\mathbf{E}(\mathbf{r}) = \int \rho(\mathbf{r}') \frac{\mathbf{r} - \mathbf{r}'}{|\mathbf{r} - \mathbf{r}'|^3} \, d^3 \mathbf{r}', \tag{2}$$

where $\rho(\mathbf{r})$ is the *charge density*, equal to the ratio of the charge Δq placed in the volume $\Delta r_1 \times \Delta r_2 \times \Delta r_3$ around the point $\mathbf{r}$, and the volume itself:

$$\rho(\mathbf{r}) = \Delta q / (\Delta r_1 \Delta r_2 \Delta r_3).$$

Some calculations are required to show that the electric field $\mathbf{E}$ given by (2) satisfies the following pair of equations:

$$\operatorname{div} \mathbf{E} \equiv \nabla \cdot \mathbf{E} = 4\pi\rho, \tag{3}$$

$$\operatorname{curl} \mathbf{E} \equiv \nabla \times \mathbf{E} = 0, \tag{4}$$

where the differential operator ∇ is defined as

$$\nabla = \mathbf{i} \frac{\partial}{\partial x} + \mathbf{j} \frac{\partial}{\partial y} + \mathbf{k} \frac{\partial}{\partial z}.$$

These equations are sufficient to describe electrostatics, i.e. the interaction of static charges.

Coulomb also experimented with magnetics, and found the same inverse square law for the mechanical force experienced by one small magnet in the presence of another small magnet. At this time, there were no connections between electricity and magnetism, despite the number of similarities in their properties. Many researchers at the beginning of the 19th

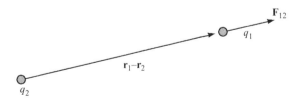

Figure 4.1 $\mathbf{F}_{12}$ is a force acting on a point charge q_1 located at $\mathbf{r}_1$. The force is created by the point charge q_2 located at $\mathbf{r}_2$. The force is directed along the line connecting the two charges.

century tried to connect the two phenomena. The first breakthrough came with experiments by Hans Christian Oersted (1777–1859), who discovered in 1820 that moving electric charges, *electric currents*, influence a magnet in exactly the same way as magnets do. The experiments were continued by Andre Marie Ampère (1775–1836). Only a few months after the publications of Oersted's results, Ampère presented to the French Academy of Sciences a paper in which he showed that not only is there a mechanical force between an electric current and a magnet, but there is also a mechanical force between two neighbouring electric circuits. In contemporary notation, his findings are expressed by the formula known as Ampère's law:

$$\mathbf{F}_{12} = \frac{I_1 I_2}{c^2} \frac{d\mathbf{l}_1 \times (d\mathbf{l}_2 \times \mathbf{r}_{12})}{|\mathbf{r}_{12}|^3}. \tag{5}$$

Here $\mathbf{F}_{12}$ is the force acting between segments $d\mathbf{l}_1$ and $d\mathbf{l}_2$ of the electric circuits (see Fig. 4.2), I_1 and I_2 are the corresponding electric currents, and c is a coefficient. In this form, Ampère's law looks similar to Coulomb's law (1). To push the analogy even further and to quantify the force, it is convenient to introduce the *magnetic field* $\mathbf{B}$ defined by the equality

$$\mathbf{F}_{12} = \frac{I_1}{c}(d\mathbf{l}_1 \times \mathbf{B}).$$

The vector $\mathbf{B}$ can be now obtained from Ampère's law (5) as

$$\mathbf{B} = \frac{I_2}{c}\frac{d\mathbf{l}_2 \times \mathbf{r}_{12}}{|\mathbf{r}_{12}|^3}.$$

It is possible to generalize the last equation in terms of the *current density* $\mathbf{J}(\mathbf{r}')$:

$$\mathbf{B}(\mathbf{r}) = \frac{1}{c}\int \mathbf{J}(\mathbf{r}') \times \frac{\mathbf{r} - \mathbf{r}'}{|\mathbf{r} - \mathbf{r}'|^3}\, d^3 r'. \tag{6}$$

The current density is related to the charge density by the continuity equation

$$\frac{\partial \rho}{\partial t} + \mathbf{\nabla} \cdot \mathbf{J} = 0, \tag{7}$$

which states that any change in electric charge is due to an inflow or an outflow of electric current. Once again, it is straightforward to check that the magnetic field $\mathbf{B}$ satisfies the following pair of equations:

$$\text{curl } \mathbf{B} \equiv \mathbf{\nabla} \times \mathbf{B} = \frac{4\pi}{c}\mathbf{J}, \tag{8}$$

$$\text{div } \mathbf{B} \equiv \mathbf{\nabla} \cdot \mathbf{B} = 0. \tag{9}$$

These two equations are similar to the electrostatic equations (3) and (4), and represent the main equations of magnetostatics. They are sufficient to describe the magnetic field generated by steady flows of electric charges.

What happens if the electric current is not steady? How can one incorporate the dynamics and insert time derivatives in (3), (4), (8), and (9). The first astonishing answer came in 1831 when Michael Faraday (1791–1867) discovered the phenomena of magnetic induction. The effect that Faraday first observed was the appearance of an electric current in one circuit when another nearby circuit containing a battery was completed or broken. He also observed that the same effect can be obtained if the second circuit has a steady electric current and is moved relative to the first circuit, or if a magnet is moved into or out of the first circuit. Faraday

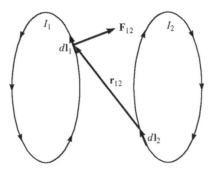

Figure 4.2 Ampère's law for the interaction between two electric currents.

interpreted these observations as indication of the fact that a changing magnetic field causes a change in the electric field, which in turn causes motion of electric charges. In mathematical form, the last statement is formalized by the equation that replaces (4) for the case of a time-dependent magnetic field:

$$\mathbf{\nabla} \times \mathbf{E} + \frac{1}{c}\frac{\partial \mathbf{B}}{\partial t} = 0. \tag{10}$$

This equation expresses Faraday's law of magnetic induction.

Let us return now to Ampère's law (8). This was derived under the assumption of steady current flows. What term has to be added to the equation to generalize it for arbitrary time-dependent currents? Adding an as-yet unknown term T to the left-hand side of (8) and applying the operation div $\equiv \mathbf{\nabla}\cdot$ to both sides of the equation, we find that

$$\mathbf{\nabla} \cdot \mathbf{T} = \frac{4\pi}{c}\mathbf{\nabla} \cdot \mathbf{J}.$$

Here we have used the well-known identity $\mathbf{\nabla} \cdot \mathbf{\nabla} \times = 0$ (i.e. div curl $= 0$). The right-hand side of the last equation can be rewritten in terms of the charge density rather than the current density using the continuity equation (7):

$$\mathbf{\nabla} \cdot \mathbf{T} = -\frac{4\pi}{c}\frac{\partial \rho}{\partial t}.$$

As we know from Coulomb's law (3), the charge density is equal to $\mathbf{\nabla} \cdot \mathbf{E}/4\pi$. This means that the last equation can be rewritten as

$$\mathbf{\nabla} \cdot \mathbf{T} = -\frac{1}{c}\frac{\partial}{\partial t}\mathbf{\nabla} \cdot \mathbf{E},$$

giving the term T as $-\frac{1}{c}\frac{\partial \mathbf{E}}{\partial t}$. This term was introduced by James Clerk Maxwell (1831–1879) and called the *displacement current* because in the final modification of (8) it stands as a correction to the electric current **J**:

$$\mathbf{\nabla} \times \mathbf{B} = \frac{4\pi}{c}\mathbf{J} + \frac{1}{c}\frac{\partial \mathbf{E}}{\partial t}. \tag{11}$$

Collecting together the equations describing magnetic and electric fields, (3), (9), (10), and (11), we obtain the system of differential equations known as *Maxwell's equations*:

$$\nabla \cdot \mathbf{E} = 4\pi\rho, \quad \nabla \times \mathbf{B} = \frac{4\pi}{c}\mathbf{J} + \frac{1}{c}\frac{\partial \mathbf{E}}{\partial t}, \tag{12}$$

$$\nabla \cdot \mathbf{B} = 0, \quad \nabla \times \mathbf{E} + \frac{1}{c}\frac{\partial \mathbf{B}}{\partial t} = 0. \tag{13}$$

These equations, although not in this mathematical form, were presented by Maxwell before the Royal Society of London in 1864, and were published in the *Philosophical Transactions* in 1865 in a paper called 'A dynamical theory of the electromagnetic field'. Maxwell also showed that the equations in the absence of charges and currents allow, as a solution, a wave propagation of the electric and magnetic fields, with the speed of the waves being equal to the constant c in the equations. These wave solutions were later identified with light propagation, which resulted in the interpretation of c as the speed of light in vacuum, which is approximately 3×10^8 m s^{-1}.

The publication of Maxwell's paper stimulated further interest in electromagnetic phenomena, and especially their experimental manifestations. Although there were noticeable debates about the theory, it became widely accepted after Heinrich Hertz (1857–1894) experimentally produced electric waves in 1887 using a spark discharge as a source of the oscillating current.

To sum up the material of this section, let us state the points most important for our future goals:

1. The electric and magnetic fields are different manifestations of the electromagnetic field.

2. The field and charges are complementary to each other in the sense that the field is created by charges and is responsible for the mediation of the electromagnetic force between them, while the charges are influenced by the force that is propagated by the field.

3. The classical dynamics of the electromagnetic field is described by Maxwell's equations (12) and (13) together with Newton's equations of motion or the charges in the presence of the electric and magnetic forces.

2   GAUGE INVARIANCE AND GEOMETRY

This section is devoted to the gauge invariance of electrodynamics. We will see that Maxwell's equations obey a symmetry under local transformations that looks like the gauge symmetry defined in Chapter 3. This is the bridge that connects electromagnetism and our main subject.

Let us look again at (12) and (13). The equation $\nabla \cdot \mathbf{B} = 0$ prompts us to use the identity $\nabla \cdot \nabla \times = 0$ and to introduce a new variable $\mathbf{A}$ such that

$$\mathbf{B} = \nabla \times \mathbf{A}. \tag{14}$$

A change of variables from $\mathbf{B}$ to $\mathbf{A}$ reduces the number of Maxwell's equations and hence simplifies the consideration.

Following this line, we substitute (14) into the second equation in the pair (13):

$$\mathbf{\nabla} \times \mathbf{E} + \frac{1}{c}\frac{\partial \mathbf{B}}{\partial t} = \mathbf{\nabla} \times \left(\mathbf{E} + \frac{1}{c}\frac{\partial \mathbf{A}}{\partial t} \right) = 0. \tag{15}$$

This means that the electric field $\mathbf{E}$ can be expressed as

$$\mathbf{E} = -\frac{1}{c}\frac{\partial \mathbf{A}}{\partial t} - \mathbf{\nabla}\Phi. \tag{16}$$

The last term does not violate (15), owing to the identity $\mathbf{\nabla} \times \mathbf{\nabla}\cdot = 0$, and thus has to be added to give a general solution. This leaves us with only the first pair of Maxwell's equations:

$$\nabla^2\Phi + \frac{1}{c}\frac{\partial}{\partial t}\mathbf{\nabla}\cdot\mathbf{A} = -4\pi\rho, \qquad \nabla^2\mathbf{A} - \frac{1}{c^2}\frac{\partial^2\mathbf{A}}{\partial t^2} - \mathbf{\nabla}\cdot\left(\mathbf{\nabla}\cdot\mathbf{A} + \frac{1}{c}\frac{\partial\Phi}{\partial t}\right) = -\frac{4\pi}{c}\mathbf{J}, \tag{17}$$

written in terms of the *vector potential* $\mathbf{A}$ and the *scalar potential* Φ, which give the physical electric and magnetic fields as

$$\mathbf{B} = \mathbf{\nabla} \times \mathbf{A}, \qquad \mathbf{E} = -\frac{1}{c}\frac{\partial \mathbf{A}}{\partial t} - \mathbf{\nabla}\Phi. \tag{18}$$

Equations (17) and (18) have an amazing property: they stay the same if instead of the fields $\mathbf{A}$ and Φ one uses fields $\mathbf{A}'$ and Φ' defined by the relation

$$\mathbf{A}' = \mathbf{A} + \mathbf{\nabla}\Lambda, \qquad \Phi' = \Phi - \frac{1}{c}\frac{\partial\Lambda}{\partial t}, \tag{19}$$

with an arbitrary function $\Lambda(\cdot)$. It is easy to check this property directly from (17) and (18) or by reminding ourselves that (17) have been written originally in terms of the fields $\mathbf{E}$ and $\mathbf{B}$ so that it will be sufficient to check the invariance for the relations (18) only. In the last case, the invariance is immediately obvious.

Do the transformations (19) look familiar? If the scalar and vector potentials are unified in one four-component vector $A \equiv \{A_i\} = (-\Phi, (\mathbf{A})^1, (\mathbf{A})^2, (\mathbf{A})^3)$ and time and space are identified with four-dimensional space–time M so that an element $x = (x^1, x^2, x^3, x^4)$ of M corresponds to the space point $\mathbf{x} = (x^2, x^3, x^4)$ and the time $t = x^1/c$, then the transformations (19) take the form

$$A'_\mu = A_\mu + \frac{\partial}{\partial x^\mu}\Lambda, \qquad \mu = 1, 2, 3, 4.$$

In this form, as one can persuade oneself by looking at formula (13) of Chapter 3, they coincide exactly with the change of the connection field A under the gauge transformation in a fibre bundle with multiplicative structure group:

$$A^q_\mu = q(x)A_\mu q^{-1}(x) + \frac{\partial q(x)}{\partial x^\mu}q^{-1}(x) = A_\mu + \frac{\partial}{\partial x^\mu}\log q(x), \qquad \mu = 1, 2, 3, 4.$$

A further geometrical analogy comes with the relations (18) and the curvature tensor calculated from the connection A. As formula (7) of Chapter 3 states, for the multiplicative structure group, the elements of the curvature tensor have the form

$$R_{\nu\mu} = \frac{\partial A_\mu}{\partial x^\nu} - \frac{\partial A_\nu}{\partial x^\mu}.$$

This gives, for example, the element R_{12} equal to

$$R_{12} = \frac{\partial A_2}{\partial x^1} - \frac{\partial A_1}{\partial x^2} = \frac{1}{c}\frac{\partial(\mathbf{A})^1}{\partial t} + (\nabla\Phi)^1 = -(\mathbf{E})^1.$$

This is not an offhand observation. The whole matrix $\|R_{\nu\mu}\|$ can be expressed in terms of components of the electric and magnetic fields:

$$\|R_{\nu\mu}\| = \begin{pmatrix} 0 & -(\mathbf{E})^1 & -(\mathbf{E})^2 & -(\mathbf{E})^3 \\ (\mathbf{E})^1 & 0 & (\mathbf{B})^3 & -(\mathbf{B})^2 \\ (\mathbf{E})^2 & -(\mathbf{B})^3 & 0 & (\mathbf{B})^1 \\ (\mathbf{E})^3 & (\mathbf{B})^2 & -(\mathbf{B})^1 & 0 \end{pmatrix}.$$

This means that the electric and magnetic fields are actually elements of the curvature tensor $\|R_{\nu\mu}\|$ calculated from the connection field A. One can take a further step and observe that the second pair of Maxwell's equations (13) coincide exactly with the Bianchi identities (equation (9) of Chapter 3) for the elements of the curvature tensor. Furthermore, the gauge invariance of (18) is a result of the corresponding gauge invariance of the curvature tensor.

All of these geometrical analogies make the idea of constructing a purely geometrical theory of electromagnetism very appealing. Indeed, if the physical fields are the elements of the curvature tensor, the auxiliary four-vector A is the connection, and the dynamical equations (Maxwell's equations) are gauge-invariant, one might wonder if it is possible to formulate some first principles in purely geometrical terms and derive Maxwell's classical electrodynamics as a mathematical consequence. In the next section, we see how this task can be accomplished.

3   ELECTRODYNAMICS AS A GAUGE THEORY

When talking about gauge theories, one usually starts with a description of the corresponding fibre bundle. The base space of our fibre bundle will be the four-dimensional space–time M described in the previous section. We also provide the space M with a rule for calculating a 'length', or interval, of its elements: the 'length' of element $x = (x^1, x^2, x^3, x^4)$ is equal to

$$\|x\| = \sum_{\mu,\nu=1}^{4} x^\nu x^\mu g_{\mu\nu} = -(x^1)^2 + (x^2)^2 + (x^3)^2 + (x^4)^2, \tag{20}$$

with the matrix g defined as

$$\|g_{\mu\nu}\| = \|g^{\mu\nu}\| = \begin{pmatrix} -1 & 0 & 0 & 0 \\ 0 & 1 & 0 & 0 \\ 0 & 0 & 1 & 0 \\ 0 & 0 & 0 & 1 \end{pmatrix}.$$

We take the complex plane with coordinates $z = x + iy$ as the fibre[1] and add the structure group G, which will be the group of multiplications by complex numbers $e^{i\phi}$ of unit modulus. Our aim is to define classical dynamics for the components of a connection field iA. The imaginary unit i stands here to show that it is the phase ϕ that will be gauged.

To define the dynamics, we start with the following first principles.

---

[1] This choice of fibre space will be explained in Section 5.

1. Classical trajectories of the connection $A(\cdot)$ starting at time t_i and ending at time t_f minimize the integral $\mathcal{A}$ called the *action*:

$$\mathcal{A} = \int_{t_i}^{t_f} dt \int_M d^3x \, \mathcal{L}(A).$$

This assumption is known as the *principle of minimal action*. The function $\mathcal{L}$ is called the *Lagrangian* of the system.

2. The classical dynamics is gauge-invariant, which means that the equations of motion do not change under the gauge transformations associated with the structure group G.

3. In the four-dimensional space–time M there is no preferred direction, so that all coordinates have equal rights. More precisely, we postulate a symmetry of the dynamics with respect to rotations in the space M such that the 'length' of space elements is kept constant. This is a form of the main principle of the *Special Theory of Relativity*. We also require a symmetry of the dynamics with respect to arbitrary translations in the space. The reason to include these assumptions is that Maxwell's equations, besides gauge invariance, are also symmetric with respect to these space–time rotations and translations.

4. The Lagrangian is a local function of the connection, i.e. it can contain only the field A and its derivatives, but not integrals. This provides local equations of motion.

5. The dynamical equations for the field A are linear, so as to obey the superposition principle: a field created by a system of charges is the vector sum of fields generated by each particular charge.

The first assumption says that all dynamical rules are defined by a single function, the Lagrangian: as soon as the Lagrangian is known the derivation of the equations of motion is a pure problem of variational calculus. All the other assumptions specify the form of the Lagrangian. Assumptions 2 and 3 state that the Lagrangian, as a key point in the construction of the classical dynamics, has to be invariant under gauge transformations and rotations in the base space. In other words, the Lagrangian has to be built from invariants of these symmetries. Assumption 4 adds that the invariants have to be local.

Now we start to construct the Lagrangian of the connection field. We have learnt in Section 6 of Chapter 3 that the simplest local gauge invariant is the curvature tensor $\|R_{\nu\mu}\|$. It has, however, space indices, and can be used only in invariant combinations such as

$$\sum_{\mu=1}^{4} R_{\mu\mu} g^{\mu\mu}.$$

As we already pointed out, this sum is equal to zero since the curvature tensor is antisymmetric and all diagonal elements $R_{\mu\mu}$ vanish. The next invariant quantity is

$$\sum_{\mu,\nu=1}^{4} R_{\nu\mu} R_{\nu\mu} g^{\mu\mu} g^{\nu\nu}.$$

This does not have any space indices left, and is therefore symmetric under the space rotations and translations. It is also gauge-invariant and local. Moreover, since it is quadratic in $R_{\nu\mu}$ and hence, in A, it will generate linear equations of motion. It is possible to show that there are no other viable structures for the Lagrangian $\mathcal{L}$ that obey the five first principles. Finally, we arrive at the following Lagrangian for our dynamical system:[2]

$$\mathcal{L}_A = \frac{c}{8\pi} \sum_{\mu,\nu=1}^{4} R_{\nu\mu} R_{\nu\mu} g^{\mu\mu} g^{\nu\nu}, \tag{21}$$

where $R_{\nu\mu}$ are the elements of the curvature tensor:

$$R_{\nu\mu} = i\left(\frac{\partial A_\mu}{\partial x^\nu} - \frac{\partial A_\nu}{\partial x^\mu}\right).$$

We do not prove it here, but the dynamical equations for the trajectories that minimize the functional $\int_{t_i}^{t_f} dt \int_M d^3 x \mathcal{L}(A)$ with the Lagrangian (21) are Maxwell's equations (17) in the absence of charges, and the physical observables (the electric and magnetic fields) are given by the gauge-invariant elements of the curvature tensor up to a factor i. This means that we have achieved our objective and represented electrodynamics as a geometric theory based on locality, symmetries, and the minimal action principle. To take account of charges, one has to enlarge the set of dynamical variables and include cross-sections of the fibre bundles along with the connection field. We postpone discussion of this matter until Section 5.

4   WEYL'S GAUGE THEORY

We have seen in the previous section that electrodynamics can be constructed axiomatically as the gauge dynamics of a connection vector field. Readers might be surprised, however, with our choice of structure group. Indeed, the only thing that we actually used was the fact that the group is a group of multiplications with a single parameter: N parameters would lead to an N-component vector for the component A_μ, which is definitely not what we have in electrodynamics: the scalar and vector potentials are real numbers. There are two options to choose from if one is interested in a one-parameter multiplication group:

1. Multiplications by $e^{i\phi}$, which we employed in the calculations in the last section – this is the so-called $U(1)$ group.

2. Multiplications by any positive number – the dilatation group.

In the framework of classical physics, the complex numbers do not play any fundamental role, and hence it would be natural to choose the second option and try to find a physical explanation of the dilatational gauge invariance principle. This is exactly the line of thought that led Hermann Weyl to his gauge theory of electrodynamics formulated in 1919. This first ever gauge theory, although it was later rejected, has had a great deal of influence on the theoretical physics of this century.

It is absolutely straightforward to see that all arguments of the previous section are valid for the dilatation group exactly as they were applied to the group $U(1)$, with one exception: the factor i will never appear. It is very appealing to accept this gauge theory and to try to find a physical motivation for the use of dilatation invariance. At that time, physicists were under the huge influence of General Relativity Theory, the theory of gravity that was proposed by Albert Einstein in 1915. We will touch upon this theory in Section 6, but, in a few words for

---

[2] The prefactor is dictated as a matter of convenience only.

now, Einstein's idea was to connect the curvature of our physical four-dimensional space–time and the gravitational force. While the Special Theory of Relativity deals with flat space and requires the dynamics to be symmetric with respect to global rotations in this space, General Relativity studies curved spaces where the coordinates can be defined only locally and the corresponding rotational symmetry also has to be local. Gauge invariance with respect to this local rotational symmetry leads to the introduction of a gauge field that corresponds to gravity. Weyl's original idea was to enlarge the gauge group and include in it dilatations of vectors together with rotations. In this way, gravity would be unified with electromagnetism in a single geometrical theory – the cherished aspiration of Weyl, Einstein, and many other physicists.

According to Weyl's idea, there is no well-defined 'length' of physical vectors in the tangent plane, and only a ratio of 'lengths' can be defined. This statement is equivalent to the statement that the physical dynamics has to be gauge-invariant, with the dilatation group as the structure group. In a certain sense, this means that there is no fundamental 'length' that can gauge other objects (see Fig. 4.3). This, by the way, explains why Weyl introduced the word 'gauge' into the name of his theory – the name that is now associated with all gauge-invariant theories with various structure groups. Unfortunately for Weyl's theory, in physics there do exist such gauge 'lengths' that break the gauge invariance. They are connected with masses of particles.

In the Special Theory of Relativity, there is the following formula for the energy E of a particle with mass m and momentum $\mathbf{p}$:

$$E/c = \sqrt{\mathbf{p} \cdot \mathbf{p} + m^2 c^2},$$

where c is the speed of light. This implies that the 'length' of the four-dimensional vector of energy–momentum $p^\mu = (E/c, \mathbf{p})$ can be calculated as

$$\|p\| = \sum_{\mu=1}^{4} p^\mu p^\mu g_{\mu\mu} = -E^2/c^2 + \mathbf{p} \cdot \mathbf{p} = -m^2 c^2.$$

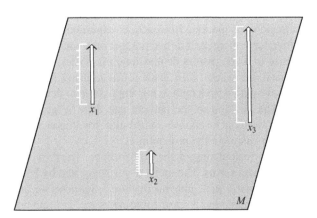

Figure 4.3 Gauge invariance in Weyl's theory. The 'length' of vectors is measured by a ruler, but this ruler can have arbitrary units. Then the only information available after the measurement is a ratio of the 'lengths'.

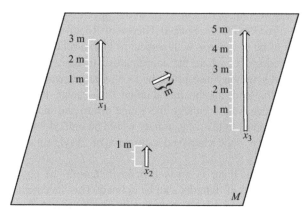

Figure 4.4   Mass of a particle as a unit of the gauge ruler.

This last equation shows that the mass of the particle establishes the characteristic 'length' of the energy–momentum vector (Fig. 4.4), which cannot be changed arbitrarily unless the mass is unobserved. This inconsistency was discussed by several people, including Einstein. After some unsuccessful efforts to improve the theory and to accommodate the critics, Weyl eventually gave it up. This effectively completes the story of Weyl's interpretation and the first gauge theory based on the dilatation group. It took 18 years to develop a framework of quantum theory that allowed physicists to find a physical reason for the gauge invariance with $U(1)$ structure group and to overcome the difficulties of Weyl's theory.

5   QUANTUM ELECTRODYNAMICS

Before the beginning of the 20th century, physicists believed that the world could be described by Newton's laws. Systems might be very complex and contain a huge number of particles but, in principle, their description could be obtained from a (possibly very large) system of classical equations of motion. However, as experiments became more and more subtle, a new picture of nature emerged. It turned out that on a small enough scale, the laws of classical mechanics cease to work. Waves demonstrate properties of point particles, quanta, and point particles behave like waves. This leads to a confusing picture. For example, if a particle behaves like a wave with wavelength λ, it is impossible to determine where physically the particle is located. The position of the particle can then be given only with a certain measure of probability. *Quantum mechanics* substitutes for classical mechanics on small scales and explains how to calculate the probabilities.

There are several ways of calculating of the probabilities. They are all equivalent, so we choose the one most convenient for us. The method was suggested by Richard Feynman, and is therefore known as Feynman's path integral method.[3] Suppose we are interested in the quantum dynamics of a system that has a set of coordinates $x = \{x^j\}$ and on a classical level is

---

[3] A few facts on path integrals are collected in the Appendix on quantum field theory methods at the end of this book.

described by a Lagrangian $L(x)$. This means that the classical trajectory that starts at time t_i at the point with coordinates x_i and ends up at time t_f at the point with coordinates x_f minimizes the action functional

$$A = \int_{t_i}^{t_f} L(x)\,d\tau. \tag{22}$$

The condition of minimization is sufficient to derive the classical equations of motion and thus to define the classical dynamics. In Feynman's picture of quantum mechanics, the system can, with a certain probability, follow *any* trajectory that starts at point $x(t_i) = x_i$ (Fig. 4.5). The conditional probability to find the system at time t_f with coordinates x_f is then given by a sum, or more precisely an integral, over all trajectories that start at point $x(t_i) = x_i$ and evolve to point $x(t_f) = x_f$:

$$P(x_f, t_f | x_i, t_i) = \left| \int Dx(\cdot)\, e^{i/\hbar A} \right|^2 / N. \tag{23}$$

Here N is a normalization factor, the functional A is given by (22), i is the imaginary unit, and $\hbar$ is the so-called Planck's constant. When Planck's constant tends to zero, the classical trajectory that minimizes the action A gives the overwhelming contribution to the integral (23), and the path integral reduces to the contribution of the classical trajectory (see Section 5 of the Appendix for further details). Quantum mechanics reduces to the classical case.

There is one strange thing about (23), namely the appearance of the imaginary unit i and the corresponding squared modulus. From what we said above, it would be natural to expect an integral over trajectories with positive probabilities. Why do we use complex numbers? The reason for this is the strange quantum probabilistic calculus: instead of characterizing a

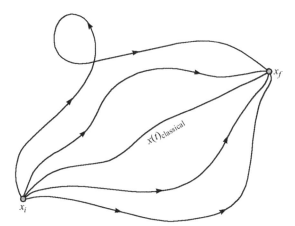

Figure 4.5 Feynman's interpretation of quantum mechanics: with certain probability, a particle can follow any path. The probability to arrive at point x_f from point x_i is the sum over all possible paths connecting the points.

state with a probability P, one has to use a complex number ψ called an *amplitude* and related to the probability by

$$P = |\psi|^2.$$

Moreover, to find a probability of event I or event II that are mutually exclusive, one has to sum ψ_I and ψ_{II} rather than P_I and P_{II}:

$$P_{(I \text{ or } II)} = |\psi_I + \psi_{II}|^2 = P_I + P_{II} + 2\psi_I\psi_{II}.$$

The last term represents interference, and demonstrates the wave nature of particles. Equation (23) is a generalization of the last equation to the case where the mutually exclusive events are the evolutions of the system along different trajectories.

The quantum probabilistic calculus has another strange feature directly connected with our discussion of gauge theories: the fundamental quantity ψ is defined by observable probabilities up to a phase factor $e^{i\phi}$, which can be chosen arbitrarily. Differences of phases can be observed, but the phase itself cannot. The complex plane of quantum amplitudes ψ can be rotated without any change in the physical system. The choice of the basis frame in the complex plane is a mere matter of convention and should be irrelevant for any practical matter. Any theory compatible with quantum laws has to be constructed in such a manner that it does not depend on a particular choice of the coordinate system in the complex plane of the quantum amplitudes, or, in other words, has to be gauge-invariant, with the gauge group being multiplications by phase factors $e^{i\phi}$. As we saw in Section 3, introducing a connection in such a theory will be equivalent to introducing an electromagnetic field. The complete theory of electromagnetism is thus a theory in the fibre bundle with space–time as the base space and the complex planes as the fibres. The theory has a set of dynamical variables that comprises cross-sections[4] ψ representing charged particles and the connection representing the electromagnetic field.

To develop quantum electrodynamics, we apply the path integral formalism and use the Lagrangian (21) for the gauge field. However, we also need a Lagrangian for the matter fields, the charges. As we will see, the dynamical variables that correspond to the charges are cross-sections of the fibre bundle. To construct a Lagrangian to govern the dynamics of cross-sections, we once again use the same first principles that were used in Section 3 to define the Lagrangian of the gauge field. First of all, the locality and gauge invariance of the theory require that the Lagrangian has to be a function of the cross-sections ψ and their covariant derivatives

$$D_\mu \psi(x) = \frac{\partial \psi}{\partial x^\mu} - iA_\mu \psi.$$

Furthermore, the Lagrangian has to be a real number – otherwise the minimal action principle does not make sense. This means that, besides the cross-section ψ, the Lagrangian has to contain the complex-conjugate field $\bar{\psi}$, which enters in such a way that the Lagrangian as a whole is a real function of the dynamical variables. We also have to remember about the symmetry of the dynamics with respect to arbitrary translations and rotations in the base

---

[4] Cross-sections are functions on the base with values in the fibre. See Section 3 of Chapter 3.

space, as it was defined in Section 3. The simplest non-trivial Lagrangian that satisfies all of these criteria is given by the expression

$$\mathcal{L}_m = \sum_{\mu=1}^{4} i\bar{\psi}\gamma^\mu D_\mu \psi - m\bar{\psi}\psi, \tag{24}$$

where γ^μ and m are some real numbers. Indeed, terms constant and linear in ψ and $\bar{\psi}$ do not affect the calculation of the optimal trajectory, and hence can be disregarded. Then the Lagrangian collects the first non-trivial terms: terms quadratic in ψ and $\bar{\psi}$ and with the smallest possible order of the covariant differentiation. We do not allow higher terms in ψ and $\bar{\psi}$, because these terms would bring nonlinear equations of motion for the cross-sections even in the absence of the electromagnetic field, and would reflect an action of additional forces that we want to exclude. This leaves us with only one degree of freedom in the construction procedure – the number of covariant derivatives, which in (24) is taken to be 0 and 1. One can imagine other numbers of covariant derivatives, for example 2. In this case, the Lagrangian will have the form:

$$\mathcal{L}_m = \sum_{\mu,v=1}^{4} g^{\mu\mu}g^{\mu\mu}\overline{D_v\psi}D_\mu\psi + m^2\bar{\psi}\psi, \tag{25}$$

which also looks simple. If one drops the requirement of space–time symmetry then there are other possible constructions, such as

$$\mathcal{L}_m = \bar{D}_t\bar{\psi}\psi + \frac{1}{2m}\sum_{v=2}^{4} \bar{D}_v\bar{\psi}D_v\psi + \lambda\bar{\psi}\psi. \tag{26}$$

This is the Lagrangian for matter fields in non-relativistic quantum electrodynamics, and the parameter m is the mass of the particles. We have settled on (24) rather than (25), since experiment agrees with the former structure for quantum electrodynamical systems. In reality, life is slightly more complicated because of the existence of internal angular momentum of electrons, the spin, so that ψ is a vector-function (a 'spinor') and the coefficients γ^μ are matrices. This is the only correction that has to be made (24) to transform it into the Lagrangian for charged particles in Quantum Electrodynamics.

Collecting together the terms in (21) and (24), we obtain the complete Lagrangian for the system of charges and the electromagnetic field:

$$\mathcal{L} = \mathcal{L}_A + \mathcal{L}_m = \frac{c}{8\pi}\sum_{\mu,v=1}^{4} R_{v\mu}R_{v\mu}g^{\mu\mu}g^{vv} + \sum_{\mu=1}^{4} i\bar{\psi}\gamma^\mu D_\mu\psi - m\bar{\psi}\psi. \tag{27}$$

One can check that the dynamical equations dictated by the Lagrangian give Maxwell's equations (17) in the presence of charges, with the charge density and current density defined as

$$\rho = \bar{\psi}\gamma^1\psi, \quad J^i = \bar{\psi}\gamma^{i-1}\psi.$$

Introduced in this way, the densities obey the continuity equation

$$\frac{\partial\rho}{\partial t} + \mathbf{\nabla}\cdot\mathbf{J} = 0$$

on the trajectories that minimize the action with the Lagrangian (27). Therefore we have found a geometrical description of electrodynamics in terms of objects of a fibre bundle geometry. To move from the classical picture to the quantum one, we have to calculate the path integral (23) with the Lagrangian (27) inserted as the action functional.

6 OTHER FUNDAMENTAL GAUGE THEORIES

We have seen that quantum electrodynamics is a theory of a connection field interacting with cross-sections of a fibre bundle with structure group $U(1)$, which is equivalent to the group of plane rotations. The natural generalization of this construction would be a theory with another, more complicated gauge group. If this new group contains the $U(1)$ group then the new theory will reproduce electrodynamics as well as *describing other forces*. This very idea is behind all modern theories of fundamental interactions and attempts at the grand unification of forces. Moving step by step, we will see how different structure groups correspond to all presently known fundamental forces, namely the weak nuclear interaction, the strong nuclear interaction, and gravity.

6.1 Weak Interactions

The *weak nuclear interaction* is the interaction responsible for β-decay:

$$n \to p + e + \bar{\mu}.$$

and similar processes. This last equation illustrates the nuclear process of decay of a neutron n into a proton p, electron e, and antineutrino $\bar{\nu}$. This process conserves electric charge and produces light particles e and $\bar{\nu}$, which are called *leptons*. They are not affected by the second nuclear interaction – the strong interaction. Since the initial neutron was electrically neutral, the process cannot be governed by the electromagnetic interaction, and one has to introduce a new kind of force – the so-called weak nuclear force. The name 'weak' is explained by the fact that the relevant dimensionless quantity characterizing the interaction is small.[5]

The first theory of the weak interaction was proposed by Enrico Fermi in the 1930s. The theory postulated a contact form of the interaction, which in the first approximation could explain the observed experimental behaviour of weakly interacting particles. However, any attempt to calculate corrections to the first approximation was doomed because the higher-order terms diverged. Besides, in contrast to electrodynamics, Fermi's theory was a contact theory and did not require any field to transfer the interaction.

The commonly accepted and experimentally verified theory of unified electromagnetic and weak interactions was proposed by Sheldon Glashow, Abdus Salam, and Steven Weinberg, who shared the Nobel Prize for Physics in 1979 for this development. The theory is a gauge theory in which the structure group is a product of the $U(1)$ group and the $SU(2)$ group. The $SU(2)$ group is the group of rotations of two-dimensional complex vectors that leave the lengths of vectors constant. We already know that the factor $U(1)$ has to be introduced to get electromagnetism from the theory. The required $U(1)$ gauge invariance is responsible for the

---

[5] The dimensionless quantity $\alpha = g^2/\hbar c$ is approximately $1/30$ at the nuclear scale 10^{-16} cm. Here g is the weak coupling constant, c is the speed of light, and $\hbar$ is Planck's constant. For comparison, the corresponding quantity for the strong interaction is ~ 0.1 at the same distance, and diverges at distances around 10^{-14} cm. For the electromagnetic interaction, the characteristic quantity $\alpha = e^2/\hbar c \simeq 1/137$.

elimination of the dependence on definition of quantum phases. The second, more complicated, group performs a similar role: the $SU(2)$ gauge invariance states that in weak
interactions some particles can be rearranged in pairs, such as (e, v), such that substitution
of one particle of the pair by another does not change the weak interaction picture. Let us be
more precise. Since both the electron e and the neutrino v are quantum particles and have to
be described by quantum amplitudes, the state of a particle that is either the electron or the
neutrino is given by the vector

$$\Psi = \begin{pmatrix} \psi_e \\ \psi_v \end{pmatrix}, \quad \|\Psi\| \equiv |\psi_e|^2 + |\psi_v|^2 = 1,$$

rather than a single complex number. The *principle of $SU(2)$ gauge invariance* establishes
that, as far as the weak interaction concerned, the vector $(1, 0)$ is as good for the description of
the matter as the vector $(0, 1)$ or any general vector Ψ that has a probability of $|\psi_e|^2$ for a
particle to be an electron and a probability $|\psi_v|^2$ to be a neutrino. This is a formalization of
our previous assertion that electrons and neutrinos play the same roles in acts of weak
interactions. Now, if one starts with the $U(1) \times SU(2)$ gauge invariance and follow the
strategy outlined for Quantum Electrodynamics, one ends up with Glashow–Salam–Weinberg
theory of the electroweak interaction.

Once again, real life is more complicated. There are many different leptons, they have
spins, the gauge symmetry is spontaneously broken at some length scale, and so on. These
peculiarities are extremely important to explain various experiments. However, what we want
to emphasize here is that the central point in the development of the theory was the
postulation of gauge invariance and the corresponding geometrical formulation.

6.2   Strong Forces

The nucleus consists of protons and neutrons. The force that keeps them together is the result
of the *strong nuclear interaction*. Originally, protons and neutrons were believed to be
elementary particles and their interaction was attributed to the exchange of other elementary
particles, mesons. When the number of observed 'elementary' particles became large,
physicists started to look for ways to classify them. This gave birth to the quark hypothesis
pioneered by Murray Gell-Mann at the beginning of the 1960s.

According to the contemporary picture, there exist six kinds of true elementary particles,
quarks, which are called 'up' (u), 'down' (d), 'charmed' (c), 'strange' (s), 'top' (t), and
'bottom' (b). Together with their antiparticles, they constitute 'building' blocks for all other
particles participating in strong interactions, such as protons, neutrons, and mesons. The
quarks possess an internal degree of freedom, *colour*, which has three possible states, named
'red' (r), 'green' (g), and 'blue' (b). The theory of strong interactions describes forces acting
between the coloured quarks, and has the corresponding name of *Quantum Chromodynamics
(QCD)*. This is a gauge theory that states the following *$SU(3)$ gauge invariance principle*:
quarks with different colours can be exchanged with each other without change in the strong

interaction dynamics. Similarly to our consideration of the weak interaction, we can represent the state of a quark by a vector of quantum amplitudes

$$\Psi = \begin{pmatrix} \psi_r \\ \psi_g \\ \psi_b \end{pmatrix}, \quad \|\Psi\| \equiv |\psi_r|^2 + |\psi_g|^2 + |\psi_b|^2 = 1,$$

which corresponds to the probabilities $|\psi_r|^2$ to have the 'red' colour, $|\psi_g|^2$ to have the 'green' colour, and $|\psi_b|^2$ to have the 'blue' colour. The gauge-invariance principle says that quarks with vectors $(1, 0, 0)$, $(0, 1, 0)$, and $(0, 0, 1)$ behave in strong interactions in absolutely the same way as a quark with the general vector Ψ. Therefore the particular choice of coordinate frame in the colour space is irrelevant for any physical purposes, and can be changed arbitrarily without altering the dynamical rules.

The strong interaction is carried by the particles of the gauge fields, *gluons*. The net effect of the virtual exchange of gluons is to produce a force that tends to bind quarks together into systems that are colour-neutral. This is an important property of the theory, since bare coloured quarks have never been observed, and it is now a common belief that single quarks cannot be met in nature. This rule also prohibits the observation of an isolated gluon, since they also carry colours.

The next step was to unify together electroweak interactions and strong interactions. This was done in the framework of the so-called Standard Model, which is a gauge theory with gauge group $U(1) \times SU(2) \times SU(3)$, which comprises the gauge group of the electroweak theory $U(1) \times SU(2)$ and the gauge group of the theory of strong interactions $SU(3)$. It turns out that the Standard Model is more robust than its separate elements: some unpleasant 'anomalies' that are present in the electroweak theory and the theory of strong interactions cancel each other in the unified theory. As a result of this and other theoretical and experimental successes, the Standard Model is commonly recognized as the candidate for the role of the theory of fundamental forces.

6.3   Gravity

In 1908, the Polish mathematician Hermann Minkowski demonstrated that the Special Theory of Relativity formulated by Albert Einstein in 1905 has a simple geometrical interpretation. He showed that the results of Special Relativity are equivalent to the statement that four-dimensional space–time is symmetric with respect to certain rotations and translations in it. These do not include all rotations of the space, but only those that do not change the 'length' of vectors as defined in (20):

$$\|x\| = -(x^1)^2 + (x^2)^2 + (x^3)^2 + (x^4)^2.$$

This 'length', or interval therefore does not depend on the choice of coordinate system introduced globally in the space–time. And neither do any physical laws. In physical language, the last phrase means that physical laws look exactly the same in all coordinate systems in space that move with a constant speed relative to each other. If, however, the relative speed varies then one can conclude that there exists a force that acts on an object associated with one of the coordinate systems. This in turn will change the form of the physical laws expressed in this coordinate system: things look differently in a falling lift. For example, if a person in the falling lift throws a ball, this ball flies along a straight line as seen by the person in the lift (can you imagine anyone sitting in a falling lift and watching flying objects?). However, the same thrown ball follows a parabolic trajectory for an observer who stands on the ground (see Fig. 4.6). The curved character of the trajectory for the observer on the ground reflects the action of the force of gravity on the ball. One can look at the parabolic trajectory as a straight trajectory but in curved space. This consideration binds together gravity and space–time curvature.

We know from Chapter 3 that the existence of curvature prevents us from introducing a global coordinate system in the space. This means that in the presence of the gravitational interaction, one has to be satisfied with a set of local coordinates and their consistency rules. Special Relativity is transformed to the symmetry of the local coordinates with respect to rotations. But since the coordinates are local, the rotations are local as well. The requirement of a theory to be symmetric under local rotations is a *gauge-invariance principle, with the group of local rotations as the gauge group.* The components of the corresponding

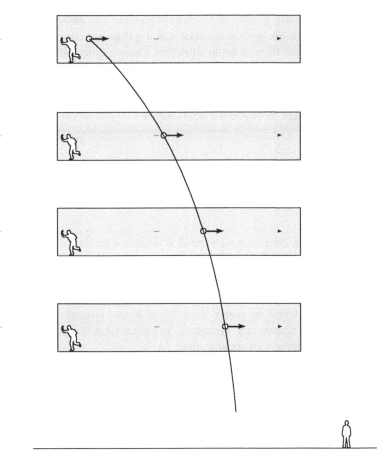

Figure 4.6 The dynamics of a thrown ball looks different for an observer standing on the ground and an observer sitting in a falling lift. The first sees a parabolic trajectory; for the second, the trajectory is a straight line. In the second case, there is no indication of gravity.

connection are called Christoffel symbols (we have already met them in Section 3 of Chapter 3). They are calculated using the metric tensor, which is effectively the dynamical variable. It defines the space–time curvature associated with the force gravity.

Although from the point of view of principle gravity is quite similar to other fundamental gauge theories, there are several considerable differences. These make the theory of gravity extremely difficult to quantize. That is why, despite the fact that the classical theory of gravity, General Relativity, is widely accepted and has been confirmed by many experiments, up to now there is no satisfactory quantum theory of gravitational forces.

7   ONCE MORE ON WEYL'S THEORY

The final comment in this chapter concerns Weyl's theory. As we saw, Weyl's theory was the first gauge theory proposed to unify gravity and electromagnetism. The theory was rejected because all attempts to motivate the use of the dilatational gauge invariance contradicted fundamental physical properties of the real world. However, Chapter 2 demonstrated that the dilatation gauge group appears absolutely naturally in a financial setting. There, *dilatational gauge invariance means that financial dynamics is independent of a particular choice of asset units.* The corresponding connection fields are prices and discount factors. We proceed with a construction of the financial gauge theory in the next chapter.

8   SUMMARY

- The classical dynamics of the electromagnetic field is described by Maxwell's equations (12) and (13) together with Newton's equations of motion for charged particles in the presence of electric and magnetic forces.

- The dynamics can be formulated in purely geometrical terms, starting with five first principles: gauge invariance, rotational invariance in space–time, the minimal-action principle, locality, and the principle of superposition.

- Electrodynamics is a gauge theory with gauge group $U(1)$, which is a group of redefinitions of the quantum phase.

- Theories of all fundamental interactions – strong nuclear interaction, the weak nuclear interactions, and gravity – are gauge theories. The interaction fields arise to preserve the local gauge invariance of the theories.

- Weyl's theory was the first gauge theory introduced to describe electromagnetism. It was later rejected, but has returned as a gauge theory of financial market dynamics. The corresponding gauge group is the group of dilatations.

9   FURTHER READING

1. An interesting account of the early history of studies of electromagnetism is given in Buckley (1927). For more on personal details and stories of people mentioned in the first section, see Cajori (1935).
2. There exist a number of textbooks on classical electrodynamics. This chapter follows Jackson (1975).
3. Any reader left unsatisfied by the explanations of quantum laws in this chapter can remedy this by turning to the excellent informal introduction to quantum mechanics and quantum electrodynamics by Feynman (1985).
4. Introductions to gauge theories can be found in Moriyasu (1983), Ryder (1985), and Faddeev and Slavnov (1980).
5. Descriptions of Weyl's theory can be found in Weyl (1919), Moriyasu (1983), and Bergmann (1979).
6. A description of the history of gauge theory is given in Yang (1977).

5

Fibre Bundles in Finance: Gauge Field Dynamics

W E saw in Chapter 4 how one can develop a gauge theory starting with a few initial first principles. This chapter and the next two examine the possibility of applying the same methodology in the search for a model of fast market reaction. Once again, we start with some assumptions and derive a statistical description of the market dynamics that governs the market response on mispricing opportunities. As readers will see, the assumptions are quite natural and intuitively appealing. Moreover, they can be further relaxed to include more realistic market features.

As we have already discussed in Chapter 2, the financial market obeys, at least approximately, a gauge symmetry – symmetry with respect to the local rescaling of asset units accompanied by the corresponding change of prices and discount factors. In Section 5, we review some facts that suggest that the symmetry is indeed only approximate and is violated by market imperfections. Since the violations are tiny, they can be disregarded at first and introduced as a perturbation later. This leaves us with a gauge theory of the financial market. However, this does not fix the theory completely. Some additional assumptions about the market and market participants are required. These additional assumptions distinguish models of fast market response from those of long-term dynamics. Nevertheless, whatever these additional assumptions are, the gauge invariance is a common feature of all these theories and provides a general framework for all of them. In later chapters, we deal mainly with fast market dynamics and return to a long-term picture in Chapter 9.

Our experience with gauge theories gained from Chapter 4 shows that there are *two distinctive types of dynamical variables inherent in gauge theories*. They are interconnected and have to be considered simultaneously in order to provide a non-trivial dynamical theory. The first type is the connection field, the gauge field, which is responsible for the mediation of the interaction. The field appears in the theory to preserve a local gauge invariance, the existence of which is one of the first principles. The variables of the second type are the cross-sections of the fibre bundle, which are gauged by the connection and represent matter fields. Following this line, below we consider both the financial connection field and the cross-sections, namely the prices and the money. This chapter concentrates on the construction of the gauge field dynamics, while the next two chapters deal with the cross-sections.

As we have learnt in previous chapters, the connection is a rule for comparing elements of fibres associated with different points of a base. In a financial setting, the points of the base correspond to different assets and the elements of the fibres stand for a number of the asset units. The comparison of two elements is then essentially a comparison of the asset units, which is accomplished in terms of mutual prices and discount factors. Thus the connection comprises the prices and rates of return. We formalize this consideration in Section 1, where the general lattice construction of the relevant fibre bundle is given and the connection is specified. The corresponding continuous versions of the base are introduced in Section 4. The first principles, the main assumptions needed to construct the dynamics of the gauge field, are formulated and discussed in Section 2. After this, following the analogy with the $U(1)$ gauge theory described in Sections 3 and 5 of Chapter 4, we develop a statistical description of price dynamics in the absence of money flows. It will be shown in Section 4 that in the case of continuous time, the constructed stochastic price dynamics produces quasi-Brownian stochastic processes widely used in financial mathematics. The introduction of money flows in later chapters makes the price dynamics more complicated and more realistic.

1 FIBRE BUNDLES: FORMAL CONSTRUCTIONS

In this section, we formalize the previous consideration of financial fibre bundles given in Chapter 2.[1] More precisely, we give a description of the relevant fibre bundles, we construct the parallel transport rules using elements of the structure group, and we give an interpretation of the parallel transport operators. The corresponding curvature is also defined, and is shown to be equal to the rate of excess return on the elementary plaquette arbitrage operation. These facts are used later to construct the gauge dynamics of the parallel transport factors. We first consider a general discrete base, and deal with the continuous case in Section 4.

1.1 Construction of the Discrete Base

To define the fibre bundle, we shall construct the base first. Suppose we want to model a financial system with $N + 1$ types of assets. This number N can be equal to 1 for the simplest system (dollar, pound) or can be as large as 500 to embrace dollars and shares in the S&P500 market index. Let us order the complete set of assets and label them by numbers from 0 to N. The set can be represented on a two-dimensional plane as $N + 1$ points. The dimension of the embedding space is purely a matter of convenience, and can be chosen arbitrarily. To add the time in the construction we attach a copy of a $\mathbb{Z}$-lattice[2] to the each asset point. We prefer discretized time, since there is a natural time step and all real trades happen discretely. All together, this gives the prebase set $L_0 = \{0, 1, 2, \ldots, N\} \times \mathbb{Z}$ (see Fig. 5.1). Any point of the prebase is completely characterized by the pair of numbers (i, n), where the first indicates the asset number and the second shows the moment of time. In this notation, an event associated with the point (i, n) happened at moment of time n with the ith asset.

The next step in the construction is to define the *connectivity* of the prebase. The connectivity is important to define all possible paths on the base, and hence the corresponding parallel transports. To do this, we start with the introduction of a matrix of links

---

[1] In this section we follow Ilinski (2000a).
[2] That is, the set of all integer numbers $\{\ldots, -1, 0, 1, 2, \ldots\}$.

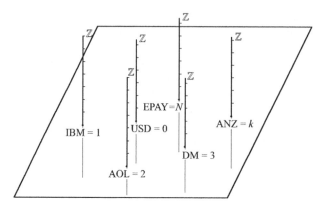

Figure 5.1 The prebase $L_0 = \{0, 1, 2, \ldots, N\} \times \mathbb{Z}$. Points on the plane represent the assets while the set $\mathbb{Z} \equiv -\infty, \ldots, -1, 0, 1, 2, \ldots, \infty$ indicates all possible time moments. The time is measured in quanta Δ.

$\Gamma : L_0 \times L_0 \rightarrow \{0, \pm 1\}$. This is defined by the following rule: for any two elements of the base $x \equiv (i, n) \in L_0$ and $y \equiv (k, m) \in L_0$, the element of the matrix of links $\Gamma(x, y)$ is zero,

$$\Gamma(x, y) = 0,$$

except for the following cases:

1. $i = k$ and $n = m - 1$ under the condition that the ith security exists at a moment that is not an expiration date for the security:

$$\Gamma(x, y) = 1, \qquad \Gamma(y, x) = -1.$$

2. $n = m$, $i \neq k$, and at the nth moment of time the ith asset can be exchanged for some quantity of the kth asset at some rate (see Fig. 5.2). We assume that the transaction is instant. In this case,

$$\Gamma(x, y) = 1.$$

When the elements of the matrix of links are non-zero, we say that the corresponding points are connected. The definition states that the points of the base are connected if they represent the same security and consecutive moments of time, or they belong to the same time instant and can be exchanged.

Using the matrix $\Gamma(., .)$ we can define a *curve* in the base. A curve $\gamma(x, y)$ in L_0 that links two points $x, y \in L_0$ is a set of points $\{x_j\}_{j=1}^p$ of the base such that:

1. The first and last points of the set coincide with the endpoints of the curve:

$$x_1 = x, \qquad x_p = y.$$

2. For all $p - 1$ segments (x_j, x_{j+1}), the elements of the matrix of links are non-zero:

$$\Gamma(x_j, x_{j+1}) = \pm 1 \quad \forall j = 1, \ldots, p - 1.$$

The notion of a curve allows us to finally define the base. The whole L_0 can be divided into a set of connected components. A connected component is a maximal set of elements of L_0

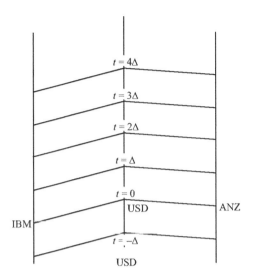

Figure 5.2 Points representing dollars and IBM shares are connected only if they correspond to the same moment of time. There is no link between IBM and ANZ shares, since they cannot be directly exchanged.

that can be linked by some curve for any pair of elements. The base L is defined now as the connected component containing US dollars at, say, 15.30 of 17 June 1999. This completes the construction of the base of the fibre bundle. Examples of bases for simple models of a stock exchange, a foreign exchange, and the European call option are depicted in Figs. 5.3, 5.4, and 5.5.

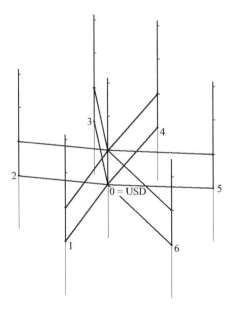

Figure 5.3 Base for the simple stock exchange. All shares are traded in US dollars.

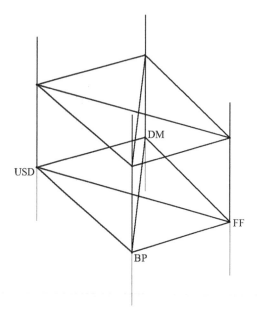

Figure 5.4 Base for the FOREX market.

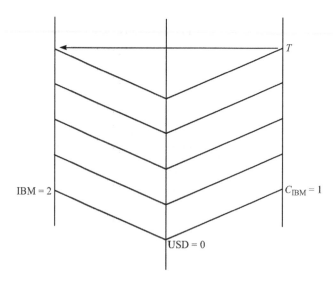

Figure 5.5 Base for the European call option on IBM shares with expiration date T. The arrow at the expiration time indicates that $\Gamma((1, T), (2, T)) = 1$ but $\Gamma((2, T), (1, T)) = 0$, and the option can be exchanged on shares but not vice versa.

1.2   Structure Group

As explained in Chapter 2, the structure group G to be used in the financial framework is the group of dilatations. This is the group of maps g of $\mathbb{R}_+ \equiv [0, +\infty)$ to $\mathbb{R}_+$ that act by multiplication of any $x \in \mathbb{R}_+$ by some positive constant $\lambda(g) \in \mathbb{R}_+$:

$$g(x) = \lambda(g) \cdot x.$$

The group is actually a group of rescalings of asset units (the values of which are elements of $\mathbb{R}_+$) with rescaling factor $\lambda(g)$. The transition functions of a fibre bundle with this structure group correspond below to various prices, exchange rates, and discount factors.

1.3   Fibres

As is already clear from our choice of the representation of the structure group, the fibre that we will work with is $\mathbb{R}_+$:

$$F = \mathbb{R}_+ \equiv [0, +\infty).$$

The interpretation of this fibre is absolutely straightforward: the statement 'element f of fibre F_i is equal to 5' means that the element represents 5 units of the ith asset. The units are fixed in some way, but can be changed arbitrarily. This will cause the corresponding change of the element f, which is accomplished by multiplication by a rescaling factor, i.e. by an action of the structure group.

This fibre bundle is a space of money flows, or cash-debts flows. To understand why this is so, let us consider a *cross-section s*. In this context, $s(x \equiv (i, m))$ gives the number of units of the ith asset at the moment of time m. Thus the cross-section describes the time evolution of an initial money allocation $s(i, 0)$, $i = 0, \ldots, N$: at time $t = 0$, one had $s(0, 0)$ units of the 0th asset, $s(1, 0)$ units of the 1st asset, and so on, while at the moment of time $t = m$, the corresponding quantities are $s(0, m), s(1, m), \ldots, s(N, m)$. The space of all cross-sections is the space of all possible scenarios of money movements, or money flows. Using the language of Feynman's path integrals, this is a space of all trajectories. It will be used as a space for the integration of quantities, which will be functionals of the cross-sections. The main property of the integrands will be local gauge invariance, i.e. invariance under a local action of the structure group G.

Now, when the base, the fibres, and the structure group are constructed, we define the fibre bundle E as a trivial one: $E = L \times F$. The projection maps are trivial and we do not stop to describe them.

1.4   Parallel Transport, Curvature, and Arbitrage

As defined in Chapter 3, a connection is a rule for the parallel transport of an element of a fibre from one point of a base, say point x, to another point, point y. An operator $U(\gamma)$ of parallel transport along the curve γ belongs to the structure group, and acts from the fibre F_x to the fibre F_y:

$$U(\gamma): F_x \rightarrow F_y.$$

Unless we deal with a continuous base, we do not need to introduce a vector field of the connection but rather have to deal with elements of the structure group G. Thus we use the lattice formulation introduced in Section 7 of Chapter 3. By definition, an operator of parallel transport along a curve γ, $U(\gamma)$, is defined as the product of operators of parallel transport along the links that constitute the curve γ:

$$U(\gamma) = \prod_{i=1}^{p-1} U(x_i, x_{i+1}), \qquad \gamma \equiv \{x_i\}_{i=1}^{p-1}, \qquad x_1 = x, \quad x_p = y.$$

This means that we are left to define only the operators of parallel transport along elementary links. Since $U(\gamma) = U^{-1}(\gamma^{-1})$,[3] this restricts us to a definition of those operators along elementary links with a positive connectivity. Summing up, the rules for parallel transport in the fibre bundle are completely defined by the set of parallel transport operators along elementary links with positive connectivity and operators of parallel transport along asymmetric links. The definition of this set is equivalent to the definition of parallel transport in the fibre bundle. Since the connectivity was defined by the possibility of asset movements in 'space' and time, it allows us to give an interpretation of parallel transport. In Section 1.1, two principle kinds of links with positive connectivity were defined. The first one connects two points (i, n) and $(i, n + 1)$ and represents a deposition of the ith asset for one unit of time. This deposition then results in a multiplication of the number of asset units by an interest factor (or internal rate of return factor) calculated as:

$$U((i, n), (i, n + 1)) = e^{r_i \Delta} \in G,$$

where Δ is the time unit and r_i is an appropriate rate of return for the ith asset. In the continuous limit, r_i becomes a time component of the corresponding connection vector field at the point $(i, \Delta n)$. In a similar way, the parallel transport operator is defined for the second kind of elementary links, i.e. links between points (i, n) and (k, n) if there is a possibility to change at the nth moment a unit of the ith asset to $S_n^{i,k}$ units of the kth asset:

$$U((i, n), (k, n)) = S_n^{i,k} \in G.$$

In general, an operator of parallel transport along a curve is a factor by which a number of asset units is multiplied as a result of an operation represented by the curve. The results of parallel transport along two different curves with the same boundary points are not equal for a generic set of parallel transport operators. A measure of the difference is the curvature tensor R. Its elements are equal to the resulting multipliers[4] after parallel transport along a loop encircling all elementary plaquettes with non-zero links in the base L:

$$R_{\text{plaquette} \to 0} = \prod_m U_m - 1.$$

The index m runs over all plaquette links, $\{U_m\}$ are the corresponding parallel transport operators, and agreement about orientation is implied.

We will now show that the elements of the curvature tensor are, in fact, excess returns on the operation corresponding to the encircled plaquettes. Let us consider an elementary plaquette that involves two different assets. We will call them for now share and cash (see Fig.

---

[3] If γ^{-1} exists – which is not always the case: a derivative can be exchanged with some underlying quantity, but not vice versa.
[4] See the last section of Chapter 3 for the definition and discussion.

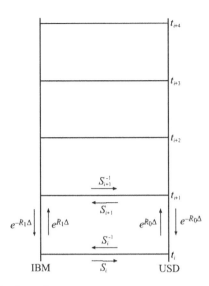

Figure 5.6 Elementary cash–share plaquette.

5.6). Suppose that the assets can be exchanged with each other, with some exchange rate S_i. This means that one share is exchanged on S_i units of cash at some moment t_i, with the reverse rate for the cash-to-share operation is S_i^{-1}. The exchange rates S_i are quoted on a set of equidistant times $\{t_i\}_{i=1}^{N}$, with some time step $\Delta = t_{i+1} - t_i$. The interest rate for cash is r_0, so that between two subsequent times t_i and t_{i+1}, the volume of cash is increased by factor $e^{r_0 \Delta}$. The shares are characterized by a rate r_1. As we will show later, the rate r_1 is related to the average rate of return of the share. Considering an elementary (arbitrage) operation between two subsequent times t_i and t_{i+1}, there are two possibilities for an investor who possesses a cash unit at the moment t_i and wants to get shares by the moment t_{i+1}. The first is to put cash on a bank deposit with interest rate r_0 at the moment t_i, withdraw money back at the moment t_{i+1} and buy shares for price S_{i+1} each. In this way, an investor gets $e^{r_0 \Delta} S_{i+1}^{-1}$ shares at the moment t_{i+1} for each unit of cash he invested at the moment t_i. The second way is to buy the shares for price S_i each at the moment t_i. Then, at the moment t_{i+1}, the investor will have $S_i^{-1} e^{r_1 \Delta}$ shares for each unit of cash at the moment t_i. If these two numbers, $e^{r_0 \Delta} S_{i+1}^{-1}$ and $S_i^{-1} e^{r_1 \Delta}$, are not equal then there is a profitable opportunity, an arbitrage.[5] Indeed, suppose that $e^{r_0 \Delta} S_{i+1}^{-1} < S_i^{-1} e^{r_1 \Delta}$; then, at the moment t_i, an arbitrageur can borrow one unit of cash, buy S_i^{-1} shares, and get $S_i^{-1} e^{r_1 \Delta} S_{i+1}$ units of cash from selling shares at the moment t_{i+1}. The value of this cash discounted to the moment t_i is $S_i^{-1} e^{r_1 \Delta} S_{i+1} e^{-r_0 \Delta} > 1$. This means that $S_i^{-1} e^{r_1 \Delta} S_{i+1} e^{-r_0 \Delta} - 1$ is an arbitrage excess return on the operation. If $e^{r_0 \Delta} S_{i+1}^{-1} > S_i^{-1} e^{r_1 \Delta}$ then the arbitrageur can borrow one share at the moment t_i, sell it for S_i units of cash, put cash in the bank, and buy $S_i e^{r \Delta} S_{i+1}^{-1}$ shares at the moment t_{i+1}. We have an arbitrage situation again.

Let us consider the following quantity:

$$R^{(2)} = S_i^{-1} e^{r_1 \Delta} S_{i+1} e^{-r_0 \Delta} + S_i e^{r_0 \Delta} S_{i+1}^{-1} e^{-r_1 \Delta} - 2. \tag{1}$$

---

[5] Remember, there is no uncertainty in the problem at present.

This is the sum of excess returns on the plaquette arbitrage operations. In the continuous limit, $R^{(2)}/2\Delta$ converges to the square of the curvature tensor element. The absence of the arbitrage is equivalent to the equality

$$S_i^{-1}e^{r_1\Delta}S_{i+1}e^{-r_0\Delta} = S_ie^{r_0\Delta}S_{i+1}^{-1}e^{-r_1\Delta} = 1,$$

and we can use the quantity (1) to measure the arbitrage as an excess rate of return on an arbitrage operation. We have seen in Section 7 of Chapter 3 that the expression $S_i^{-1}e^{r_1\Delta}S_{i+1}e^{-r_0\Delta} - 1$ represents a lattice regularization of an element of the curvature tensor along the plaquette with links $(1, 2)$, $(2, 3)$, $(3, 4)$, $(4, 1)$. This allows us to rewrite (1) in a more formal way as

$$R^{(2)} = U_1 U_2 U_3^{-1} U_4^{-1} + U_3 U_4 U_2^{-1} U_1^{-1} - 2$$
$$= (R_{1234} + 1) + (R_{1234} + 1)^{-1} - 2.$$

In this form, it can be generalized to other plaquettes, such as 'space'–'space' plaquettes. For example, in a simple model of Foreign Exchange with three currencies 1, 2, and 3 (see Fig. 5.7) the 'space'–'space' element of the curvature tensor is equal to

$$R_{123} = S_{12}S_{23}S_{31} - 1,$$

and the cross-rate arbitrage can be characterized by the quantity

$$R^{(2)} = S_{12}S_{23}S_{31} + S_{21}S_{13}S_{32} - 2.$$

The last point to add in this section is the notion of gauge transformation. A gauge transformation means a local change of the scale in the fibres:

$$f_x \to g(x)f_x \equiv f_x', \quad f_{x(x')} \in F_{x(x')}, \quad g(x) \in G, \quad x \in L$$

together with the following transformation of the parallel transport operators:

$$U(y, x) \to g(y)U(y, x)g^{-1}(x) \equiv U'(y, x) \in G.$$

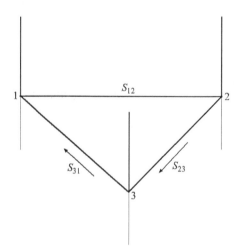

Figure 5.7   Cross-rate arbitrage for a simple Foreign Exchange with three currencies.

It is easy to see that the parallel transport operation commutes with the gauge transformation:

$$g(y)(U(y,x)f_x) = U'(y,x)f_x',$$ (2)

and the curvature tensor is invariant under the transformation:

$$U_1 U_2 U_3^{-1} U_4^{-1} = U_1' U_2'(U_3')^{-1}(U_4')^{-1}.$$ (3)

2 BASIC ASSUMPTIONS

We know already that prices and discount factors have a geometrical meaning: they are elements of the structure group of the fibre bundle. They are responsible for parallel transport in 'space' and time directions. However, this does not say anything yet about their dynamics. We address this question now.

At first sight, the dynamics is difficult to specify, since it is not restricted, and any attempt to formulate dynamical rules will seem to be arbitrary and insufficiently motivated. However, as we will see below, some simplified dynamics can be derived from a few quite general and natural assumptions. The main point of the present analysis is an assumption about local gauge invariance, with the dilatation group as the gauge group.

Assumption I: Gauge-Invariant Dynamics

We have already discussed this assumption in Chapter 2, and we will further examine its practical validity in Section 6 of this chapter. Here we formulate the assumption as the statement that *all observable properties of the financial environment, and, in particular, rules of dynamical processes, do not depend on the choice of the units of the assets in question*. This means that all effects of, say, changes of currency units or shares splits may be eliminated by a corresponding change of rates and prices. This natural assumption allows us to make a step to a specification of the dynamics. Indeed, owing to gauge invariance, all quantities that govern the dynamics have to be constructed from gauge-invariant objects. The gauge invariance essentially dictates the nature of the dynamical rules. However, to specify the dynamics, we need some other assumptions.

Assumption 2: Intrinsic Uncertainty

The real financial environment *is intrinsically uncertain*, so that there exist non-zero probabilities to get excess rates of returns different from those in an entirely certain environment. Exchange rates, prices, and interest rates fluctuate, and there can be local 'mispricings' and 'profitable' opportunities. We assume that elements of the curvature tensor R, as well as prices and rates, are random variables whose statistical properties have to be defined.

In what follows, we assume that this randomness is a reflection of the influence of factors other than price-driven money flows, since the latter will be accounted for directly. Such factors include news announcements that have to be taken into account to adjust a price. Another example of such a factor is trading that is not price-driven. A company may have some spare money to invest temporarily in stocks or bonds and make a 'buy' order that is not price-driven. Or, alternatively, it may require to sell some financial assets to carry its main business activity, which will also generate a non-price-driven 'sell' order. Overnight, week-end, and public holiday market gaps are ascribed to the same group, since they are not associated with any money flows unless the overnight stops in trading are modelled directly. We assume that changes in price due to these factors occur at random.

Assumption 3: Minimal-Action Principle

In a fully rational and certain economic environment, there should be no possibility to have 'something from nothing', i.e. to have higher return than the riskless rate of return. In more general form, *the excess rate of return, i.e. the deviation of the rate of return from the riskless rate, on any kind of operations takes the smallest possible value* that is allowed by the external economic environment. This means that the *action*[6] functional can be defined as an increasing function of the deviations, and the set of prices and discount factors realized in a certain and rational financial market has to minimize this functional.

If no restrictions are applied to the prices and the trade is free trade, all the deviations have to be zero. It is known, however, that external regulations can create an arbitrage situation, and this situation can last for some period of time. This is typical of a currency market when a state wants to support or weaken its own currency to achieve its political objectives. Tax arbitrage presents another example. These restrictions have to be modelled explicitly, and enter the model as external conditions. What the postulate says is that, in these circumstances, the observable mispricing has to be minimal if not zero.

In the case of an uncertain environment, by definition, all price and discount factors can be realized. We require, however, that the most probable configurations of the random connection are the configurations with minimal absolute value of the excess rate of return, and other configurations are distributed symmetrically around them.[7] This provides a smooth transition from uncertainty to certainty for all observable quantities as the parameter of uncertainty tends to zero. This also causes the zero average excess rate of return.

Assumption 4: Locality

We assume *local dynamics of the prices and discount factors* in a complete theory. This locality means that, if a theory is complete, the dynamics of an asset is directly influenced by Γ-connected assets only. By definition, two points in the base L are Γ-connected if there exists a possibility of exchanging the assets. The locality postulate states the following for the exchange factor U_{xy} between points $x = (i, n)$ and $y = (k, m)$:

1. Such a factor exists if the corresponding element of the matrix of links $\Gamma((i, n), (k, m))$ is non-zero.

2. U_{xy} is a function of other exchange factors U_{xz} and U_{wy} (such that $\Gamma(x, z)$ and $\Gamma(w, y)$ are non-zero) and the money flows $M_{x,z}$ and $M_{w,y}$ along the links:

$$U_{xy} = f(\{U_{xz}, M_{xz}\}_{\Gamma(x,z)}, \{U_{wy}, M_{wy}\}_{\Gamma(w,y)}).$$

---

[6] We use the terminology of Chapter 4 and the Appendix on quantum field theory methods.
[7] Thus skewed price distributions will be generated by money flows or other external interactions.

As an example, we can take the world stock market. Prices of stocks can be explicit functions of prices of other stocks quoted in the same currency and of exchange rates of the currency and other currencies, but not of prices of stocks quoted in different currencies. These latter prices, however, can enter the game implicitly through the dynamics of the connected prices and money flows. Thus a decrease in return of one kind of shares will lead to money outflow from this asset and a corresponding inflow into other assets. Changes in the prices of assets in which money flows is a reaction to the money flows rather than a direct result of the initial drop in return of the first shares.

It is necessary to emphasize that everything said above applies to a complete theory only. If a model is designed to describe a subsystem rather than the complete system, it may be non-local to reflect omitted elements of the comprehensive theory. As an example, one can consider a stock market where price movements are generally correlated owing to fundamental reasons. In a model of fast market reaction, this correlation will not be modelled directly, and has to be introduced as a non-local interaction for the connection. To construct models for market subsystems, one needs then a correspondence principle.

Assumption 5: Correspondence Principle

When money flows do not enter the theory, the theory has to be equivalent to standard mathematical finance. This means in particular that in the continuous-time limit, we will obtain correlated quasi-Brownian walks for the prices and discount factors, and will reproduce the results of portfolio theory and derivative pricing. Therefore, in this approach, non-trivial stochastic processes for prices result from the presence of money flows. Indeed, it will be shown in the next two chapters, one can introduce money flows and use some first principles to develop their dynamics in such a way that statistical properties of price movements will be in good agreement with real data analysis.

Therefore the complete theory including prices and money flows is a generalization of mathematical finance, not an alternative to it. The new element is the emphasis on the explicit presence of money flows and their influence on prices. When this element is dropped, the model have to provide the standard results. This requirement serves as a correspondence principle.

Assumptions 1–5 above constitute the complete set of first principles needed to formulate the rules of stochastic dynamics of prices and discount factors. We formulate the dynamical description in the next section, in close analogy with the corresponding consideration of electrodynamics in Section 3 and 5 of Chapter 4.

3 CONSTRUCTION OF THE DYNAMICS

In this section, we derive a description of stochastic dynamics based on the assumptions discussed in the previous section.

We start with Assumption 2, which states that the financial market is intrinsically uncertain. Therefore prices and rates can be characterized by probabilities rather than some fixed values. The joint probability distribution of prices and rates gives probabilities to find particular values of the parallel transport factors U on every elementary link in the base L, which is a complete description of a system. We will call a particular set of values of the parallel transport factors, a *configuration* and denote it by $\{S, r\}$. Thus the probability distribution of configurations is the principal quantity to construct.

First of all, it is convenient to rewrite the probability distribution in the exponential form

$$P(\{S, r\}) = Ne^{-A_g(\{S,r\})},$$

where N is a normalization factor and $A_g(\{S, r\})$ is a new functional, which we call the *action*. This last equation represents nothing more than a convenient notation. In this notation, additivity of the action in terms of some variables means the statistical independence of these variables.

The next step is to use Assumption 1 and provide the gauge-invariant formulation. To ensure gauge invariance, the measure of integration has to be gauge-invariant, and the prices and rates of a configuration have to enter the action in the form of products along closed curves in the base L. From a geometrical point of view, these products are the operators of parallel transport along the curves. One can check that the only combinations of $\{U_{ik}\}$ that stay constant under a general gauge transformation are the products such as $U_{12}U_{23}, \ldots, U_{n1}$. Moreover, since at present we do not restrict the functional dependence of the action on the products, we can, without loss of generality, restrict the set of cyclic parallel transports to parallel transport along elementary plaquettes in the base, i.e. curves that cannot be reduced to a pair of other curves by the addition of an existing link in the base (see Fig. 5.8). Figure 5.9 shows that sometimes further reductions are possible. Instead of the operators of parallel transport along the elementary plaquettes $U_{\text{plaquette}}$, one can use the elements of the lattice curvature tensor R:

$$R_{\text{plaquette}} = U_{\text{plaquette}} - 1.$$

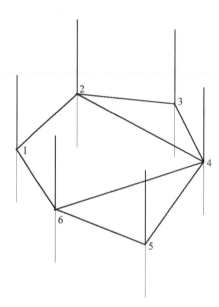

Figure 5.8 The plaquette 2342 is an elementary one, in contrast to the plaquette 124561, which is not. In the latter case, one can add a link between points 4 and 6 to get a pair of curves 12461 and 4564. The operator of parallel transport along the curve 12456 is the product of the corresponding operators along the curves 12461 and 4564.

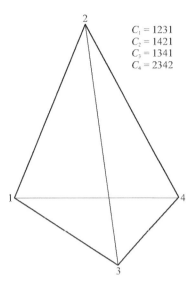

$C_1 = 1231$
$C_2 = 1421$
$C_3 = 1341$
$C_4 = 2342$

Figure 5.9 All cycles C_1, C_2, C_3, and C_4 are curves along the elementary plaquettes. However, the parallel transport along the cycle C_4 can be represented as the result of consecutive parallel transports along the cycles C_1, C_2, and C_3. Here one can choose the operators of any three elementary parallel transports to be variables in the action functional.

This allows us to represent the action as a series expansion in terms of the elementary plaquette curvatures R:

$$A_g(\{S, r\}) = \sum_{\{\gamma_1, \gamma_2, \ldots, \gamma_n\}} \alpha_{\gamma_1, \gamma_2, \ldots, \gamma_n} (R_{\gamma_1} + 1)(R_{\gamma_2} + 1) \cdots (R_{\gamma_n} + 1), \qquad (4)$$

where the sum is taken over all possible sets of elementary plaquettes (including their orientation) with some arbitrary coefficients $\alpha_{\gamma_1, \gamma_2, \ldots, \gamma_n}$.

Equation (4) gives the general form of a gauge-invariant action. Any gauge-invariant dynamics of a gauge field system has to be described by an action of this type. To define the coefficients $\alpha_{\gamma_1, \gamma_2, \ldots, \gamma_n}$ one needs to use Assumptions 3–5. Given any particular situation, one has to define $\{\alpha\}$ in such a way that the probability distribution function of the problem in question in the absence of money flows will coincide with the model probability function with action (4). As an example, we consider general cases of linear and quadratic actions, and discuss their meaning.

3.1 Linear Actions

The general form of the action that is linear in the curvatures R can be written as

$$A_g(\{S, r\}) = \sum_{\gamma_n} \alpha_{\gamma_n} (R_{\gamma_n} + 1). \qquad (5)$$

Here the sum is taken over all elementary plaquettes γ_n including different orientations. Assumption 3 states that the configuration with zero arbitrage has to be the most probable one, and configurations with larger arbitrage are less probable than the configurations with smaller arbitrage. This leads to the equality

$$\alpha_{\gamma_n} = \alpha_{\gamma_n}^{-1} > 0,$$

which means that the coefficient corresponding to an elementary plaquette does not depend on the orientation. This allows us to rewrite (5), up to a numerical constant, as

$$
\begin{aligned}
A_g(\{S, r\}) &= \sum_{\text{plaquettes } p} \alpha_p[(R_p + 1) + (R_p + 1)^{-1} - 2] \\
&= \sum_{\text{plaquettes } p} \alpha_p(U_p + U_p^{-1} - 2) \\
&= \sum_{\text{plaquettes } p} \alpha_p R_p^{(2)},
\end{aligned}
\tag{6}
$$

where the sum is taken already over different elementary plaquettes, disregarding the orientation. We will use the action in this form later.

To illustrate the meaning of the action, we consider once again a two-asset (we call them cash and shares) system. The first issue to mention here is that of gauge fixing. Since the action is gauge-invariant, it is possible to perform a gauge transformation that will not change the dynamics but will simplify further calculations. In lattice gauge theory (see Creutz, 1983), there are several standard choices of gauge fixing, one of which is to use the axial gauge. In the axial gauge, elements of the structure group are taken constant on links in the time direction (we keep them as $e^{r_{0,1}\Delta}$). One also has to fix one of the exchange rates (an element along the 'space' direction at some particular chosen time). Below we fix the price of the shares at moment $t = 0$, taking it to be S_0. This means that in the situation of the ladder base, the only dynamical variable is the exchange rate (price) as a function of time, and the corresponding measure of integration is the invariant measure dS_i/S_i.

Starting with (6) and defining $t_i = i\Delta$, $i = -\infty, \ldots, \infty$, we arrive at the following action as a function of $\{S_i\}$:

$$
A_g(\{S_i\}) = \sum_{i=-\infty}^{\infty} \alpha_i(S_i^{-1} e^{r_1\Delta} S_{i+1} e^{-r_0\Delta} + S_i e^{r_0\Delta} S_{i+1}^{-1} e^{-r_1\Delta} - 2).
\tag{7}
$$

Choosing $\alpha_i = 1/2\Delta\sigma_i^2$ it is not difficult to see that in the limit $\Delta \to 0$, the expression (7) converges to the integral

$$
A_g(S(\cdot)) = \frac{1}{2} \int_{-\infty}^{\infty} d\tau \, \frac{1}{\sigma^2(\tau)} \left(\frac{\partial S(\tau)}{\partial \tau} \bigg/ S(\tau) - \mu \right)^2,
\tag{8}
$$

which corresponds to the geometrical random[8] walk with time-dependent volatility $\sigma(\tau)$ and average rate of share return

$$
\mu = r_0 - r_1.
\tag{9}
$$

To prove this, we first introduce $S(\tau_i)$ as

$$S(\tau_i) = S(t_i + \Delta/2).$$

---

[8] The actions for random walks are described in the Appendix on field theory methods.

This allows us to represent the term $S_i^{-1} e^{r_1 \Delta} S_{i+1} e^{-r_0 \Delta}$ to leading orders in Δ as

$$[1 + (r_1 - r_0)\Delta + (r_1 - r_0)^2 \Delta^2/2] \frac{S(\tau_i)(1 + \Delta S'/2S + \Delta^2 S''/8S)}{S(\tau_i)(1 - \Delta S'/2S + \Delta^2 S''/8S)}$$

$$\simeq \times [1 + (r_1 - r_0)\Delta + (r_1 - r_0)^2 \Delta^2/2]$$

$$\times \left(1 + \frac{\Delta S'}{2S} + \frac{\Delta^2 S''}{8S}\right)\left[1 + \frac{\Delta S'}{2S} - \frac{\Delta^2 S''}{8S} + \frac{\Delta^2}{4}\left(\frac{S'}{S}\right)^2\right]$$

$$\simeq 1 + \left(\frac{S'}{S} + r_1 - r_0\right)\Delta + \Delta^2(r_1 - r_0)\frac{S'}{S} + \frac{\Delta^2}{2}\left(\frac{S'}{S}\right)^2 + \frac{\Delta^2}{2}(r_1 - r_0)^2$$

$$= 1 + \left(\frac{S'}{S} + r_1 - r_0\right)\Delta + \frac{\Delta^2}{2}\left(\frac{S'}{S} + r_1 - r_0\right)^2.$$

Similarly, the term $S_i e^{r_0 \Delta} S_{i+1}^{-1} e^{-r_1 \Delta}$ can be expanded as

$$S_i e^{r_0 \Delta} S_{i+1}^{-1} e^{-r_1 \Delta} \simeq 1 - \left(\frac{S'}{S} + r_1 - r_0\right)\Delta + \frac{\Delta^2}{2}\left(\frac{S'}{S} + r_1 - r_0\right)^2.$$

Substituting these expressions into (7) and keeping in mind that $\alpha_i = 1/2\sigma_i^2 \Delta$, we obtain

$$\mathcal{A}_g(\{S(\cdot)\}) = \frac{1}{2} \sum_{i=-\infty}^{\infty} \frac{1}{\sigma_i^2} \left(\frac{S'(\tau_i)}{S(\tau_i)} + r_1 - r_0\right)^2 \Delta,$$

which in the limit $\Delta \to 0$ converges to the expression (8).

We conclude, therefore, that the action (6) describes geometrical random walks of prices, with volatilities varying across the assets and the time intervals. Introducing time-dependent rates r_0 and r_1, one can also generate time-dependent rates of return.

It is easy to give an interpretation of the relation (9). The system as a whole is not conservative, and both the interest rate r_0 and the rate r_1 come from outside the system (from banks and the corresponding company production). Imagine that the world is certain and that, because of the company production, the capitalization of the firm has increased. For this amount, new shares with the same price S_1 have been issued and no cash dividends have been paid (these are so-called stock dividends). The number of new shares for each old share is equal to $e^{r_1 \Delta}$. This means that the cumulative (old) share will have a price $S_1 e^{r_1 \Delta}$, while the original price (at zero time) was S_0. Taking into account discounting and certainty, we end up with the following expression:

$$S_1 = e^{(r_0 - r_1)\Delta} S_0,$$

which tells us that the rate of return on the share must be equal to $r_0 - r_1$. After introducing an uncertainty, the last expression turns into an average rate of return on the share.

Linear actions can be derived from the general actions (4) under assumptions of locality and small arbitrage fluctuations measured by means of $R^{(2)}$.

3.2   Quadratic Actions

The general form of the action that is quadratic in the curvatures R is represented as

$$A_g(\{S, r\}) = \sum_{\gamma_n \gamma_m} \alpha_{\gamma_n \gamma_m} R_{\gamma_n} R_{\gamma_m}. \tag{10}$$

Here the sum is taken over all elementary plaquettes γ_n and γ_m, including different orientations. In close analogy with the analysis that we carried out in the case of linear actions, it is possible to show that in the case of a system comprising 'cash' and N stocks, as action (10) that is local in time,

$$A_g(\{S, r\}) = \sum_{i=-\infty}^{\infty} \sum_{l,m=1}^{N} \alpha_{lm,i}[(S_{l,i}e^{r_0\Delta}S_{l,i+1}^{-1}e^{-r_l\Delta} - 1)(S_{m,i}e^{r_0\Delta}S_{m,i+1}^{-1}e^{-r_m\Delta} - 1)$$

$$+ (S_{m,i}^{-1}e^{r_m\Delta}S_{m,i+1}e^{-r_0\Delta} - 1)(S_{l,i}^{-1}e^{r_l\Delta}S_{l,i+1}e^{-r_0\Delta} - 1)],$$

$$\alpha_{lm,i} = \alpha_{ml,i} = \frac{1}{2\Delta}(\sigma^2)_{lm}^{-1},$$

generates in the continuous-time limit stochastic processes for stock returns that have time-varying variances and *non-zero correlation coefficients* both across the stocks and in time:

$$A_g(\{S, r\}) = \int_{-\infty}^{\infty} d\tau \sum_{l,m=1}^{N} \frac{1}{2}(\sigma^2(\tau))_{lm}^{-1}\left(\frac{S_l'}{S_l} + r_l - r_0\right)\left(\frac{S_m'}{S_m} + r_m - r_0\right).$$

This type of model suits the description of assets with a priori correlations that are not due to price-driven money flows. The reader will find further examples of quadratic actions in Chapters 8 and 9, where general asset pricing and derivative pricing are examined.

It is clear that the linear and quadratic actions are very particular cases of the general action (4). They are sufficient to model simple random processes such as geometrical random walks of prices and rates, and can be considered as approximations for the cases where the arbitrage fluctuations are sufficiently small that one can limit the general action (4) to the first non-trivial terms only. It has to be noted, however, that, as shown in the next chapter, even these simple actions, provided with the money flows terms, can produce a realistic statistical description.

4   CONTINUOUS FIBRE BUNDLES

In Section 2, we constructed a fibre bundle with discrete base. Although, as we will show in later chapters, this space is sufficient to describe the speculative behaviour of traders, one need a continuous version of this construction when portfolio analysis or derivative pricing are concerned. Indeed, the discrete picture does not allow one to describe situations where a market participant invests in several assets, with some part of her wealth in each of them. As we have already explained in Chapter 2, the fractions of the wealth kept in different assets, together with time, play the role of coordinates in the base, and replace the point-like base.

First of all, let us consider a simple two-asset example, which will later be generalized to the case of an arbitrary number of assets. In the case of two assets (say dollars and shares), the space of all possible portfolios is parametrized by a real number x, which is the fraction of wealth of a portfolio invested in shares. Thus the base B is the product of two real axes $\mathbb{R}$

$$B = \mathbb{R} \times \mathbb{R}$$

and the fibre is the semi-axis $\mathbb{R}_+$. A point of the fibre bundle with coordinates $(b = (x, t), f)$ represents a portfolio at time t such that it comprises f units of the basis portfolio associated with the point b and its wealth fraction invested in shares is equal to x. The general form of the basis portfolios is $a(b) = (a_1(b), a_2(b))$, which represents a portfolio with a_1 units of cash and a_2 units of shares and is subject to the constraint

$$x = \frac{a_2 S(t)}{a_1 + a_2 S(t)},$$

where S is the price of a unit of shares in units of cash. We recover the lattice situation when x is restricted to two values only: $x = 0, 1$. The first case corresponds to a pure dollar portfolio and the second to a pure stock portfolio. The freedom to choose the prices of the basis portfolio is analogous to the freedom to choose the asset units in the discrete case. A choice of prices of basis portfolios for each point of the base is equivalent to a choice of a gauge fixing, and gauge invariance requires that no observable quantity should depend on it.

Using the notation $b_\mu = (x, t)$ for coordinates on the base, the components of the connection vector field are defined as

$$A_\mu \, db_\mu = \frac{(a_1^{g_{db_\mu}} + a_2^{g_{db_\mu}} S)(b + db_\mu)}{(a_1 + a_2 S)(b)} - 1$$

where $(a_1^{g_{db_\mu}}, a_2^{g_{db_\mu}})$ is the portfolio that is the result of the parallel transport of $(a_1, a_2)(b)$ along the curve db_μ. The parallel transport along the space directions is, as before, dictated by exchange of portfolios according to their values. Portfolios with different stock ratios but the same price will be exchanged one-to-one, or, equivalently, transformed one-to-one under parallel transport. Parallel transport in time is defined by the time evolution of the portfolio components according to their discount factors, exactly as in the discrete-base case.

Having defined the connection vector field, one can calculate the elements of the curvature tensor as

$$R_{\mu\nu} = \frac{\partial A_\nu}{\partial b^\mu} - \frac{\partial A_\mu}{\partial b^\nu}. \tag{11}$$

The elements of the curvature tensor are gauge-invariant, and hence one can use any convenient gauge for the calculation. In what follows, we choose a gauge fixing that leads to a zero value of A_1:

$$a(x, t) = \left(1 - x, \frac{x}{S(t)}\right).$$

All basis portfolios have unit price, and for any particular moment of time can be exchanged one-to-one. This means that parallel transport in the x direction is trivial and A_1 is equal to zero.

As time changes from t to $t + \Delta$, the portfolio $a(x, t) = (1 - x, x/S(t))$ transforms to the portfolio

$$a'(x, t + \Delta) = \left(e^{r_0\Delta}(1 - x), \frac{e^{r_1\Delta}x}{S(t)} \right)$$

which has to be expressed in terms of basis portfolios $a(x, t + \Delta) = (1 - x, x/S(t + \Delta))$. To this end, we rewrite the portfolio a' as

$$a'(x, t + \Delta) = \left(e^{r_0\Delta}(1 - x), e^{r_1\Delta} \frac{S(t + \Delta)}{S(t)} \frac{x}{S(t + \Delta)} \right)$$

$$= \left(e^{r_0\Delta}(1 - x) + e^{r_1\Delta} \frac{S(t + \Delta)}{S(t)} x \right) a(y, t + \Delta)$$

and define y as

$$y = \frac{e^{r_1\Delta}xS(t + \Delta)/S(t)}{e^{r_0\Delta}(1 - x) + e^{r_1\Delta}xS(t + \Delta)/S(t)}.$$

We see that the time evolution leads to parallel transport in both time and 'space' directions that is a direct consequence of the time dependence of the price S. The time evolution causes the parallel transport of a basis portfolio $a(x, t)$ to $(e^{r_0\Delta}(1 - x) + e^{r_1\Delta}S(t + \Delta)x/S(t))$ units of the basis portfolio $a(y, t + \Delta)$. Since the parallel transport in the 'space' direction is trivial, the time component of the connection vector field can be easily found as

$$A_0(x, t) = \lim_{\Delta \to 0} \frac{1}{\Delta} \left(e^{r_0\Delta}(1 - x) + e^{r_1\Delta} \frac{S(t + \Delta)}{S(t)}x - 1 \right) = (1 - x)r_0 + x\left(r_1 + \frac{d \log S(t)}{dt} \right).$$

This gives the elements of the curvature tensor as

$$R_{10} = -R_{01} = \frac{\partial A_0}{\partial x} = r_1 - r_0 + \frac{d \log S(t)}{dt}, \tag{12}$$

in complete agreement with the continuous limit of the lattice curvature:

$$R_{10} = e^{r_1\Delta}S(t + \Delta)S^{-1}(t)e^{-r_0\Delta} - 1 \to \Delta\left(r_1 - r_0 + \frac{d \log S(t)}{dt} \right). \tag{13}$$

To clarify further the relationship between the continuous and discrete cases, we note that the gauge fixing used above is analogous to the following lattice gauge: one chooses stock units to cost one cash unit, which makes the unit of stock equal to $1/S(t)$ part of the share with the price $S(t)$. This results in the fact that the operator of parallel transport along the 'space' link is the identity operator and the operators of parallel transport along the time direction are the operators of multiplication by $e^{r_0\Delta}$ for cash and $e^{r_1\Delta}S(t + \Delta)/S(t)$ for stocks. The lattice curvature along an elementary plaquette does not depend on the gauge fixing, and is equal to

$$R = e^{-r_0\Delta} \cdot 1 \cdot \frac{S(t + \Delta)}{S(t)} e^{r_1\Delta} \cdot 1 - 1,$$

in agreement with (13), and converges in the limit of continuous time to the same value

$$R_{10} = r_1 - r_0 + \frac{d \log S(t)}{dt}.$$

This type of gauge fixing is more convenient when one is dealing with portfolios.

Now we are ready to consider a more general case of a stock market consisting of 'cash' and N securities. The space B_0 of all possible portfolios consists of the subspace of $\mathbb{R}^{N+1}$ with coordinates $(x_0, x_1, \ldots, x_N)$ such that

$$x_0 + x_1 + x_2 + \cdots + x_N = 1.$$

The base B of the fibre bundle is the product of the space B_0 and the time axis $\mathbb{R}$:

$$B = B_0 \times \mathbb{R}.$$

We keep the dilatation group as the structure group and $\mathbb{R}_+$ as the fibre.

At each point $b = (x, t)$ of the base, one can define a basis portfolio $a(b) = (a_0, a_1, a_2, \ldots, a_N)$ that consists of a_i asset units of the ith type:

$$x_i = a_i \Big/ \sum_{i=0}^{N} a_i S_i \quad \forall i = 0, \ldots, N. \tag{14}$$

Here S_i is the price of the ith asset unit measured in terms of the zeroth asset, the cash. Thus $S_0 = 1$. The portfolios $a(x, t)$ are the unit portfolios associated with a generic point b of the base. The gauge-invariance principle requires that the market dynamics has to be independent of the particular choice of asset units and of the particular choice of the unit portfolios provided that they obey (14). The meaning of an element f of the fibre attached to a point b of the base is that f is the number of unit portfolios $a(b)$. Therefore the point (f, b) of the fibre bundle corresponds to f units of the basis portfolios $a(b)$. The whole fibre bundle is the space of all possible portfolios constructed from the $i = 1, \ldots, N$ assets at any moment of time.

Using $b = \{b_\mu\} = (x_1, \ldots, x_N, t)$ as coordinates on the base, the components of the connection vector field are defined as

$$A_\mu \, db_\mu = \frac{\sum_{i=0}^{N} a_i^{g_{db_\mu}}(b + db_\mu) S_i(b + db_\mu)}{\sum_{i=0}^{N} a_i(b) S_i(b)} - 1,$$

with the corresponding formulae for the elements of the curvature tensor given by (11). To calculate the elements of the curvature tensor, we choose the following basis portfolios:

$$a(x, t) = \left(1 - \sum_{i=1}^{N} x_i, \frac{x_1}{S_1(t)}, \ldots, \frac{x_N}{S_N(t)} \right). \tag{15}$$

As before, all basis portfolios have unit price and for any particular moment of time can be exchanged one-to-one. A shift on dx_i in the ith space direction changes the point $(1 - \sum_{k=1}^{N} x, x_1, \ldots, x_i, \ldots, x_N)$ to the point $(1 - \sum_{k=1}^{N} x_k - dx_i, x_1, \ldots, x_i + dx_i, \ldots, x_N)$ and therefore corresponds to the exchange of some quantity of 'cash' to some quantity of the ith asset. Owing to the choice of the basis portfolios the parallel transports in the space directions are trivial:

$$A_\mu = 0 \quad \text{for all space indices } \mu = 1, \ldots, N.$$

To find the time component of the connection vector field, one has to consider the time evolution of portfolios. As time changes from t to $t + \Delta$, the portfolio $a(x, t)$ given by (15) transforms to the portfolio

$$a'(x, t + \Delta) = \left(e^{r_0 \Delta} \left(1 - \sum_{i=1}^{N} x_i \right), e^{r_1 \Delta} \frac{S_1(t + \Delta)}{S_1(t)} \frac{x_1}{S_1(t + \Delta)}, \ldots, e^{r_N \Delta} \frac{S_N(t + \Delta)}{S_N(t)} \frac{x_N}{S_N(t + \Delta)} \right).$$

This has to be expressed in terms of basis portfolios $a(x, t + \Delta)$:

$$a'(x, t + \Delta) = \left(\left(1 - \sum_{i=1}^{N} x_i \right) e^{r_0 \Delta} + \sum_{i=1}^{N} e^{r_i \Delta} \frac{S_i(t + \Delta)}{S_i(t)} x_i \right) a(y, t + \Delta).$$

The ratios y_i corresponding to the point y are defined as

$$y_i = \frac{e^{r_i \Delta} x S_i(t + \Delta) / S_i(t)}{\left(1 - \sum_{i=1}^{N} x_i \right) e^{r_0 \Delta} + \sum_{i=1}^{N} e^{r_i \Delta} \frac{S_i(t + \Delta)}{S_i(t)} x_i}.$$

Once again, we see that the time evolution leads to parallel transport in both the time and space directions. This results in parallel transport of a basis portfolio $a(x, t)$ to

$$\left(1 - \sum_{i=1}^{N} x_i \right) e^{r_0 \Delta} + \sum_{i=1}^{N} e^{r_i \Delta} \frac{S_i(t + \Delta)}{S_i(t)} x_i$$

units of the basis portfolio $a(y, t + \Delta)$. Since the parallel transports in the space directions are trivial, the time component of the connection vector field can be found as

$$A_0(x, t) = \lim_{\Delta \to 0} \frac{1}{\Delta} \left[\left(1 - \sum_{i=1}^{N} x_i \right) e^{r_0 \Delta} + \sum_{i=1}^{N} e^{r_i \Delta} \frac{S_i(t + \Delta)}{S_i(t)} x_i - 1 \right]$$

$$= r_0 \left(1 - \sum_{i=1}^{N} x_i \right) + \sum_{i=1}^{N} x_i \left(r_i + \frac{d \log S_i(t)}{dt} \right).$$

This gives the elements of the curvature tensor as

$$R_{i0} = -R_{0i} = \frac{\partial A_0}{\partial x^i} = r_i - r_0 + \frac{d \log S_i(t)}{dt}, \tag{16}$$

with all others zero. This again agrees with what has been derived in the continuous-time limit of lattice curvature constructions.

One can see that since the curvature elements calculated in the limit of continuous time for the discrete and continuous cases coincide, the dynamical theories of the gauge field in fibre bundles with discrete and continuous bases are equivalent in this limit. The local-in-time quadratic theories derived in Section 3 have action

$$A_g = \int dt \sum_{ik} \alpha_{ik} R_{i0} R_{k0},$$

which generates the same dynamics whether a continuous or a discrete base is considered. This is not the case, however, for the matter fields. The continuous base is considerably richer from the point of view of modelling, and allows one to treat diversification and speculative behaviour on the same ground while the discrete base is restricted to a particular type of speculative behaviour. The price for this generality comes with realizing that the continuous-base case is much more complicated for both analytical and numerical studies than theories with discrete bases.

Let us now turn to the mutually exchangeable assets. Since the general construction is cumbersome and we do not use it anywhere else in later chapters, we do not give a general description, but illustrate it with the example of a simple Foreign Exchange with three mutually exchangeable assets labelled 1, 2, and 3 (see Fig. 5.7). Each pair of assets (i, k) has its exchange rate S_{ik}, which means the possibility of swapping one unit of the ith asset to S_{ik}

units of the kth asset. Obviously, $S_{ik} = S_{ik}^{-1}$. The base of the fibre bundle is the four-dimensional space

$$B = B_0 \times \mathbb{R}, \qquad B_0 = \mathbb{R}^3,$$

which contains a three-dimensional portfolio ratio space and the time xis. The points of B_0 are labelled by coordinates (z, x_2, x_3), where x_2 and x_3 for $z = 0$ are the ratios of the portfolio wealth kept in the second and third assets and measured in units of the first asset. The variable z is an auxiliary coordinate whose meaning will become clear later. For the space B_0, there exists a projection operator Pr such that all points in B_0 have a unique projection onto the plane $z = 0$:

$$\text{Pr} : (z, x_2, x_3) \rightarrow (0, x_2 - z, x_3 + z).$$

A shift along the z axis corresponds after the projection to exchange of the second and the third assets with exchange rate S_{23}, while shifts along the x_2 and x_3 axes correspond to exchanges of the second and third assets with the first. The projection operator identifies the portfolio structures with equal ratios, and allows one to define new types of curves on the plane $(z = 0, x_2, x_3)$. These curves start at points of the plane, and evolve in the three-dimensional space, and then the endpoint is projected back to the plane. To see how this works, we consider a path describing a chain exchange of assets: one unit of the first asset is exchanged for S_{12} units of the second, which, in turn, are exchanged with rate S_{23} for the third asset, which is consequently exchanged back for the first asset with rate S_{31}. On the base, this chain exchange corresponds to the path

$$(0, 0, 0) \rightarrow (0, 1, 0) \rightarrow (1, 1, 0) \rightarrow (1, 1, -1).$$

Now the projection operator can be used to formally close the loop:

$$\text{Pr}(1, 1, -1) = (0, 0, 0).$$

The additional dimension and the projection operator provide the possibility to describe exchange between the second and the third assets. Two points in the plane $(z = 0, x_2, x_3)$ can be connected now not only by curves lying in the plane but also by curves above and below the plane with the endpoint projected back to the plane.

As before, one can associate a parallel transport along the curves and define the corresponding connection vector field using the discount rates and the exchange rates. For each point $b = (x, t)$ of the base, one can define a basis portfolio $a(b) = (a_1, a_2, a_3)$ consisting of a_i asset units of the ith type. We will use the following gauge:

$$a(b) = \left(1 - x_2 - x_3, \frac{x_2 - z}{S_{21}(t)}, \frac{x_3 + z}{S_{31}(t)} \right).$$

As has already been explained, the parallel transports along the x_2 and x_3 axes are trivial and the corresponding components of the connection vector field are equal to zero. To find the component of the connection along the z axis, we start with the portfolio $a(b)$ and exchange dz/S_{21} units of the second asset with $S_{23} \, dz/S_{21}$ units of the third. This will transform the portfolio $a(b)$ to the portfolio

$$a^g(b) = \left(1 - x_2 - x_3 + x_2 - dz + x_3 + dz \, \frac{S_{23} S_{31}}{S_{21}} \right) a(b'),$$

where the point b' is defined as

$$t' = t, \quad x_2' = \frac{x_2 - dz}{1 + dz\,(S_{23}S_{31}S_{12} - 1)}, \quad x_3' = \frac{x_3 + dz\,S_{23}S_{31}S_{12}}{1 + dz\,(S_{23}S_{31}S_{12} - 1)}.$$

Again we see that the exchange leads to parallel transports in the x_2, x_3, and z directions. But since the parallel transports in the x_2 and x_3 directions are trivial, the z component of the connection vector field can be found as

$$A_z(x, t) = \lim_{dz \to 0} \frac{1}{dz}[(1 + dz\,(S_{23}S_{31}S_{12} - 1) - 1] = S_{12}S_{23}S_{31} - 1.$$

The curvature R_{123} calculated along the infinitesimal loop

$$(1 - x_2 - x_3, x_2, x_3) \xrightarrow{S_{12}} (1 - x_2 - x_3 - \Delta, x_2 + \Delta, x_3)$$
$$\xrightarrow{S_{23}} (1 - x_2 - x_3 - \Delta, x_2, x_3 + \Delta) \xrightarrow{S_{31}} (1 - x_2 - x_3, x_2, x_3)$$

coincides with the lattice curvature calculated from the lattice plaquette 1231 in Section 1. Note that the formula (11) does not apply here, because of the multivalued nature of the set of paths.

To conclude this subsection, we give a list of expressions for the remaining components of the connection vector field and the corresponding elements of the curvature tensor. The derivation of these expressions is straightforward, and follows the procedure explained in detail before. The components of the connection vector field are

$$A_t(x, t) = r_1(1 - x_2 - x_3) + (x_2 - z)\left(r_2 + \frac{d \log S_{21}}{dt}\right) + (x_3 + z)\left(r_3 + \frac{d \log S_{31}}{dt}\right),$$

$$A_{x_2}(x, t) = 0, \quad A_{x_3}(x, t) = 0, \quad A_z(x, t) = S_{12}S_{23}S_{32} - 1,$$

and the elements of the curvature tensor

$$R_{x_2, x_3, z} \equiv R_{123} = S_{12}S_{23}S_{31} - 1,$$

$$R_{x_2, t} = r_2 - r_1 + \frac{d \log S_{21}}{dt}, \qquad R_{x_3, t} = r_3 - r_1 + \frac{d \log S_{31}}{dt}$$

$$R_{z, t} = r_3 - r_2 + \frac{d \log S_{32}}{dt} + \frac{d}{dt}[\log S_{12}S_{23}S_{31} - (S_{12}S_{23}S_{31} - 1)].$$

One can see that the expressions for the elements of the curvature tensor coincide with the corresponding quantities calculated on the discrete base in the continuous-time limit, except for the case of $R_{z,t}$. The latter also contains a term with the time derivative of the expression $\log S_{12}S_{23}S_{31} - (S_{12}S_{23}S_{31} - 1)$, which is of order $(S_{12}S_{23}S_{31} - 1)^2/2$ and can be neglected for small arbitrage fluctuations.

We see that in the case of mutually exchangeable assets, the continuous formulation again appears to be equivalent to the lattice formulation unless money flows are introduced. To expand on the last consideration, for the general case of $N + 1$ assets with K pairs of mutually exchangeable assets, one has to introduce a K-dimensional space B_0 following the method that we sketched above for the case $N = 2$, $K = 3$. The parallel transport and the connection vector field can be introduced in a similar way, but we do not stop here for the details.

5   GAUGE INVARIANCE: PRACTICAL ISSUES

There is no perfect symmetry in nature. Gauge symmetry is not perfect either. Market reality breaks the symmetry and makes it only approximate. In this section, we examine splits as gauge symmetry operations and consider two major sources of the market imperfections that violate the gauge symmetry. These are transaction costs and psychological factors. We also comment on observations of uneven distribution of numbers in prices. This is often cited as an example of gauge symmetry violations. It will be shown that this is not so, and that scale invariance and an uneven distribution of digits can coexist.

5.1   Splits and Devaluations

The stock split is an act decided by the board of directors of a company to destroy old shares and to issue new ones with a new par value.[9] Afterwards, the number of shares in the circulation is larger than before, with an exact ratio defined by the size of the split. If, for example, a company goes through a 2-for-1 split, the shareholder with 100 shares with par value \$2 will receive 200 shares with new par value \$1. No other figures change for the shareholder. His share in the company wealth stays the same, as do all the company's fundamentals. A reverse split performs the inverse operation where the number of shares is reduced by a ratio defined by the reverse split. So, a shareholder with the same 100 shares with par value \$2 will receive 50 shares with new par value \$4 under the the reverse 2-for-1 split. Once again, nothing changes with the reverse split except for this nominal difference. The splits and the reverse splits are particular examples of a gauge transformation, and we expect them not to change the financial dynamics. Empirical studies as well as common experience, however, suggest that splits do change the dynamics and therefore violate gauge invariance.

Bar-Yosef and Brown (1977) examined the average behaviour of stock returns for 219 splits that occurred between 1945 and 1965. They found that the stocks tended to have a positive abnormal return prior to the split. Grinblatt et al (1984) reported an apparent market inefficiency during the splits. They showed that if shares were bought the day before the ex-distribution date, the date of definition of the ownership of the new shares, and were sold the next day after the ex-distribution date, then, on average, an investor would make an abnormal return of 1%. Effects of splits on a market were also discussed by Fama et al (1969) and Charest (1978), who also found anomalous market behaviour associated with splits. Copeland (1979) demonstrated that trading volume rises less than proportionally to the split ratio, which clearly demonstrates an impact of splits on stock market dynamics.

Besides their direct impact, splits can cause changes in other gauge-invariance-breaking factors. For example, Conroy et al (1990) showed that splits influence the bid–ask spread, causing it to increase. We will see in the next subsection that in a typical situation, bid–ask spreads violate gauge invariance. Therefore this channel of gauge-symmetry violation by splits has also to be taken into account.

If one is concerned with a currency market, splits are equivalent to devaluation of a national currency decided by the government. Statistically, these are rarer events and are more

---

[9] The subsection on splits follows the classic book by Sharpe et al (1995).

susceptible to external political influence, which makes them difficult to analyse. In general, experience shows that devaluations generate qualitatively similar effects to stock splits. As an example, the devaluation of the Russian rouble 1000-for-1 in 1997 moved exchange rates and internal prices up, although it is difficult to quantify to what extent this increase in prices was due to the devaluation and to what extent it was due to other economic and political reasons.

As a result, we have to admit that splits and devaluations generally change market dynamics and violate gauge invariance, although the violation is comparatively insignificant.

5.2 Transaction Costs

In 1975, the Securities Acts Amendments terminated the system of fixed commissions in the USA. Brokers are free to set commissions or to negotiate them with customers. With the development of electronic trade and internet services, commissions are one of the factors of competition between brokerage firms. Many firms provide additional free benefits to their customers, such as real-time market quotes and security analysis, that are effectively paid by commissions.

Generally, commissions depend both on the price and on the number of bought or sold shares. Typically, commission as a percentage of the order value decreases with number of shares and their price. As an example, we consider commissions asked by Charles Schwab & Co., Inc., effective 23 November 1998. First of all, they state an overriding minimum of $39 per trade and define the commission rate as follows:

Transaction size	Commission rate
$0–2499	$30 + 1.7%
$2500–6249	$56 + 0.66%
$6250–19 999	$76 + 0.34%
$20 000–49 999	$100 + 0.22%
$50 000–499 999	$155 + 0.11%
$500 000+	$255 + 0.09%

With considerably larger rates applying for 'penny stocks' with price less than $1. Orders placed using Charles Schwab internet services will be charged $29.95 for up to 1000 shares or $0.03 per share for trades over 1000 shares. This example shows that the commissions violate gauge invariance: the dependences on both the number of shares and the fixed amount in commissions are not gauge-invariant. Splits of shares are gauge transformations, but they change the number of shares corresponding to the same wealth, and hence lead to different commissions. The existence of a fixed part in commissions makes the commission per share directly dependent on the price and also makes it violate the symmetry. In general, *commissions break gauge symmetry*. However, if the assumption about the commissions per share as a fixed percentage of the share price is a good enough approximation, one can neglect the symmetry violation, and the model with commissions will be gauge-invariant.

Another source of transaction costs is the bid–ask spread. A stock is purchased at the dealer's asked price and sold at the bid price, which is lower. The bid–ask spread constitutes compensation of a market-maker for providing liquidity. This can also be considered as a price faced by a buyer or a seller to make a transaction in a hurry.

The bid–ask spread is influenced by several factors. Loeb (1983) showed that the capitalization of a company (its share price multiplied by the number of shares outstanding) is one of the factors. He showed that the average bid–ask spread decreased continuously from 6.5% for small firms to 0.52% for large firms. The larger the capitalization of the firm the greater the liquidity, which, in turn, reduces the bid–ask spread. Analysing stocks with the same level of liquidity, one might then expect that the bid–ask spread is proportional to the price, and hence preserves gauge invariance. Unfortunately, this is not generally the case.

For an illustration, we consider, stocks traded in NASDAQ and constituting the ISDEX internet stock index. Table 5.1 gives the bid and ask prices S_b and S_a, the bid–ask spread $S_a - S_b$, the average prices $(S_a + S_b)/2$, the inverse average prices $2/(S_a + S_b)$, and the relative bid–ask spread $2(S_a - S_b)/(S_a + S_b)$. Gauge invariance requires a constant relative bid–ask spread as a function of inverse price. Figure 5.10 shows however, that there is considerable dependence of the relative bid–ask spread on the inverse price:

$$\frac{2(S_a - S_b)}{S_a + S_b} \simeq 0.0007 + \frac{\$0.0982 \cdot 2}{S_a + S_b}.$$

This shows that *the relative bid–ask spread tends to decrease as a function of price, thus violating gauge symmetry.* The relative bid–ask spread is typically of the order of 1%, and often can be neglected or approximated by a constant. In these cases, the corresponding model will remain gauge-invariant.

5.3 Psychological Factors

During an intraday trade, and (partially) on an interday scale as well, one can observe that certain prices serve as support and resistance levels. Often these levels coincide with integer or half-integer values of prices. One example of such a situation is shown in Fig. 5.11.

The origin of these patterns lie in the psychological peculiarities of traders' behaviour. One possible explanation is that traders tend to set for themselves the easily recognizable price levels as barriers to activate their 'buy' or 'sell' orders. There is no rational excuse to set integers or any other special numbers to be the barriers, and the choice might be dictated by pure lame aesthetic reason. However, this tends to be a rather self-reinforcing effect for some (maybe short) period of time. Besides, for practical reasons, prices are quoted in units of fractions of, say, USD, and are usually $\frac{1}{8}$, $\frac{1}{16}$, or $\frac{1}{32}$.

It is clear that the market dynamics demonstrating this type of price behaviour violates gauge invariance. Integers or any over-special numbers cannot influence the gauge dynamics, since, in the gauge-invariance picture, prices can be rescaled, changing integer values of the price to non-integer values without changing the dynamics. Thus, psychological factors have to be put into the group of symmetry-breaking ones.

5.4 Uneven Distribution of Numbers in Prices

Another argument put forward against gauge invariance is the uneven distribution of digits in prices (see Ley, 1996; Hill, 1998; Pietronero et al, 1998). It was observed that, for example,

Table 5.1

29 March 1999	Bid ($)	Ask ($)	Bid–ask spread ($)	Average ($)	Inverse average (1/$)	Relative bid–ask spread
GNET	138.9375	139	0.03125	138.96875	0.007195862	0.000224871
CNET	96	96.125	0.0625	96.0625	0.010409889	0.000650618
CMGI	186.5625	186.875	0.15625	186.71875	0.005355649	0.00083682
SPLN	45.5	45.9375	0.21875	45.71875	0.021872864	0.004784689
GCTY	113.375	113.9375	0.28125	113.65625	0.0879846	0.002474567
XCIT	147.1875	147.375	0.09375	147.28125	0.006789731	0.000636537
RNWK	126.875	127.25	0.1875	127.0625	0.007870143	0.001475652
DCLK	191.125	191.5	0.1875	191.3125	0.00522705	0.000980072
BCST	114.5	114.6875	0.09375	114.59375	0.008726479	0.000818107
SONE	73.5	73.625	0.0625	73.5625	0.013593883	0.000849618
EGRP	59.1875	59.25	0.03125	59.21875	0.016886544	0.000527704
VRSN	138.25	138.875	0.3125	138.5625	0.00721696	0.0022553
EBAY	147.75	147.8125	0.03125	147.78125	0.006766758	0.000211461
XMCM	71.125	71.25	0.0625	71.1875	0.01404741	0.000877963
CNCX	79.1875	79.9375	0.375	79.5625	0.012568735	0.004713276
LCOS	90.375	90.625	0.125	90.5	0.011049724	0.001381215
INSP	87.25	87.5	0.125	87.375	0.011444921	0.001430615
PSIX	43.25	43.6875	0.21875	43.46875	0.023005032	0.005032351
ATHM	159.625	159.6875	0.03125	159.65625	0.006263457	0.000195733
VRIO	46.4375	46.5	0.03125	46.46875	0.021519839	0.000672495
BVSN	66.25	66.3125	0.03125	66.28125	0.015087223	0.000471476
NSOL	104.375	104.5	0.0625	104.4375	0.009575105	0.000598444
SEEK	81.4375	81.5	0.03125	81.46875	0.012274645	0.000383583
EXDS	144.8125	144.875	0.03125	144.84375	0.006903991	0.00021575

MSPG	91.875	92.5	0.3125	92.1875	0.010847458	0.003389831
USWB	42	42.125	0.0625	42.0625	0.023774146	0.001485884
YHOO	175	175.875	0.4375	175.4375	0.005700036	0.002493766
ISSX	79.75	80.875	0.5625	80.3125	0.012451362	0.007003891
PTVL	17.25	17.4375	0.09375	17.34375	0.057657658	0.005405405
AMZN	150	151	0.5	150.5	0.006644518	0.003322259
AOL	131.375	131.6875	0.15625	131.53125	0.007602756	0.001187931
ELNK	62	62.75	0.375	62.375	0.016032064	0.006012024
INKT	82.5	82.625	0.0625	82.5625	0.012112036	0.000757002
AXNT	31.75	32.375	0.3125	32.0625	0.031189084	0.009746589
CSCO	109.9375	110	0.03125	109.96875	0.009093492	0.000284172
BYND	22.5625	22.875	0.15625	22.71875	0.044016506	0.006877579
OMKT	14.0625	14.1875	0.0625	14.125	0.07079646	0.004424779
BRCM	60.9375	61	0.03125	60.96875	0.016401845	0.000512558
ONSL	34.0625	34.25	0.09375	34.15625	0.029277219	0.002744739
NTKI	15.0625	15.5	0.21875	15.28125	0.065439673	0.014314928
VOCLF	11.125	11.4375	0.15625	11.28125	0.088642659	0.013850416
TFSM	44.375	45.5	0.5625	44.9375	0.022253129	0.012517385
CDNW	17.125	17.25	0.0625	17.1875	0.058181818	0.003636364
CYCH	15.25	15.4375	0.09375	15.34375	0.065173116	0.00610998
SDTI	17.6875	17.875	0.09375	17.78125	0.056239016	0.005272408
NETA	32	32	0	32	0.03125	0
EGGS	17.75	17.75	0	17.75	0.056638028	0
COOL	21.75	21.75	0	21.75	0.045977011	0

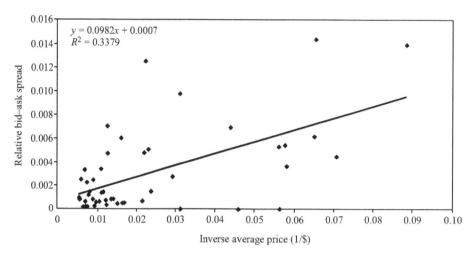

Figure 5.10   Relative bid–ask spread as a function of the inverse average price for stocks in ISDEX internet stocks index, 29 March 1999. Trading of Netscape (NSCP) was halted. The least-squares fit shows that there is a considerable dependence of the bid–ask spread on the inverse average price, which violates gauge symmetry.

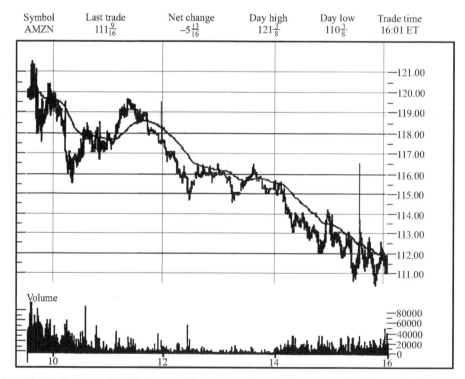

Figure 5.11   Integer and half-integer numbers serve as levels of support and resistance for the intraday trade.

probabilities to find the first digits in prices are distributed non-uniformly between numbers from 1 to 9. Indeed, the first three integers 1, 2, and 3 have together a frequency of 60%, while the other six values from 4 to 9 appear in only 40% of the cases. This empirical fact is considered a demonstration of gauge-invariance breaking, since a rescaling of prices seems to deprive the numbers 1, 2, and 3 of any particular importance. Below, we show why this argument is flawed and the uneven distribution alone does not necessarily mean gauge-symmetry violation.

The effect is not specific to stock prices, but has been reported for many natural phenomena, such as the areas of lakes, lengths of rivers, and molecular weights of chemical compounds (Benford, 1938). Benford found an empirical law for the probability distribution $P(n)$ of the first digit, *Benford's law*:

$$P(n) = \log\left(\frac{1+n}{n}\right).$$

Figure 5.12 (Pietronero et al, 1998) shows how this law fits the empirical distribution of first digits in stock market prices.

The uneven distribution of numbers in prices could be explained by psychological reasons. Reasons of convenience could be another explanation when the prevalence of the number 1 in the first digit is explained by a tendency to assign price values of order of unity in local currency. To check this hypothesis, Pietronero et al (1998) expressed prices in different currencies. They repeated their analysis of Zurich market prices expressed in pesetas and Madrid stock prices expressed in Swiss francs. As a result, they found that Benford's law is independent of the units adopted. Therefore one can conclude that the uneven distribution does not violate the gauge invariance.

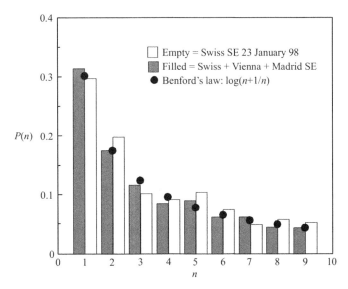

Figure 5.12 First-digit distribution for prices of the Madrid, Vienna, and Zurich stock markets on 23 January 1998. Taken from Pietronero et al (1998). Reproduced with kind permission of the authors.

To see why this is so, we start with the scaling invariant probability distribution function of price S, which has the general form of a power law:

$$P(S) = \text{const} \times S^{-\alpha}.$$

It is easy to see that under the rescaling transformations $S \to \lambda S$, the distribution function reproduces itself:

$$P(\lambda S) = \text{const} \times \lambda^{-\alpha} S^{-\alpha} = \text{const}' \times S^{-\alpha},$$

since the constant multiplier is determined by the normalization condition $\int dS\, P(S) = 1$. To find now the probability $\prod$ for the first digit to be n, we have to calculate the following sum:

$$\prod(n) = \sum_{i=0}^{\infty} \int_{n \times 10^i}^{(n+1) \times 10^i} dS\, \text{const} \times S^{-\alpha}.$$

Evaluating the integral for $\alpha \neq 1$ for every i, we derive the following expression:

$$\prod(n) = \sum_{i=0}^{\infty} \frac{\text{const}}{1 - \alpha} [(n+1)^{1-\alpha} \times 10^{i(1-\alpha)} - n^{1-\alpha} \times 10^{i(1-\alpha)}]$$

$$= \frac{\text{const} \times [(n+1)^{1-\alpha} - n^{1-\alpha}]}{\alpha - 1} \sum_{i=0}^{\infty} 10^{i(1-\alpha)},$$

which, after normalization, gives the distribution function as

$$\prod(n) = [(n+1)^{1-\alpha} - n^{1-\alpha}] / \sum_{k=1}^{9} [(k+1)^{1-\alpha} - k^{1-\alpha}]. \tag{17}$$

In the limit $\alpha = 1$, the last equation converges to Benford's law as plotted on Fig. 5.12:

$$\prod(n) = \log\left(\frac{n+1}{n}\right).$$

Therefore we conclude that *it is possible to obtain an uneven distribution of the first digits of quantities distributed according to a scale-invariant law.*

As a final comment, we note that, in fact, any decreasing probability distribution of prices will provide uneven distributions of first digits. To illustrate this statement, one can consider a distribution function that is not scale-invariant:

$$P(S) = \text{const}_1 \times S^{-\alpha_1} + \text{const}_2 \times S^{-\alpha_2},$$

with $\alpha_1, \alpha_2 > 1$. After calculations analogous to those above, he following distribution function of the first digits can be derived:

$$\prod(n) = \frac{N \times \text{const}_1}{1 - \alpha_1} [(n+1)^{1-\alpha_1} - n^{1-\alpha_1}] + \frac{N \times \text{const}_2}{1 - \alpha_2} [(n+1)^{1-\alpha_2} - n^{1-\alpha_2}],$$

with normalization factor N. Both terms on the right-hand side are decreasing functions of n, which makes the sum decreasing as well. This generates an uneven distribution of the first digits for non-scale-invariant distribution $P(S)$. It is straightforward to generalize this example to a series of terms provided that all the series converge and it is possible to interchange integration and summation. This example shows that the uneven distribution of first digits is not a peculiar phenomenon but rather a general property of decreasing distributions, and has nothing to do with scale invariance. In contrast, scale invariance is a quite restrictive requirement that singles out power-law distributions.

The market imperfections listed above do exist in real market life. They make gauge symmetry only approximate and require gauge-fixing terms in market models. We have to note that only certain types of market imperfections break the symmetry. Thus transaction costs proportional to the price can be easily included in models without breaking gauge symmetry. This means that most imperfections, in principle, can be accounted for in gauge-invariant terms, leaving the rest as a gauge-fixing perturbation. We have seen that generally the perturbation is small, and can be either ignored or taken into account using perturbative methods.

6 SUMMARY

- A financial market can be described as a fibre bundle. It is possible to define fibre bundles both with discrete and with continuous bases.

- A fibre bundle with a discrete base is appropriate to describe speculative behaviour. A fibre bundle with a continuous base suits portfolio analysis and derivative pricing as well as speculative behaviour modelling.

- Fibre bundles with continuous bases are considerably more difficult to analyse.

- A general gauge-invariant stochastic dynamics of the gauge field representing prices and discount factors can be constructed from some natural first principles.

- Two simple forms of the action functional for the gauge field – the linear and quadratic actions – are shown to converge in the limit of continuous time to the geometrical Brownian motion for prices with time-dependent parameters and mutual correlation. Other types of stochastic models emerge when more complicated actions are analysed.

- Market imperfections such as transaction costs violate gauge symmetry. However, these violations are tiny, and can be either neglected or introduced as a perturbation.

6

Dynamics of Fast Money Flows: I

I INTRODUCTION

In Chapter 5, we introduced a gauge-invariant dynamics of prices and rates. As mentioned before, a complete theory has to include the connection field and the money flows, which are gauged by the connection. This chapter takes the first step in gauge modelling of money flows, and concentrates on fast speculative behaviour. This means that we will be interested in the dynamics of a liquid market on a time scale from one minute to a few trading days. To simplify the analysis, the case of just one traded asset will be considered. Since in real life one can hardly extract one asset that will not be influenced by other assets traded in the market, the closest analogue of this model situation is the trading of the whole market portfolio. This is why, to test the model of this chapter, we use the results of an analysis of high-frequency data for the S&P500 market index rather than individual shares or other financial instruments.

We start in Section 2 with a review of the recent analysis of high-frequency data for the most liquid markets, paying particular attention to the statistical analysis of high-frequency data for S&P500. Here we describe an experimentally observed time scaling of the probability distribution function of returns, the time evolution of the kurtosis, and correlators. We argue that the behaviour of these quantities is characteristic of the market, and hence should be described by a model.

Section 3 gives a set of first principles that we use to construct the money flows dynamics. We proceed with the formal construction of the dynamics in Section 4. Here the exposition begins with the case of a single investor, and is generalized to the case of many investors using the standard language of creation–annihilation operators. Those who encounter this language for the first time are advised to look through Section 1 of the Appendix on methods of quantum field theory at the end of the book. The representation in terms of creation–annihilation operators leads directly to the functional integral (Section 2 of the Appendix) for the money flows action that is derived in Section 4. Section 5 is devoted to the derivation of Farmer's term for the direct impact of trades on price changes. In Section 6, we discuss the modelling of an interaction term that describes an interaction among traders and various biases in their decisions. We compare the gauge model with other models for fast market dynamics in Section 7.

Results of analytical and numerical studies of the gauge model and a comparison with market empirics are presented in Section 8. The central result is the possibility of connecting the clearly non-Gaussian behaviour of prices reviewed in Section 2 with the active trading behaviour of speculators who profit from the temporary mispricing of assets. Thus, starting with a geometrical random walk for prices and including money flows, we will be able to fit the statistical quantities calculated for the real prices. The style of Section 8 is purely descriptive, and it does not contain any complicated mathematics. The interested and mathematically oriented reader will find a detailed derivation of the analytical form of the probability distribution function in Section 10 at the end of this chapter. Others can just look through this section to make sure that it is not that easy.

2   FAST PRICE DYNAMICS: MODELS AND EMPIRICS

In this section, we give a concise description of the main empirical observations concerning high-frequency market dynamics. In what follows, the principal attention will be paid to a dynamics of stock market indices, although the main features hold for other liquid markets such as Foreign Exchange markets and futures markets.

As described in Chapter 1, the first stochastic model for price movements was suggested by Bachelier in 1900. However, this model allowed prices to become negative, which is definitely not the case in the real market. Based on empirical evidence Osborn (see Osborn, 1959; Samuelson, 1965) found that returns rather than prices have to be treated as dynamical variables and described by Brownian motion.[1] Soon after, it was realized that the returns, strictly speaking, do not follow Brownian motion, and are characterized by probability distributions with higher central peak and 'fatter' tails (see Mandelbrot, 1963; Fama, 1965). Estimating the tails of the probability distribution of cotton prices on a time scale of months, Mandelbrot suggested that the probability distribution could be better fitted by the Levy stable process[2] (see Bertoin, 1996). The symmetric Levy flight, in contrast to Brownian motion, is composed of independent random steps distributed according to the symmetric Levy stable distribution

$$L_\alpha(Z, \Delta t) = \frac{1}{\pi} \int_0^\infty e^{-\gamma \Delta t q^\alpha} \cos(qZ)\, dq, \qquad 0 < \alpha \leq 2, \tag{1}$$

rather than the Gaussian distribution

$$G(Z, \Delta t) = \frac{1}{\sqrt{4\pi\gamma\Delta t}} e^{-Z^2/(4\gamma\Delta t)}. \tag{2}$$

In fact, as the index α tends to 2, the distribution (1) converges to the distribution (2) and the scaling parameter γ appears to be related to the volatility σ by

$$\sigma^2 = 2\gamma.$$

Although the Levy distribution can be successfully used to fit the probability distributions across various markets (the reader will find examples for stocks, bonds and currencies markets in Peters, 1994), an obvious problem that confronts anyone who favours the distribution (1) is the infinite second moment $\langle Z^2 \rangle$ for any index α except $\alpha = 2$. The

---

[1] Thus Osborn first pointed out the importance of the analysis of gauge-invariant returns in contrast to non-invariant prices.
[2] Which is also called Levy walk or Levy flight.

second moment is the square of the volatility of the return, which one would like to be finite to agree with empirical studies. This obstacle delayed wide practical applications of the Levy distribution in finance for more than 20 years.

The Levy distribution is not the only proposal to fit the market data. The most popular choices are the following:

1. The scaled-t distribution

$$f(x) = \frac{\Gamma((v + 1)/2)}{\Gamma(v/2)\sqrt{\pi(v - 2)\sigma^2}} \left(1 + \frac{x - \mu}{(v - 2)\sigma^2}\right)^{-(v+1)/2},$$

where $\Gamma(\cdot)$ is the gamma function, μ and σ^2 are the location and dispersion parameters respectively, and $v > 0$ is a degree-of-freedom parameter. This distribution was used by Praetz (1972), Blattberg and Gonedes (1974), Gray and French (1990), Piero (1994), and Aparicio and Estrada (2000) to fit the distribution of returns on various time scales. It was found that this distribution fits the observed data better than many competing alternatives for time spans starting with one trading day.

2. Leptokurtic distribution generated by a mixture of distributions (for the discrete-time analogue, see Fama, 1965; Clark, 1973; Epps and Epps, 1976; Kon, 1984; Aparicio and Estrada, 2000; S.J. Taylor, 1986). Recently the same idea was applied to the case of the high-frequency FOREX market (see Ghashghaie et al, 1996) and to high-frequency market index dynamics (see Kornilovitch, 1998).

3. Stochastic volatility models

4. ARCH–GARCH models.

5. Fractional Brownian motion.

To make our exposition self-contained, we give a short description of last three types of models.

2.1   Models

Models with Stochastic Volatility

In stochastic volatility models, one assumes that the price follows Brownian motion but with a random volatility. The first class of these models comprises models that have the volatility as a function of the price (see Geske, 1979; Rubinstein, 1983; Bensoussan et al, 1994):

$$\frac{dP}{P} = \sigma(P)\,dW + \mu\,dt.$$

The rationale behind the models is the following. Suppose that a firm has a debt and its share price represents the surplus of the firm's assets over debt. If one assumes that the firm's assets fluctuate as geometrical Brownian motion, the volatility of the share prices depends on the price level. Indeed, it grows significantly when the assets fall and debts become more important, and it falls when the assets rise and the debt factor becomes irrelevant. Thus the volatility in this approach is negatively correlated with the share price. Cox and Russ (1976) considered a particular case of the above model, the Constant Elasticity of Variance model, which specifies the volatility dependence as $\sigma(P) = \sigma P^{\alpha-1}$, with $0 < \alpha < 1$.

The next class of stochastic volatility models describe the volatility as an independent quasi-Brownian process (see Scott, 1987; Wiggins, 1987; Hull and White, 1987, 1988; Stein and Stein, 1991; Heston, 1993):

$$\frac{dP}{P} = \sigma \, dW + \mu(\sigma, \rho) \, dt, \quad d\sigma = f(\sigma, \rho) \, dB + \gamma(\sigma, \rho) \, dt, \quad dB \, dW = \rho \, dt.$$

Stochastic volatility models formulated in continuous time are especially suited for derivative pricing. Moreover, all of them were introduced in this context. While continuous-time models provide the natural framework for asset pricing, discrete-time models are ideal for the statistical and descriptive analysis of the patterns in price changes.

ARCH–GARCH Models

ARCH–GARCH models (see Engle, 1982; Bollerslev, 1986; Bollerslev et al, 1992) attempt to explain volatility clustering. The basic idea behind the autoregressive conditional hetero-scedasticity (ARCH) models is that many markets have active and passive periods when large (small) fluctuations are followed by further large (small) ones. The most general zero-mean ARCH process, the ARCH(n) process, is defined as a sequence of random variables $\{\epsilon_t\}$ such that ϵ_t is chosen at time t from a set of random variables characterized by a Gaussian distribution with zero mean and standard deviation σ_t:

$$\sigma_t = \alpha_0 + \sum_{i=1}^{n} \alpha_i \epsilon_{t-i}.$$

For ARCH(1), the unconditional variance of ϵ_t is finite for $\alpha_1 < 1$ and is calculated as

$$\sigma^2 = \frac{\alpha_0}{1 - \alpha_1},$$

while the kurtosis[3] is equal to

$$\kappa = \frac{3(1 - \alpha_1^2)}{1 - 3\alpha_1^2}$$

(for details, see Engle, 1982). The Generalized ARCH, the GARCH(p, q) process, differs from the ARCH by its additional flexibility in the definition of σ_t:

$$\sigma_t = \alpha_0 + \sum_{i=1}^{p} \alpha_i \epsilon_{t-i} + \sum_{i=1}^{q} \beta_i \sigma_{t-i}.$$

GARCH(1, 1), the simplest GARCH process, has finite unconditional second and fourth moments if the parameters obey the following conditions:

$$1 - \alpha_1 - \beta_1 > 0, \qquad 1 - \beta_1^2 - 2\alpha_1\beta_1 - 3\alpha_1^2 > 0.$$

Empirical analysis (see Akgiray, 1989) shows that the value of $\beta_1 = 0.9$ is preferred to describe stock market data. This value, together with α_0 and α_1 calculated from market

---

[3] Defined by (6) in Section 2.2.

variance and kurtosis, were used by Mantegna and Stanley (1998) to obtain a very good fit of the probability distribution function for the S&P500 index with a time interval $\Delta t = 1$ minute.

Fractional Brownian Motion

Fractional Brownian motion was proposed by Mandelbrot and van Ness (1968; see also Mandelbrot, 1982). It has statistical features that are self-similar over time, and it possesses persistence, which creates trends and cycles.

Essentially, fractional Brownian motion can be regarded as the $(\frac{1}{2} - H)$th fractional derivative of regular Brownian motion:

$$B_H(t) = \frac{1}{\Gamma(H + \frac{1}{2})} \int_0^t (t - \tau)^{H-1/2} \, dB(\tau),\tag{3}$$

with the Hurst exponent $0 < H < 1$. For the case $H = \frac{1}{2}$, this definition converges to regular Brownian motion, but for other values of H, it gives a highly correlated process. It is easy to show that

$$\langle |B_H(t) - B_H(t')|^2 \rangle = |t - t'|^{2H},$$

and the autocovariance function decays with the time lag t as $|t|^{2H-2}$ (Mandelbrot and van Ness, 1968). The main motivation for using the model (3) is that it demonstrates the scaling property observed for volatilities in real markets (see below). Fractional Brownian motion possesses a long memory, and can be used to model returns if such long-term memory is observed in the market. In practice, the returns have short-term memory, in contrast to their absolute values, which demonstrate long-term memory effects. This is why the fractional processes are more suited to describe the absolute value of returns or higher moments. Figure 6.1 shows that fractional Brownian motion has a Gaussian profile.

The idea of fractional integration can be applied to other models, such as ARCH–GARCH models. For reviews of long memory processes, models, and applications of fractional integration, see Baillie (1996) and Granger and Ding (1996).

Truncated Levy Flights

Mantegna and Stanley (1995) proposed to model price returns as the Levy flight with a probability distribution function (PDF) exponentially truncated at the wings. The truncation makes the moments of the returns finite, and thus removes the main problem in applications of Levy flights. At the same time, the model has a probability distribution function that is in good agreement with the observable data in the high-frequency regime and demonstrates the scaling behaviour typical of market indices. The finiteness of the second moment provides, according to the Central Limit Theorem, the convergence of the probability distribution for truncated Levy flights to the normal distribution. Therefore one might expect that after 10 or so steps, the resulting PDF will have a Gaussian profile. It turned out, however, that the convolution of truncated Levy distributions converges to a Gaussian profile very slowly (Mantegna and Stanley, 1994), and it might take thousands of steps to get the normal shape for the probability distribution function. This is just enough to describe the high-frequency regime and to converge to Brownian motion in the long-time limit.

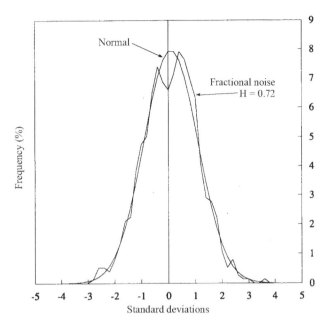

Figure 6.1 Probability distribution function for fractional Brownian motion with index $H = 0.72$, in comparison with a Gaussian profile. From *Fractal Market Analysis: Applying Chaos Theory to Investment and Economics*, by E.E. Peters, Copyright © 1994 John Wiley & Sons, Inc. Reprinted by permission of John Wiley & Sons, Inc.

Let us now turn to results of empirical studies of fast market dynamics, which are essential to test the models listed above.

2.2   Empirical Results[4]

Probability Distribution Function (PDF)

Mantegna and Stanley (1995) analyzed 1 447 514 records of the S&P500 index during the period from January 1984 to December 1989. Although they studied price increments rather than returns, they stated that the results obtained remain the same for returns. As the principal result of their study, Mantegna and Stanley found that the central region (see Fig. 6.2) of the PDF can be very well fitted by the Levy distribution (1) with parameters $\alpha = 1.40 \pm 0.05$ and $\gamma = 0.00375$ (Fig. 6.3 gives a similar fit for the GBP/USD exchange rate PDF). They also showed that the scaling property of the Levy distribution (1),

$$L_\alpha(Z/(\Delta t)^{1/\alpha}, 1) = (\Delta t)^{1/\alpha} L_\alpha(Z, \Delta t), \tag{4}$$

---

[4] For a short review of empirical study of high-frequency data, see also Bouchaud and Cont (1998) and Guillaume et al (1997). The reader might be interested to look at a recent collection of research papers on high-frequency studies in Dunis and Zhou (1998).

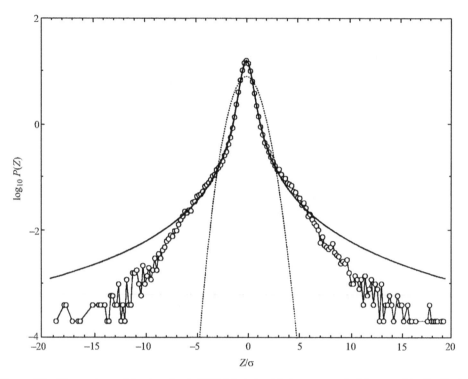

Figure 6.2 Comparison of the $\Delta t = 1$ min PDF (circles) with the symmetrical Levy stable distribution (1) with index $\alpha = 1.4$ and scale parameter $\gamma = 0.00375$ (solid line). The dotted line shows the Gaussian distribution (2) with the same standard deviation σ. The price increments Z are normalized to this value so that Z/σ is approximately equal to the return. Nearly exponential deviations from the Levy distribution are observed for $Z/\sigma \geq 6$. Reprinted by permission from R.M. Mantegna and H.E. Stanley, *Nature* **376**, 46–49, Copyright © 1995 Macmillan Magazines Ltd.

is observed for real data for time Δt in the range 1–1000 minutes. Figure 6.4 demonstrates how the PDFs for different Δt collapse on the same curve, which can be approximated in the central regions by the Levy distribution and has an exponential cut-off.

The scaling behaviour becomes even more transparent if one examines the probability of returns to the origin, $P(0)$, which is the value of the PDF at the peak. For the Levy distribution (1), $P(0)$ can be calculated explicitly, and is equal to

$$P(0, \Delta t) \equiv L_\alpha(0, \Delta t) = (\Delta t)^{-1/\alpha} \frac{\Gamma(1/\alpha)}{\pi \alpha \gamma^{1/\alpha}}. \tag{5}$$

The reader can see that the probability of return to the origin has a power-law behaviour if calculated from the Levy distribution. As Mantegna and Stanley demonstrated, the real data also obey this power-law. Figure 6.5 shows the probability of return to the origin as a function of time, thus supporting the scaling hypothesis.[5] The scaling starts to break down on time

---

[5] From a practical point of view, the study of scaling behaviour from $P(0)$ is very useful, since most events belong to the central region of the PDF and hence provide good statistics for real-time indicators. In contrast, empirical studies of the wings of the distributions are much harder, because one has to analyse rare events.

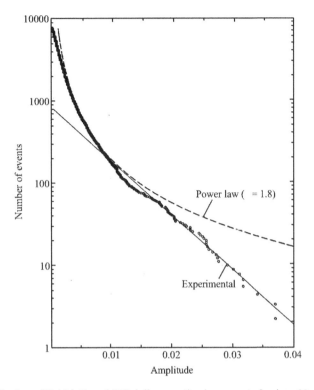

Figure 6.3   Distribution of British Pound/US dollar negative increments for $\Delta t = 30$ min, in the period 1991–1995. The 'near tail' of the distribution can be fitted by a power law, which clearly overestimates the 'far tails'. The latter is well represented by an exponential fall-off. Reprinted from *Physica* **A263**, J.P. Bouchaud, pp. 415–426, Copyright © 1999, with permission from Elsevier Science.

scales of a few trading days and converges to the Gaussian law with $\alpha = 2$ on time scales of two weeks to one month.

Other financial markets have also been examined. Studies of high-frequency regimes for the Milan Stock Exchange (Mantegna, 1991), the Paris Stock Market index CAC40 (Zajdenweber, 1994; Bouchaud and Sornette, 1994), and Foreign Exchange markets give scaling behaviour with scaling index varying from 1.5 to 1.7. Matacz (1997) studied the Australian All Ordinaries Share Market index (AOI), and found scaling behaviour (5) with index $\alpha = 1.2$. Therefore we can conclude that the self-similarity of the PDF and the Levy PDF fitting of the central part of the distributions are well-observed properties of well-developed financial markets.

The study of the 'fat' tails of the PDF is another way to reveal the scaling behaviour. Gopikrishnan et al (1999) found that for the S&P500 index $P(g > x)$, the cumulative distribution of normalized returns

$$g = \frac{\log S(t + \Delta t) - \log S(t) - \langle \log S(t + \Delta t) - \log S(t) \rangle}{\langle [\log S(t + \Delta t) - \log S(t) - \langle \log S(t + \Delta t) - \log S(t) \rangle]^2 \rangle^{1/2}},$$

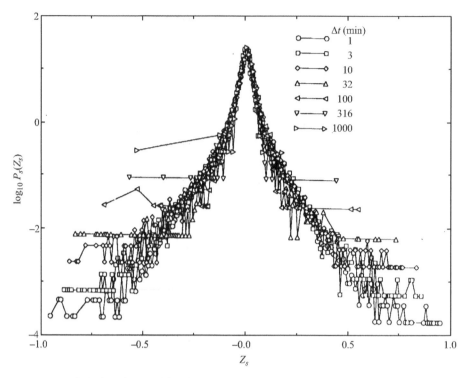

Figure 6.4 Scaled plot of probability distributions. All the data collapse on the $\Delta t = 1$ min PDF by using the scaling transformation (4) with scaling parameter $\alpha = 1.4$. The points outside the average behaviour define the noise level of that specific distribution. Reprinted by permission from R.M. Mantegna and H.E. Stanley, *Nature* **376**, 46–49, Copyright © 1995 Macmillan Magazines Ltd.

has power-law asymptotic behaviour

$$P(g > x) \sim \frac{1}{x^{\alpha_1}}.$$

For the central region of the PDF, $0.5 < g < 3$, they estimated $\alpha_1 \simeq 1.65$, which is close enough to the expected power law for the Levy flight PDF. However, for $3 < g < 50$, the index demonstrates quite different behaviour:[6]

$$\alpha_1 = 3.05 \pm 0.04 \quad \text{positive tail},$$
$$\alpha_1 = 2.94 \pm 0.08 \quad \text{negative tail}.$$

This is well outside the range $0 < \alpha \le 2$ characteristic of the Levy distribution (1). Similar values of the exponent α_1 were found for individual stocks (see Gopikrishnan et al, 1998).

---

[6] Similar results hold for the Hang-Seng (Hong Kong) and NIKKEI (Tokyo) Stock Market indices (Gopikrishnan et al, 1999).

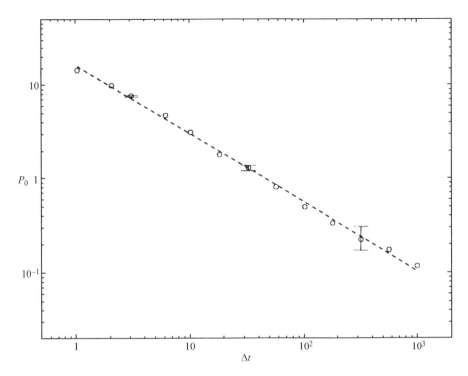

Figure 6.5 Probability of return to the origin $P(0)$ as a function of the time sampling. A power-law scaling behaviour is observed for time intervals spanning three orders of magnitude. The slope of the best-fit line is -0.712 ± 0.025, which corresponds to $\alpha = 1.40 \pm 0.05$. Reprinted by permission from R.M. Mantega and H.E. Stanley, *Nature* **376**, 46–49, Copyright © 1995 Macmillan Magazines Ltd.

This shows that the Levy distribution is indeed only a good fit for the central region of the PDF.

Another key characteristic of the 'fat' tails of the PDFs is the kurtosis, which is the ratio of the fourth moment and the squared variance:

$$\kappa(\Delta t) = \frac{\langle \{\log(S(\Delta t)/S(0)] - \langle \log[S(\Delta t)/S(0)] \rangle \}^4 \rangle}{\langle \{\log[S(\Delta t)/S(0)] - \langle \log[S(\Delta t)/S(0)] \rangle \}^2 \rangle^2} - 3. \tag{6}$$

It is known (see Müller et al, 1990; Baillie and Bollersley, 1989, 1991) that the kurtosis decreases with increasing time windows, which also means that the tails lose weight. Cont (1997, Fig. 3) depicts this fact for the S&P500 index futures. This also suggests that the kurtosis decays as a power law. We will see below that the same data can be fitted without references to a power law in the framework of our model (see Fig. 6.18).

Correlation Coefficients

It is well known that correlations between returns disappear quickly (Fama, 1970; Lo, 1991; Goetzman, 1993; Mills, 1993; Lux, 1996), and the correlation coefficient for returns

$$C_{r\Delta t}(t) = \frac{\langle\{\log[S(\Delta t)/S(0)] - E_{\Delta t}(0)\}\{\log[S(\Delta t + t)/S(0)] - E_{\Delta t}(t)\}\rangle}{\langle\{\log[S(\Delta t)/S(0)] - E_{\Delta t}(0)\}^2\rangle},$$

$$E_{\Delta t}(t) = \langle\log[S(t + \Delta t)/S(t)]\rangle,$$

decays exponentially (see Fig. 6.6). This was always considered to be an empirical proof of the Efficient Market Hypothesis. However, other correlation coefficients

$$C_{k,\Delta t}(t) = \frac{\langle\{|\log[S(\Delta t)/S(0)]|^k - E_{\Delta t}^{(k)}(0)\}\{|\log[S(\Delta t + t)/S(0)]|^k - E_{\Delta t}^{(k)}(t)\}\rangle}{\langle\{|\log[S(\Delta t)/S(0)]|^k - E_{\Delta t}^{(k)}(0)\}^2\rangle},$$

$$E_{\Delta t}^{(k)}(t) = \langle|\log[S(t + \Delta t)/S(t)]|^k\rangle,$$

demonstrate quite different behaviour. Generally $C_{k,\Delta t}(t)$ have long-term memory and decay as some power law (Ding et al, 1993; Lux, 1996; Cont, 1997; Gopikrishnan et al, 1999). Figure 6.7 reveals the power-law behaviour of the correlation coefficients C_1 calculated for the S&P500 index. This type of behaviour is typical of other markets as well. This shows that, in contrast to the returns, the volatility and the corresponding higher-order quantities have a long memory and cannot be modelled by processes with short-term memory such as random walks (Brownian or truncated Levy) or GARCH–ARCH models.

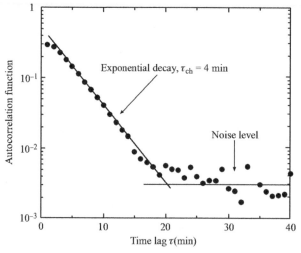

Figure 6.6 Exponential decay of the correlation coefficient for the S&P500 index. Reprinted by permission from P. Gopikrishnan, M. Meyer, L. A. N. Amaral, and H. E. Stanley, *Phys. Rev.* **E60**, 5305–5316 (1999). Copyright © 1999 The American Physical Society.

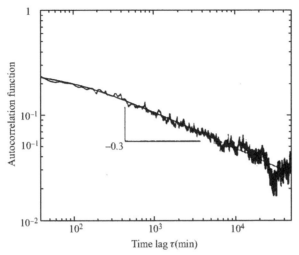

Figure 6.7 The correlation coefficient of absolute returns for the S&P500 index. Reprinted by permission from P. Gopikrishnan, M. Meyer, L. A. N. Amaral, and H. E. Stanley, *Phys. Rev.* **E60**, 5305–5316 (1999). Copyright © 1999 The American Physical Society.

Volatility

The volatility $\sigma^2(T) = \langle\{\log[S(T)/S(0)] - \langle\log[S(T)/S(0)]\rangle\}^2\rangle$ on an interday time scale has been studied for a long time (see Peters, 1994, and references therein). It was noted that, in the long run, the volatility as a function of the time delay T goes as a power law

$$\sigma^2(T) \sim T^\beta, \tag{7}$$

where the index β is approximately equal to 1, the value predicted from the Brownian motion model.

The availability of tick-by-tick data opened the way for research on the intraday volatility scaling (see Dunis and Zhou, 1998). For the S&P500 index, it was found (see Mantegna and Stanley, 1996; Gopikrishnan et al, 1999) that $\beta \simeq 0.7$ for time scales $T < 20\,\text{min}$, beyond which β is approximately equal to 0.5 (see Fig. 6.8). The last value is consistent with the absence of correlations in returns at longer time scales.

For the FOREX market, the scaling was reported for the mean absolute values of returns (Müller et al, 1990) and for higher moments (Ghashghaie et al, 1996; Galluccio et al, 1997). The reported scaling exponents for the FOREX market are quite different from the counterparts calculated for the stock market, and vary from paper to paper.

One might consider the volatility itself as a random variable, and study its PDF. For the S&P500 index this was done in Cizeau et al (1997). The authors examined a data set over 13 years from January 1984 to December 1996, and studied the quantity

$$v_{T=n\Delta t}(t) = \frac{1}{n}\sum_{t'=t}^{t+n-1}\left|\frac{\log[S(t'+\Delta t)/S(t')]}{\langle|\log[S(t'+\Delta t)/S(t')]|\rangle_d}\right|.$$

Here Δt was taken to be equal to 30 minutes to exclude correlations of the returns, and the notation $\langle\,\rangle_d$ in the denominator means an average value at the same time of day averaged

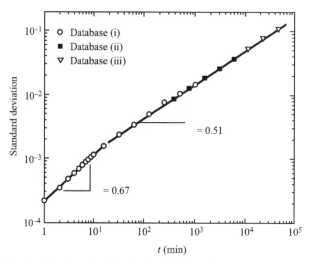

Figure 6.8 Scaling law for the volatility for the S&P500 index. Reprinted by permission from P. Gopikrishnan, M. Meyer, L. A. N. Amaral, and H. E. Stanley, *Phys. Rev.* **E60**, 5305–5316 (1999). Copyright © 1999 The American Physical Society.

over all days of the data set. The denominator was included to eliminate the U-shaped dependence with high market activity in the morning and in the afternoon and much lower activity over noon. It was found in Cizeau et al (1997) that the PDF for v_T can be well fitted by a log-normal distribution (see Fig. 6.9), thus supporting the stochastic volatility models.

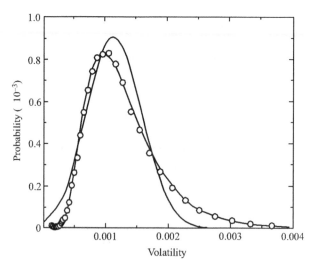

Figure 6.9 PDF for volatilities for $T = 300$ min for the S&P500 index (circles), compared with a log-normal distribution (solid line) and a Gaussian distribution (dashed line). Reprinted from *Physica* **A245**, P. Cizeau, Y. Liu, M. Meyer, C.-K. Peng and H.E. Stanley, pp. 441–445, Copyright © 1997, with permission from Elsevier Science.

Multifractal Behaviour

In the same way as in (7), one can consider other moments. Therefore we introduce the scaling exponents β_k, defined as

$$\mu_k(T) \equiv \langle |\log[S(T)/S(0)] - \langle \log[S(T)/S(0)]\rangle|^k \rangle \sim T^{\beta_k}. \tag{8}$$

For $k = 2$, the moment μ_2 is equal to the square of the volatility and $\beta_2 = \beta$. The scaling exponents were studied in Ghashghaie et al (1996) and Galluccio et al (1997) for the FOREX market and in Gopikrishnan et al (1999) for the S&P500 index. All the studies demonstrated that the scaling exponents do not obey a one-parameter scaling

$$\beta_k = k\beta_1,$$

thus showing so called multifractal behaviour for short and intermediate times T. For USD/DM, it was found in Galluccio et al (1997) that

$$\beta_k \simeq 1.1 + 0.22k \quad \text{as} \quad k \to \infty$$

if the physical time is changed to the 'inner' time

$$\tau(t) = \int_0^t \sigma(t')\, dt'.$$

Figure 6.10 gives the moments for the S&P500 index at different time scales (Gopikrishnan et al, 1999). All studies show a crossover to Gaussian scaling exponents $\beta_k = k/2$ in the long-time T limit.

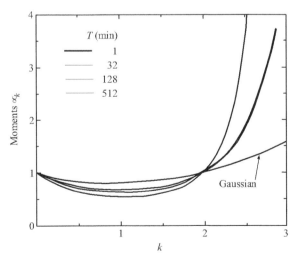

Figure 6.10 Multifractal behaviour of moments for the S&P500 index. Reprinted by permission from P. Gopikrishnan, M. Meyer, L. A. N. Amaral, and H. E. Stanley, *Phys. Rev.* **E60**, 5305–5316 (1999). Copyright © 1999 The American Physical Society.

Returning to the models of price dynamics we see the following:

1. The truncated Levy flight model mainly fits the PDF and possesses the required scaling property and the exponentially decaying correlation coefficients, but fails to produce stochastic volatility and long-term memory for higher moments.

2. Fractional Brownian motion, although it exhibits the scaling property for PDF and the volatility, does not have an exponentially decaying correlation coefficient Cr. Moreover, it has a clear Gaussian PDF (Fig. 6.1), in contrast to the empirical results.

3. GARCH–ARCH models can fit the PDF profile for a particular time horizon, but show scaling behaviour with much higher scaling index for $P(0)$ (Mantegna and Stanley, 1998). Besides, they have exponentially decaying correlation coefficients for volatilities, which contradicts the empirical existence of long memory.

4. Continuous-time stochastic volatility models can, in principle, fit both the PDF profile and the scaling exponent for $P(0)$. However, as for ARCH–GARCH models, they have exponentially decaying correlation coefficients for volatilities.

To eliminate some of these problems, one can consider the following model for returns r_n:

$$r_n = \epsilon_n y_n,$$

where ϵ is a random sign variable with zero mean and exponentially decaying correlations, and y_n is a positive random variable with a long memory modeled by fractional differentiation of an ARCH–GARCH type of model. This will ensure the short-term memory for the returns while providing a realistic PDF shape and the long-term memory for higher moments. However, even this type of model cannot generate the multiscaling behaviour observed for real returns, which may, in fact, be only apparent and result from a single-parameter scaling model with a long transition period (Bouchaud et al, 2000) or the PDF truncation (Nakao, 2000).

3 MONEY FLOWS: FIRST PRINCIPLES

In this short section, we formulate the first principles that will be used later to give a formal description of the dynamics as in Ilinski (1997).

1. We assume a perfect capital market environment, i.e. there is always the possibility of placing money in a deposit and borrowing without any restrictions and at the same interest rate.

2. For short-time investment horizons (intraday range), traders do not think about the corresponding risk. Thus traders are risk-neutral. The risk associated with intraday trading is comparatively small, and traders are in the 'near-certain' situation.[7] In the framework of the expected utility formalism, this leads to approximate risk-neutrality. In real life, traders have their own expectations of price movements during their investment horizon; they believe in these expectations, and do not consider it risky to act. Since there is no risk in the game, no one wants to diversify his portfolio to reduce the risk. This allows us to use

---

[7] Marginally uncertain.

lattice bases for the fibre bundles (see Section 2 of Chapter 5). The behaviour that will be modelled is purely speculative behaviour.

3. We assume that there is a smallest time in the systems (smallest investment horizon) which is equal to Δ. The transactions are instant.

4. There are transaction costs. Their presence is not just an unimportant complication. The transaction costs play the role of inertia for money flows, and stabilize the system. Although we will neglect the transaction costs in the next section to simplify the calculations, the general model takes them into account.

5. The dynamics is gauge-invariant. This means that functionals[8] that govern money flow trajectories with fixed endpoints have to be constructed from products of elements of the structure group along the trajectories.

6. Investors tend to be rational and try to maximize their profit from the securities; i.e., in the absence of irrationality, money flows by the most profitable trajectory subject to given boundary conditions. If, say, an investor starts today in dollars and wants to be in pounds tomorrow, the set of transactions he makes is such that giving the initial number of dollars the number of pounds is maximal. This leaves us with the governing functional, which is an increasing function of the product of structure group elements along the trajectory. Long-term dynamics will deal with more complicated forms of the functionals, but they still have to be constructed from the products of structure group elements to satisfy the gauge invariance condition.

   Formally, an investor wants to maximize the following functional, the *action*, of a value of his investment,

$$s(C) = \log(U_1 U_2, \dots U_N), \tag{9}$$

by a certain choice of the strategy that results in the corresponding trajectory C in the assets 'space'–time. Here $\{U_i\}_{i=i}^{N}$ are elements of the structure group, which are equal to the exchange (price) or interest factors. These factors result from a choice of the investor's behaviour at the ith step on the trajectory C, where the boundary points (at times $T = 0$ and $T = N$) are fixed. For example, an investment strategy C_0 to keep money in dollars today and change it into pounds tomorrow (horizon $\Delta = 1$ day) will result in the following expression for the action:

$$s(C_0) = \log[e^{r_1 \Delta} S_{12}(\Delta)].$$

The increasing function must be the logarithm to ensure additivity of the functional, thus ensuring that maximizing the functional on every step maximizes it on the whole trajectory.

7. Investors' strategy is not always optimal, *i.e.* investors are bounded-rational (Simon, 1969; Sargent, 1993; Conlisk, 1996). This is due to:
   (i) the intrinsic fallibility of their beliefs (as discussed in Chapter 1);
   (ii) incomplete information in their hands;
   (iii) the complicated nature of the utility personal function;
   (iv) the large number of parameters influencing the choice;
   (v) investors' (or managers') internal objectives.

---

[8] Playing the role of utility functionals.

This means that the flow of real wealth is uncertain, and money flow trajectories fluctuate around the most profitable trajectory (the 'classical trajectory'). Thus, in this model, the 'smart money' and the 'noise' traders physically coincide: for part of the time traders behave as the 'smart money', and for part of the time as the 'noise' traders (Black, 1986).

8. As soon as this type of behaviour is assumed, one has to describe the trajectories in a probabilistic way, as was done for the gauge field in Chapter 5. To mimic the features of the bounded rationality that we sketched above, we define the following Boltzmann-type probability weight for a certain trajectory C with N steps:

$$P(C) \sim e^{\tilde{\beta}' s(C)/T} \equiv e^{\tilde{\beta}s(C)}, \tag{10}$$

with some 'effective temperature' $1/\tilde{\beta}$, which represents a measure of the average bounded rationality of investors per unit time. This choice of probability weight corresponds to the so-called multinomial Logit model (see Luce, 1959; McFadden, 1973, 1976; Marsili, 1999). The multinomial Logit model appears in the problem of decision-making by a population of utility maximizer agents with a random utility

$$U(C) = s(C) + \epsilon(C),$$

where $\epsilon(C)$ are independent variables with Gumbel distribution:[9] Prob($\epsilon \leq x$) = exp($-e^{-x}$). The same model arises if one wants to construct a probabilistic model of decision-making under bounded rationality that satisfies the axiom of independence from irrelevant alternatives, namely that the relative odds $p(x)/p(y)$ in a binary choice between x and y are not affected if a third alternative z is added. The same multinomial Logit model was derived recently (see Marsili, 1999) in the situation where a single decision-maker has a multiparametric utility function that however, has a small number of most important parameters. Therefore the choice (10) of probability weight is absolutely consistent with the origin of the bounded rationality we mentioned earlier. The Logit model has been successfully tested on econometric data (McFadden, 1973) and in experiments in strategic contexts (McKelvey and Palfrey, 1995).

9. Fractal Market Hypothesis: there are many investment horizons with identical dynamical rules but rescaled parameters (Peters, 1994).

Later in this chapter, we use a linear and homogeneous action for the gauge field (see Section 3 of Chapter 5). This action is local in the sense that it is given by the sum over plaquettes of the excess return on the corresponding local arbitrage operation. At the same time, the action for the cash-debt flows is non-local and is defined by a curve in the 'space–time' base. This is the only difference in the action constructions for the gauge field and the matter fields.

In the simple model of this chapter, we do not consider 'debt' flows, i.e. we assume that there is no possibility to go short.[10] However, the derivation presented below can easily be generalized to the case of 'debt' flows by adding money flows that *minimize* rather than

---

[9] The limiting distribution of normalized extreme values of a large number of variables whose distribution falls faster than any power as $x \to \infty$.

[10] The action for 'debt' flows is given in Section 4 without a derivation, which is straightforward.

maximize the action (9) and have the opposite sign for the 'temperature' $\tilde{\beta}$ (for details, see Ilinski, 1997).

4 DYNAMICS CONSTRUCTION FOR A SINGLE INVESTMENT HORIZON

Let us now turn our attention to the functional integral representation for the transition probability for the money flows for a single investment horizon. It is convenient to start with one investor and then generalize the consideration to many investors using creation–annihilation operators (as explained in Sections 1 and 2 of the Appendix on methods of quantum field theory).

In what follows, we want to describe a simple stock market with only one traded asset, labelled by index 2, and cash labeled by index 1. This prompts us to deal with the 'ladder' base of the fibre bundle (Fig. 5.6 in Chapter 5). The asset will be called 'shares'. The price of one unit of shares is denoted by S and the corresponding rates are r_1 and r_2. The notation for the investor horizon is Δ or h.

4.1 Single-Investor Case

It was shown in the previous section that the weight $P(C)$ of a trajectory C with initial and final points (x_i, x_f) in 'space'–time is proportional to $e^{\tilde{\beta}s(C)}$. However, if we want to compare trajectories with different initial and (or) final points, we have to transport them to the same endpoints. Keeping in mind the above discussion, this means that the weight $P(C)$ has to be defined in a more general form:

$$P(C) \sim e^{\tilde{\beta}s(\phi_f^{-1}(x_f)C\phi_i(x_i))} \equiv e^{\tilde{\beta}\log[\phi_f^{-1}(x_f)U_N U_{N-1},\ldots,U_1\phi_i(x_i)]}. \tag{11}$$

Here $\phi_i(x_i)$ and $\phi_f(x_f)$ are factors that represent a price of one unit of assets at the initial and final points x_i and x_f. In principle, it is irrelevant how we fix the prices, or, equivalently, what we use as a global numeraire. However, it is better to do this in such a way that the intrinsic symmetry of the problem,

$$\text{cash} \rightarrow \text{shares}, \quad \text{shares} \rightarrow \text{cash}, \quad S \rightarrow S^{-1}, \quad r_1 \rightarrow r_2, \quad r_2 \rightarrow r_1,$$

is kept. The easiest way is to fix the gauge so that at the original and the final times a unit of shares will cost a unit of cash. This means that, in this gauge, the unit of cash in the initial and final moments is equal to $\sqrt{S}$ (where S is the real price of the share in currency units, say dollars) and the unit of shares is equal to $1/\sqrt{S}$ times the real share. If we express $\log[\phi_f^{-1}(x_f)U_N U_{N-1},\ldots,U_1\phi_i(x_i)]$ in real units, $\phi(x_{(i,f)})$ is defined as

$$\phi(x_{(i,f)}) = S^{1/2}(T_{i,f}) \quad \text{for } x_{i,f} = (\text{cash}, T_{i,f}),$$

and

$$\phi(x_{(i,f)}) = S^{-1/2}(T_{i,f}) \quad \text{for } x_{i,f} = (\text{shares}, T_{i,f}).$$

The latter definitions of $\phi(x_{(i,f)})$ and additivity of the logarithm in (9) results in the non-normalized N-step transition probability for an investor

$$\Pi(t_N; t_0) = D^{-1}(t_N)P(t_N; t_{N-1})P(t_{N-1}; t_{N-2})\cdots P(t_1; t_0)D(t_0) \qquad (12)$$

where the matrices $P(t_i; t_{i-1})$ are defined as (tc is a relative transaction cost)

$$P(t_i; t_{i-1}) = \begin{pmatrix} e^{\tilde{\beta}r_1\Delta} & (1-tc)^{\tilde{\beta}}S_i^{\tilde{\beta}} \\ (1-tc)^{\tilde{\beta}}S_i^{-\tilde{\beta}} & e^{\tilde{\beta}r_2\Delta} \end{pmatrix},$$

and the matrix $D(t)$ has the form

$$D(t) = \begin{pmatrix} S^{\tilde{\beta}/2}(t) & 0 \\ 0 & S^{-\tilde{\beta}/2(t)} \end{pmatrix}.$$

The matrices act on vectors

$$\rho = \begin{pmatrix} p_1 \\ p_2 \end{pmatrix},$$

which give the probability to be in cash (p_1) or in shares (p_2). It is straightforward to check now that the one-step transition probability obeys the principal symmetry property:

$$P_{ik}(S, r_1, r_2) = P_{ki}(S^{-1}, r_2, r_1),$$

which returns us to the discussion after (11). This ensures the corresponding symmetry for the multistep transition probabilities.

The matrix $P(t_i; t_{i-1})$ can be represented as a product of three factors,

$$P(t_i; t_{i-1}) = T_i U(t_i; t_{i-1}) T_{i-1}^{-1},$$

where the matrix of the gauge transformation T_i is defined as

$$T_i = \begin{pmatrix} e^{\tilde{\beta}r_1 t_i} & 0 \\ 0 & e^{\tilde{\beta}r_2 t_i} \end{pmatrix}.$$

and the matrix $U(t_i; t_{i-1})$ has the form

$$U(t_i; t_{i-1}) = \begin{pmatrix} 1 & (1-tc)^{\tilde{\beta}}e^{-\tilde{\beta}(r_1-r_2)t_{i-1}}e^{-\tilde{\beta}r_1\Delta}S_i^{\tilde{\beta}} \\ (1-tc)^{\tilde{\beta}}e^{\tilde{\beta}(r_1-r_2)t_{i-1}}e^{-\tilde{\beta}r_2\Delta}S_i^{-\tilde{\beta}} & 1 \end{pmatrix}.$$

The matrix $U(t_i; t_{i-1})$ can be considered as a lattice version of the continuous-time evolution operator $\hat{U}(t_i; t_{i-1})$, which satisfies the Schrödinger-like equation

$$\frac{\partial}{\partial t}\hat{U} = H\hat{U}, \qquad (13)$$

with the initial condition

$$\hat{U}(t \to t', t') = \begin{pmatrix} 1 & 0 \\ 0 & 1 \end{pmatrix}$$

and Hamiltonian

$$H(t) = \begin{pmatrix} 0 & \gamma S^{\tilde\beta}(t)e^{-\tilde\beta r_1 \Delta}e^{-\tilde\beta \mu t} \\ \gamma S^{-\tilde\beta}(t)e^{-\tilde\beta r_2 \Delta}e^{\tilde\beta \mu t} & 0 \end{pmatrix}, \tag{14}$$

where $\gamma \equiv (1 - tc)^{\tilde\beta}/\Delta$ and $\mu = r_1 - r_2$. In this form, the generalization of the problem to the case of many investors is straightforward. We note that the time step Δ appears in the denominator. However, this should not worry the reader, since it does not appear in the final lattice action and re-emerges only in continuous-time calculations. There it stands for the smallest time scale in the theory, the time cut-off.

4.2   Risk Factors

Before going further, we want to make a short note concerning risk in the model. As we said above, the model deals with short-time investments and neglects the risk describing purely speculative behaviour. Since our aim is to model the short-time behaviour of the market, we believe that risk consideration does not play a role – traders anticipate future prices (using Technical Analysis, pattern recognition, or simply their nose), and they are reluctant to examine the risk of the decision. Moreover, if they believe that the price is heading in this or that direction, the decision is not risky for them at all, because they believe they know the future. Therefore the risk has not appeared in the calculations. However, if one wants to introduce risk into the model at this stage, it is possible to change the matrices $P(t_i; t_{i-1})$ to include the risk factor q:

$$P_q(t_i; t_{i-1}) = \begin{pmatrix} e^{\tilde\beta r_1 \Delta} & (1 - tc)^{\tilde\beta}S_i^{\tilde\beta} \\ (1 - tc)^{\tilde\beta}S_i^{-\tilde\beta} & q^{-\tilde\beta \Delta}e^{\tilde\beta r_2 \Delta} \end{pmatrix},$$

Here the factor $q > 1$ represents an investor's reluctance to take a risk by reducing the probability of being in the risky asset. The matrices $P_q(t_i; t_{i-1})$ will return us again to the Hamiltonian (14), with the only difference being that r_2 will be changed to $r_2 - \log q$, giving

$$\mu \to \bar\mu = \mu + \log q. \tag{15}$$

Thus the only signature of the risk is the change of the average return μ to $\bar\mu$. The relation (15) is a common risk adjustment, and the last term is the price for the risk that is required by traders. In what follows, we never use $\bar\mu$.

The appearance of the factor q in the expression for P_q can be viewed as a change in the action functional (9). Indeed, if one adds to the functional (9) the term describing a 'potential' with support at points of the base representing shares:

$$s_p(C) = \log(q^{\Delta}n), \quad n = \text{number of time steps spent in shares,}$$

the resulting action functional will generate the transition probability P_q. We use this observation in Chapter 8 to model money flows in Arbitrage Pricing Theory.

4.3 Many-Investors Case

Following our previous considerations, the amount of money that an investor posesses is irrelevant to describing his possible strategy, i.e. his trajectories in the 'space'–time. Indeed, since this amount is a not gauge-invariant quantity and can be changed arbitrarily to any other value, it cannot define anything in the theory according to our assumption of gauge invariance. An investor with one dollar will behave in the same manner as an investor with two dollars. However, if we want to deal with many *indistinguishable* investments, we need to gauge them to the same unit amount at some initial time moment. In this way, we no longer talk about investors, but rather about cash and share units available for the trading operations at the initial time moment.[11] Making this transition, we effectively assume that all investors have identical statistical behaviour, although a particular choice for each of them can be different at each step.

The easiest way to generalize the results of the previous subsection to the case of many 'investors' is to use the formalism of creation–annihilation operators (Section 1 of the Appendix on methods of quantum field theory). In simple terms, the creation operator $\psi_{i,k}^{+}$ acts on a state with n units of the ith asset at time k and produces a state with $n + 1$ units, thus effectively 'creating' an additional asset unit. Similarly, the annihilation operator $\psi_{i,k}$ acts on a state with n units of the ith asset at time k and produces a state with $n - 1$ units, thus effectively 'annihilating' one asset unit. The combination $\psi_{i,k+1}^{+}\psi_{i,k}$ 'kills' a unit at time k and 'creates' a unit at time $k + 1$, therefore describing the propagation of the unit in time. Other asset movements can also be presented in this way. This language is very convenient to describe systems with a large number of units, especially if the number is not constant.

There is a simple recipe to generalize the description of a single investor to many investors using creation–annihilation operators. One has to start with a single-investor Schrödinger equation (13),

$$\frac{\partial}{\partial t}\hat{U} = H\hat{U},$$

but this time with the initial condition

$$\hat{U}(t \rightarrow t') = \hat{I} \quad \text{(the identity operator)},$$

and with the Hamiltonian $\hat{H}$ written in terms of creation–annihilation operators of cash units $(\hat{\psi}_1^{+}, \hat{\psi}_1)$ and share units $(\hat{\psi}_2^{+}, \hat{\psi}_2)$:

$$H = \gamma f(t)\hat{\psi}_1^{+}\hat{\psi}_2 + \gamma f'(t)\hat{\psi}_2^{+}\hat{\psi}_1. \tag{16}$$

Here we also introduce the notation

$$f(t) \equiv S^{\tilde{\beta}}(t)e^{-\tilde{\beta}r_1\Delta}e^{-\tilde{\beta}\mu t},$$
$$f'(t) \equiv S^{-\tilde{\beta}}(t)e^{-\tilde{\beta}r_2\Delta}e^{\tilde{\beta}\mu t}.$$

In the case of a single investor, at each point of time, there are only two possible locations – cash or shares – which returns us to the 2-by-2 matrix problem and reproduces the Hamiltonian (14).

---

[11] This is why in what follows we often put the word 'investor' in inverted commas.

The next standard step in the derivation of a functional integral representation is to use the coherent states generated by the operators $\hat{\psi}^+_{1,2}$ and $\hat{\psi}_{1,2}$ (see Section 2.2 of the Appendix). We use the following set of coherent states:

$$|\psi\rangle = \sum_{n,m=0}^{\infty} \frac{1}{n!m!} (\psi_1\hat{\psi}^+_1)^n(\psi_2\hat{\psi}^+_2)^m|0\rangle, \qquad \langle\bar{\psi}| = \langle 0| \sum_{n,m=0}^{\infty} \frac{1}{n!m!} (\bar{\psi}_1\hat{\psi}^+_1)^n(\bar{\psi}_2\hat{\psi}^+_2)^m.$$

Here $|0\rangle$ is the state where there are no investors at all, and $\bar{\psi}$ and ψ are the usual complex numbers. The main properties of coherent states that we use to derive the functional integral are

$$\frac{1}{2\pi i} \int dz\, d\bar{z}|z\rangle\langle\bar{z}|e^{-\bar{z}z} = I, \qquad \langle\bar{z}|z\rangle = e^{\bar{z}z},$$

$$\langle\bar{z}|\hat{\psi}^+_k|z\rangle = \bar{z}_k\langle\bar{z}|z\rangle, \qquad \langle\bar{z}|\hat{\psi}_k|z\rangle = z_k\langle\bar{z}|z\rangle.$$

These properties are sufficient to generate an expression for the matrix element of the evolution operator $\hat{U}$ in the coherent state representation in terms of a lattice functional integral (as explained in Section 2.2 of the Appendix):

$$\langle\bar{\psi}_N|\hat{U}(t = t' + N\Delta', t')|\psi_0\rangle = e^{\bar{\psi}_{1,0}\psi_{1,0}+\bar{\psi}_{2,0}\psi_{2,0}} \int \prod_{k=1,2} \prod_{i=1}^{N-1} d\bar{\psi}_{i,k}\, d\psi_{k,i}$$

$$\times \exp\Bigg[\sum_{i=0}^{N-1} \Big(\bar{\psi}_{1,i+1}\psi_{1,i} - \bar{\psi}_{1,i}\psi_{1,i} + \bar{\psi}_{2,i+1}\psi_{2,i} - \bar{\psi}_{2,i}\psi_{2,i}$$

$$+ \frac{\Delta'(1-tc)^{\bar{\beta}}}{\Delta} e^{-\bar{\beta}(r_1-r_2)t_i} e^{-\bar{\beta}r_1\Delta} S_i^{\bar{\beta}} \bar{\psi}_{1,i+1}\psi_{2,i}$$

$$+ \frac{\Delta'(1-tc)^{\bar{\beta}}}{\Delta} e^{\bar{\beta}(r_1-r_2)t_i} e^{-\bar{\beta}r_2\Delta} S_i^{-\bar{\beta}} \bar{\psi}_{2,i+i}\psi_{1,i}\Big)\Bigg].$$

In the lattice version, the smallest time step Δ' is equal to the time Δ, and we rediscover, after the gauge transformation $\bar{\psi}_{k,i} \to e^{\bar{\beta}r_k t_i}\bar{\psi}^+_{k,i}$, $\psi_{k,i} \to e^{-\bar{\beta}r_k t_i}\psi_{k,i}$, the functional integral given in Ilinski (1997),

$$\langle\bar{\psi}_N|\hat{U}(t' + N\Delta, t')|\psi_0\rangle = e^{\bar{\psi}_{1,0}\psi_{1,0}+\bar{\psi}_{2,0}\psi_{2,0}} \int D\bar{\psi}_1\, D\psi_1\, D\bar{\psi}_2\, D\psi_2\, e^{\bar{\beta}s1},$$

with the action for cash flows

$$s1 = \frac{1}{\bar{\beta}} \sum_{i=0}^{N-1} [\bar{\psi}_{1,i+1}e^{\bar{\beta}r_1\Delta}\psi_{1,i} - \bar{\psi}_{1,i}\psi_{1,i} + \bar{\psi}_{2,i+1}e^{\bar{\beta}r_2\Delta}\psi_{2,i} - \bar{\psi}_{2,i}\psi_{2,i}$$

$$+ (1-tc)^{\bar{\beta}} S_i^{\bar{\beta}} \bar{\psi}_{1,i+1}\psi_{2,i} + (1-tc)^{\bar{\beta}} S_i^{-\bar{\beta}} \bar{\psi}_{2,i+i}\psi_{1,i}]. \qquad (17)$$

Using this expression for the matrix elements in the coherent state representation, it is easy to obtain the transition probability in the occupation number representation simply by integrating over $\bar{\psi}$ and ψ:[12]

$$P((n, m), (n_1, m_1), t, t') = S(t)^{-\frac{\bar{\beta}(n-m)}{2}} S(t')^{\bar{\beta}\frac{(n_1-m_1)}{2}}$$

$$\times \int d\psi \, d\bar{\psi} \, \langle \bar{\psi}_N | \hat{U}(t, t') | \psi_0 \rangle \bar{\psi}_{1,0}^{n_1} \bar{\psi}_{2,0}^{m_1} \psi_{1,N}^{n} \psi_{2,N}^{m} e^{-\bar{\psi}_N \psi_N - \bar{\psi}_0 \psi_0} n! m!$$

Here $\Pi((n, m), (n_1, m_1), t, t')$ is the un-normalized transition probability for the transition from the state at time t' with n_1 investors in cash and m_1 investors in shares to the state at time t with n investors in cash and m investors in shares. Thus it gives the generalization of the single-investor matrix $P(t_i, t_{i-1})$ in (12) to the case of many investors.

In the same way, the functional integral for the debt flows can be derived as (Ilinski, 1997)

$$\langle \chi_N | \hat{U}(t' + N\Delta, t') | \chi_0 \rangle = e^{\bar{\chi}_{1,0} \chi_{1,0} + \bar{\chi}_{2,0} \chi_{2,0}} \int D\bar{\chi}_1 \, D\chi_1 \, D\bar{\chi}_2 \, D\chi_2 \, e^{\bar{\beta} s 1'},$$

with the action for debt flows:

$$s1' = \frac{1}{\bar{\beta}} \sum_i [\bar{\chi}_{1,i+1} e^{-\bar{\beta} r_1 \Delta} \chi_{1,i} - \bar{\chi}_{1,i} \chi_{1,i} + \bar{\chi}_{2,i+1} e^{-\bar{\beta} r_2 \Delta} \chi_{2,i}$$

$$- \bar{\chi}_{2,i} \chi_{2,i} + (1 + tc)^{-\bar{\beta}} S_i^{-\beta} \chi_{1,i+1}^{+} \chi_{2,i} + (1 + tc)^{-\bar{\beta}} S_i^{\beta} \bar{\chi}_{2,i+1} \chi_{1,i}]. \tag{20}$$

Uing these formulae, one can calculate the un-normalized transition probability for debt flows using the analogue of (19). It is interesting to note that in the absence of the transaction costs, (20) may be transformed to (17) by reversing the signs of r_i and inverting the prices S. This corresponds to the transformation from negative to positive interaction constant.[13] The transaction costs make this symmetry only approximate:

$$(1 + tc)^{-\bar{\beta}} \simeq (1 - tc)^{\bar{\beta}} \quad \text{for } tc \ll 1.$$

In the absence of restructuring of debts (i.e. one kind of debts cannot be transformed to another kind), the last terms containing S drop out. Then the action takes the especially simple form:

$$s1_0' = \frac{1}{\bar{\beta}} \sum_i (\bar{\chi}_{1,i+1} e^{-\bar{\beta} r_1 \Delta} \chi_{1,i} - \bar{\chi}_{1,i} \chi_{1,i} + \bar{\chi}_{2,i+1} e^{-\bar{\beta} r_2 \Delta} \chi_{2,i} - \bar{\chi}_{2,i} \chi_{2,i}), \tag{21}$$

and does not affect the price dynamics. This is the case that we study later.

---

[12] The particular choice of the factors $n!$ and $m!$ in (19) is explained by the following relation:

$$P((n, m), (n_1, m_1), t, t') = \left\langle 0 \frac{1}{n! m!} (\hat{\psi}_1)^N (\hat{\psi}_2)^m \hat{U}(t, t') (\hat{\psi}_1^+)^{n_1} (\hat{\psi}_2^+)^{m_1} | 0 \right\rangle, \tag{18}$$

which is different from the usual quantum mechanics expression, since here we do not calculate an amplitude but rather the transition probability itself. The proof of this relation can be found in Section 2.3 of the Appendix
[13] The electric charge in electrodynamics.

4.4 Lattice Gauge Theory

Let us have another look at the functional (17):

$$s1 = \frac{1}{\tilde{\beta}} \sum_{i=-\infty}^{\infty} [\bar{\psi}_{1,i+1} e^{\tilde{\beta}r_1 \Delta} \psi_{1,i} - \bar{\psi}_{1,i} \psi_{1,i} + \bar{\psi}_{2,i+1} e^{\tilde{\beta}r_2 \Delta} \psi_{2,i} - \bar{\psi}_{2,i} \psi_{2,i}$$

$$+ (1 - tc)^{\tilde{\beta}} S_i^{\tilde{\beta}} \bar{\psi}_{1,i+1} \psi_{2,i} + (1 - tc)^{\tilde{\beta}} S_i^{-\tilde{\beta}} \bar{\psi}_{2,i+1} \psi_{1,i}],$$

and take the continuous-time limit. This transforms the functional to the form

$$s1 = \frac{1}{\tilde{\beta}} \int dt \left(\frac{\partial \bar{\psi}_1}{\partial t} \psi_1 + \tilde{\beta} r_1 \bar{\psi}_1 \psi_1 + \frac{\partial \bar{\psi}_2}{\partial t} \psi_2 + \tilde{\beta} r_2 \bar{\psi}_2 \psi_2 + \gamma S^{\tilde{\beta}}(t) \bar{\psi}_1 \psi_2 + \gamma S^{-\tilde{\beta}}(t) \bar{\psi}_2 \psi_1 \right),$$

with $\gamma = (1 - tc)^{\tilde{\beta}}/\Delta$. Now we make the following steps:

1. Change $\tilde{\beta}$ to $i\tilde{\beta}$, which corresponds to a transition from the dilatation group to the $U(1)$ group.

2. Change the 'space'–time ladder to a square lattice on a plane with lattice spacing a. The index $k = 1, 2$ now goes from $-\infty$ to ∞.

3. Denote $\tilde{\beta} r_k$ by $A_1(k, t)$ and $S^{i\tilde{\beta}}(t)$ by $e^{-iA_2(k,t)a}$.

This leads to the following expression for the new action:

$$s1 = \frac{1}{\tilde{\beta}} \int dt \sum_{k=-\infty}^{\infty} \left(\frac{\partial \bar{\psi}_k}{\partial t} \psi_k + iA_1(k, t) \bar{\psi}_k \psi_k + \gamma \bar{\psi}_k e^{-iA_2(k,t)a} \psi_{k+1} + \gamma \bar{\psi}_{k+1} e^{iA_2(k,t)a} \psi_k \right).$$

It is absolutely straightforward to check that in the continuous limit, this action converges to the functional

$$s_{\lim} = \frac{1}{a\tilde{\beta}} \int dt \int dx \left[\frac{\partial \bar{\psi}}{\partial t} \psi + iA_1(x, t) \bar{\psi} \psi - \gamma a^2 \left(\frac{\partial \bar{\psi}}{\partial x} + iA_2(x, t) \bar{\psi} \right) \left(\frac{\partial \psi}{\partial x} - iA_2(x, t) \psi \right) + \gamma \bar{\psi} \psi \right].$$

Using the definition of the covariant derivatives

$$D_t = \frac{\partial}{\partial t} - iA_1(x, t), \qquad D_x = \frac{\partial}{\partial x} - iA_2(x, t),$$

we finally arrive at the action for matter fields in non-relativistic quantum electrodynamics:

$$s_{\lim} = \frac{1}{a\tilde{\beta}} \int dt \int dx (D_t \bar{\psi} \psi - \gamma a^2 \bar{D}_x \bar{\psi} D_x \psi + \gamma \bar{\psi} \psi).$$

which the reader has already seen in Section 5 of Chapter 4: equation (26). Therefore we can conclude that the theory we have described in this section is an analogue of non-relativistic quantum electrodynamics with the dilatation gauge group instead of the $U(1)$ group and on the discrete 'space'–time ladder instead of physical space–time. The action (17) is a lattice action, and the whole theory is a lattice gauge theory. The parameter γa^2 plays the role of the inverse mass of the particles. One can see that large transaction costs $tc \sim 1$ correspond to heavy massive particles, which cannot move fast. The transaction costs therefore represent the inertia in the system that stops money reacting to small mispricing and stabilizes the system.

5   FARMER'S TERM

In this section, we want to return for a while to the gauge field dynamics. In Section 3.1 of Chapter 5, we derived the linear action for the gauge field, which for the 'ladder' base looks like

$$
\mathcal{A}_g(\{S_i\}) = \sum_{i=-\infty}^{\infty} \alpha_i (S_i^{-1} e^{r_2 \Delta} S_{i+1} e^{-r_1 \Delta} + S_i e^{r_1 \Delta} S_{i+1}^{-1} e^{-r_2 \Delta} - 2)
$$

$$
= \sum_{i=-\infty}^{\infty} \alpha_i [\exp(\log S_{i+1} - \log S_i - \mu \Delta)
$$

$$
+ \exp(-\log S_{i+1} + \log S_i + \mu \Delta) - 2].
$$

In the limit of small $-\log S_{i+1} + \log S_i + \mu \Delta$, the last expression is approximately equal to

$$
\mathcal{A}_g(\{S_i\}) = \sum_{i=-\infty}^{\infty} \alpha_i (-\log S_{i+1} + \log S_i + \mu \Delta)^2. \tag{22}
$$

In what follows, we use the latter action with the parameters $\{\alpha_i\}$ all equal to $\beta \equiv 1/\sigma^2 \Delta$.

As the reader will remember, in the derivation in Chapter 5 of the actions for the gauge field and therefore of (22), it was emphasized that an impact on the prices from speculative money flows has to be accounted for separately. In the presence of money flows, the action (22) has to contain an additional term responsible for the change of prices due to the market impact of 'buy' and 'sell' orders. We derive this term following the paper by Farmer (1998).

It is well known that large 'buy' orders tend to increase the price, while large 'sell' orders tend to decrease it. Since for any buyer there is a seller, it is not obvious that this actually makes sense: if the buyer drives the price up, the seller drives the price down! The answer is that the traders are not equally patient, which causes an asymmetric price impact. The market maker who simultaneously offer to buy at a bid price and to sell at a higher ask price is paid the premium in the form of the bid–ask spread for providing liquidity selling to the buyer, even if other sellers are more patient and do not want to sell immediately. The market maker does not have a directional view, and receives the bid–ask spread as a compensation for his service. Thus effectively the trades are transactions between buyers, sellers, and the market maker. Having unbalanced demand or supply, the market maker shifts the price up or down. This is what we mean by saying that 'buy' orders push the price up and 'sell' orders push the price down.

There are many complications in this apparently simple scheme. The discussion of some of them, such as different types of orders, the information impact of trades, competition between market makers, and the indirect marker impact, can be found in Farmer (1998). Here we derive the simplest model for the direct market impact on price that is caused by unbalanced market orders.

We denote the current market price by S, the size of the market order placed at this price[14] by N, and the market price at which the order is filled by $\tilde{S}$. To derive the model, we assume the following:

---

[14] With the convention that positive N corresponds to a 'buy' order and negative N to a 'sell' order

1. The price $\tilde{S}$ is always finite, and is an increasing function of the order size N:

$$\tilde{S} = \tilde{S}(S, N).$$

2. If there are no orders, there is no market impact:

$$\tilde{S}(S, 0) = S.$$

3. There is no arbitrage: it is impossible to make profits by repeatedly trading through a circuit.[15]

4. Gauge invariance: nothing depends on the currency units. Thus the only possible combination for prices to enter is $\tilde{S}/S$.

$$\tilde{S}/S = \phi(N).$$

These assumptions uniquely define the market impact function ϕ. Assumption 3 says that for a sequence of trades with sizes N and $-N$, the resulting change in the price should be zero:

$$\tilde{S}(\tilde{S}(S, N), -N) = S.$$

By Assumption 1, $\tilde{S}$ is an increasing function of N and, for fixed S, its inverse exists. Taking the inverse function of both sides of the last expression, we arrive at the equality

$$\tilde{S}(S, N) = \tilde{S}^{-1}(S, -N), \tag{23}$$

which says that buying and selling have inverse market impact. The next step is to consider a circuit of trades with sizes N_1, N_2, and $-N_1 - N_2$. Once again, by Assumption 3, this circuit should not generate any change in price:

$$\tilde{S}(\tilde{S}(\tilde{S}(S, N_1), N_2), -N_1 - N_2) = S.$$

Taking the inverse of both sides of this last equation and using (23), we derive the *additivity* condition:

$$\tilde{S}(\tilde{S}(S, N_1), N_2) = \tilde{S}(S, N_1 + N_2),$$

which is therefore equivalent to Assumption 3. Assumption 4 allows us to transform it to the form

$$\phi(N_1)\phi(N_2) = \phi(N_1 + N_2).$$

This functional equation has a general solution

$$\phi(N) = e^{N/\lambda},$$

where the parameter λ is a scale factor that normalizes the order size and can be called *liquidity*. This gives the following formula for the direct market impact:

$$\tilde{S} = Se^{N/\lambda}, \quad \text{or} \quad \log \tilde{S} - \log S = \frac{N}{\lambda}. \tag{24}$$

---

[15] The circuit is a sequence of trades that sum to zero.

This means that in the presence of money flows, (22) has to be changed to

$$A_g(\{S_i\}) = \sum_{i=-\infty}^{\infty} \beta \left(\log S_{i+1} - \log S_i - \mu\Delta - \frac{N_i}{\lambda} \right)^2, \tag{25}$$

where $\{N_i\}$ is a stream of (unbalanced) orders. We will call the last term Farmer's term. Figure 6.11 illustrates (24) for the example of VERTICALNET INC (VERT) as traded 15 June 1999 (see Fig. 6.12 for the corresponding intraday chart). One can see that the agreement is not perfect. In fact, as was pointed in Farmer (1998), small size trades tend to be noisier and to generate changes higher than predicted by (24), while large orders tend to generate smaller impacts. This may be explained by the policy of market makers to stabilize the market and to avoid big changes: big changes corresponding to large orders tend to be accumulated during some period from a series of small-order changes.

The market impact derived above in the situation of a quasi-equilibrium environment can be connected with the supply–demand mechanism of price formation. Assume that an increasing supply function $C(z)$ intersects a decreasing demand function $D(z)$ at some point $z_e = \log S_e$. If the supply and demand functions change by δC and δD, then, to first order, the change in the equilibrium price will be

$$\log \tilde{S}_e - \log S_e = \frac{\delta D - \delta C}{C'(z_e) - D'(z_e)}.$$

This last equation is transformed into (24) if one introduces the notation $N = \delta D - \delta C$ and $\lambda = C'(z_e) - D'(z_e)$: the market impact (24) is consistent with the classical arguments of demand and supply.

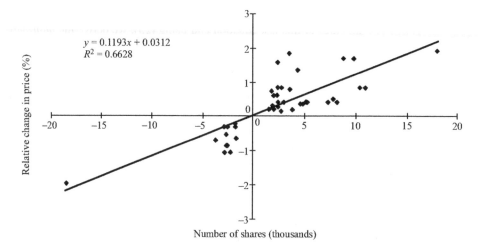

Figure 6.11   Illustration of market impact on the example of VERTICALNET INC (VERT). The chart is obtained by analyzing tick-by-tick data for first the 150 minutes of trading, 15 June 1999. Trades of less than 500 shares were not considered. Adverse price movements are omitted. The total number of records was 290. Small orders are accumulated in groups with a volume of 1500 or more. The relative change of price was calculated using the average of the bid and ask prices.

Symbol	Last trade	Net change	Day high	Day low	Trade time
VERT	58	$+1\frac{5}{16}$	$61\frac{1}{4}$	56	16:00 ET

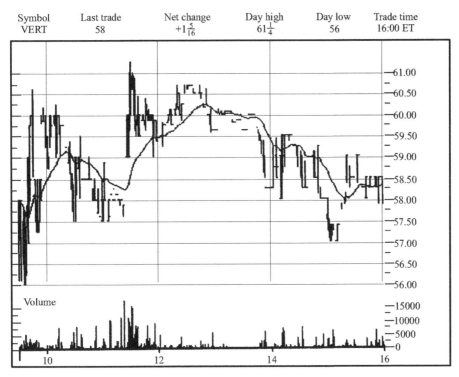

Figure 6.12   Intraday chart for VERT as traded 15 June 1999.

6   INTERACTION

Farmer's term represents an interaction between the gauge field and the money flows. Another source of interaction comes into the theory if one wants to include an effective interaction between traders to incorporate the 'herd' effect and pattern recognition.

Before doing this, it is convenient to change the gauge to express the action (and later the interaction) in terms of returns rather than in terms of the price itself. To this end, we make the following change of variables:

$$\psi_{1,i} \to \sqrt{S_i^{\tilde{\beta}/2}}\psi_{1,i}, \quad \psi_{2,i} \to \sqrt{S_i^{-\tilde{\beta}/2}}\psi_{2,i}, \quad \psi_{1,i}^+ \to \sqrt{S_i^{-\tilde{\beta}/2}}\psi_{1,i}^+, \quad \psi_{2,i}^+ \to \sqrt{S_i^{\tilde{\beta}/2}}\psi_{2,i}^+. \quad (26)$$

We also put r_1 and μ equal to zero to simplify the analysis. Then the single-investor probability matrix takes the form

$$P(t_i; t_{i-1}) = \begin{pmatrix} e^{-\Delta y_i \tilde{\beta}/2} & e^{-\Delta y_i \tilde{\beta}/2} \\ e^{\Delta y_i \tilde{\beta}/2} & e^{\Delta y_i \tilde{\beta}/2} \end{pmatrix}, \quad (27)$$

where $\Delta y_i \equiv \log(S_{i+1}/S_i)$ is the return on the time step Δ. In this form, it can be easily normalized; the normalization factor is $2\cosh(\tilde{\beta}\Delta y_i)$. After the transformation (26), one unit of shares costs one unit of cash, the symmetry between cash and shares is preserved, and the boundary terms $\phi_{i,f}$ are equal to one. This choice of gauge significantly simplifies further analytical investigation of the model.

In the presence of the interaction, the matrix (27) has to be changed to

$$P(t_i, t_{i-1}) = \frac{1}{2\cosh(\beta\Delta y_i)} \begin{pmatrix} e^{-\beta\Delta y_i - v_i} & e^{-\beta\Delta y_i - v_i} \\ e^{\beta\Delta y_i + v_i} & e^{\beta\Delta y_i + v_i} \end{pmatrix}, \tag{28}$$

where $v_i \equiv v(n_{k,i}, y_i; n_{k,i-1}, y_{i-1})$ are functions of the logarithm of asset price y and the distribution of speculators $(n_{k,i} \equiv n_k(t_i)$, the number of speculators in the kth asset).

The simplest possible choice that we consider here is an interaction mimicking the 'herd' effect. In this case, a trader is biased to buy if other traders buy, and to sell if other people sell. Suppose M is the total number of investors.[16] It is easy to give an expression that catches this behaviour:

$$v_i = -\frac{\xi_1}{M^2}[(n_{1,i} - n_{1,i-1}) - (n_{2,i} - n_{2,i-1})]. \tag{29}$$

For $\xi_1 > 0$, the potential is negative if more traders go in cash than in shares, thus increasing the probability to be in cash according to (28). One can also model the 'anti-herd' behaviour associated with 'smart' money by defining the potential with negative ξ_1.

The herd-following does not maximize the possible profit, especially if the time for the change of mood is larger than the time horizon. One can see this from Fig. 6.13, which shows trajectories of the logarithm of price and $n_1/M - 1/2$ obtained as solutions of the quasiclassical dynamical equations for small times derived in the next chapter. The reader can see that the trajectories demonstrate an oscillatory pattern, and traders can benefit from using this pattern. Indeed, following the herd would suggest buying in regions I and II (effectively close to the left boundary of region I, since the region is larger than the time step) and selling in regions III and IV (effectively close to the left boundary of region III). This strategy is far from optimal. Let us consider the potential[17]

$$v = \theta(1/2 - n_1/M + a)\left(-2\xi[\Delta(n_1/M - 1/2)]^k - \alpha_1\Delta(n_1/M - 1/2)\frac{\Delta y}{n_1/M - 1/2}\right). \tag{30}$$

Here k is some odd integer, ξ and α_1 are positive numerical constants, a is a parameter that defines the width of the top and bottom regions, and $\theta(x)$ is the Heaviside step function: $\theta(x > 0) = 1$ and zero otherwise. Using this potential, a trader can make his profit bigger by trading more often, as Fig. 6.14 demonstrates. In region I, $\Delta(n_1/M - 1/2)$ is large and negative and Δy is almost zero. This means that in this region, the only relevant term in (30) is the first one. This generates the bias to buy. In region II, the first term loses its strength while Δy is positive and grows, and $\Delta(n_1/M - 1/2)$ and $n_1/M - 1/2$ are both negative, which all together results in the generation of the bias to sell, making profit after buying at the bottom. In region III, the second term changes sign and causes the buy bias. In region IV, and in region I, the only relevant term is the first one, which is negative and causes the selling bias, making profit at the top. The θ function leads to a zero bias in regions V and VI. If traders are allowed to go short, the potential has to be changed to generate sell-short signals in these regions. In general, the interaction term allows the modelling of any effects that the reader finds to be important in any particular circumstances.

---

[16] Which is equal to the total number of cash and share units available at some original moment of time for speculation.
[17] In this formula, $\Delta(n_1/M - 1/2) = n_{1,i}/M - n_{1,i-1}/M$. Do not confuse it with the time step Δ.

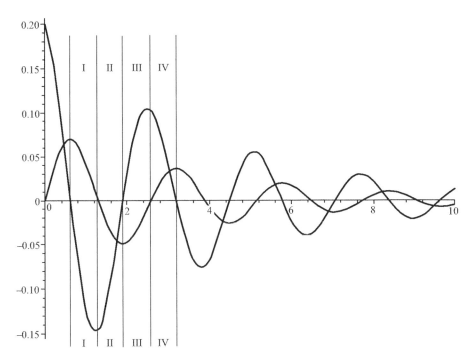

Figure 6.13 Trading on the 'herd' effect. Solution of the equations of motion for $n_1/M - 1/2$ (solid), the density of investors in cash measured from the equilibrium value, and $y = \tilde{\beta} \log S$ (dashed). Traders have a bias to buy in regions I and II, and to sell in regions III and IV. Time is measured in investment horizons Δ.

The θ function is difficult to deal with analytically. That is why, in our analytical calculations, we simplify the potential by dropping the θ function:

$$v = -2\xi[\Delta(n_1/M - 1/2)]^k - \alpha_1 \Delta(n_1/M - 1/2)\frac{\Delta y}{n_1/M - 1/2}. \tag{31}$$

The θ function makes the PDF asymmetric with respect to change of sign of y: $y \rightarrow y$.[18] That is why neglecting the θ function in the model with cash flows effectively only corresponds to an approximation of symmetric market reaction. We keep this approximation in what follows. Equation (31) will be used as the potential in Section 10 to derive an analytical expression for the PDF. However, there is no need for this simplification if one is interested in numerical simulations based on the model.

In what follows, we introduce many investment time horizons. This means that the model consists of many types of investors, and each type is characterized by the particular time horizon, which we have previously denoted by Δ. While the time horizons are different, the dynamics of the different types are identical (except for numerical constants that are scaled with time). In this construction, we follow the Fractal Market Hypothesis (Peters, 1994).

---

[18] We have seen in Section 2 that the symmetry of real PDFs is indeed only approximate. Furthermore, introducing debt flows with a potential that has a complementary θ function will almost restore the symmetry.

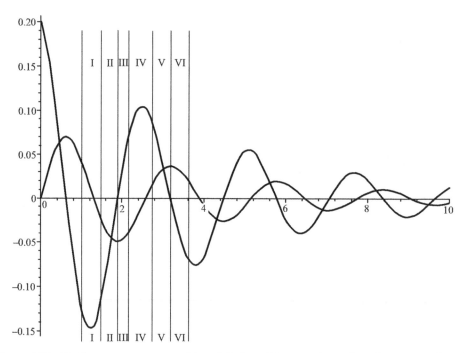

Figure 6.14 Trading on pattern recognition. Solution of the equations of motion for $n_1/M - 1/2$ (solid), the density of investors in cash measured from the equilibrium value, and $y = \tilde{\beta} \log S$ (dashed). Traders have a bias to buy in regions I and III, to sell in regions II and IV, and to stay away in regions V and VI. Time is measured in investment horizons Δ.

7 COMPARISON WITH OTHER MICROSCOPIC MODELS

One of the features of the gauge model formulated above is the homogeneity of the traders set. In earlier models, traders have often been divided into 'smart', who trade rationally, and 'noisy', who follow a fad (see e.g. De Long et al, 1990a,b, 1991; Bak et al, 1997; Arifovich, 1996; Youssefmir and Huberian, 1997; in LeBaron et al, 1999). One can argue that for the consideration of short-time trades, this differentiation is not appropriate. Indeed, all high-frequency market participants are professional traders with years of experience. Unsuccessful traders quickly leave the market and do not affect the dynamics. At the same time, each of the traders has their own view on the market and their own anticipations. That is why their particular decision can be only modelled in a probabilistic way. In this sense, the traders are not strictly rational but 'quasi-rational', and the corresponding market where the *quasi*rational investors deal can be called a *quasi*-effective market (Ilinski and Stepanento, 1998).

Levy et al (1994, 1995) proposed a microscopic model (the LLS model) for market dynamics using homogeneous investors with different look-back periods, which are analogous to the notion of the investment horizon that we use in this book. However, all traders with the same look-back period make the same decisions, and the decision is defined by the assumption that the future return is equal to one of the look-back period returns with equal probability. These two elements make the model less applicable to short-time dynamics modelling.

The herd effect has been incorporated into several models (see Bak et al, 1997; Cont and Bouchaud, 1997; Bouchaud and Cont, 1998). In Bak et al (1997), some of the market participants copied other (more skilled) ones. In Cont and Bouchaud (1997), the herd effect was introduced by allowing the traders to form stochastic clusters. Being intended for fund managers and financial analysts, the model may be applicable for interday time scales rather than for intraday trading.

The gauge model formulated above is a microscopic model. In this sense it is complementary to the phenomenological Langevin-type model suggested in Bouchaud and Cont (1998), where the market dynamics was governed by a system of coupled equations for a price and the number of 'buy–sell' orders in the presence of external noise. The equation that coupled the number of orders and the price is similar to Farmer's equation (24), but it deals with the price rather than the logarithm of the price, and therefore is not gauge-invariant. As we will show in the next chapter, the gauge model allows one to derive macroscopic (hydrodynamic-type) equations for price and money flows, but the equations have a different structure from those of Bouchaud and Cont (1998). In particular, the risk aversion term does not appear in the gauge consideration, since the goal is to describe the short-time dynamics, where the risk aversion is irrelevant.

The important feature of the gauge model is the presence of traders with many different horizons. It is known that there are conventional intraday time horizons, such as 1, 10, 30, 60, and 400 minutes, which, however, have a certain measure of idealization. In Section 10, we use a continuous set of time horizons between minimal, h_{min}, and maximal, h_{max}, time horizons to describe the spread and uncertainty in the definition of time horizons. This means that the model contains a set of money flows defined by the matrices (19), with the corresponding parameters h and $\tilde{\beta}$. The suggested model therefore includes the Fractal Market Hypothesis (FMH), which states that a stable market consists of traders with different time horizons but identical dynamics. This chapter introduces the 'microscopic' gauge model for the dynamics. It is also important to note that, for every horizon, the investors are acting in the background connection field created by a play in longer time horizons. Therefore the model of this chapter is a model with the information cascade studied recently by Müller et al (1997). They studied the absolute values of returns on different time scales, and found that the changes over longer intervals have a stronger influence on those over shorter time frames than vice versa. This has been interpreted as an information flow from long-time horizons to small-time ones. The cascade scenario is a central feature in the analogy between short-term speculative trading and hydrodynamical turbulence that was proposed by Ghashghaie and co-authors (Ghashghaie et al, 1996; Breymann et al, 2000) to explain the scaling properties of the FOREX rates and their correlations.

It would be fair to say that the scaling properties in the gauge model are consequences of the existence of the many horizons, in contrast to many models that are designed to explain scaling behaviour with a set of traders with only one characteristic trading time. These include phenomenological nonlinear models (see Levy and Solomon, 1996a,b; Levy et al, 1996a,b), the stochastic clustering model (Cont and Bouchaud, 1997), and multi-agent numerical simulations (see Bak et al, 1997; Caldarelli et al, 1997; Lux and Marchesi, 1999). For earlier multi-agent simulations,[19] see De Grauwe et al, 1993; Palmer et al, 1994).

---

[19] As far as I know Stigler (1964) contains the first price simulation. He studied the impact of security market regulation rules, and illustrated his point with the artificial market model.

Since the gauge model described above relies on the Fractal Market Hypothesis, we would like to examine the motivation underlying the FMH to make the consideration self-contained (for a detailed treatment of the FMH and the relevant empirical tests, see Peters, 1994). The FMH states that the *stable* market consists of traders with all possible time horizons $\{h_i\}$. When the price falls more than several σ_i (a characteristic price fluctuation in the time window h_i, for example the standard deviation of the price increments in time step h_i), then the traders with time horizon h_i tend to sell and the market stability requires somebody to buy, because otherwise the price would continue to fall and the market would become unstable. The assumption is that the traders who buy have large time horizons h_k, $k > i$, since for them the price fall is still in the limit of their σ_k, so they consider the situation a bargain and buy low. The existence of stability on all time scales leads to the existence of all time horizons, and instability can occur only when some long-time horizons shrink (owing to political uncertainty, market hysteria, or the like). It is not obvious (and, in general, wrong) that market participants with different time horizons can be modelled in the same way. Indeed, fund managers are directed by arguments different from intraday traders. However, for short times, all market participants have the same objective and methodology, and therefore can be modelled in the same framework but with different parameter values (which are scaled according to their investment horizons). The observed scaling properties of the statistical data seem to support the hypothesis (Peters, 1994). In short, according to the FMH, the scaling properties are due entirely to the hierarchy of time horizons, but the particular form of the distributions and correlators depends essentially on the model dynamics.

In this chapter, we have not applied a constraint on the total number of the traded shares. This differs drastically from other models, where the constraint (and the corresponding demand–supply price determination mechanism) plays a central role. In the present approach, as we discussed above, Farmer's term plays the role of the classical demand–supply mechanism. Moreover, since the total number of time horizons is huge and contains not only the short-time horizons considered but also long horizons that are outside the scope of the model, it seems that the influence of the constraint on the dynamics of each time-horizon group is almost negligible, and we have dropped it to simplify the analysis. This corresponds to the assumption that the number of traded lots is extremely large and a considerable part of the lots are in the hands of the market makers and longer-time investors, which is quite realistic.

To conclude this section, we mention the work by Kornilovitch (1998), who studied the possibility of modelling the S&P500 PDF using a weighted sum of PDFs of generalized Brownian motions with inertia, with different parameter values. In his picture, the market exists in various phases (calm with inertia and volatile Gaussian) with characteristic PDFs, and the observable PDF has to be taken as a sum of the PDFs weighted with the probabilities of the phases (92% and 8%). One can argue, however, that the situation where the inertia (or memory) exists in the active phase and price movements are directed by the active trade rather than randomly incoming news is more realistic. Moreover, it is possible to look at the model from the FMH point of view. It can be shown that the inertia term in the equations of Kornilovitch (1998) can be derived from the gauge model presented above in the approximation of small price and money flow fluctuations. The different phases then represent the trades of traders with different time horizons, and the weighted sum contains the probabilities of such trades occurring during the specified time period.[20]

---

[20] Roughly, during time h_i, the majority of trades are due to traders with horizons h_i or less, and a comparatively small number of trades are due to the occasional trades of traders with $h_k > h_i$.

8   STATISTICAL PROPERTIES OF THE MODEL

In this section, we describe quantitative results for the gauge model introduced in previous sections. As the reader will see, they are in qualitative agreement with the empirical results listed in Section 2, and the agreement can be made better and better by further refinements to the model.

We start with the PDF profile and the scaling relation observed for the probability of return to the origin $P(0, \Delta t)$ (see Section 2.2). In Section 10, we give the derivation of an expression for the PDF in the limit of an infinite number of traded units (both cash and shares), large Farmer's liquidity $\lambda = \alpha^{-1}$, and zero transaction costs. The transition matrix for a single investment horizon used in the calculation is given by (28),

$$P(t_i, t_{i-1}) = \frac{1}{2 \cosh(\tilde{\beta} \Delta y_i)} \begin{pmatrix} e^{-\tilde{\beta} \Delta y_i - v_i} & e^{-\tilde{\beta} \Delta y_i - v_i} \\ e^{\tilde{\beta} \Delta y_i + v_i} & e^{\tilde{\beta} \Delta y_i \mid v_i} \end{pmatrix},$$

with the potential v given by (31),

$$v = -2\xi[\Delta(n_1/M - 1/2)]^k - \alpha_1 \Delta(n_1/M - 1/2)\frac{\Delta y}{n_1/M - 1/2}.$$

Here y_i is the logarithm of the price, and $n_{1,i}$ and $n_{2,i}$ are the numbers of 'investors' in cash and shares at moment i. The transition probability for the returns is taken to be a Gaussian PDF with Farmer's term:

$$P_0(\Delta t, 0) = \frac{1}{\sqrt{2\pi \Delta t}} \exp\left(-\frac{[\Delta y_i + \frac{\alpha}{M}(\Delta n_{1,i} - \Delta n_{2,i})]^2}{2\sigma^2 \Delta t}\right).$$

We then use the Fractal Market Hypothesis and introduce a continuous set of investment horizons spanning the range from h_{min} to h_{max} with the parameters scaled as

$$\alpha_1(h) \sim h^{-1-\gamma}, \quad \xi(h) \sim h^{-1}, \quad \tilde{\beta}(h) \sim h^{-\gamma}.$$

with γ being some specified exponent (for S&P500, $\gamma \approx 0.71$).

Then the PDF for this model can be written as (see Section 10 for details):

$$P(y, T; 0, 0) = \frac{1}{\sigma\sqrt{2\pi T}} \exp\left[-\frac{\left(y - \alpha \int_{h_{min}}^{h_{max}} dh\, \theta(T - h)z(y)\right)^2}{2\sigma^2 T} \right.$$

$$\left. + \int_{h_{min}}^{h_{max}} dh\, [\theta(T - h)\xi(h)z^2(y) - \alpha_1(h)yz(y)]\right], \qquad (32)$$

with the function $z(y)$ given by

$$z(y) \equiv \tanh\left(\frac{h}{T}\tilde{\beta}(h)y\right).$$

A typical profile of the PDF is shown in Fig. 6.22 in Section 10.

There are several things to note about the PDF (32):

1. It converges to a Gaussian PDF for large times. Indeed, the only signature of the money flows in (32) is the presence of the function $z(y)$, which tends to zero for large times T. The characteristic crossover time is defined by the parameter $\tilde{\beta}$, which is a measure of the bounded rationality of players.

2. The PDF is approximately invariant under the scaling

$$T \to \lambda T, \qquad h \to \lambda h, \qquad y \to \lambda^{\gamma} y,$$

which is a property that real PDFs possess, as Figs. 6.4 and 6.5 demonstrate. The scaling is broken by the Gaussian term y^2 and by the integration limits $h_{\max}$ and $h_{\min}$. This causes a breakdown of the scaling when the times become comparable to the maximal investment horizon and when the Gaussian term starts to be important, i.e. at the region of crossover from 'Levy' to Gaussian behaviour.

3. The corrections to the Gaussian disappear in the limit of purely 'noise' traders, who do not consider their potential profit as a motivation for transactions, i.e. in the limit $\tilde{\beta} \to 0$.

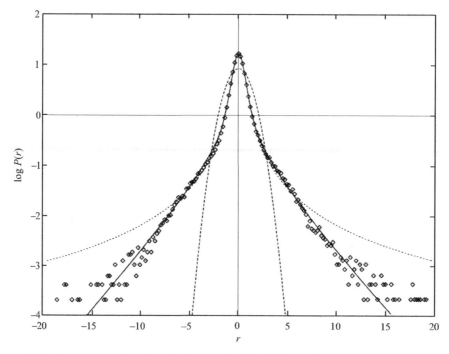

Figure 6.15 Comparison of the $\Delta = 1$ min theoretical (solid line) and observed (squares) probability distribution of the return $P(r)$ (Mantegna et al, 1995). The long-dashed line shows the Gaussian distribution with the standard deviation σ equal to the experimental value 0.0508. Values of the return are normalized to σ. The short-dashed line is the best-fit symmetrical Levy stable distribution (Mantegna et al, 1995). From K. Ilinski and A. Stepamento, *Advances in Complex Systems* **1**, 143–148 (1998). Reproduced by permission of Hermes Science Publications.

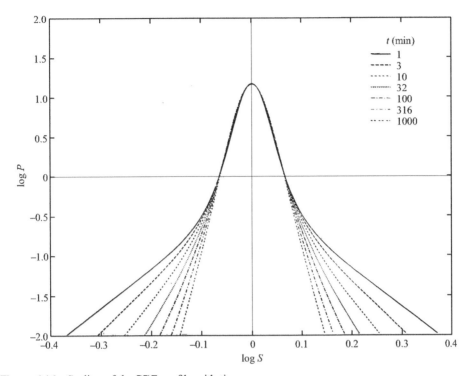

Figure 6.16   Scaling of the PDF profile with time.

4. In fact, the correction is governed by a number of traders (read as money available for trading). The corrections disappear when no money is available.

Figures 6.15, 6.16, and 6.17 (Ilinski and Stenamento, 1998) depict the PDF profile for a single (1 min) horizon, the scaling of the PDFs with time, and the scaling of $P(0)$ for a similar model with the interactions (29) and (31) but with (truncated) Gaussian averaging over the initial distribution of the capital across cash and shares and different values of the parameters.[21] Figure 6.18 also shows the time evolution of the kurtosis calculated from the PDF in comparison with empirical observations. It is possible to argue that the fit of the kurtosis as derived from the gauge model is as good as the power-law fit of Cont (1997). To summarize, one can see that there is almost perfect coincidence of the PDF-related quantities calculated from the gauge model and the empirical one.

The next step is to describe the dynamical characteristics of the gauge model, i.e. the correlation coefficients and moments as functions of time. It is very difficult to calculate these quantities analytically, and some kind of numerical study has to be done. The following results were obtained using Monte Carlo simulations[22] for the model with the 'pure herd' interaction and six investment horizons: 1, 3, 9, 27, 81 and 243 minutes. Figures 6.19 and 6.20 show the correlation coefficient of returns and the correlation coefficient of absolute

---

[21] The parameter values were chosen to fit the PDF profile to real data for the S&P500 empirical PDF (Fig. 6.4).
[22] I am grateful to Alexandra Ilinskaia for these numerical simulations.

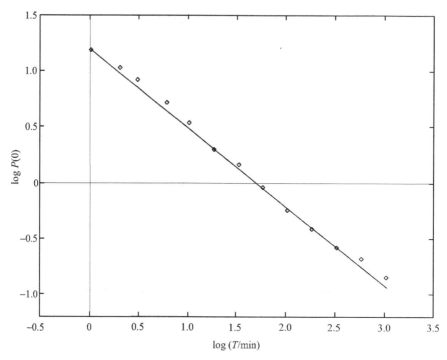

Figure 6.17 Theoretical (solid line) and experimental (squares) probability of return to the origin (to get zero return) $P(0)$ as a function of time. The slope of the best-fit straight line is -0.712 ± 0.025 (Mantegna et al, 1995). The theoretical curve converges to the Brownian value 0.5 as time tends to one month. From K. Ilinski and A. Stepamento, *Advances in Complex Systems* **1**, 143–148 (1998). Reproduced by permission of Hermes Science Publications.

values of the returns. On comparing these with Figs. 6.6 and 6.7, one can see that there is qualitative agreement with the empirical results. The time dependence of the variance for the returns is shown in Fig. 6.21. The figure shows that there are two scaling regions – one for small times and one for large times, with corresponding exponents 1.5 and 1.04, which are close to those observed.

Our final note concerns the multifractal behaviour apparently demonstrated by market prices. The PDF obtained from the model can be considered as a form of truncated Levy flight PDF. Thus we can apply the result obtained by Nakao (2000), who showed that multiscaling properties are a consequence of the smooth truncation of the single-parameter scaling of the Levy flights. Therefore the multifractal exponents are not universal, owing to their dependence on the chosen truncation scheme, and are not of great practical interest. Another source of apparent multiscaling was identified by Bouchaud et al (2000), who argued that the apparent multiscaling is rather a feature of a long transition, which can also be the case for multifractal behaviour, of the moments in real markets.

We have shown that that the deviation of the distribution function from a log-normal distribution may be explained by active trading behaviour of speculators. Let us now make some final remarks:

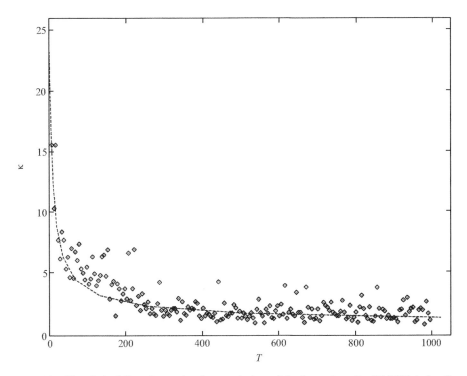

Figure 6.18 The dashed line shows the time evolution of the kurtosis κ for S&P500 index futures (October 1991–September 1995) calculated from the PDF in comparison with empirical observations (Cont, 1997: points, with kind permission of the author).

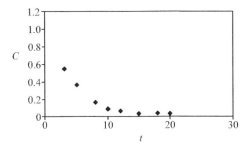

Figure 6.19 The correlation coefficient of the returns.

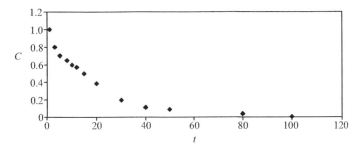

Figure 6.20 The correlation coefficient of the absolute values of the returns.

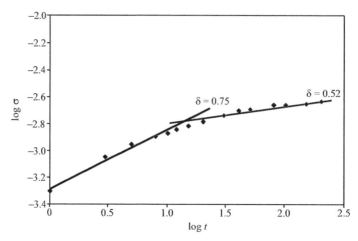

Figure 6.21   Variance of the returns as a function of time.

1. Above, we considered a very simple model of a stock exchange where only one kind of securities is traded. The analysis can be generalized to a more realistic situation with a set of traded securities. Following this line, it is possible to construct a dynamical portfolio theory that in the equilibrium limit will coincide with standard portfolio theory (see Chapter 8). In the dynamical theory, time-dependent correlation functions will play the role of response functions of the market to an external perturbation such as new information or a change in the macroeconomic environment. Taking the corrections into account will lead to a time-dependent modification of Arbitrage Pricing Theory (see Chapter 8).

2. Since the non-Markovian and non-quasi-Brownian character of real price walks do not allow the Black–Scholes no-arbitrage analysis to be applied, the virtual arbitrage opportunities and corresponding money flows have to be considered. The money flows, being responsible both for the deviation of the probability distribution function of the underlying asset prices from quasi-Brownian walks and, at the same time, for restoring virtually violated no-arbitrage constraints, must cause corrections to the Brownian walks based arbitrage-free equation for prices of derivatives. These corrections then account for both the non-quasi-Brownian walks of the prices and the violation of the no-arbitrage constraint. We discuss the corrections in Chapter 9 in a gauge model derivative pricing.

3. It turns out to be very difficult even for a simple model to get analytical results that display the behaviour that is found numerically. The situation becomes even worse for the portfolio generalizations or for the derivative pricing problem. On the other hand, there are well-studied numerical methods to simulate lattice gauge theory, which constitutes the essence of all these models. We have to admit that it is better to have correct numerical results than wrong (due to inevitable simplifications) analytical ones.

9   SUMMARY

- The real market has clearly non-Gaussian behaviour – at least for small enough times. It is characterized by a non-Gaussian PDF profile and (apparent) multifractal correlation coefficients.

- No single standard model can completely describe this behaviour.

- It is possible to construct a stochastic description of money flows based on the gauge-invariance assumptions and some other first principles.

- The simplest gauge models can produce statistical characteristics of return that strongly resemble the real market characteristics, thus working better than the standard models. At the same time, these are microscopic models – in contrast to the mainly phenomenological common models.

10 PROBABILITY DISTRIBUTION FUNCTION – ANALYTICS

In this final section, we derive an explicit analytical expression[23] for the PDF of the return in the model in the limit of an infinite number of 'investors' $M \to \infty$ and large Farmer's liquidity α^{-1}.

As was said before, we assume that speculators adjust their positions every time step $\{h_i\}$. The transition matrix for the speculator in the time interval $h = t_i - t_{i-1}, i = 1, \ldots, N$ (with N the number of steps), is given by the matrix (see (28))

$$P(t_i, t_{i-1}) = \begin{pmatrix} P_{11} & P_{12} \\ P_{21} & P_{22} \end{pmatrix} = \frac{1}{2\cosh(\tilde{\beta}\Delta y_i)} \begin{pmatrix} e^{-\tilde{\beta}\Delta y_i - v_i} & e^{-\tilde{\beta}\Delta y_i - v_i} \\ e^{\tilde{\beta}\Delta y_i + v_i} & e^{\tilde{\beta}\Delta y_i + v_i} \end{pmatrix}, \tag{33}$$

where v_i is some potential and

$$\Delta y_i \equiv y_i - y_{i-1}, \qquad y_i \equiv \log(S_i e^{-\mu t_i}).$$

In Section 5, we discussed possible interaction potentials. Here we use the potential (31):

$$v = -2\xi[\Delta(n_1/M - 1/2)]^k - \alpha_1\Delta(n_1/M - 1/2)\frac{\Delta y}{n_1/M - 1/2},$$

with $k = 1$. Using the conservation law $n_{1,i} + n_{2,i} = M$ and the notation

$$x_i = \frac{2n_{1,i} - M}{M}, \qquad \Delta x_i \equiv x_i - x_{i-1} \qquad \forall i,$$

the potential can be rewritten as

$$v_i = -\xi\Delta x_i - \alpha_1\Delta x_i\frac{\Delta y}{x_i}.$$

We start by noting that in the absence of speculators, the (bare) probability distribution function for return is given by the Gaussian distribution

$$P_0(t_i, t_{i-1}) = \frac{1}{\sigma\sqrt{2\pi h}}\exp\left(-\frac{(\Delta y_i)^2}{2\sigma^2 h}\right), \tag{34}$$

with the volatility of the asset σ. It will be shown below that there exists a crossover to the Gaussian PDF for large times in the presence of money flows. Therefore σ is the volatility of the return on large time scales when the effects caused by the speculators' presence disappear.

---

[23] The method was suggested by Alexander Stepanenko. It turns out to be sufficiently robust to include various types of interaction.

This means that the bare volatility σ has to be chosen to be equal to the scaled volatility for the observed PDF at the times when the PDF has converged to the Gaussian.

In the presense of the speculators, one needs to consider the joint transition probability of price and speculators' decisions. Our goal then is to extract the PDF for the price from the joint probability. To this end, we start with the case of only one investment horizon, and observe that many investment horizons do not complicate the calculation, which allows a straightforward generalization of the results to the case of many horizons.

We start with a single investment horizon h, and write the joint probability (un-normalized in general) as

$$\tilde{W}(t_i, t_{i-1}) = \frac{1}{\sigma\sqrt{2\pi h}} \exp\left(-\frac{[\Delta y_i + \frac{\alpha}{M}(\Delta n_{1,i} - \Delta n_{2,i})]^2}{2\sigma^2 h}\right)$$

$$\times \sum_{j=0}^{n_{1,i-1}} \sum_{k=0}^{M-n_{1,i-1}} C_{n_{1,i-1}}^j C_{M-n_{1,i-1}}^k P_{21}^j P_{11}^{n_{1,i-1}-j} P_{12}^k P_{22}^{M-n_{1,i-1}-k} \delta_{n_{1,i-1}-j+k, n_i}, \quad (35)$$

where the conservation law $n_{1,i} + n_{2,i} = M$ has been used again. Substituting (33) into (35), we get the compact expression

$$\tilde{W}(t_i, t_{i-1}) = \frac{1}{\sigma\sqrt{2\pi h}} \exp\left(-\frac{(\Delta y_i + \alpha\Delta x_i)^2}{2\sigma^2 h} + (M - 2n_{1,i})(\tilde{\beta}\Delta y_i + v_i)\right) \frac{C_M^{n_i}}{2^M \cosh^M(\tilde{\beta}\Delta y_i)}.$$
$$(36)$$

Since the number of traders M is assumed to be very large ($M \to \infty$), one can use Stirling's formula

$$m! \simeq e^{-m} m^m \sqrt{2\pi m}$$

to derive the asymptotic formulae for the binomial coefficients, keeping n/M finite:

$$C_M^{n_i} \approx \frac{2^M}{\pi}\sqrt{\frac{2\pi}{M(1-x_i^2)}} \exp\left(-\frac{M}{2}(1+x_i)\log(1+x_i) - \frac{M}{2}(1-x_i)\log(1-x_i)\right). \quad (37)$$

This results in the following expression for the transition probability:

$$\tilde{W}(t_i, t_{i-1}) \approx \frac{1}{\sigma\pi} \frac{1}{\sqrt{M(1-x_i^2)h}} \exp\left[-\frac{(\Delta y_i + \alpha\Delta x_i)^2}{2\sigma^2 h} + \xi x_i \Delta x_i + \alpha_1 \Delta y_i \Delta x_i\right.$$
$$\left. -M\left(\tilde{\beta}\Delta y_i x_i + \log\cosh(\tilde{\beta}\Delta y_i) + \frac{1}{2}(1+x_i)\log(1+x_i) + \frac{1}{2}(1-x_i)\log(1-x_i)\right)\right].$$
$$(38)$$

The normalized joint transition probability is expressed as

$$W(t_i, t_{i-1}) = \tilde{W}(t_i, t_{i-1})\left(\int_{-\infty}^{\infty} dy_i \sum_{n_i=0}^{M} \tilde{W}(t_i, t_{i-1})\right)^{-1}$$

$$\approx \tilde{W}(t_i, t_{i-1})\left(\int_{-\infty}^{\infty} dy \frac{M}{2}\int_{-1}^{1} dx_i \tilde{W}(t_i, t_{i-1})\right)^{-1}. \quad (39)$$

We now have to calculate the normalization factor in the denominator. As $M \to \infty$, the integral over x_i in (39) can be calculated using the saddle-point method. The saddle point is

$$x_i^* = -\tanh(\tilde{\beta}\Delta y_i) \equiv -z_i, \tag{40}$$

and hence

$$\frac{M}{2}\int_{-1}^{1} dx_i\, \tilde{W}(t_i, t_{i-1})$$

$$= \frac{1}{\sigma\sqrt{2\pi h}}\exp\left(-\frac{[\Delta y_i - \alpha(z_i + x_{i-1})]^2}{2\sigma^2 h} + \xi z_i(z_i + x_{i-1}) - \alpha_1 \Delta y_i(z_i + x_{i-1})\right). \tag{41}$$

As the volatility σ is small ($\sigma \sim 10^{-4}$ for S&P500, where time is measured in minutes) the integral over y_i can also be calculated using the saddle-point method. If α can be considered a small parameter and the corresponding term neglected, the saddle point y_i^* has a very simple form:

$$y_i^* = y_{i-1}, \qquad z_i \approx \tilde{\beta}\Delta y_i = 0, \tag{42}$$

and (with the same accuracy) the normalization factor is approximately equal to one:

$$\int_{-\infty}^{\infty} dy_i\, \frac{M}{2}\int_{-1}^{1} dx_i\, \tilde{W}(t_i, t_{i-1}) \approx 1. \tag{43}$$

Hence the normalized transition probability is equal to (38):

$$W(t_i, t_{i-1}) = \tilde{W}(t_i, t_{i-1}) \tag{44}$$

The PDF for prices is given by the transition probability summed over the final distribution of speculators:

$$\tilde{P}(t_i, t_{i-1}) = \frac{M}{2}\int_{-1}^{1} dx_i\, W(t_i, t_{i-1}). \tag{45}$$

Because of (38) and (44), we have the following equality:

$$\tilde{P}(t_i, t_{i-1}) = \frac{1}{\sigma\sqrt{2\pi h}}\exp\left(-\frac{[\Delta y_i - \alpha(z_i + x_{i-1})]^2}{2\sigma^2 h} + \xi z_i(z_i + x_{i-1}) - \alpha_1 \Delta y_i(z_i + x_{i-1})\right). \tag{46}$$

In a similar way, the corresponding many-step analogue of (45) is defined as follows:

$$\tilde{P}(t_N, t_{N-k-1}) = \int_{-\infty}^{\infty} dy_{N-k}\, \frac{M}{2}\int_{-1}^{1} dx_{N-k}\tilde{P}(t_N, t_{N-k})W(t_{N-k}, t_{N-k-1}) \tag{47}$$

Let us use this last equation to find the expression for $\tilde{P}(t_N, t_{N-k})$ by mathematical induction. The induction hypothesis is prompted by (46):

$$\tilde{P}(t_N, t_{N-k}) = \frac{1}{\sigma\sqrt{2\pi k h}}\exp\left(-\frac{[y_N - y_{N-k} - \alpha(z_N^{(k)} + x_{N-k})]^2}{2\sigma^2 k h}\right.$$

$$\left. + \xi z_N^{(k)}(z_N^{(k)} + x_{N-k}) - \alpha_1(y_N - y_{N-k})(z_N^{(k)} + x_{N-k})\right), \tag{48}$$

where

$$z_N^{(k)} \equiv \tanh\left(\frac{\tilde{\beta}(y_N - y_{N-k})}{k}\right). \tag{49}$$

The basis of the induction is (46) itself.

We test the hypothesis (to simplify notation, we put $k = N - 1$ in (47)):

$$\tilde{P}(t_N, t_0) = \int_{-\infty}^{\infty} dy_1 \frac{M}{2} \int_{-1}^{1} dx_1 \frac{1}{\sigma^2 \pi h \sqrt{2\pi M(N-1)(1-x_1^2)}}$$

$$\times \exp\Bigg[-\frac{[y_N - y_1 - \alpha(z_N^{(N-1)} + x_1)]^2}{2\sigma^2(N-1)h} - \frac{[y_1 - y_0 + \alpha(x_1 - x_0)]^2}{2\sigma^2 h}$$

$$+ \xi z_N^{(N-1)}(z_N^{(N-1)} + x_1) - \alpha_1(y_N - y_1)(z_N^{(k)} + x_{N-k}) + \xi x_1(x_1 - x_0)$$

$$- \alpha_1(y_1 - y_0)(x_1 - x_0) - M\bigg(\beta \Delta y_1 x_1 + \log \cosh(\tilde{\beta}\Delta y_1)$$

$$+ \frac{1}{2}(1 + x_1)\log(1 + x_1) + \frac{1}{2}(1 - x_1)\log(1 - x_1)\bigg)\Bigg], \tag{50}$$

and, calculating the integral over x_1 in the same manner as in (40), we get

$$x_1^* = -z_1. \tag{51}$$

This leads us to the equation for $\tilde{P}(t_N, t_0)$:

$$\tilde{P}(t_N, t_0) = \int_{-\infty}^{\infty} dy_1 \frac{1}{\sigma^2 2\pi h \sqrt{(N-1)}} \exp\Bigg(-\frac{[y_N - y_1 - \alpha(z_N^{(N-1)} - z_1)]^2}{2\sigma^2(N-1)h}$$

$$- \frac{[y_1 - y_0 - \alpha(z_1 + x_0)]^2}{2\sigma^2 h} + \xi z_N^{(N-1)}(z_N^{(N-1)} - z_1) - \alpha_1(y_N - y_1)(z_N^{(N-1)} - z_1)$$

$$+ \xi z_1(z_1 + x_0) - \alpha_1(y_1 - y_0)(z_1 + x_0)\Bigg). \tag{52}$$

Evaluating the integral over y_1 again using the saddle-point method ($1/\sigma^2 \gg 1$), we get the solution of the saddle-point equation:

$$y_1^* = \frac{y_N + (N-1)y_0}{N}. \tag{53}$$

This results in a simple expression for the variable z_1,

$$z_1 = z_N^{(N-1)} = \tanh\left(\frac{\tilde{\beta}(y_N - y_0)}{N}\right) = z_N^{(N)}, \tag{54}$$

and therefore in the final expression for $\tilde{P}(t_N, t_0)$:

$$\tilde{P}(t_N, t_0) = \frac{1}{\sigma\sqrt{2\pi Nh}} \exp\left(-\frac{[y_N - y_0 - \alpha(z_N^{(N)} + x_0)]^2}{2\sigma^2 Nh}\right.$$

$$\left. + \xi z_N^{(N)}(z_N^{(N)} + x_0) - \alpha_1(y_N - y_0)(z_N^{(N)} + x_0)\right). \tag{55}$$

So we have completed the induction and proved the form of the transition probability summed over speculators' degrees of freedom. Now one can either average over the initial distribution of investors or take $x_0 = 0$, which corresponds to equidistribution at the initial time. For the sake of simplicity, we choose the second option here, but in the situation of a real market, one has rather to go for the first. In this way, the initial market conditions such as a rising or falling market can be taken into account. Thus, in our case, the final answer for the single-horizon PDF is

$$\tilde{P}(t_N, t_0) = \frac{1}{\sigma\sqrt{2\pi Nh}} \exp\left(-\frac{[y_N - y_0 - \alpha(z_N^{(N)})]^2}{2\sigma^2 Nh} + \xi(z_N^{(N)})^2 - \alpha_1(y_N - y_0)z_N^{(N)}\right). \tag{56}$$

This last expression can be rewritten in the more tractable form

$$P(y, T; 0, 0) = \frac{1}{\sigma\sqrt{2\pi T}} \exp\left(-\frac{[y - \alpha z(y)]^2}{2\sigma^2 T} + \xi z^2(y) - \alpha_1 yz(y)\right), \tag{57}$$

introducing the function

$$z(y) \equiv \tanh\left(\frac{h}{T}\tilde{\beta}y\right). \tag{58}$$

This completes the calculation in the case of a single investment horizon. Figure 6.22 shows the PDF profile for $\sigma^2 T = 1$, with the parameters

$$\alpha = 2.5, \quad \alpha_1 = 5, \quad \xi = 2.12, \quad h\tilde{\beta}/T = 15.$$

The reader can see that the profile is similar to Fig. 6.15, and indeed resembles the real-market PDF depicted in Fig. 6.4. For large times $T \to \infty$, the function $z(y)$ converges to zero and we recover the Gaussian PDF for returns.

To modify the calculation and introduce many investment horizons, we observe that in calculating integrals over y_i, the only terms that contributed to the saddle-point equations came from the Gaussian distribution (34). So, in the presence of speculators with several (J) investment horizons, we can repeat all the steps to get the similar result:[24]

$$P(y, T; 0, 0) = \frac{1}{\sigma\sqrt{2\pi T}} \exp\left(-\frac{\left(y - \sum_{j=1}^{J}\theta_j\alpha z_j(y)\right)^2}{2\sigma^2 T} + \sum_{j=1}^{J}\theta_j\xi_j z_j^2(y) - \sum_{j=1}^{J}\theta_j\alpha_{1,j}z_j(y)y\right),$$

$$\tag{59}$$

---

[24] Here we neglect a possible interaction between different horizons.

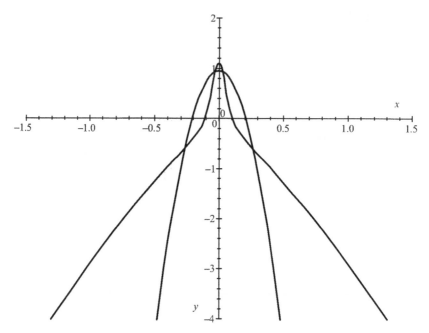

Figure 6.22 Typical profile for the PDF (57). The parameters are $\sigma^2 T = 1$, $\alpha = 2.5$, $\alpha_1 = 5$, $\xi = 2.12$, and $h\tilde{\beta}/T = 15$. The solid line is the normalized PDF (57), and the dashed line is the Gaussian distribution with the same standard deviation 0.15.

where the parameters ξ_j and $\tilde{\beta}_j$ correspond to speculators with jth investment horizon, and the functions $z_j(y)$ and θ_j are defined as

$$z_j(y) \equiv \tanh\left(\frac{h_j}{T}\tilde{\beta}_j y\right), \qquad \theta_j \equiv \theta(T - h_j). \qquad (60)$$

In the last equation, $\theta(x)$ is the Heaviside step function. Equation (59) is a basis for a multihorizon treatment.

In the case where the horizons are distributed continuously, (59) transforms to

$$P(y, T; 0, 0) = \frac{1}{\sigma\sqrt{2\pi T}}\exp\left(-\frac{\left(y - \alpha\int_{h_{\min}}^{h_{\max}} dh\,\theta(T - h)z(y)\right)^2}{2\sigma^2 T}\right.$$

$$\left. + \int_{h_{\min}}^{h_{\max}} dh[\theta(T - h)\xi(h)z^2(y) - \alpha_1(h)yz(y)]\right), \qquad (61)$$

with the function $z(y)$ being given by

$$z(y) \equiv \tanh\left(\frac{h}{T}\tilde{\beta}(h)y\right).$$

We can now use the Fractal Market Hypothesis and define the parameters for each investment horizon so that the overall PDF will exhibit approximate scaling invariance. For this, we impose on (61) the following scaling for the parameters in the model:

$$\alpha_1(h) \sim h^{-1-\gamma}, \quad \xi(h) \sim h^{-1}, \quad \tilde{\beta}(h) \sim h^{-\gamma}. \tag{62}$$

where γ is some specified exponent (for S&P500, $\gamma \approx 0.71$). Then the PDF (59) is approximately invariant under the scaling

$$T \to \lambda T, \qquad h \to \lambda h, \qquad y \to \lambda^\gamma y,$$

which is the property that real PDFs possess, as Figs. 6.4 and 6.5 demonstrate. The scaling will be broken by the Gaussian term and by the integration limits in (61). This causes a breakdown of scaling when the times become comparable to the maximal investment horizon and when the Gaussian term starts to be important, i.e. at the region of crossover from 'Levy' to Gaussian behaviour. Figures 6.15 and 6.16 were obtained using this type of consideration.

7

Dynamics of Fast Money Flows: II

'In brief, the new work says that returns are predictable from past returns, dividend yields, and various term-structure variables.'

Eugene F. Fama (Fama, 1991)

The weak form of the Efficient Market Hypothesis (EMH) excludes predictions of future market movements from historical data and thus prohibits the use of Technical Analysis (TA). However TA is widely used by traders and speculators, who steadfastly refuse to consider the market as a 'fair game' and, what is important, survive with such beliefs. Below we conjecture that TA and the EMH correspond to different time regimes, and show[1] how some technical analysis predictions for short times can be obtained from the same gauge model that in the previous chapter generated realistic statistical data for larger times.

I INTRODUCTION

For many decades, people who deal with securities have been divided into two groups. The first group 'feels' the market, listens to how the market 'breathes', and treat the market as a live being (see Roosevelt, 1998). They analyse historical data for prices and volumes, draw patterns and construct indicators, i.e. make use of the machinery of Technical Analysis (see Pring, 1991, Chande and Kroll, 1994; Achelis, 1995). They are technicians. If somebody asks them whether the price is a random process, their answer will be emotional and strongly negative. No one trader would agree that his job is equivalent to throwing a dice. In the same time, the second group, roughly speaking, assumes that the price is a random process, the game is fair, and the market is efficient. Indeed, as standard textbooks put it (see e.g. Blake, 1990), even the weak form of the Efficient Market Hypothesis (EMH) states that all the relevant information from historical data is encoded in the current price, and hence the only ingredient that is able to influence future prices is new information. The information is unpredictable and random. This excludes predictions of future market movements from

---

[1]This chapter follows Ilinskaia and Ilinski (1998).

historical data, i.e. makes the technical analysis invalid. The EMH lays a basis for financial analysis with many outcomes such as modern portfolio theory and derivative pricing.

The conflict has lasted for years. Many efforts have been made to check the EMH. This led to the belief that 'the evidence for weak-form market efficiency is very strong' and that 'technical analysts are deluding themselves about their ability to predict future price movements' (Blake, 1990). At the same time, there have been a number of statistical estimates of the TA prediction accuracy (see e.g. Sweeney, 1986; Brock et al, 1992; Levich and Thortas, 1993; Morris, 1995; Ilinskaia and Ilinski, 1997) that excluded a purely random process. In brief TA is more often right than wrong, but it cannot be used thoughtlessly and it is not a 'Holy Grail' (Pring, 1993).

Traders and speculators mainly stick with TA, while quantitative analysts base their strategies on the EMH. The difference between players suggests that the conflict is due to different time horizons. From this point of view, TA predictions result from an internal deterministic dynamics that brings the market to equilibrium. The market has a long memory (see the review of empirical results in the previous chapter) and the dynamics might not be as fast as the EMH assumes. We show below that, in fact, TA and the EMH can be observed in the same model for market relaxation, and the regime depends only on a time scale. More precisely, we show that the TA indicators and the corresponding predictions are consistent with the model for short times while for longer times the model produces the EMH state with realistic statistical data.

In a certain sense, the situation with the EMH and TA slightly resembles the conflict in physics between Schrödinger and Laplacian determinism at the beginning of the century. Let us recall that the Laplacian (or classical) picture implies the possibility of determining the future state of a dynamical system precisely subject to the condition that the current state is completely known. Schrödinger's determinism implies that only the probability of the future states of the system can be predicted. The conflict is due to the fact that all we can see around us is deterministic (exactly as an extreme apologist for TA may say), but the theory predicts a vital influence of quantum fluctuations for long enough times (for example, a car can tunnel through a wall if we wait long enough). However, for sufficiently small times, any quantum system behaves classically. Following this line, we show in the gauge model that as time goes by the deterministic TA regime is substituted by the EMH regime in the course of a relaxation equilibration process.

This chapter is organized as follows. In the next two sections, we briefly describe the main issues of TA and the EMH to make the consideration self-contained. In Section 4, we derive dynamical equations for the gauge model in the small-time limit, and show how the model leads to TA behaviour in this limit. In Section 5, some econometric issues of the price adjustment process will be discussed. The results of this section can be applied to the parameter estimations in Chapters 8 and 9. The chapter is concluded with a few final remarks concerning the gauge model studied in Chapter 6 and in this chapter.

2 TECHNICAL ANALYSIS

Technical Analysis in general can be defined as a set of methods for predicting future prices that is based on 'mathematical' rather than economic calculations. It was developed for purely utilitarian purposes, namely are to get a profit from speculations playing with stocks and commodities and, later, with derivatives[2]. In the same way that fundamental analysis is a job for economists, is a field for engineers.[3]

Leaving aside patterns of classical TA, Elliott wave theory (Prechter and Frost, 1995), Japanese candlesticks (Morris, 1995) and Renkos (Nison, 1994), where the recognition of patterns is quite subjective, it is possible to say that TA consists of a set of simple indicators calculated from previous volumes and prices. The indicators produce 'buy' and 'sell' signals, and can be verified using historical data.[4] It is clear that there are a huge number of combinations of prices and volumes that are potential indicators, but only few of them survive after testing against real data.

Mathematically, TA is very simple, and cannot be compared with the complicated financial mathematics involved in portfolio theory, pricing and hedging. This has led to a certain degree of disbelief in TA. Another source of doubt concerns the possibility of constructing a trading plan, i.e. an algorithm that can substitute for a trader. Indeed, the market consists of human beings, reflects human psychology, and cannot be put in a finite set of simple equations. Supporters of TA argue that the basic principles of economic theories are not very complicated either, although they developed to describe the same market. Concerning the trading plan, there is an opinion that the plan is useful to save the financial and emotional potential of traders in an uncertain and rapidly changing informational environment (Hartle, 1998). From this point of view, it is analogous to walking in a forest when one has lost one's way—it is better to go straight ahead rather than making loop after loop like a drunk sailor.

In brief, TA, although controversial, is popular among investors and is widely used by professional traders[5]. It is not risk-free. Clear signals do not come very often, and it is hard to collect statistics and make money from them. The situation in a market changes with time, and it is important to adjust the TA toolkit to it. This fact also smears the statistics. However, as traders put it, there are certain market patterns, and TA is more often right than wrong[6].

There exists a huge literature on TA methods (for references see Achelis,1995), and we do not intend here to give any kind of review of the subject. All that we will do is to describe a few of the TA indicators that will be mentioned later in this chapter. They will, however, illustrate the general idea behind TA.

First, we consider the price Rate-of-Change (ROC) indicator (Appel and Hitschler, 1980). This displays the difference between the current price and the price N periods of time ago, similarly to the common momentum indicator:

$$ROC = S_{\text{now}} - S_{-N}.$$

The rationale behind the ROC indicator is the well-recognized phenomenon that securities prices surge ahead and retract in a cyclical motion. This wavelike action is generally considered as a result of changing expectations as buyers and sellers struggle to control

---

[2]See Chapter 1 for a short historical review.

[3]This does not mean, however, that there is no place for fundamental economic information in TA. For example, it was shown in Ilinskaia and Ilinski (1997) how to incorporate fundamental information in the correlation of companies' share prices into TA to construct new correlative indicators, using the example of two principal energy supply companies in Russia. One can argue that the background for general multi-asset consideration is given by Mantegna's ultrametric trees (Mantegna, 1998) as constructed for stocks in the DJIA and the S&P500 index.

[4]This does not imply, however, that the indicators will work in the future.

[5]Taylor and Allen (1992) demonstrated that a majority of FOREX traders use TA methods.

[6]There are a number of economic papers devoted to the study of return predictability (see e.g. Lo and MacKinlay, 1988; Fama and French, 1988; DeBondt and Thaler, 1985; Campbell and Shiller, 1988; Campbell, 1987; Lakonishok and Maberly, 1990). See also Fama (1991) for a discussion of market efficiency in connection with predictability tests.

prices. A trader has to choose the time step and the 'overbought'–'oversold' lines, which depend on the security and overall market conditions. The indicator generates the 'buy' signal when the indicator crosses the 'oversold' line in upswing. Similarly, the 'sell' signal is generated when the indicator crosses the 'overbought' line in downswing (see Fig. 7.1).

The next example is Williams' % R indicator W_n. It is given by the formula

$$W_n = -100 \frac{H_n - C}{H_n - L_n}.$$

Here C is a last closing price, and H_n and L_n are the highest and lowest prices for the last n time periods. The indicator oscillates in the range between -100 and 0. The undervalued zone lays in range -100 and $-80(-70)$, while the overvalued zone spans from -20 to 0. As for the ROC, the 'buy' ('sell') signal comes when the indicator leaves the undervalued (overvalued) zone. Both ROC and Williams' %R are very simple and easy to use methods.

The Positive Volume Index (PVI) and the Negative Volume Index (NVI) (Achelis, 1995) are the examples of a TA toolkit of another kind. In contrast to the previous two indicators, which use only prices, the PVI and the NVI use the trading volumes as well. These indicators are defined by the following formulae:

$$PVI_n = PVI_{n-1}[1 + \theta(V_n - V_{n-1})r_n], \tag{1}$$

$$NVI_n = NVI_{n-1}[1 + \theta(V_{n-1} - V_n)r_n], \tag{2}$$

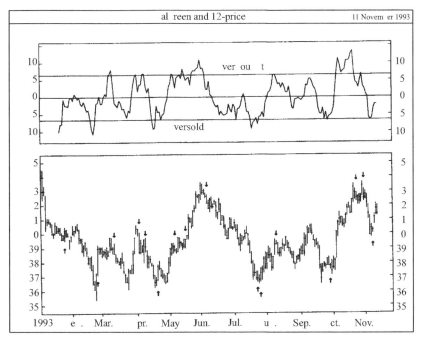

Figure 7.1 Application of 12-day ROC indicator. The 'overbought' line is placed at 6.5 and the 'oversold' line is placed at -6.5. Reprinted from S.B. Achelis, *Technical Analysis from A to Z*. Irwin Professional Publishing, 1995.

where r_n and V_n are the return and trade volume in the nth period, and $\theta(x)$ is the Heaviside step function defined as $\theta(x > 0) = 1$, with zero value otherwise. One of the interpretations of the PVI assumes that in the periods when volumes increase, the crowd of 'uninformed' investors reign in the market. These periods contribute to the PVI. Conversely, in periods with decreasing volume, the 'smart money' is quietly taking positions which is reflected by the NVI. We shall see in Section 4 that the 'classical' dynamics of the single-asset gauge model leads to predictions of the NVI and the PVI indicators. The fact that the 'classical dynamics' is consistent with both the NVI and the PVI indicators can be interpreted as a consequence of the absence of pure 'noise traders' and 'smart money' in the model. 'Buy' and 'sell' signals appear when the indices cross their own moving averages. Statistical estimations of the indicators' accuracy and further references can be found in Achelis (1995).

3   EFFICIENT MARKET HYPOTHESIS

In Section 1 we formulated a conflict between TA and the Efficient Market. Indeed, if, according to EMH, any relevant information is already included in prices, then there is no way to predict prices from historical data, as TA assumes. We show now that the conflict is apparent, and stems from an inaccurate definition of the EMH.

Let us define the Efficient Market as a superposition of the Rational Expectation Hypothesis and the Orthogonality Property (LeRoy, 1989; Cuthbertson, 1996). The *Rational Expectation Hypothesis* states the following:

1. Agents are rational, i.e. they use any possibility to get more than less if the possibility occurs.

2. There exists a perfect pricing model, and all market participants know this model.

3. Agents have all relevant information to incorporate into the model.

Using the model and the information, the rational agents form an expectation value of the future return $E_t R_{t+1}$. This expectation value can differ from the actual value of the return R_{t+1} on a estimation error $\epsilon_t = R_{t+1} - E_t R_{t+1}$. The *Orthogonality Property* implies the following:

1. ϵ_{t+1} is a random variable that appears owing to new incoming information.

2. ϵ_{t+1} is independent on the full information set Ω_t at time t, and

$$E_t(\epsilon_{t+1} | \Omega_t) = 0.$$

If agents have a wrong model then the model gives a systematic error, and some serial correlation of ϵ_{t+1} and ϵ_τ (with $\tau < t + 1$) emerges. For example, if

$$\epsilon_{t+1} = \rho \epsilon_t + \delta_t,$$

where ρ is a parameter of the serial correlation and δ_t is a white noise, then the following occur:

1. $E_t(\epsilon_{t+1}|\Omega_t) \neq 0$.

2. $E_t R_{t+1}$ is not the best expectation, i.e. the model is wrong.

Indeed, we can improve the model using $\tilde{E}_t R_{t+1}$ as a new model expectation:

$$\tilde{E}_t R_{t+1} = E_t R_{t+1} + \rho(R_t - E_{t-1} R_{t-1}).$$

If agents do not improve the model in this way, they are irrational and there exists the possibility of a superprofit. That is why some tests of market efficiency concentrate on the existence of serial correlations and superprofit. Fama (1970) gives a review of early empirical results on the EMH. An excellent review of various tests and recent results can be found in Cuthbertson (1996). Almost all of them show that the EMH does not hold (at least using existing pricing models as candidates for the role of the perfect model).

What is important for our goal here is that the perfect pricing model $E_t R_{t+1}$ is formed using all relevant information and, in particular, historical data.[7] Let us consider an example. If the arrival of new information increases the return of a security compared with other securities with the same measure of risk then rational traders buy the profitable security and sell others until the returns no longer equalize.[8] This equalization (relaxation) process is not infinitely fast – it takes some time to recognize the mispricing and to take advantage of it. This fact has to be accounted for in the perfect pricing model. Knowledge of how the relaxation goes can be obtained from available information and the *historical data*. This means that analysis of historical data and underlying market forces is extremely important for the construction of a model of future price dynamics or, more precisely, the dynamics of the expected future prices.[9] At this point, we return to TA, which is a set of empirical (phenomenological) rules for expected future price predictions and the corresponding investment decisions. The comparison of characteristic times of the return fluctuations and the market relaxation defines the applicability of TA. If we assume that the relaxation time is much less than the time between perturbations, we return to the simplified EMH definition, with all relevant information included in the price. If the changes are also assumed to be statistically independent and identically distributed, we end up with random walks. Following this line, one can argue that the consideration of two typical time scales resolves the conflict between the TA and Market Efficiency.

Summarizing, Technical Analysis can be considered as a phenomenological method for the construction of a mean price model for future prices. It uses price history to estimate market relaxation, and is valid when the relaxation time is not zero. Real prices are stochastically distributed around the mean price, and this constitutes the Efficient Market Hypothesis. We now show how these TA predictions for small times can be obtained from the same gauge model that we studied in the previous chapter, where it was shown how the model generates a realistic statistical description.

---

[7]Fama (1970) pointed out that the historical data, in fact, are important to estimate the statistical properties of the returns, in particular, the probability distribution functions.

[8]We assume that this arrival of new information does not change the 'risk' that investors associate with the security.

[9]Some authors agree that TA should be accounted for in the pricing model, but they argue that its purpose is to account for the presence of 'noise' traders who use TA. This scenario also leads to re-emergence of TA patterns. This does not contradict the point of view elaborated in the text, where the patterns are associated with collective market forces, since these forces can be caused by quasirational (partially noise) traders whose presence we account for in the gauge model.

4   SHORT-TIME DYNAMICAL EQUATIONS

In Section 4 of Chapter 6, it was shown that the transition probability from the state with price $S(0)$ and (n_1, m_1) traders in (cash, shares) to the state with price $S(T)$ and corresponding trader distribution (n, m) can be written in terms of the functional integral[10].

$$P(S(T), (n, m)|S(0), (n_1, m_1)) = \frac{1}{n!m!} S(T)^{-\tilde{\beta}\frac{(n-m)}{2}} S(0)^{\tilde{\beta}\frac{(n_1-m_1)}{2}} \int d\psi \ d\bar\psi \bar\psi_{i,0}^n \bar\psi_{2,0}^m \bar\psi_{1,N}^n \psi_{2,0} \psi_{2,N}^m$$

$$\times e^{-\bar\psi_N \psi_N - \bar\psi_0 \psi_0} I(\bar\psi, \psi, S(0), S(t))). \tag{3}$$

In the continuous-time limit, the functional integral $I(\bar\psi, \psi, S(0), S(T)))$ takes the form

$$I(\bar\xi, \xi, S(0), S(T))) = \int Dy \ D\bar\psi_1 \ D\psi_1 \ D\bar\psi_2 D\psi_2 e^{s_1}, \tag{4}$$

with the action

$$s_1 = -\frac{1}{2\sigma^2} \int_0^T \left(\frac{d(y - \frac{\alpha}{M}\bar\psi_2\psi_2 + \frac{\alpha}{M}\bar\psi_1\psi_1)}{dt} \right)^2 dt$$

$$+ \int_0^T dt \left(\frac{d\bar\psi_1}{dt}\psi_1 + \frac{d\bar\psi_2}{dt}\psi_2 + \frac{1}{\Delta}e^{\tilde\beta y}\bar\psi_1\psi_2 + \frac{1}{\Delta}e^{-\tilde\beta y}\bar\psi_2\psi_1 \right) \tag{5}$$

and the boundary conditions for integration trajectories

$$\psi_i(0) = \xi_i, \qquad \bar\psi_i = \bar\xi_i, \qquad y(0) = \log(S(0)), \qquad y(T) = \log(S(T)).$$

Let us denote the number of traded lots (both money and shares) by M. We now derive the equation on the saddle-point trajectories that give the main contribution in the small time limit to the functional integral (3)–(5) (see Section 5 of the Appendix on methods of quantum field theory). In quantum physics, the equations for the saddle points of such functional integrals actually coincide with the classical equations of motion for the underlying classical system. That is why the corresponding saddle-point approximation is called *quasiclassical*.

To extract the short-time behaviour, we measure the time t in terms of the smallest time interval in the system, i.e. in units of the time horizon Δ:

$$t \to t/\Delta.$$

Since the full number of asset units M is large, we use the standard field-theoretical trick and change the fields $\bar\psi$, and ψ to the 'hydrodynamical' variables ρ and ϕ:[11]

$$\bar\psi_i = \sqrt{M\rho_i}e^{\phi_i}, \qquad \psi_i = \sqrt{M\rho_i}e^{-\phi_i}.$$

We also change $\tilde\beta y$ to y. The variable $\rho_i(t)$ is proportional to the density of money flows at point i at time t, while $\phi_1(t) - \phi_2(t)$ is connected with the corresponding velocity of the

---

[10]At present, we consider the single-investment-horizon case.
[11]Thus we get rid of many small 'particles', and concentrate on the macroscopic characteristics of the system.

flows. Indeed, the operator for the number of 'investors' in cash (shares), $\psi_{1(2)}^+\psi_{1(2)}$, has the following form in the coherent state representation:

$$\bar{\psi}_{1(2)}\psi_{1(2)} = M\rho_{1(2)},$$

and is proportional to the fields $\rho_{1(2)}$. Similarly, the operator for the current from shares to cash, $\psi_1^+\psi_2$, has the representation

$$\bar{\psi}_1\psi_2 = M\sqrt{\rho_1\rho_2}\,e^{\phi_1-\phi_2}.$$

In these variables, the action takes the form

$$S(\rho,\phi) = M\int_0^{T/\Delta} dt \left[-\frac{1}{2\sigma^2\Delta\tilde{\beta}^2 M}\left(\frac{d(y+\alpha\tilde{\beta}\rho_1 - \alpha\tilde{\beta}\rho_2)}{dt}\right)^2 \right.$$

$$\left. + \frac{d\phi_1}{dt}\rho_1 + \frac{d\phi_2}{dt}\rho_2 + 2\sqrt{\rho_1\rho_2}\,\cosh(\phi_1 - \phi_2 + y) \right], \tag{6}$$

up to boundary terms that do not contribute to the equations of motion. The functional integral can be rewritten as

$$I(\bar{\psi},\psi,S(0),S(T))) = \int Dy\, D\phi_1\, D\phi_2\, D\rho_1\, D\rho_2 e^{s(\rho,\phi,y)}.$$

Let us now assume that the coefficients

$$\alpha_1 = 2\alpha\tilde{\beta}$$

and $2\sigma^2\Delta\tilde{\beta}^2 M$ are finite. Then the appearance of the large external multiplier M is a key point for the calculation of the above functional integral using the saddle-point method. Indeed, as M tends to infinity the only relevant contributions to the integral are given by the 'classical' trajectories, which are defined by the minimization equations

$$\frac{\delta s(y,\rho,\phi)}{\delta y} = 0, \qquad \frac{\delta s(y,\rho,\phi)}{\delta \rho_i} = 0, \qquad \frac{\delta s(y,\rho,\phi)}{\delta \phi_i} = 0.$$

This means that the equations define the joint dynamics of prices and money flows for times of order of Δ. Using the explicit form (6) and the fact that

$$\rho_1 + \rho_2 = 1,$$

it is easy to check that the last equations can be written as

$$\frac{1}{2\sigma^2 \Delta \tilde{\beta}^2 M} \frac{d^2(y+\alpha_1\rho_1)}{dt^2} + \sqrt{\rho_2\rho_1} \sinh(\phi_1 - \phi_2 + y) = 0, \tag{7}$$

$$\frac{\alpha_1}{\sigma^2 \Delta \tilde{\beta}^2 M} \frac{d^2(y+\alpha_1\rho_1)}{dt^2} + \frac{d\phi_1}{dt} + \sqrt{\frac{\rho_2}{\rho_1}} \cosh(\phi_1 - \phi_2 + y) = 0,$$

$$\frac{d\phi_2}{dt} + \sqrt{\frac{\rho_1}{\rho_2}} \cosh(\phi_1 - \phi_1 + y) = 0,$$

$$-\frac{d\rho_1}{dt} + 2\sqrt{\rho_2\rho_1} \sinh(\phi_1 - \phi_2 + y) = 0,$$

$$\frac{d\rho_2}{dt} + 2\sqrt{\rho_1\rho_2} \sinh(\phi_1 - \phi_2 + y) = 0. \tag{8}$$

The first important note concerns (7). Indeed, combining (8) and (7) we find the equation

$$\frac{2}{\sigma^2 \Delta \tilde{\beta}^2 M} \frac{d^2 y}{dt^2} = \frac{d\rho_2}{dt} - \frac{d\rho_1}{dt} - \frac{2\alpha_1}{\sigma^2 \Delta \tilde{\beta}^2 M} \frac{d^2 \rho_1}{dt^2},$$

which, after integration, gives us the first-order differential equation

$$\frac{dy}{dt} = \frac{M\sigma^2 \Delta \tilde{\beta}^2}{2}(\rho_2 - \rho_1) - \alpha_1\rho_1 + \left(\frac{d(y+\alpha_1\rho)}{dt} - \frac{M\sigma^2 \Delta \tilde{\beta}^2}{2}(\rho_2 - \rho_1) \right)(0).$$

The relation $\rho_1 + \rho_2 = 1$ immediately gives the equality

$$\frac{d\rho_1}{dt} + \frac{d\rho_2}{dt} = 0.$$

This last equality can also be found directly from the sum of the equations in (8). This allows us to express ρ_2 as $1 - \rho_1$, and we finally get the equations of motion as

$$\frac{dy}{dt} = \sigma^2 \Delta \tilde{\beta}^2 M \left(\frac{1}{2} - \rho \right) - 2\alpha_1 \sqrt{(1-\rho)\rho} \, \sinh(v + y)$$

$$+ \left(\frac{d(y+\alpha_1\rho)}{dt} - M\Delta\sigma^2 \tilde{\beta}^2 \left(\frac{1}{2} - \rho \right) \right)(0),$$

$$\frac{dv}{dt} = \left(\sqrt{\frac{\rho}{1-\rho}} - \sqrt{\frac{1-\rho}{\rho}} \right) \cosh(v+y) + 2\sqrt{(1-\rho)\rho} \, \sinh(v+y),$$

$$\frac{d\rho}{dt} = 2\sqrt{(1-\rho)\rho} \, \sinh(v+y). \tag{9}$$

Here we have introduced the notation $\rho \equiv \rho_1$ for the relative number of 'traders' in cash and $v = \phi_1 - \phi_2$.

One can combine the first two equations of (9) to reduce the number of equations in (9) and to get a system of two ordinary differential equations for ρ and $\tilde{y} = y + v$:

$$\frac{d\rho}{dt} = 2\sqrt{(1-\rho)\rho} \ \sinh \tilde{y},$$

$$\frac{d\tilde{y}}{dt} = \sigma^2 \Delta \tilde{\beta}^2 M\left(\frac{1}{2} - \rho\right) + 2(1 - \alpha_1)\sqrt{(1-\rho)\rho} \ \sinh \tilde{y}$$

$$+ \left(\sqrt{\frac{\rho}{1-\rho}} - \sqrt{\frac{1-\rho}{\rho}}\right) \cosh \tilde{y} + \left(\frac{d(y + \alpha_1 \rho)}{dt} - M\Delta\sigma^2 \tilde{\beta}^2 \left(\frac{1}{2} - \rho\right)\right)(0).$$

This system is easy to solve numerically. Figure 7.2 and 7.3 show the typical solutions of the equations for the parameters

$$M = 40, \qquad \sigma^2 \Delta = 0.04, \qquad \tilde{\beta} = 2.5, \ \alpha = 0.3,$$

and the initial conditions

$$\rho = 0.5, \qquad y(0) = 0.2, \qquad \frac{dy}{dt}(0) = 0, \qquad \frac{d\rho}{dt}(0) = \sinh 0.2, \qquad v(0) = 0.$$

This example corresponds to a 'shock' when the market at equilibrium ($\rho_1 = \rho_2 = 0$, $y = v = 0$) received 'positive' information about the stock, which lifted its price to $y = 0.2$. The following wavelike market dynamics reduces the mispricing and brings it eventually to zero. During this period of relaxation, the price oscillates owing to the

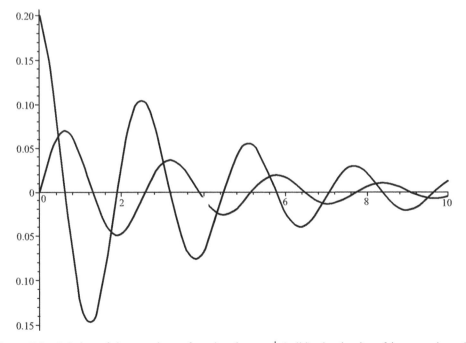

Figure 7.2 Solution of the equations of motion for $\rho - \frac{1}{2}$ (solid), the density of investors in cash measured from the equilibrium value, and $y = \tilde{\beta} \log S$ (dashed). The values of the parameters are given in the text.

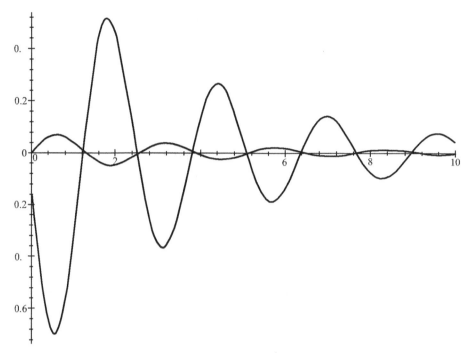

Figure 7.3   Solution of the equations of motion for $\rho - \frac{1}{2}$ (solid), the density of investors in cash measured from the equilibrium value, and the return $\beta \, dy/dt$ (dashed). The value of parameters are given in the text.

overreaction of the market participants. The period of the oscillations and the characteristic relaxation time both depend on the parameters of the model. In fact, if the parameter α is small enough, the relaxation will be changed to speculative enhancement of the oscillations. Figure 7.4 shows this situation for $\alpha = 0.1$. Figures 7.5 and 7.6 shows examples of intraday price charts demonstrating the same oscillatory behaviour.

We now turn to TA. Our goal is to show that the solutions of the derived equations (9) indeed resemble the situation of the real financial markets, and are consistent with some standard TA tools.

Let us estimate the performance of the TA indicators for our model. The first trivial example is the price Rate-of-Change (ROC) indicator, which we described in Section 2 and which is simply the return. We get 'buy' and 'sell' signals at points where the security return line crosses some predefined levels. One can see that for our idealized description these signals anticipate reversals in the underlying security's price.

Two other indicators that we described in Section 2 can also be easily recognized for our model. They are the Positive Volume Index (PVI) and the Negative Volume Index (NVI). These indicators are more complicated, since they involve the trading volume as well as the price.

We plot the NVI and the PVI for our model and estimate the connection between their behaviour and price movements (see Fig. 7.7). First of all, one can see that both the PVI and the NVI trend in the same direction as prices, which agrees with the TA arguments. Another important point is that the NVI's reversal points in this model always anticipate those of the

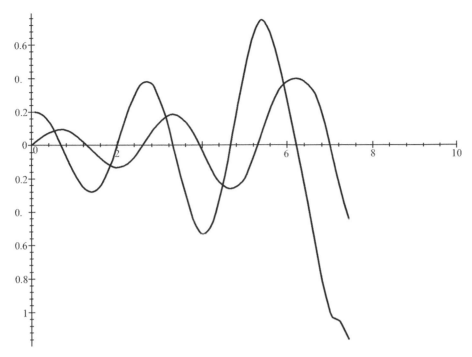

Figure 7.4 Enhancement of the oscillations for small values of α.

Sym ol	Last trade	Net c an e	Day i	Day low	Trade time	Volume
VE T	88	$7\frac{1}{16}$	$89\frac{3}{8}$	80	16:03 ET	100

Figure 7.5 Oscillatory pattern for intraday trading of VERTICALNET (VERT), 24 March 1999.

Sym ol	Last trade	Net c an e	Day i	Day low	Trade time
S E	$68\frac{1}{2}$	$2\frac{1}{2}$	$70^{\perp}$	$67\frac{5}{8}$	16:00 ET

Figure 7.6 Oscillatory pattern for intraday trading of SAFEGUARD SCIENTIFIC (SFE), 10 April 1999.

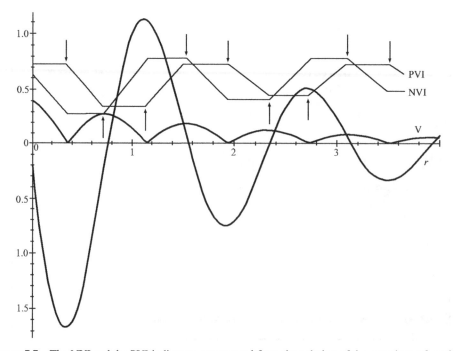

Figure 7.7 The NVI and the PVI indicators constructed from the solution of the equations of motion.

PVI, which is very reasonable if we compare the behaviour of crowd-following and informed investors. Indeed, when calculating the NVI, we take into account only days when the volume decreases and the 'smart money' is believed to take positions. The PVI, in contrast, counts only days when volume increases, i.e. crowd-following investors are in the market. That is why it seems to be natural that the NVI, which reflects 'smart money' behaviour, reacts earlier to changing of the market situation than the PVI. The fact that both indicators are consistent with the solutions of the equations of motion reflects the mixed description of 'smart' and 'noisy' traders in the gauge model.

Therefore we can state that *the gauge model is consistent with the TA phenomenological rules of market relaxation for small enough time*. To answer the question why the TA toolkit also works at sufficiently large times, we have to return to the model with many time horizons. Indeed, all calculations of this chapter have been done for a single investment horizon. To model a realistic market, as we have seen in Chapter 6, one has to include many investment horizons with similar dynamics. This will deform the clear oscillatory charts for the price and bring many characteristic cycles with a similar structure. This cross-time similarity can indeed be observed in the market, and it is accounted for in the TA in the form of multiframe analysis.

5   ECONOMETRIC ISSUES OF PRICE ADJUSTMENT

In the previous section, we saw that the equilibration dynamics depends on the values of the model parameters, which are difficult to quantify. Although it is difficult to develop a robust procedure for estimating all the internal parameters in the model, there is one statistical quantity that does reflect the dynamics and thus the internal parameters and that is comparatively easy to estimate. This is the speed of the price equilibration, or the price adjustment. The importance of this quantity for us is also explained by the fact that, as we will see in Chapters 8 and 9, the models that can be derived from first principles use the speed of adjustment rather than the unobserved internal parameters. Some econometric methods for the parameter estimation are the subject of this section.

Amihud and Mendelson (1987) and Damodaran (1993) studied partial price adjustment with white noise specifying the log-price process as

$$P(t) = P(t-1) + \lambda[V(t) - P(t-1)] + \epsilon(t), \tag{10}$$

where λ is the speed of adjustment,[12] $\epsilon(t)$ is the white noise term, and $V(t)$ is the intrinsic value of the stock, which is assumed to follow the random process

$$V(t) = V(t-1) + \mu + e(t),$$

with a white noise innovation term $e(t)$. The model produces an iterative expansion for the observed returns $R(t) = P(t) - P(t-1)$:

$$R(t) = \lambda\mu + \lambda \sum_{j=0}^{\infty} (1-\lambda)^j[e(t-j) - \epsilon(t-1-j)] + \epsilon(t).$$

---

[12]Here we assume that the speed of adjustment is stationary. The impact of non-stationarity was investigated analytically by Theobald and Yallup (1998).

In order that the return series remain finite, the adjustment factor λ has to be in the range $0 < \lambda < 2$.

It is not difficult to obtain a simple formula for λ. Indeed, the autocovariance for lag one and two can be derived as

$$\text{cov}(R(t), R(t-1)) = \frac{\lambda}{2-\lambda}[(1-\lambda)\,\text{var}(e(t)) - \text{var}(\epsilon(t))]$$

and

$$\text{cov}(R(t), R(t-2)) = \frac{\lambda(1-\lambda)}{2-\lambda}[(1-\lambda)\,\text{var}(e(t)) - \text{var}(\epsilon(t))].$$

This results in the following expression for the adjustment factor:

$$\lambda = 1 - \frac{\text{cov}(R(t), R(t-2))}{\text{cov}(R(t), R(t-1))}. \tag{11}$$

Using this last expression, the speed of adjustment can be estimated from the transaction data. Alternatively, one can rearrange (10) in the form (Theobald and Yallup 1999)

$$R(t) = (1-\lambda)R(t-1) + \lambda[V(t) - V(t-1)] + \epsilon(t) - \epsilon(t-1),$$

so that, after substituting of the equation for the intrinsic value $V(t)$, the returns are expressed as

$$R(t) = \lambda\mu + (1-\lambda)R(t-1) + \epsilon(t) - \epsilon(t-1). \tag{12}$$

Theobald and Yallup (1999) used the last equation to find the speed of adjustment as the autoregression coefficient. They also compared the performance of various estimators, and applied the estimators to show that small capitalization stocks exhibit lower speeds of adjustment.

In practice, all real data has to be adjusted to market imperfections, such as the existence of spread, thin trading, and delayed prices. Several econometric techniques have been suggested to incorporate these factors.[13] One of the ways to account for the non-trading impacts may be modelled by relating the observed returns $R(m, t)$ to the 'true' returns as (Dimson,1979; Theobald and Price, 1984; Cohen et al, 1986)

$$R_m(t) = \sum_{i=0}^{q} w(i)R(t-i) + r(t),$$

where $r(t)$ is an i.i.d error term, $w(i)$ is the deterministic proportion of the measured return deriving from the 'true' returns occurring i periods ago, and q is the longest time lag influencing the current measured return. In the latter case, the estimator (11) can be derived in the following form (Theobald and Yallup, 1999)

$$\lambda = 1 - \frac{\text{cov}(R_m(t), R_m(t-2-q))}{\text{cov}(R_m(t), R_m(t-1-q))},$$

[13]Stoll and Whaley (1990) suggested simple model to incorporate the spread effect. Huang and Stoll (1997) developed a very general model to include the presence of adverse selection together with inventory and processing costs. Thin trading was considered by Miller et al (1994).

while (12) becomes

$$R_m(t) = \lambda\mu + (1 - \lambda)R_m(t - 1)$$
$$+ \sum_{i=0}^{q} w(i)[\lambda e(t - i) + \epsilon(t - i) - \epsilon(t - 1 - i)]$$
$$+ r(t) - (1 - \lambda)r(t - 1).$$

Again, this last equation serves to estimate the factor $1 - \lambda$ as the autoregression coefficient.

6 FINAL REMARKS ON CHAPTERS 6 AND 7

In this chapter, we have considered the relation between Market Efficiency and the applicability of Technical Analysis. As was shown above, these two aspects are not conflicting but are complementary to each other in the sense that TA reflects market relaxation dynamics and thus participates in the formulation of a market model for future expected returns in the framework of the EMH. For times much larger than the characteristic market relaxation time and with existence of asymptotic stable equilibrium, EMH reduces to the equilibrium variant of the EMH, which states that all relevant information is already accounted for in prices. At this stage, the study of price history does not help to predict future prices. This scenario is realized when the characteristic time between perturbations is considerably longer then the relaxation time. If this is not the case, the equilibrium picture will not be valid at all.

There is a practical outcome of the discussion. If one wants to construct a statistical model of market behaviour to be used later in pricing or the development of trading strategies, it is important to take into account quasi-deterministic market behaviour at short times. The practical source of information about this behaviour comes from everyday trading practice which is summed up into the form of the TA phenomenological rules. These rules can play the role of criteria for the construction of effective models. Indeed, to model a price process for a particular security, one needs to choose an action functional that will occur in functional integrals to calculate various averages. Since the choice of the action dictates the short-time 'quasi-classical' dynamics, one has to construct the functional such that the corresponding model dynamics will reproduce the essential features of the real asset prices. The convenience of the language of creation-annihilation operators lies in the fact that as soon as some price patterns are spotted and their basic origin is realized, it is absolutely straightforward to encode this origin into the model. In Chapter 6, we gave examples of the interaction terms that represent some features of realistic markets. Playing with this 'construction toy' one can model any characteristic price patterns. The pricing models developed in this way will therefore account for typical price behaviour, in contrast to widely used simple stochastic processes, which neglect it. A pricing theory based on this type of model can therefore fill the gap between equilibrium pricing and traders' practice.

Up till now, we have considered a very simple model of a stock exchange where only one kind of security is traded. The consideration can be generalized to more realistic situations with a set of traded securities. In reality, each trader watches the prices of several assets. Therefore the mutual influence of asset prices is quite important. However, even for the single-asset model, it turns out to be difficult to get analytical results that exhibit the behaviour found numerically. The situation becomes even worse for the portfolio generalizations or for derivative pricing problem. Since it is always better to have a correct numerical result rather than an inaccurate analytical one, the natural route to practical applications of this kind of model lies in the extensive use of computer power.

Let us now return to the analogy with Quantum Electrodynamics (QED) that was outlined in Chapter 2. In last three chapters, we have seen how the same underlying geometry dictates the same framework to describe the dynamics. The logic was absolutely straightforward. Let us recall the main steps:

1. Gauge invariance implies the existence of an underlying fibre bundle geometry.

2. Parallel transport on these fibre bundles is naturally defined by prices and is connected with the exchange of assets.

3. The existence of the gauge field implies that existence of fields which are gauged, i.e. the money flow fields.

4. Intrinsic uncertainty leads to the necessity to deal with functional integrals or other equivalent techniques.

5. Gauge invariance requires the construction of the theory in gauge-invariant terms, which, together with some additional first principles, fix the action functionals in the functional integrals. Instead of first principles, one can use empirical features of particular securities, such as working Technical Analysis indicators.

More or less the same steps have been used in Chapter 4 to construct physical gauge theories, and QED in particular. To make the analogy between the QED and Capital Market Theory more transparent, we give a 'dictionary' to translate one language to another in Table 7.1.

Table 7.1

QED	Capital Market Theory
Time component of connection	Interest rate
Operator of parallel transport in time	Discount factor
Operators of parallel transport in space	Exchange rates and prices
Electromagnetic field	Excess return on elementary arbitrage operation
Quantization of electromagnetic field	Uncertainty in price movements
Matter fields	Money flow fields
Quantization of matter field	Bounded rationality of traders
Gauge transformations	Change of asset units
Gauge invariance	Independence of this change
Positive (negative) charges	Securities in long (short) position
External potential	Risk
Inverse mass of particles	Transaction costs
Quasiclassical approximation	Short-time dynamics

7 SUMMARY

- The functional integral representation for the gauge model allows one to use the saddle-point approximation to derive the equations of motion for the most probable trajectories of money flows and prices.

- Solutions of the equations of motion exhibit the oscillatory behaviour typical of real markets. These oscillations are due to temporal overreaction of the market.

- The values of the parameters in the model define if the oscillations are damped or enhanced. Damped oscillations correspond to reduction of mispricing and return to the equilibrium. Enhanced oscillations correspond to speculative destabilizing behaviour and lead to non-steady states.

- The solutions of the equations of motion are consistent with some indicators developed in Technical Analysis.

- To develop a gauge model 'tailored' to a particular asset, one has to start with an analysis of patterns characteristic of the asset price on small times. This gives a 'quasiclassical' action for the system, which can later be substituted into the functional integrals to describe the statistical properties of the assets. Such model will be useful for pricing and the development of trade strategies for the asset and related securities.

8

Virtual Arbitrage Pricing Theory

Up to now, we have studied a single mispriced security and the corresponding market response. If a market consists of several securities but any interconnection between them is negligible, one can apply the model studied in the previous two chapters to describe the system and/or to develop a profitable trading strategy. Unfortunately, the real market does not fit this picture. Trades in one asset influence trades in others, which makes the system extremely complicated. Mispricing arising in one asset causes associated mispricings in other assets, thus making the original mispricing 'travel' across the market. In such a scenario, an equilibrium in one tradeable asset cannot be reached without reaching equilibria in correlated assets. Owing to this global feature of the market, characteristics of one security are determined by characteristics of related securities and the market as a whole. This general idea underlies equilibrium asset pricing theory.

Absence of mispricing is an essential part of any equilibrium pricing model. However, as we have already discussed in Chapter 1, equilibrium is a rather questionable idealization. In a dynamical market, profitable opportunities (or their illusion) occur all the time and cause money flows which, in turn, change prices and therefore the situation in the market. If all market participants agree about the 'fair' equilibrium price, the money flows will tend to reduce the mispricing and to bring the market back to the equilibrium state. In the opposite case, when the market participants have considerably different perceptions of the 'fair' price, the money flows can destabilize the market and drive it from equilibrium. In this case, the equilibrium is unstable and the whole notion of 'fair' price loses its sense. In this chapter, we consider in more detail the first case, where the mispricing is small and temporal, and the money flows drive the market towards a stable equilibrium state. In this case, fluctuations around the equilibrium state dictate corrections to the relations of the equilibrium pricing theory. These corrections disappear in the limit of absence of fluctuations or an infinitely fast market reaction.

Below we generalize Arbitrage Pricing Theory (APT) to include the contribution of virtual arbitrage opportunities following Ilinski (1999). We will model the arbitrage using the general gauge ideas considered earlier. This allows us to employ gauge methodology to construct the money flow fields that are responsible for the market reaction on arbitrage opportunities and even to use some results of Chapter 6 in the present analysis.

The chapter is constructed as follows. In the next section, we recall the basic relations of the Capital Asset Pricing Model (CAPM) and the APT. In Section 2, the APT relations are derived in the framework of a gauge theory of arbitrage. Here we also discuss a general form of the corrections due to virtual arbitrage opportunities and the corresponding money flows.

After drastic simplifications, we reduce the model essentially to the APT model, with the arbitrage return simulated by an Ornstein–Uhlenbeck stochastic process. This later model is investigated further in Sections 3 and 4. Simple analysis allows us to calculate the corrections to APT due to virtual arbitrage opportunities. The resulting relations are reduced to APT for an infinitely fast market reaction or in the absence of virtual arbitrage. Corrections to the CAPM are investigated in Section 5. Section 6 contains a discussion of the drawbacks of the model and possible ways to improve it.

I EQUILIBRIUM ASSET PRICING

To make the exposition self-contained, we give in this section a simple derivation of the main equation of the CAPM and the relations of APT. The reader who feels happy with the models is welcome to skip this section.

Let us first consider the CAPM (see Sharpe, 1964; Lintner, 1965; Mossin, 1966), and derive its main equation. To this end, we have to return to Fig. 4 of Chapter 1, which shows the efficient frontier – a set of risky portfolios such that the risk[1] is minimal while the average return is kept fixed, or the average return is maximal while the risk is fixed. If one assumes the existence of a risk-free asset with a risk-free rate of return r_0, it is possible to draw the *capital market line*, which touches the efficient frontier at the point $M = (\bar{r}_m, \sigma_m)$ and intersects the axis $\bar{r}$ at the point r_0 (see Fig. 8.1). It is easy to check that all portfolios placed on the capital market line comprise the riskless asset and the portfolio M. These portfolios are optimal, i.e. they maximize the average return for a fixed risk and minimize the risk for a fixed average return. Personal preferences of investors define only a position on the capital market line, but not the structure of the risky investment. This is known as the Separation Theorem. Since the risky part of an investment is given by the portfolio M for every investor, the portfolio M represents the *market portfolio*, i.e. the portfolio with fractions equal to the relative capitalization of the corresponding companies in the market.

This beautiful result does not say anything yet about pricing of the individual securities comprising the market. To derive an expression for the average return of a security, let us consider an inefficient portfolio with fraction x of the security i and fraction $1 - x$ of the market portfolio r_m. The average rate of return $\bar{r}_p$ and the standard deviation σ_p of the new portfolio will be given by the expressions

$$\bar{r}_p = x\bar{r}_i + (1 - x)\bar{r}_m,$$

$$\sigma_p = \sqrt{x^2\sigma_i^2 + (1 - x)^2\sigma_m^2 + 2x(1 - x)\operatorname{cov}(r_i, r_m)}.$$

Using these formulae to calculate the quantity $(d\bar{r}_p/d\sigma_p)|_{x=0}$, we find

$$\left.\frac{d\bar{r}_p}{d\sigma_p}\right|_{x=0} = \left.\frac{d\bar{r}_p}{dx}\right|_{x=0} \left(\left.\frac{d\sigma_p}{dx}\right|_{x=0}\right)^{-1} = \frac{\sigma_m(\bar{r}_i - \bar{r}_m)}{\operatorname{cov}(r_i, r_m) - \sigma_m^2}. \tag{1}$$

---

[1]Which, without going into subtleties, is taken as the standard deviation of the portfolio's return.

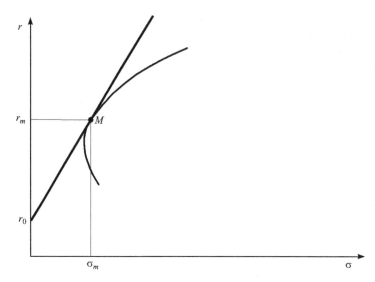

Figure 8.1   The capital market line touches the efficient frontier F at the point M $(\bar{r}_m, \sigma_m)$ and intersects the $\bar{r}$ axes at the point r_0. The portfolio M is the market portfolio.

On the other hand, the portfolio with $x = 0$ coincides with the market portfolio M, and therefore provides the following result for the quantity $(d\bar{r}_p/d\sigma_p)|_{x=0}$ calculated from the capital market line:

$$\frac{d\bar{r}_p}{d\sigma_p}\bigg|_{x=0} = \frac{\bar{r}_m - r_0}{\sigma_m}. \tag{2}$$

Equating the right-hand sides of (1) and (2), we find the following relation:

$$\frac{\sigma_m(\bar{r}_i - \bar{r}_m)}{\text{cov}(\bar{r}_i, \bar{r}_m) - \sigma_m^2} = \frac{\bar{r}_m - r_0}{\sigma_m},$$

which, after solving with respect to $\bar{r}_i$, results in the main equation of the CAPM:

$$\bar{r}_i = r_0 + \frac{\bar{r}_m - r_0}{\sigma_m^2}\,\text{cov}(\bar{r}_i, \bar{r}_m) = r_0 + \beta_i(\bar{r}_m - r_0), \qquad \beta_i = \frac{\text{cov}(\bar{r}_i, \bar{r}_m)}{\sigma_m^2}. \tag{3}$$

In this final form, the CAPM equation coincides with equation (3) of Chapter 1. It expresses an expected rate of return on a security as the sum of a risk-free return and a risk premium that is defined by the excess return on the market portfolio and the correlation of the security with the market.

Equation (3) admits a very simple interpretation. It states that the risk premium on a security is determined purely by the rate of return on the market portfolio, which is the only relevant factor in the theory. For empirical tests of this assumption, the model is normally taken in the form

$$\bar{r}_i - r_0 = \beta_i(\bar{r}_m - r_0) + a_i, \tag{4}$$

with the aim of estimating whether or not the 'intercept term' a is zero. Non-zero a_i is usually interpreted as an indication of existence of other factors influencing the return. The intercept can be also generated by the absence of a truly riskless asset (the Zero-Beta CAPM) or by differences in tax rates on dividend income and capital gains (the Post-Tax CAPM). As we will see later, virtual mispricing and the corresponding market reaction also lead to non-zero a_i, thus allowing an explanation of the intercept by the non-equilibrium nature of the market.

Empirical evidence indicates that there probably exist other sources that, together with the return on the market portfolio, define the risk premium. The most commonly accepted factors include the size of the company and the dividend policy. It was noticed that small companies have higher returns compared with large companies with the same value of β (Banz, 1981). Similarly, companies with high dividend yields give greater returns than companies with the same β but lower dividend yields. Moreover, researchers argue that changes in the book-to-market ratio,[2] in the risk-default premium, in the shape of the yield curve, in real interest rate, and in inflation are relevant factors driving the investment return[3] (for a review. see Fama, 1991). Therefore the idea was forwarded that instead of the single-factor CAPM, one has to consider multifactor pricing models with the aim of explaining the anomalies described above. This is what was started in APT (Ross, 1976). Chen et al (1986) identified the growth rate of industrial production and credit spread as the most significant factors, while the market β has only marginal explanatory power. Chan et al (1985) showed that these factors can explain, for example, the size effect. In what follows, we will not be interested in the nature of the factors, but rather will concentrate on the arbitrage consideration, taking factors as granted.

Let us now recall the standard derivation of the APT relations. Alhough the underlying mathematics is quite simple and the final equations are reminiscent of the CAPM, the basic assumptions of APT are very different from the CAPM.

The first assumption of APT is the existence of M fluctuating leading parameters, or factors, $\{\xi_j\}_{j=1}^M$ that define the prices of all $N+1$ assets such that[4]

$$\langle \xi_j \rangle_\xi = 0, \qquad \langle \xi_i \xi_j \rangle_\xi = \delta_{ij}$$

and

$$r_i = \bar{r}_i + \sum_j b_{ij} \xi_j + \epsilon_i. \tag{5}$$

Here $b_{ij} = \langle r_i - \bar{r}_i, \xi_j \rangle_\xi$ is a measure of the influence of the jth parameter on the i-th asset, and ϵ_i is a residual risk, which is independent of the factors and can be eliminated in large portfolios. To form a riskless portfolio, we pick up fractions $\{x_i\}$ such that

$$\sum_i x_i b_{ij} = 0$$

for any $j = 1, \ldots, M$ and that obey the normalization condition $\sum_i x_i = 1$. We also assume that the 0th asset is totally riskless.

The return on the portfolio is $\sum_i r_i x_i = \sum_i \bar{r}_i x_i$, and *has to be equal* to the risk-free interest rate r_0 in the case of *no arbitrage*. In simplified terms, the latter means that the return on a

---

[2] The book-to-market ratio is the ratio of the book value of the stock to its market value.
[3] In fact, Fama and French (1992) argue that the book-to-market ratio is the most powerful explanatory parameter, since it is correlated with size and leverage. See also Fama and French (1996) for a discussion of multifactor models of anomalies.
[4] $\langle A \rangle_B$ denotes an average of the quantity A with respect to the quantity B.

riskless portfolio should be equal to the riskless rate of return, which for now can be taken to be equal to the rate of the return on government bonds.[5] This leads to the equation

$$\sum_i \bar{r}_i x_i = r_0, \tag{6}$$

or, after a change of variables $x_i = y_i + \delta_{0i}$,

$$\sum_i \bar{r}_i y_i = 0,$$

subject to the constraints

$$\sum_i y_i b_{ij} = 0 \quad \forall j, \qquad \sum_i y_i = 0.$$

The solution of the equation for $\bar{r}_i$ then can be written as

$$\bar{r}_i = \alpha + \sum_j b_{ij} \gamma_j, \tag{7}$$

where α and $\{\gamma_j\}$ form a set of independent parameters. Since the 0th asset was chosen as risk-free, the coefficients $b_{0j} = 0$ for all j and $\alpha = r_0$. Equation (7) constitutes the APT relation. As we will see, it covers the CAPM relation as a particular case of a single-parameter model.

Indeed, if the only leading parameter is chosen to be a random part of a return on the market portfolio, $\xi \equiv (r_m - \bar{r}_m)/\sigma_m$, then (7) can be rewritten as

$$\bar{r}_i = r_0 + b_i \gamma, \tag{8}$$

with $b_i = \langle r_i - \bar{r}_i, r_m - \bar{r}_m \rangle / \sigma_m$. The next step is to introduce the market portfolio fractions θ_i and find an expression for the average rate of return on the market portfolio $\sum_i \theta_i \bar{r}_i$ using (8):

$$\bar{r}_m = r_0 + \sum_i \theta_i b_i \gamma.$$

This gives us the value of the variable γ as

$$\gamma = \frac{1}{\sigma_m}(\bar{r}_m - r_0). \tag{9}$$

Substituting (9) into (8), we rediscover the CAPM expression for the average rate of return:

$$\bar{r}_i = r_0 + \beta_i(\bar{r}_m - r_0),$$

with the standard definition $\beta_i = \langle r_i - \bar{r}_i, r_m - \bar{r}_m \rangle / \sigma_m^2$.

Along with the CAPM, APT is a standard model for determining the expected rate of return on individual stocks and on a portfolio of stocks (Elton and Gruber, 1995). In contrast to the CAPM, APT does not rely on any assumptions about utility functions or on the assumption that agents consider only the mean and variance of returns on possible portfolios. Taking into account critical remarks about the expected utility approach to the theory of decision-making under uncertainty and the long-running discussion about the definition of risk, this seems to be a considerable achievement. What APT does imply are homogeneous expectations, assumptions of linear factor weightings, a large enough number of securities to eliminate the specific risk, and the *no-arbitrage* condition. Being a basis for the APT and derivative pricing (Black and Scholes, 1973; Merton, 1973), the no-arbitrage assumption appears to be very reasonable and robust. Indeed, if any arbitrage possibility exists then agents (arbitrageurs)

---

[5]Here, for the sake of simplicity, we assume perfect capital market conditions, i.e. a single rate of lending and borrowing without restrictions, and absence of transaction costs and bid–ask spread; we touch on possible generalizations in the conclusions.

would use the opportunity to make an abnormal riskless profit, which itself would bring the system to equilibrium and eliminate the arbitrage opportunity. Thus the arbitrage cannot exist for long, and its lifetime depends on the liquidity of the market. This, however, does not mean that arbitrage opportunities do not exist at all and cannot influence the asset pricing, violating the APT assumption. Moreover, there exist empirical studies indicating the existence of virtual arbitrage opportunities even for very liquid markets – of the order of 5 minutes for futures on S&P500 (Sofianos, 1993) and possibly much longer for less liquid markets such as bonds markets and derivatives markets (Black et al, 1972; Galai, 1977).[6] Moreover, in the asset pricing setting, the arbitrage is not immediately detectable, which also adds to its lifetime. That is why, in this chapter, we try to overcome the no-arbitrage assumption and suggest a model to account for the existence of virtual arbitrage opportunities and their influence on asset pricing in the framework of APT.

2 GAUGE MODEL: CORRECTIONS TO APT

In this section we formulate a gauge model that is designed to describe dynamical corrections to APT. We start with the simplest non-trivial example of two risky assets and one stochastic factor. This allows us to understand the main idea behind the general calculation with an arbitrary number of assets and factors.

Let us assume that the market consists of only two risky securities and one risk-free asset. The risk-free asset has a fixed rate of return r_0, and the rates of the risky assets are defined by the relation

$$R_i = \mu_i + \delta\mu_i + b_i\xi, \qquad i = 1, 2, \tag{10}$$

where ξ is the (slowly) fluctuating leading factor that defines the prices of the securities, μ_i is the corresponding long-time average return on the ith security, and $\delta\mu_i$ is the short-time fluctuation of the return around μ_i, which is independent of ξ and is assumed to be small. These last quantities $\delta\mu_i$ are responsible for the existence of virtual arbitrage opportunities.

Using (10), the correlation matrix of the returns R_i is calculated as

$$||C_{ij}|| = \begin{pmatrix} \langle(R_1 - \mu_1)(R_1 - \mu_1)\rangle & \langle(R_1 - \mu_1)(R_2 - \mu_2)\rangle \\ \langle(R_2 - \mu_2)(R_1 - \mu_1)\rangle & \langle(R_2 - \mu_2)(R_2 - \mu_2)\rangle \end{pmatrix}$$

$$= \begin{pmatrix} b_1b_1 + \epsilon_{11} & b_1b_2 + \epsilon_{12} \\ b_2b_1 + \epsilon_{21} & b_2b_2 + \epsilon_{22} \end{pmatrix},$$

with the notation $\langle\delta\mu_i\delta\mu_j\rangle = \epsilon_{ij}$. The parameters ϵ_{ij}, as we will soon see, define the characteristic arbitrage fluctuations. As shown in Section 3 of Chapter 5, to construct an action for the asset prices, we need, in fact, the inverse correlation matrix $||C^{-1}|| = ||\alpha||$. Since the fluctuations $\delta\mu_i$ are assumed to be small, we keep only the first non-trivial terms in the ϵ_{ij} expansion and get the inverse correlation matrix as

$$||\alpha_{ij}|| = Det^{-1}\begin{pmatrix} b_2b_2 + \epsilon_{22} & -b_1b_2 - \epsilon_{12} \\ -b_2b_1 - \epsilon_{21} & b_1b_1 + \epsilon_{11} \end{pmatrix}, \qquad Det \equiv \epsilon_{11}b_2b_2 + \epsilon_{22}b_1b_1 - 2\epsilon_{12}b_1b_2.$$

$$\tag{11}$$

---

[6]We postpone the review of empirical studies of arbitrage fluctuations until Section 2 of Chapter 9.

Now, having found the correlation matrix (11), we can write a local continuous-time quadratic action for the connection field taken from Section 3.2 of Chapter 5:

$$A_g = \int_{-\infty}^{\infty} d\tau \sum_{i,j=1}^{2} \frac{1}{2} \alpha_{ij} \left(\frac{S_i'}{S_i} + r_i - r_0 \right) \left(\frac{S_j'}{S_j} + r_j - r_0 \right).$$

It was shown there that this is the simplest choice of gauge action that accommodates the correlation between the assets. Identifying S_i'/S_i with R_i, and $r_0 - r_i$ with μ_i and using the matrix (11), we arrive at the following action:

$$A_g = \int_{-\infty}^{\infty} d\tau \, \frac{1}{2Det} \{ \epsilon_{22}(R_1 - \mu_1)^2 + \epsilon_{11}(R_2 - \mu_2)^2$$

$$- 2\epsilon_{12}(R_1 - \mu_1)(R_2 - \mu_2) + [b_1(R_2 - \mu_2) - b_2(R_1 - \mu_1)]^2 \}.$$

Taking into account the fact that the fluctuations $\delta\mu_i$ are assumed to be small and that we can therefore neglect[7] terms such as $\epsilon\delta\mu$, we cast the action into the form

$$A_g = \int_{-\infty}^{\infty} d\tau \frac{1}{2} \left(\xi^2 + \frac{(b_1 \delta\mu_2 - b_2 \, \delta\mu_1)^2}{Det} \right). \tag{12}$$

In this form, the action has a particular meaning: the first term describes the slowly fluctuating factor ξ, while the second gives the fluctuations of the arbitrage return. As ϵ goes to zero and Det diverges, the second term requires that

$$\delta\mu_i = b_i \delta\gamma, \qquad i = 1, 2, \tag{13}$$

with some parameter $\delta\gamma$. Equation (13), as we know from the previous section, is exactly the condition for the absence of arbitrage in this particular case. Thus *non-zero ϵ generates fluctuations bearing virtual arbitrage opportunities.* If one consider an equilibrium situation, and hence the absence of arbitrage,[8] the only expression for μ_i consistent with (13) is

$$\mu_i = a + b_i \gamma, \qquad i = 1, 2,$$

with some parameters a and γ. In this form, the last equation represents the main APT relation (7). The interpretation of $b_i\gamma$ as a risk premium leaves the parameter a equal to r_0.

Now let us introduce the arbitrageurs' money flows. To do this, we consider a continuous fibre bundle (see Section 4 of Chapter 5 for more details). The base has coordinates (t, x_1, x_2), where t is time and x_1 and x_2 are the fractions of the portfolio placed in securities 1 and 2. This implies that the remaining $1 - x_1 - x_2$ fraction is saved in the risk-free asset. We can use the same principles for construction of the money flow action as we did in Section 3 of Chapter 6, with one difference: we add an external potential

$$-\lambda \int dt \left(\sum_{i=1}^{2} x_i b_i \right)^2,$$

---

[7]In any calculation, these terms generate contributions that are small compared with ϵ.
[8]An arbitrage causes money flows and makes the consideration non-equilibrium.

which as $\lambda \to \infty$ reduces the set of configurations with non-zero weight to the risk-free portfolios only.[9] In our simple example, these configurations have 'space' coordinates obeying the condition

$$x_1 b_1 + x_2 b_2 = 0, \tag{14}$$

or, in terms of a new arbitrary real parameter k

$$x_1 = b_2 k, \qquad x_2 = -b_1 k. \tag{15}$$

At this point, the action for the money flows defines a one-dimensional gauge field theory with the line (15) as configuration space. This theory is still difficult to deal with analytically, although numerically it is quite tractable. We can, however, simplify the problem further if we assume that arbitrageurs always choose the portfolio with the largest possible value of $|k|$. This corresponds to the situation where the decision to buy an arbitrage portfolio leads to the purchase of the maximal possible amount of the portfolio and the corresponding borrowing of money for this purchase. Since any real borrowing is finite, this leaves us with only two possible arbitrage portfolios, $(b_2 k_0, -b_1 k_0)$ and $(-b_2 k_0, b_1 k_0)$, which are characterized by a finite positive number k_0. This approximation reduces the line in configuration space to just two points, thus returning us to the lattice field theory on a ladder already studied in Chapters 6 and 7.

We saw in Section 4 of Chapter 5 that in the case of a continuous fibre bundle, it is convenient to fix the gauge such that the price of basis portfolios in each point of the base is equal to one and the corresponding components of the connection at the point $(t, \{x_i\}_{i=1}^2)$ have the form

$$A_0 = \left(1 - \sum_{i=1}^{2} x_i\right) r_0 + \sum_{i=1}^{2} x_i \left(r_0 - \mu_i + \frac{d \log S_i(t)}{dt}\right), \qquad A_1 = A_2 = 0.$$

In this gauge, the single-investor transition matrix[10] for the time step Δ has the form

$$P(t_i, t_{i-1}) = \begin{pmatrix} e^{\tilde{\beta} r_0 \Delta - \tilde{\beta} \sum_1^2 x_i (R_i - \mu_i) \Delta} & 1 \\ 1 & e^{\tilde{\beta} r_0 \Delta + \tilde{\beta} \sum_1^2 x_i (R_i - \mu_i) \Delta} \end{pmatrix},$$

which is taken directly from equation (10) of Chapter 6 and the two-point approximation for the configuration space. Taking into account that the fractions x_1 and x_2 have to obey (14) and (15), we can rewrite the transition matrix as

$$P(t_i, t_{i-1}) = \begin{pmatrix} e^{\tilde{\beta} r_0 \Delta - k_0 \tilde{\beta} (b_2 \delta \mu_1 - b_1 \delta \mu_2) \Delta} & 1 \\ 1 & e^{\tilde{\beta} r_0 \Delta + k_0 \tilde{\beta} (b_2 \delta \mu_1 - b_1 \delta \mu_2) \Delta} \end{pmatrix}.$$

After normalization and neglecting the interest rate r_0, this matrix is transformed to a form that is already familiar to the reader:

$$P(t_i, t_{i-1}) = \frac{1}{2 \cosh[k_0 \tilde{\beta} (b_2 \delta \mu_1 - b_1 \delta \mu_2) \Delta / 2]} \begin{pmatrix} e^{-k_0 \tilde{\beta} (b_2 \delta \mu_1 - b_1 \delta \mu_2) \Delta / 2} & e^{-k_0 \tilde{\beta} (b_2 \delta \mu_1 - b_1 \delta \mu_2) \Delta / 2} \\ e^{k_0 \tilde{\beta} (b_2 \delta \mu_1 - b_1 \delta \mu_2) \Delta / 2} & e^{k_0 \tilde{\beta} (b_2 \delta \mu_1 - b_1 \delta \mu_2) \Delta / 2} \end{pmatrix}.$$

This matrix has the same form as the transition matrix in equation (25) of Chapter 6, which allows us to use the results of Chapter 6. In particular, we know that the introduction of

---

[9]See Section 4.2 of Chapter 6 for a discussion of risk factors as an external potential.
[10]In the absence of transaction costs and bid–ask spread.

money flows leads to the appearance of the mean reversion for returns and an exponentially decaying correlation function with characteristic lifetime λ. This means that to the first non-trivial order, the gauge model with money flows is equivalent to the much simpler model where the arbitrage return $\mathcal{R}$ on the portfolio $(1 + b_1 - b_2, b_2, -b_1)$ follows the Ornstein–Uhlenbeck process:

$$\frac{d\mathcal{R}}{dt} + \lambda\mathcal{R} = v(t), \qquad \langle v(t)\rangle_v = 0, \qquad \langle v(t)v(t')\rangle_v = \Sigma^2\delta(t - t'). \tag{16}$$

with the parameter Σ^2 equal to Det. This is the model that we will study in detail in the following sections.

It is not difficult to generalize the above calculations to the case of many assets and leading parameters. For example, in the case of three risky assets and a single parameter, the expression (12) will be replaced by

$$A_g = \int_{-\infty}^{\infty} d\tau \frac{1}{2}\{\xi^2 + [\epsilon_{33}(b_1\delta\mu_2 - b_2\delta\mu_1)^2$$

$$+ \epsilon_{22}(b_1\delta\mu_3 - b_3\delta\mu_1)^2 + \epsilon_{11}(b_3\delta\mu_2 - b_2\delta\mu_3)^2]/Det\}. \tag{17}$$

where Det, as before, is the determinant of the correlation matrix $||C_{ij}||$, which in this case is proportional to ϵ^2. If the number of factors is equal to 2 then the corresponding action will take the form

$$A_g = \int_{-\infty}^{\infty} d\tau \frac{1}{2}\left(\xi_1^2 + \xi_2^2 + \frac{(x_1\delta\mu_1 + x_2\delta\mu_2 + x_3\mu_3)^2}{Det}\right). \tag{18}$$

where

$$x_1 = \beta_{21}\beta_{32} - \beta_{31}\beta_{22}, \qquad x_2 = \beta_{32}\beta_{11} - \beta_{12}\beta_{31}, \qquad x_1 = \beta_{22}\beta_{11} - \beta_{21}\beta_{12},$$

which are, in fact, solutions of the system for the riskless portfolios:

$$\beta_{11}x_1 + \beta_{21}x_2 + \beta_{31}x_3 = 0$$
$$\beta_{12}x_1 + \beta_{22}x_2 + \beta_{32}x_3 = 0.$$

The reader can now guess the generalization of (12), (17), and (18) to the case of arbitrary numbers of assets and factors. It has the form

$$A_g = \int_{-\infty}^{\infty} d\tau \frac{1}{2}\left[\sum_{j=1}^{M}\xi_j^2 + \sum_{sym}\alpha_i(\epsilon)\left(\sum_{k=1}^{N}\eta_{i,k}\delta\mu_k\right)^2\bigg/Det\right]. \tag{19}$$

where $\sum_{sym}$ is the sum symmetrized with respect to all indices, $\eta_{i,k}$ is the kth component of the ith basis vector in the subspace of riskless portfolios, and $\alpha_i(\epsilon)$ are some functions of ϵ. To derive (19), one needs to use a basis in the space of riskless portfolios, which is discussed in Section 4.1. The action for money flows can be constructed in the same way as was shown above, but in general one has to deal with continuous field theory rather than with lattice theory. However the main important point – the exponential decay of the mispricing correlations – is probably still valid. This allows us to use the same simplified model (16). Concluding this section, we have to admit that generally the gauge models for asset pricing are too complicated to be treated analytically, and the best way forward is the application of numerical algorithms developed in field theory.

3 EFFECTIVE EQUATION FOR A RISKLESS PORTFOLIO IN THE PRESENCE OF VIRTUAL ARBITRAGE

In the previous section we, ended up with a simple model that generalized APT and took into account the existence of virtual arbitrage. Let us look more closely at the influence of arbitrage fluctuations on the return of a riskless portfolio. Under the no-arbitrage assumption, the rate of return on a riskless portfolio consisting of a mixture of risky and risk-free assets should be equal to the single riskless rate of return,[11] which is equal to, for example, the return on government bonds. However, if we allow the existence of virtual arbitrage opportunities, the rate of return on the portfolio does not have to be equal to the rate of return on government bonds. It is unpredictable (and thus is modelled as random), and might depend on the portfolio composition. To give an intuitive example, we can imagine that if some market sector is more attractive for investors than others, then the speculative trades and resulting arbitrage fluctuations involving securities from this sector will occur more often. This will result in more arbitrage opportunities for portfolios containing the assets of the sector and the corresponding composition dependence. On the other hand, the portfolio consisting of the only riskless asset does not bear any arbitrage opportunities at all. These examples show that the random process for the arbitrage return has to be considered as portfolio-dependent, i.e. the statistical characteristics of the process have to be functions of the portfolio composition.

Consider the riskless portfolio Π created by $N+1$ assets with fractions $\{x_i\}_{i=0}^{N}$. In the case of no arbitrage, the price of the portfolio Π would satisfy the following equation:

$$\frac{d\Pi}{dt} - r_0\Pi = 0, \qquad \Pi(0) = 1, \tag{20}$$

where r_0 is the riskless interest rate. However, in the case of virtual arbitrage, the right-hand side of (20) will be changed to

$$\mathcal{R}(t, \Pi)\Pi,$$

where $\mathcal{R}(t, \Pi)$ represents the virtual arbitrage return. We are now going to discuss a general phenomenological expression for $\mathcal{R}(t, \Pi)$ and its correspondence to the model of the last section. To find an expression for $\mathcal{R}(t, \Pi)$, let us imagine that at some moment of time $\tau < t$, a fluctuation of the return (an arbitrage opportunity) appeared in the market. We then denote this instantaneous arbitrage return as $v(\tau, \Pi)$. Arbitrageurs would react to this circumstance and act in such a way that the arbitrage gradually disappears and the market returns to its equilibrium state, i.e. the absence of arbitrage. We postpone further discussion of the arbitrage mechanisms until Section 2 of the next chapter, where we will examine how empirical studies support this general scenario. What is important for us at the moment is that virtual arbitrage exists in real markets; it is eliminated by the market, but this process takes some time.

The time evolution of the arbitrage return allows a description by the differential equation

$$\frac{d\mathcal{R}}{dt} = F(\mathcal{R}), \qquad \mathcal{R}(\tau) = v(\tau, \Pi). \tag{21}$$

---

[11]Under the condition of an ideal capital market.

The general function of the market reaction $F(\mathcal{R})$ can be expanded as

$$F(\mathcal{R}) = -\lambda \mathcal{R} - \lambda_2 \mathcal{R}^2 - \lambda_3 \mathcal{R}^3 - \cdots \qquad (22)$$

If one neglects the influence of short selling restrictions, the market reaction on the arbitrage is antisymmetric with respect to the sign of $\mathcal{R}$. This leaves only odd terms in the expansion (22):

$$F(\mathcal{R}) = -\lambda \mathcal{R} - \lambda_3 \mathcal{R}^3 - \lambda_5 \mathcal{R}^5 - \cdots . \qquad (23)$$

Taking into account the fact that a typical arbitrage return is of the order of percent, one can safely neglect higher-order terms in the expansion (23), which reduces (21) to the form

$$\frac{d\mathcal{R}}{dt} = -\lambda \mathcal{R}, \qquad \mathcal{R}(\tau) = v(\tau, \Pi). \qquad (24)$$

Looking at (24), the reader will surely recognize it as the model for the arbitrage return derived in the previous section, starting with the gauge model. The parameter λ in (24) characterizes the market reaction, and is equal to the half-life of arbitrage fluctuations. It can be taken from the microscopic theory of Section 2 and expressed in terms of parameters characterizing the money flows. Alternatively, this parameter (which can be considered as the speed of adjustment) can be estimated from the market data as described in Section 5 of Chapter 7 or as

$$\lambda = -\frac{1}{t - t'} \log \left(\frac{\langle (r_\Pi - r_0)(t)(r_\Pi - r_0)(t') \rangle_{\text{market}}}{\langle (r_\Pi - r_0)^2(t) \rangle_{\text{market}}} \right), \quad t > t', \qquad (25)$$

and may well be a function of time, portfolio composition, and even prices of assets. In what follows, however, we consider λ as a constant, to get simple analytical formulae for the APT corrections. The generalization to the case of time-dependent parameters is straightforward.

The solution of (24) gives us $\mathcal{R}(t, \Pi) = v(\tau, \Pi)e^{-\lambda(t-\tau)}$, which, after summing over all possible fluctuations, leads to the following expression for the arbitrage return:

$$\mathcal{R}(t, \Pi) \equiv \int_{-\infty}^{t} e^{-\lambda(t-\tau)} v(\tau, \Pi) \, d\tau. \qquad (26)$$

Following Section 2, we specify the stochastic process $v(t, \Pi)$ as white noise with a variance $\Sigma^2(\Pi)$ that, as discussed earlier, depends on the structure of the portfolio Π:

$$\langle v(t, \Pi) \rangle_v = 0, \qquad \langle v(t, \Pi)v(t', \Pi) \rangle_v = \Sigma^2(\Pi)\delta(t - t'). \qquad (27)$$

Here again, the parameter $\Sigma^2(\Pi)$ can be expressed in terms of the underlying microscopic theory or taken from the market as

$$\Sigma^2(\Pi)/2\lambda = \langle (r_\Pi - r_0)^2 \rangle_{\text{market}}. \qquad (28)$$

To simplify the consideration, we assume here that the quantity does not depend on time, but this limitation may be overcome, in a straightforwardly manner.

Since we have introduced the arbitrage return $\mathcal{R}(t, \Pi)$, (2) has to be replaced by the following equation:

$$\frac{d\Pi}{dt} - r_0\Pi = \mathcal{R}(t, \Pi)\Pi. \qquad (29)$$

Our next step is to find an expression for the time dependence of the average price of the portfolio. To find the average price as a function of time, we use a method that is not optimal for the simple equation (29), but can be directly generalized to more complicated cases and, in particular, will be used in Chapter 9 to deal with the virtual arbitrage corrections to the Black–Scholes equation.

First of all, we rewrite (29) in the integral form

$$\Pi = \int_{-\infty}^{t} G(t, t')\mathcal{R}(t', \Pi)\Pi(t')\,dt', \tag{30}$$

where $G(t, t') = \Theta(t - t')e^{r_0(t-t')}$ is the Green function of the problem:

$$\left(\frac{d}{dt} - r_0\right)G(t, t') = \delta(t - t'), \qquad G(t, t')|_{t<t'} = 0.$$

We then iterate (29) and substitute (30) into the right-hand side of (29), which gives

$$\frac{d\Pi}{dt} - r_0\Pi = \mathcal{R}(t, \Pi)\int_{-\infty}^{t} G(t, t')\mathcal{R}(t', \Pi)\Pi(t')\,dt'. \tag{31}$$

Our next step is to average (31) over virtual arbitrage fluctuations and to obtain the effective pricing equation for the average price $\bar{\Pi}$. To first order in Σ^2/λ, it can be written as

$$\frac{d\bar{\Pi}}{dt} - r_0\bar{\Pi} = \int_{-\infty}^{t} G(t, t')K(t, t', \bar{\Pi})\bar{\Pi}(t')\,dt', \tag{32}$$

where the kernel

$$K(t, t', \bar{\Pi}) = \langle\mathcal{R}(t, \Pi)\mathcal{R}(t', \Pi)\rangle_v$$

is given by the expression (Ilinski and Stepanento,1999):

$$K(t, t') = \frac{\Sigma^2(\bar{\Pi})}{2\lambda}\theta(t - t')e^{-\lambda(t-t')} + \frac{\Sigma^2(\bar{\Pi})}{2\lambda}\theta(t' - t)e^{-\lambda(t'-t)}, \tag{33}$$

which can be easily obtained from (27). Collecting everything together, (32) and (33) are used in place of (20) in situations where virtual arbitrage opportunities exist.

To solve (32), we first note that its right-hand side is equal to

$$\int_{-\infty}^{t} G(t, t')K(t, t', \bar{\Pi})\bar{\Pi}(t')\,dt' = \int_{-\infty}^{t} e^{-\lambda(t-t')}e^{r_0(t-t')}\frac{\Sigma^2(\bar{\Pi})}{2\lambda}\bar{\Pi}(t')\,dt'.$$

We now make the approximation $\bar{\Pi}(t') = e^{r_0 t'}$, since the correction to this expression is of order $\Sigma^2(\bar{\Pi})/2\lambda$ and is irrelevant for our consideration of the right-hand side of (72) because is was derived within this order of accuracy. The approximation results in the following relation:

$$\int_{-\infty}^{t} G(t, t')K(t, t', \bar{\Pi})\bar{\Pi}(t')\,dt' = \frac{\Sigma^2(\bar{\Pi})}{2\lambda^2}e^{r_0 t}.$$

If we substitute this into (32), we obtain the approximate differential equation for the average portfolio price:

$$\frac{d\bar{\Pi}}{dt} - r_0\bar{\Pi} = \frac{\Sigma^2(\bar{\Pi})}{2\lambda^2}e^{r_0 t}, \tag{34}$$

which has the solution

$$\bar{\Pi}(t) \approx \left(1 + \frac{\Sigma^2(\bar{\Pi})}{2\lambda^2}t\right)e^{r_0 t},$$

or, to the same measure of accuracy,[12]

$$\bar{\Pi}(t) \approx e^{[r_0 + \Sigma^2(\bar{\Pi})/2\lambda^2])t}. \tag{35}$$

We use the latter expression in the next section in place of the no-arbitrage expression $\Pi(t) = e^{r_0 t}$ in APT.

Let us emphasize that we, as well as investors, are interested in the average value of the portfolio and the corresponding rate of return on the average portfolio rather than in the average rate of return on the riskless portfolio, which is exactly equal to r_0 and, in fact, is not influenced by the arbitrage. Indeed, the only valuable and material thing for an investor is the average value of her investment. She is no way interested in a mathematical quantity that is not actually connected with her wealth. At the same time, any empirical research on an interday scale deals with prices that are effectively averaged over the arbitrage noise. This means that the empirical returns are also calculated from the averaged growth factors rather than from an instantaneous return averaged over the fluctuations. The difference between the two returns is the first effect that is due solely to the presence of the virtual arbitrage.

4   CORRECTIONS TO APT

To generalize the APT relations to the case of virtual arbitrage, we have to use the derived time dependence of a riskless portfolio price in the presence of virtual arbitrage instead of having it growing with the riskless rate of return r_0 as it is done in APT. But first we define the rates of the return $\{\bar{r}'_k\}_{k=0}^N$ on the kth component of an average riskless portfolio:

$$\bar{\Pi}(t) = e^{\Sigma_i \bar{r}'_i x_i t}.$$

These are the quantities that we have to substitute for the rates of return in the APT relations. To find an expression for $\{\bar{r}'_k\}_{k=0}^N$, we return to Equation (6) of APT,

$$\sum_i \bar{r}_i x_i = r_0,$$

and replace the risk-free rate of return r_0 by the return on the riskless portfolio derived in the previous section, i.e. by $r_0 + \Sigma^2(\bar{\Pi})/2\lambda^2$, as follows from (35). This gives us an equation for $\bar{r}'_i$:

$$\sum_i \bar{r}'_i y_i = \frac{\Sigma^2(\bar{\Pi})}{2\lambda^2}, \qquad x_i = y_i + \delta_{0i}, \tag{36}$$

---

[12]There is a more straightforward way of obtaining the same expression (35) directly from (29). Indeed, it follows from (29) that

$$\bar{\Pi}(t) = e^{r_0 t} \langle e^{r_0 \int_0^t R(\tau, \Pi) d\tau} \rangle_{\mathcal{R}}.$$

Evaluating the average on the right-hand side for the Gaussian noise $\mathcal{R}$ with the correlation function (33) returns us to the expression (35).

subject to the constraints

$$\sum_i y_i b_{ij} = 0 \quad \forall j, \qquad \sum_i y_i = 0. \tag{37}$$

4.1   Basis in the Space of Riskless Portfolios

To simplify the following consideration, we introduce a convenient basis in the portfolio space such that the above constraints will take the form

$$\eta_i = 0, \qquad 0 \le i \le M,$$

in this new basis while $\{\eta_j\}_{j=M+1}^{N}$ will be the coordinates in the subspace of risk-free portfolios. To this end, we first introduce vectors $\{e'_i\}_{i=0}^{M}$:

$$e'_{0,i} = 1 \quad \forall i, \qquad e'_{i,j} = b_{ij} \quad \forall i, \qquad 1 \le j \le M.$$

These $M + 1$ vectors are linearly independent (otherwise there would be linear dependence for the factors, and the $M + 1$ constraints (37) would not be independent). The remaining $N - M$ linearly independent vectors $\{e'_i\}_{i=M+1}^{N}$ can be chosen to be arbitrary but linearly independent of $\{e'_i\}_{i=0}^{M}$. For example, if

$$b_{ij} \ne 0, \qquad 0 \le j \le N + 1 \quad \text{and} \quad 0 < i < M + 1$$

then one possible choice could be

$$e'_{i,j} = \delta_{ij} \quad \forall j, \qquad M + 1 \le i \le N + 1.$$

The next step is the Gram–Schmidt orthogonalization and normalization of the vector set $\{e'_i\}_{i=0}^{N}$, which gives us the basis set $\{e_i\}_{i=0}^{N}$. We shall start the orthogonalization with the vector e'_0:

$$e_0 = \frac{e'_0}{\sqrt{(e'_0, e'_0)}},$$

proceed with the vector e'_1 as

$$e_1 = \frac{e'_1 - (e'_1, e_0)e_0}{\sqrt{(e'_1 - (e'_1, e_0)e_0, \, e'_1 - (e'_1, e_0)e_0)}},$$

and carry on following the standard procedure:

$$e_j = \left(e'_j - \sum_{k=0}^{j-1} (e'_j, e_k)e_k \right) \bigg/ \left((e'_j, e'_j) - \sum_{k=0}^{j-1} (e'_j, e_k)^2 \right)^{1/2}.$$

It is now easy to check that in this new basis $\{e_i\}_{i=0}^{N}$, the constraints (37) can be represented as a zero projection along the first $M + 1$ basis vectors, i.e. as

$$\eta_i = 0, \qquad 0 \le M,$$

where η_i are coordinates in the new basis. Indeed, for any vector $\mathbf{y}$, the conditions

$$(\mathbf{y}, e'_j) = 0, \qquad 0 \le j \le M,$$

are exactly equivalent to the constraints (37). This also remains true after the orthogonalization,

$$(\mathbf{y}, \mathbf{e}_j) = 0, \qquad 0 \le M,$$

owing to the step-by-step nature of the procedure. Therefore any vector

$$\mathbf{y} = \sum_{j=M+1}^{N} \eta_j \mathbf{e}_j$$

represents a risk-free portfolio, and the set $\{\mathbf{e}_j\}_{j=M+1}^{N}$ is a basis in the subspace of riskless portfolios.

To express the riskless portfolios basis in terms of the original assets, we introduce the rotation matrix $U = ||U_{ik}||$:

$$U = (\mathbf{e}_0, \mathbf{e}_1, ..., \mathbf{e}_N) = \begin{pmatrix} e_{0,0} & e_{1,0} & e_{2,0} & \cdots & e_{N,0} \\ e_{0,1} & e_{1,1} & e_{2,1} & \cdots & e_{N,1} \\ \vdots & \vdots & \vdots & & \vdots \\ e_{0,N} & e_{1,N} & e_{2,N} & \cdots & e_{N,N} \end{pmatrix}. \tag{38}$$

To construct the portfolio represented by the basis vector $\mathbf{e}_j$, one just has to collect jth assets ($j = 0, \ldots, N+1$) with the fractions $e_{i,j} + \delta_{0j}$.

We are now ready to discuss the possible form of $\Sigma^2(\bar{\Pi})$ as a function of the portfolio structure, i.e. as a function of $\{y_i\}_{i=0}^{N}$ or $\{\eta_i\}_{i=M+1}^{N}$. First of all, we will not allow the existence of arbitrage fluctuations for a portfolio that consists of pure bonds, i.e. when all η_i are equal to zero. This ensures that the rate of return on government bonds is actually equal to r_0 and does not have any arbitrage corrections and that our use of r_0 is self-consistent. It means that the series expansion of $\Sigma^2(\eta)$ cannot contain a constant term. Secondly, since the virtual arbitrage return is brought in by the portfolio η, the arbitrage return on the portfolio $-\eta$ has to be equal to minus the latter, and therefore $\Sigma^2(\eta) = \Sigma^2(-\eta)$. This results in the absence of all odd terms in the expansion. Thus the series expansion of $\Sigma^2(\bar{\Pi})$ has the form

$$\Sigma^2(\bar{\Pi}) = \sum_{i,j=M+1}^{N} \Sigma^2_{ij} \eta_i \eta_j + \cdots,$$

or, equivalently,

$$\Sigma^2(\bar{\Pi}) = \sum_{i,j=0}^{N} \Sigma^2_{ij} \eta_i \eta_j + \cdots, \qquad \Sigma^2_{i\ldots k} = 0 \quad \text{for } 0 \le i, \ldots, k \le M.$$

In what follows, we keep only the first non-trivial term,[13] $(\eta, \Sigma^2 \eta)$, $\Sigma^2 \equiv ||\Sigma^2_{ik}||$, in the expansion, although the final result will be valid for the general case too.

Returning to the pricing equation (36), we substitute $\mathbf{y} = U\eta$, $\Sigma^2(\bar{\Pi}) = (\eta, \Sigma^2 \eta)$ and $\sum_i \bar{r}_i y_i = (\mathbf{r}, \mathbf{y})$, which gives us the pricing equation for $\mathbf{r}$:

$$(\bar{\mathbf{r}}, U\eta) = (\eta, \Sigma^2 \eta),$$

---

[13] In agreement with our simple gauge model of Section 2.

subject to the constraints

$$\eta_i = 0, \quad 0 \le j \le M.$$

The solution of the problem can be represented as

$$\bar{r}_i = \alpha + \sum_j b_{ij}\gamma_j + \sum_{i,k,l=0}^{N} U_{ik} \frac{\Sigma_{kl}^2}{2\lambda^2} \eta_l. \tag{39}$$

At this point, we face an unpleasant problem: a return on an asset in the portfolio depends on the structure of the portfolio. This is the second effect that stems from the presence of virtual arbitrage. However unpleasant it is, it is hardly surprising, since it was derived under the assumption of a virtual arbitrage that is portfolio-dependent. Intuitively, it is also clear: if an asset constitutes part of a 'hot' arbitrage portfolio then its rate of return will be different from assets in ('quiet') portfolios *ceteris paribus*.

To find the average growth factor for the ith asset, we have to take the sum of $e^{\bar{r}_i(\Pi)}$ weighted with the probabilities of appearance of the portfolio Π, i.e. to calculate the average value

$$\langle e^{\bar{r}_i'(\Pi)} \rangle_\Pi \equiv e^{\bar{r}_i},$$

which defines the rate of growth $\bar{r}_i$ of the average growth factor. This $\bar{r}_i$ is a counterpart of the average rate of return in the presence of virtual arbitrage, since it characterizes how rapidly the ith asset grows on average. It is easy to check that to the first non-trivial order,

$$e^{\bar{r}_i} = e^{\alpha + \sum_j b_{ij}\gamma_j} \left(1 + \sum_{k,m,l,l'=0}^{N} U_{ik} U_{im} \frac{\Sigma_{kl}^2 \Sigma_{ml'}^2}{8\lambda^4} \langle \eta_l \eta_{l'} \rangle_\Pi \right),$$

and hence, with the same measure of accuracy, the rate of growth is given by

$$\bar{r}_i = \alpha + \sum_j b_{ij}\gamma_j + \sum_{k,m,l,l'=0}^{N} U_{ik} U_{im} \frac{\Sigma_{kl}^2 \Sigma_{ml'}^2}{8\lambda^4} \langle \eta_l \eta_{l'} \rangle_\Pi. \tag{40}$$

Since the 0th asset was chosen as risk-free, the coefficients $\beta_{0j} = 0$ for all j, and so

$$\bar{r}_i = r_0 + \sum_j b_{ij}\gamma_j + \sum_{k,m,l,l'=0}^{N} U_{ik} U_{im} \frac{\Sigma_{kl}^2 \Sigma_{ml'}^2}{8\lambda^4} \langle \eta_l \eta_{l'} \rangle_\Pi - \sum_{k,m,l,l'=0}^{N} U_{0k} U_{0m} \frac{\Sigma_{kl}^2 \Sigma_{ml'}^2}{8\lambda^4} \langle \eta_l \eta_{l'} \rangle_\Pi. \tag{41}$$

This last equation looks quite complicated. It can be presented in a more compact form using matrix notation and the following matrix Δ:

$$\Delta_{ik} = \frac{1}{4\lambda^2} \left\langle \int_0^1 dz \int_0^1 dz' \left. \frac{\partial \Sigma^2(\eta)}{\partial \eta_i} \right|_{\eta=z\eta} \left. \frac{\partial \Sigma^2(\eta)}{\partial \eta_k} \right|_{\eta=z'\eta} \right\rangle_\Pi.$$

The pricing relations can then be rewritten as

$$\bar{r}_i = r_0 + \sum_j b_{ij}\gamma_j + \frac{1}{2\lambda^2}(U\Delta U^{-1})_{ii} - \frac{1}{2\lambda^2}(U\Delta U^{-1})_{00}. \tag{42}$$

In this form, the relation is valid for a general function $\Sigma^2(\eta)$. Equations (41) and (42) give a generalization of the APT relations in the case where virtual arbitrage opportunities exist. It is not difficult to check that the corrections are proportional to the square of the product of the variance of the arbitrage fluctuations and the square of a characteristic lifetime of the arbitrage. This results in the reduction of (41) and (42) to the APT expression (7) in the case of infinitely fast market reaction ($\lambda \rightarrow \infty$) or the absence of arbitrage ($\Sigma \rightarrow 0$).

5   CORRECTIONS TO CAPM

In this short section, we concentrate on a particular case of APT with only one leading parameter, which will be chosen to be a random part of the return on the market portfolio $\xi \equiv (r_m - \bar{r}_m)/\sigma_m$. As we have seen in Section 1, in this case, the standard APT relations are reduced to the CAPM equation. In this case (42) can be rewritten as

$$\bar{r}_i = r_0 + b_i \gamma + \frac{1}{2\lambda^2}(U\Delta U^{-1})_{ii} - \frac{1}{2\lambda^2}(U\Delta U^{-1})_{00}, \tag{43}$$

where $b_i = \langle r_i - \bar{r}_i, r_m - \bar{r}_m \rangle / \sigma_m$. The next step is to introduce the market portfolio fractions θ_i and find an expression for the average rate of return on the market portfolio $\sum_i \theta_i \bar{r}_i$ using (43):

$$\bar{r}_m = r_0 + \sum_i \theta_i b_i \gamma + \frac{1}{2\lambda^2} u^m - \frac{1}{2\lambda^2}(U\Delta U^{-1})_{00}$$

where we introduce the notation $u^m = \sum_i (U\Delta U^{-1})_{ii}\theta_i$. This allows us to define a value of the variable

$$\gamma = \frac{1}{\sigma_m}\left(\bar{r}_m - r_0 + \frac{1}{2\lambda^2}(U\Delta U^{-1})_{00} - \frac{1}{2\lambda^2}u^m\right),$$

and to find a final expression for the CAPM generalized to the virtual arbitrage assumption:

$$\bar{r}_i = r_0 + \beta_i(\bar{r}_m - r_0) + \frac{\beta_i}{2\lambda^2}[(U\Delta U^{-1})_{00} - u^m] + \frac{(U\Delta U^{-1})_{ii}}{2\lambda^2} - \frac{(U\Delta U^{-1})_{00}}{2\lambda^2}, \tag{44}$$

with the standard definition $\beta_i = \langle r_i - \bar{r}_i, r_m - \bar{r}_m \rangle / \sigma_m^2$. The first two terms represent the CAPM under the no-arbitrage assumption and the remaining terms are the virtual arbitrage corrections. Everything stated in the last paragraph of the previous section for APT remains true for the virtual arbitrage generalization of the CAPM, (44).

From (44), one can conclude that the the virtual arbitrage corrections effectively generate a non-zero intercept a_i in (4) for the CAPM. Moreover, in contrast to the Zero-Beta CAPM, these corrections are non-linear functions of betas, $\{\beta_i\}_{i=1}^N$, since, by construction, the basis vectors $\{\mathbf{e}_i\}_{i=1}^N$ and the matrix elements U_{ik} are β-dependent. Figure 8.2 shows the linear and quadratic fitting curves drawn for empirical intercepts. One can see that the data suggest a non-linear dependence. A non-zero quadratic term was also found by Fama and MacBeth (1974), but was believed to be insignificant on average.

To take one further step, we assume the diagonal approximation for the matrix Δ:

$$\Delta_{ij} = \Delta \delta_{ij} \quad for \quad 1 \leq i \leq N+1, \quad \text{and zero otherwise.}$$

In this case the matrix elements $(U\Delta U^{-1})_{ii}$ can be written as

$$(U\Delta U^{-1})_{ii} = \Delta \sum_{k=2}^{N} e_{k,i}^2.$$

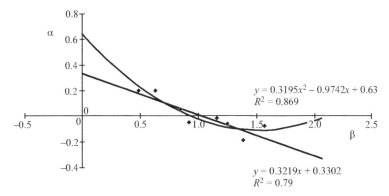

Figure 8.2 Intercept a as a function of β. The data are taken from Black et al (1972), who analyzed monthly rates of return 1926–1966. The solid line is the best-fit linear function $y \approx 0.32(1 - x)$. The dashed line is the best-fit quadratic polynomial.

The sum on the right-hand side of this equation represents contributions to the arbitrage correction for the ith security from the basis arbitrage portfolios. This allows us to write (44) in the form

$$\bar{r}_i = r_0 + \beta_i(\bar{r}_m - r_0) + \frac{\beta_i \Delta}{2\lambda^2}\left(\sum_{k=2}^{N} e_{k,0}^2 - \sum_{i=1}^{N}\sum_{k=2}^{N}\theta_i e_{k,i}^2\right) + \frac{\Delta}{2\lambda^2}\sum_{k=2}^{N}\left(e_{k,i}^2 - e_{k,0}^2\right).$$

It is possible to check that for close betas, $e_{k,0}^2$ and $e_{k,i}^2 - \sum_{j=1}^{N}\theta_i e_{k,j}^2$ are small,[14] so that the last equation is approximately

$$\bar{r}_i \simeq r_0 + \beta_i(\bar{r}_m - r_0) + \frac{\Delta}{2\lambda^2}(1 - \beta_i)\sum_{k=2}^{N} e_{k,i}^2,$$

which shows that the intercept changes sign at $\beta_i = 1$ and becomes negative for $\beta > 1$, in agreement with Fig. 8.2. It also demonstrates that, owing to the presence of the term $\sum_{k=2}^{N} e_{k,i}^2$, which is β-dependent, the intercept is a non-linear function of β, and can be approximated by a linear function only in the vicinity of $\beta = 1$. This distinguishes the intercept originating from virtual arbitrage from the intercept derived in the Zero-Beta CAPM, which predicts a linear dependence of the intercept on $1 - \beta_i$.

Summarizing, one can argue that the non-zero intercepts observed in empirical tests of the equilibrium CAPM can be at least partially explained by the non-equilibrium dynamics of the market. The fact that typical empirical intercepts are small supports the hypothesis of small market fluctuations around an equilibrium, and justifies our previous approximations.

6 DISCUSSION

In conclusion, we have introduced virtual arbitrage opportunities in the framework of Arbitrage Pricing Theory, and have derived corrections to the APT pricing relations. These

---

[14] And vanish identically for equal betas.

corrections disappear as $\Sigma \rightarrow 0$ or $\lambda \rightarrow \infty$, i.e. when there are no arbitrage fluctuations or the speed of market reaction to the mispricing is infinite (which corresponds to extremely liquid markets).

In the course of the analysis, we faced two major problems specific to the presence of arbitrage. The first is the necessity to analyse growth factors rather than the corresponding rates of return. The second effect is the dependence of the growth factor of an asset on the structure of riskless portfolios that include the asset. This forced us to introduce an average over all riskless portfolios, and reduced the problem to the calculation of the matrix Δ:

$$\Delta_{ik} = \frac{1}{4\lambda^2} \left\langle \int_0^1 dz \int_0^1 dz' \left. \frac{\partial \Sigma^2(\eta)}{\partial \eta_i} \right|_{\eta=z\eta} \left. \frac{\partial \Sigma^2(\eta)}{\partial \eta_k} \right|_{\eta=z'\eta} \right\rangle_\Pi, \tag{45}$$

which is an essentially new element. We have already mentioned that $\Sigma^2(\Pi)$ can be obtained from the market using (28). This means that Δ, in principle, can also be obtained from arbitrage portfolios presented in the market following (45). One of the possible numerical procedures to detect arbitrage portfolios was suggested by Garman (1976). However, the most economical procedure for the evaluation still has to be worked out. It might, for example, be reasonable to consider only the most frequent arbitrages and reduce the space of the relevant riskless portfolios. Another option is to study the main factors generating arbitrage opportunities and carry out a factor analysis similar to the original APT. For the moment, we leave this as an open question that requires further investigation.

As mentioned above, the estimation of the model parameters can be a very complicated task, since one has to identify virtual arbitrage portfolios in the market. It might be hard to distinguish a deviation from APT that is an arbitrage from deviations that are not. One can argue, however, that, from a practical point of view, it almost does not matter: the parameters estimated from the market will reflect both effects, thus playing the role that implied volatilities play in derivative pricing. The model with adjustment parameters is bound to do at least as well as the model without them, because in the worst-case scenario these parameters will be put equal to zero.

The model might seem to be inconsistent because the time dynamics of the arbitrage return are introduced into a fundamentally static two-period APT relationship. The inconsistency is, however, only apparent. The arbitrage dynamics and dynamics of leading factors operate on very different time scales. If the arbitrage is important for intraday trading and, to a certain extent, for interday trading, the characteristic time of changes in fundamental factors is of the order of months or even years. This means that, on a day time scale, the leading factors are constant and therefore one can use a two-period model to describe their dynamics. Let us now discuss some obvious drawbacks of the model and ways to improve it.

First of all, we have to admit immediately that it would be more difficult to carry out empirical tests of Virtual Arbitrage Pricing Theory than of APT, because the additional terms in (41) do not in any way make life easier, while even empirics for the CAPM and APT (see Black et al, 1972; Fama and MacBeth, 1974; Roll and Ross, 1980, 1984; Chen, 1983; Lakonishok and Shapiro, 1986; Chen et al, 1986; Chan and Chen, 1988; Lehmann and Modest, 1988; Fama and French 1992; Shanken, 1992; Clare and Thomas, 1994; Campbell et al, 1997, Chapters 5 and 6) have not yet produced any decisive result. Furthermore, all critical comments on APT analysis can be extended to the presented model, except for the no-arbitrage constraint. Homogeneous expectations, the absence of a clear recipe of how to measure the factors ξ_i, and the possible time dependence of the parameters of the model are three obvious points to criticize. These are not new problems, and many efforts to overcome them have been undertaken. It is possible to demonstrate that the virtual arbitrage model can be improved using these methods in the same manner as for no-arbitrage APT analysis. This, in principle, allows one to include the transaction costs, taxes, and market imperfection in the present model by rederiving the 'bare' APT relations and then adding the virtual arbitrage with minor modifications.

The second point concerns the market reaction to the arbitrage opportunity, or, qualitatively the form of $\mathcal{R}(t, \Pi)$ in (26). It may be argued that the market reaction is not exponential as assumed in (24), but has another functional dependence. This dependence can be found from statistical analysis of stock prices and then included in the equation for $\mathcal{R}(t, \Pi)$ (in particular, the functional dependence can change with time, for example, which makes λ in (24) a function of τ). This certainly complicates the model, but leaves the general framework intact.

Another point to consider is the absence of correlations between virtual arbitrage opportunities that we have assumed, i.e. the white noise character of the process $v(t, \Pi)$ in contrast to what was reported by Lo and MacKinlay (1999). It is clear that some correlations can be included in the model by appropriate substitution of the relations in (27). Such generalizations, although making analytical study almost impossible, allow one to proceed with numerical analysis for the model.

Finally, the model contains new parameters such as Σ and λ defined by (28) and (25) from the market data. It might appear that time-independent parameters are not a good enough approximation and that both Σ and λ are functions of time as a consequence of intermittent boosts of market activity. Furthermore, the parameter λ might actually depend on the structure of the portfolio in exactly the same manner as Σ because of particular sector preferences of arbitrageurs. Both situations can be processed in a similar manner to the simplest case that we considered above.

7 SUMMARY

- It is possible to formulate a gauge model to analyse asset pricing and to re-derive the relations of Arbitrage Pricing Theory and the Capital Asset Pricing Model.

- The gauge model allows the introduction into the theory of virtual arbitrage and the modelling of the market reaction to it.

- The gauge model can be reduced to a model where the arbitrage return is modelled by a stochastic Ornstein–Uhlenbeck process. It is possible to derive the same model on the grounds of purely phenomenological considerations.

- Averaging growth factors with respect to the stochastic process gives rise to corrections to APT. They disappear in the limit of the absence of arbitrage or of infinitely fast market reaction.

- These corrections represent a non-linear intercept in the APT and CAPM relations, and are in reasonable agreement with empirical data.

9

Derivatives

'Because options are specialized and relatively unimportant financial securities, the amount of time and space devoted to the development of a pricing theory might be questioned.'

Robert C. Merton (Merton, 1973)

Derivatives are a vast area, and many books have been published on the subject. This chapter does not pretend in any sense to cover the field. It concentrates on only one aspect: non-quilibrium versus equilibrium derivative pricing. In this short introduction, I would like to bring the reader's attention to the following facts. First of all, over-the-counter (OTC) derivatives comprise the main body of derivatives outstanding, in contrast to exchange-traded contracts. However, the pricing methodology used for OTC derivatives does not differ from the pricing of openly traded contracts. Secondly, although the modelling of financial derivatives is hardly a new problem, the models are not as perfect as some people might think. In particular, the no-arbitrage assumption is not as safe as it seems to be, especially for OTC derivatives. Finally, consistent allowance for arbitrage considerably complicates the mathematical treatment and requires new pricing solutions. This general line will guide us to the central issue of this chapter: consideration of the influence of virtual arbitrage on the derivative prices.

Being suitable instruments for both hedging and speculating, derivatives have become extremely popular among practitioners. This popularity explains the steady growth of the derivative markets. It is amazing to see how in the five years to the end of 1998, the notional[1] amount of exchange-traded derivatives rose from \$7.7 trillion to \$13.5 trillion, while the notional for (OTC) derivatives changed from \$8.7 trillion to almost \$51 trillion, thus together summing to \$64 trillion of notional for the derivatives outstanding (Plender, 1999). This is a huge amount of money. According to the annual report of the Bank for International Settlement, the notional amounts of just interest-rate and currency-related positions in OTC derivatives are now comparable to the total cash positions in global banking and securities markets.

Since derivatives are not a particularly new kind of financial arrangement, and have in fact existed for hundreds of years, it is not surprising that the problem of valuation and pricing of derivatives has attracted the efforts of economists and mathematicians. Bachelier was the first to suggest a way to calculate the 'fair' price for an option, based on his stochastic picture of

---

[1]The face value of all stocks, bonds, currencies, and other assets on which derivatives are derived.

market movements. Samuelson improved the procedure by taking the log-normal rather than the normal distribution function for the asset prices. But the real birth of derivative pricing was the publication of the work of Black and Scholes (1973) and Merton (1973). The original model was simple enough to provide final results using programmable pocket calculators. It had only a few variables, and a trader could work out the price of a contract in seconds. Moreover, the approach also prescribed a set of actions that had to be taken to make riskless money if the estimated price and the market price were different, i.e. it described an arbitrage strategy. In the last 25 years, an army of quantitative analysts (quants) and researchers have updated the model to include many realistic features in it. Stochastic interest rates, leptokurtic probability distributions for underlying assets, dependence on many assets, discrete hedging and transaction costs, price jumps, credit risk, stochastic volatility, local volatility, and surfaces—this is just a short list of the improvements to the Black–Scholes model. The number of papers dealing with the subject is huge and grows constantly. The influx of new recruits from physics and mathematics to the field of quantitative finance has stimulated the development of more and more complicated models. This poses an obvious question: is there any need to develop the pricing models further? Or, if a market is too complicated to be properly modelled, why not proceed with simple models and make the necessary phenomenological adjustments? Some practitioners clearly would support this line. As Jessica James from Bank One put it: 'There is very little need for improvements. Unfortunately, many academic physicists spend a lot of time searching for new ways of pricing options, when they could better direct their energies elsewhere' (James, 1999).

It is very tempting to take the message literally: enough of models, price valuation is not a problem. However, the statistical data do not quite support this view. As Fig. 9.1 shows, about 20% of losses on derivatives trading are attributed to incorrect valuation, and this amounts to billions of dollars (Stix, 1998). This makes the 'model risk', i.e., the risk incurred due to the possibility of incorrect valuation of derivative prices and inappropriate hedging strategies, comparable to other sources of risk inherent in derivatives trading. Looked at from this perspective, investing in modelling already does not seem to be a waste of money.

What most practitioners argue against is the thoughtless exploitation of models relying on obscure mathematics. They see an inbalance between the complicated mathematics involved

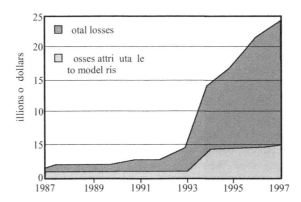

Figure 9.1 Incorrect valuation for derivatives can cause losses, as expressed in the concept of 'model risk'. The cumulative dollar figure for model risk from 1987 to 1997 comprises about 20% of all publicly disclosed losses. Reprinted from G. Stix, *Scientific American*, May 1998, pp. 70–75.

and the original approximations made. Despite the many improvements listed above, the paradigm of the modelling has hardly changed since Black's and Scholes' paper. It is the same stochastic nature for the price of underlying stocks and interest rates, equilibrium pricing, and the no-arbitrage assumption. These are themselves approximations, and so introduce inevitable errors, which are even harder to estimate and which can be fatal. The best example is the financial crash of 1987. The use of an equilibrium pricing model for a clearly non-equilibrium process led to the wrong hedging strategy and exacerbated the situation. In this case, both the stochastic process for the price and the no-arbitrage assumption were clearly out of place (Jacobs, 1999). Another example is the 'flight to quality' after the Russian crisis of 1998, when an increased difference between swap and bond yields broke the no-arbitrage calculations (Kestenbaum, 1999). In these cases, a complicated stochastic calculus can elaborate on corrections of a few percent to a stochastic no-arbitrage model, which may well be negligible compared with the errors inherited from the basic assumptions. This is what physicists call excessive precision.

Let us now take a closer look at the no-arbitrage assumption. Basically, it means that there is no riskless profit in the market. If, for some reasons, a mispricing appears, it is immediately exploited and washed out by market participants who specialized in arbitrage. As soon as *they believe* in the no-arbitrage price, they drive the price to its no-arbitrage value, restore the equilibrium in the market, and make a nice profit. The picture looks logical and robust. It implies, however, that there are always some of them about and that their impact is sufficient to influence the market price and bring it to its no-arbitrage value. In talking about the arbitrageurs, we always think of a large liquid market with many traders, and visualize them as 'locals' on LIFFE[2] who stand[3] in the trading pit, fit and ready. As a matter of fact, on LIFFE, the number of traders standing in each trading pit is about a dozen, and most of them work for brokerage houses executing clients' orders rather than trading arbitrage. We can now define the *small mispricings* as those that can be eliminated by arbitrageurs' actions – actions that return the system to its equilibrium state. By this definition, the states with the small fluctuations belong to the attraction region of the equilibrium state. In the opposite case, if arbitrageurs cannot (or do not want to) eliminate the mispricing, the system does not evolve to its no-arbitrage equilibrium state, which therefore loses its importance for pricing. In what follows, we deal mainly with small fluctuations, although, from a practical point of view, the case of large fluctuations is most important (and, as usual, difficult to analyse). Non-equilibrium pricing is treated in the last section of this chapter.

If a derivative is exchange-traded, it is the market that decides its price using the supply–demand mechanism. In the case where a model gives a price that is different from the price on the market, it does not immediately mean that one can make riskless profit, because one effectively bets on ones model, taking, as a result, the 'model risk'. Studies show that anticipated future volatilities, and thus future prices, decoded from the market prices work better than any model – traders know their job. Broadly speaking, there is not much practical sense in pricing exchange-traded derivatives,[4] and this is not what most of the quants in banks do. The number of quants soared when a new industry emerged: OTC client-tailored derivatives. As we have seen, their aggregated notional is several times larger than the notional for the exchange-traded derivatives, they are not openly traded, and their price is not,

---

[2]London International Financial Futures Exchange.
[3]The open outcry system came to its end in April 2000 but the main picture drawn here is still valid.
[4]Unless one trades a model-based arbitrage or wants to test an economic model.

in fact, defined by the market mechanism. The final details of a deal are known only to the two counterparties. Thus there is often no third party to influence the price and eliminate the mispricing if it exists. In this setting, the quant's job is to estimate the 'fair' price using parameters extracted from other liquid instruments,[5] to suggest the corresponding hedging strategy, and then to pass it to a trader who makes the deal with a price that can differ, sometimes substantially, from the quant's price.

At this point, we face a paradoxical situation:

1. The no-arbitrage assumption, which is the basis of all standard pricing models, is valid for openly traded derivatives where there is not much need in pricing;

2. Most real everyday pricing problems concern OTC derivatives whose market does not have an infrastructure of arbitrageurs, thus making the no-arbitrage assumption questionable.

One can argue therefore that to price OTC derivatives, it is important to include, in one or another way, the existence of a mispricing to make the results more realistic.

We must admit that arbitrage is a nuisance in calculations. Indeed, the no-arbitrage assumption is essential in the justifications of all contemporary mathematical methods used in derivative pricing. The origin of this ubiquitousness lies in a fundamental theorem according to which the no-arbitrage assumption allows the existence of a martingale measure (which may be not unique), with the price as the average discounted payoff with respect to this measure (for details, see Cox and Ross, 1976; Harrison and Pliska, 1981; Sundaram, 1997; Duffie, 1992). This justifies an intuitively clear view of the price of a derivative as the average of its final payoff, and allows one to calculate prices for various underlying processes. The corresponding mathematics is particularly useful when partial differential equations cannot be written at all or are difficult to analyse, as is the case for interest rate derivatives. The presence of virtual arbitrage fluctuations violates the assumptions of the fundamental theorem, and requires an updating of the martingale methodology. In what follows, to find prices, we average over the arbitrage fluctuations, which is, strictly speaking, an approximation (arbitrage causes a specific risk that cannot be hedged and therefore requires accounting for the price of the risk). In this form, one can consider an arbitrage return as an additional stochastic factor[6] similar to a stochastic interest rate but with a much shorter relaxation time, and thus one can easily generalize the martingale approach to this case.

What is even more unpleasant in the existence of an arbitrage is its dynamical nature. Indeed, as mentioned before, an arbitrage precludes an equilibrium picture and thus an equilibrium pricing. Generally, one has to model a decision-making process in response to the market fluctuations or a process that essentially defines the dynamics of the prices towards (or away from) the equilibrium. All this complicates the models and makes them less testable, which can be regarded as a price of being more realistic.

In this chapter, we try to find corrections to no-arbitrage derivatives pricing due to the presence of a virtual arbitrage. In a certain sense, derivative pricing is a very particular case of the portfolio theory that consider portfolios consisting of underlying assets and the corresponding derivatives. This is why our analysis of derivative pricing under virtual

---

[5]Such as exchange-traded futures, OTC FRA, and swaps whose quotes are supplied by major brokerage houses.
[6]I am grateful to J.M. Lasry, who pointed this out to me.

arbitrage will be very similar to the analysis carried out in the previous chapter for the case of general portfolios. We will see how to apply gauge principles to describe the system and to develop an easy-to-use recipe to update no-arbitrage models to virtual arbitrage ones. In practice, this means the following chain of actions: choose your favourite no-arbitrage model with stochastic volatility, discrete hedging and whatever else you would like to include, introduce virtual arbitrage terms estimated from the market parameters, and finally gauge the parameters to enhance the model performance. Exactly as we had for the corrections to APT and the CAPM, the new model is bound to work at least as well as the no-arbitrage model, because the latter constitutes a particular case of the former.

This chapter is organized as follows. To make the text self-contained, in the next section, the main definitions and some standard results of no-arbitrage derivative pricing are collected. In Section 2, we give a stylized review of empirical analysis of arbitrage fluctuations in real markets. We will argue that even for liquid and stable markets, there exist short-lived profitable arbitrage opportunities that can be accounted for in the modelling, while if a market goes through a large event, the mispricing can reach enormous values. In Section 3, a general gauge framework is applied to derivative pricing. This model is used in Section 4 to discuss a general form of corrections and to derive a simplified phenomenological pricing model. The latter allows us to obtain in Section 5 an effective equation for a derivative price with virtual arbitrage under the assumption of quasi-Brownian underlying price motion, thus generalizing the Black–Scholes equation. Section 6 contains exact results for forwards and European call and put options. In Section 7, we describe the effect of transaction costs and bid–ask spread on arbitrage strategies. Section 8 concludes the chapter and the book. Here we introduce a model that does not assume a quasi-equilibrium market, and is suitable for pricing derivatives in non-equilibrium markets. The mispricing plays the very important role of the variable that characterizes the state of the market.

I DERIVATIVE PRICING UNDER THE NO-ARBITRAGE ASSUMPTION

In this section, we give a simple introduction to financial derivatives and an almost rigorous derivation of the Black–Scholes equation using standard no-arbitrage arguments. The reader who is familiar with the subject is advised to skip this section.

A financial derivative is a financial instrument whose value is defined by values of other (underlying) financial variables. These underlying variables may be prices of stocks, bonds or other derivatives, interest rates, exchange rates, market indices, and so on. Some particular derivatives (such as warrants) have been known for centuries, but after the introduction in 1973 of exchange-traded derivatives on stocks in the USA, trading in derivatives became a really huge industry.[7] Most exchange-traded derivatives are call and put options and futures, while swaps, forwards, and other derivatives dominate in OTC trading. Let us give a definition of these derivatives.

The call option gives a right but not an obligation to buy a certain number of shares (or any prespecified underlying asset) at the fixed (strike) price E. If the right can be used at the *final* moment of the (expiration) time T only, the call option is called European. In contrast, the

---

[7]For an introduction to practical aspects, see e.g. Dubofsky (1992) and Hull (1997).

American call option provides the right to buy the underlying asset at the strike price at *any* time before the expiration time T. The put options guarantee the same rights not for buying but for selling of the shares. Since the American option gives an investor more freedom, it is more valuable. In general, the prices of the options are non-zero, and depend on the price of the underlying asset. The only time when the option price can be zero is the expiration time, subject to the case where the underlying asset price is less than E (for call options) or more than E (for put options).

A forward contract is an agreement between two parties to buy or sell an asset at a certain time in the future for a certain price. This agreement is a security, and can be traded. The price of the agreement clearly depends on the underlying asset price, and can be positive as well as negative. A negative price means that to close the position an additional amount should be paid. During the life of the contract, this price can grow to a large amount. That is why the counter-parties in forward contracts bear the credit risk, i.e. the risk that the losing party will default on the obligation at the final time, with the gaining party losing the its total profit. Forward contracts gave birth to futures contracts. These are very similar to forward contracts, but with two main differences: first, there exists a centralized clearing; secondly, there is a marking-to-market procedure according to which the daily change of the price is transferred to or from the parties' accounts. This minimizes the credit risk, since the clearing house has a high credit rating and the possible losses are limited to the daily profit only.

There is a number of models to estimate derivative prices and hedging ratios. The most popular is based on the original Black–Scholes no-arbitrage condition, the quasi-Brownian character of the underlying price, and a constant interest rate. Below we assume that the underlying asset is a share and that its price follows geometrical Brownian motion

$$\frac{dS}{S} = \mu\, dt + \sigma\, dW,$$

where dW is a Wiener process, μ is the average rate of return on the share, and σ is the standard deviation of the return (the so-called volatility).[8] The derivative price, C, is determined by the share price S. We also assume that the derivative price is not influenced by other factors. This means that $C(t, S)$ is a non-stochastic function of the stochastic parameter S, which means that for given t and S, $C(t, S)$ has a definite value. In what follows, we need the following fact, which is known as the Itô lemma:

$$df(t, S) = \frac{\partial f}{\partial t}\, dt + \frac{\partial f}{\partial S}\, dS + \frac{S^2 \sigma^2}{2} \frac{\partial^2 f}{\partial S^2}\, dt + o(dt), \tag{1}$$

where $f(t, S)$ is an arbitrary function of t and S.[9] Using the Itô lemma for the derivative price $C(S, t)$, we get the following equation describing derivative price movement:

$$dC(t, S) = \left(\frac{\partial C}{\partial t} + \frac{S^2 \sigma^2}{2} \frac{\partial^2 C}{\partial S^2}\right) dt + \frac{\partial C}{\partial S}\, dS + o(dt). \tag{2}$$

The right-hand-side of this equation contains dS, so the derivative price motion is stochastic. However, we can construct a portfolio from the derivative and the underlying shares that will

---

[8]Though our derivation is not, strictly speaking, rigorous, it gives the correct result and allows one to understand the basic idea. A formal derivation can be found in a number of textbooks on mathematical finance (see e.g. Duffie, 1992).
[9]The function f is assumed to be smooth.

be risk-free. Indeed, let us consider a portfolio Π consisting of the derivative and $\partial C/\partial S$ shares in the short position. The price movement of the portfolio is

$$d\Pi = \left(\frac{\partial C}{\partial t} + \frac{S^2\sigma^2}{2}\frac{\partial^2 C}{\partial S^2}\right)dt + o(dt). \tag{3}$$

Here we omit the term $Sd(\partial C/\partial S)$ that describes a change of the portfolio structure but not the portfolio value. Since in the last equation there is no longer a dS term, the portfolio is risk-free and has to grow at the risk-free interest rate r_b on a bank deposit:[10]

$$\frac{\partial C}{\partial t} + \frac{S^2\sigma^2}{2}\frac{\partial^2 C}{\partial^2 S} = \left(C - S\frac{\partial C}{\partial S}\right)r_b,$$

which is the celebrated Black–Scholes equation. It describes all derivatives, and the specific of a concrete derivative is encoded in boundary conditions only. For example, the boundary condition for the futures contract is

$$C(S, T) = S - E,$$

while for the European call it takes the form

$$C(S, T) = (S - E)\theta(S - E).$$

There are several directions to follow if one wants to make the original Black–Scholes scheme more realistic. For example, as we saw in Chapter 6, the underlying price process is not in reality geometrical Brownian motion, and has 'fatter' tails and non-constant volatility. Interest rates are not constant, and their stochastic modelling is the central issue in interest rate derivatives pricing. Another problem is concerned with transaction costs. Above, we considered the continuous-time limit and neglected $o(dt)$ in (2). This means that the portfolio of shares and cash (the hedging portfolio) has to be rearranged continuously, which leads to, strictly speaking, infinite transaction costs. To avoid this problem and include these transaction costs, one has to keep finite time steps, and therefore cannot neglect $o(dt)$ any longer. This results in the impossibility of perfect hedging and the necessity to price the residual risk. We are not going into further details here and for a discussion of these and other important issues direct the reader to various textbooks.[11] In the rest of this chapter, we will concentrate on a single assumption that was essential to the above analysis – the no-arbitrage condition.

2 ARBITRAGE OR NO-ARBITRAGE: SOME EMPIRICAL RESULTS

Reading the mathematical finance literature creates the impression that arbitrage opportunities are rare and practically unimportant events. However, we can spot an arbitrage whenever we look around. The areas vary from cross-track betting on major horse races (Hausch and Ziemba, 1990) to the UK – EU car market. But only financial markets provide a vast source of data to allow statistical studies of arbitrage. As has been mentioned before, it is difficult to analyse an arbitrage for OTC instruments, because the relevant data are scarce and often not

---

[10]The next section explains the economics behind this no-arbitrage assumption.
[11]See e.g. Hull (1997) and Wilmott (1998).

available. That is why empirical studies concentrate on exchange-traded derivatives[12] and, in particular, on futures contracts on major market indices such as, for example, the S&P500 index. First of all, it is much easier to define the no-arbitrage price for futures than for other derivatives with a non-linear payoff. Secondly, the index futures are very liquid, with the S&P500 futures being among the most liquid traded derivatives (see Fig. 9.2). This reduces the problem of stale prices and provide ample transaction series to analyse.

Arbitrage with index futures is the easiest of all possible arbitrage scenarios, and can be programmed directly. At the moment, according to the New York Stock Exchange weekly press releases[13] on program trading, approximately 10% of the program trading volume executed by NYSE members is related to the index arbitrage. This activity makes the market reaction very fast and the corresponding arbitrage short-lived. Therefore one might expect considerably longer arbitrage lifetimes for less liquid markets of derivatives on soft currencies and commercial papers. However, even for the most liquid futures, the arbitrage, as we will see below, is well-observed and profitable. Pure index arbitrage has almost disappeared in recent years in the USA and Europe, and has been substituted by an arbitrage with incomplete stock baskets and tax credit arbitrage. Index arbitrage, however, can still be found in Asia and Brazil and in emerging markets.

2.1 Evidence from Index-Futures Arbitrage

As we mentioned before, usually it is difficult to define a commonly accepted 'fair' price, which is essential in order to calculate a mispricing or an arbitrage. It is influenced by

Trading Liquidity: Futures

Commodity Futures	Exchange	% Margin	Effective % Margin	Contracts to Trade for Equal Dollar Profit	Relative Contract Liquidity
S & P 500	CME	6.6	12.1	1	
Treasury Bonds U.S.	CBT	2.9	9.1	8	
DAX-30 Stock Index	EUREX	5.6	9.2	2	
FT-SE 100 Index	LIFFE	4.5	6.8	3	
Treasury Notes (10 Yr)	CBT	1.6	6.8	10	
Eurodollar	IMM	0.3	23.0	65	
CAC-40 Stock Index	MATIF	2.2	3.5	7	
Long Gilt	LIFFE	0.5	1.1	1	
DJ Euro Stoxx 50 Index	EUREX	3.6	7.0	10	
Crude Oil	NYM	8.0	14.1	16	
10 Yr. Euro-Govt Bund	EUREX	1.5	14.4	20	
Treasury Notes (5 Year)	CBT	1.2	7.1	14	
Natural Gas	NYM	13.8	15.7	11	
NASDAQ 100 Index	CME	5.2	7.4	1	
Japanese Yen	IMM	4.0	13.2	6	
Soybeans	CBT	7.0	7.4	10	
Corn	CBT	4.1	7.1	40	
Wheat - Soft Red	CBT	5.6	3.8	13	
Coffee C	CSCE	11.6	10.0	4	
Euro Currency	CME	1.7	7.8	9	
Heating Oil #2	NYM	7.6	16.1	18	
Gold	NYM	9.6	25.2	21	
Swiss Franc	IMM	1.9	8.6	13	
Sugar-World #11	CSCE	10.4	9.7	32	
Soybean Meal	CBT	6.5	6.0	14	
Soybean Oil	CBT	5.0	5.7	27	
Gasoline Unleaded	NYM	7.0	16.6	19	
S & P 500 Mini	CME	11.6	12.3	6	
Wheat - Hard Red	KC	3.7	2.9	13	
Cotton #2	CTN	4.0	6.0	14	
Russell 2000 Index	CME	6.6	18.9	2	
Cocoa	CSCE	9.6	8.5	23	CBT	Chicago Board of Trade
Dow Jones Ind. Avg. Index	CBOT	5.3	10.5	4	
Silver	NYM	7.8	17.7	20	
Cattle - Live	CME	2.3	12.8	48	
Copper	NYM	6.8	13.4	28	
NEKKEI-225 Index	CME	7.4	24.6	8	
Mexican Peso	IMM	6.1	10.1	7	
Libor 1 mo	IMM	0.0	2.1	16	
Hogs	CME	6.5	10.8	23	
NYSE Composite Index	CTN	2.4	5.1	2	
Canadian Dollar	IMM	1.0	9.3	30	
Goldman Sachs Index	CME	4.6	18.0	16	
Treasury Notes (2 Yr.)	CBT	0.3	4.6	16	
British Pound	IMM	1.3	19.5	33	

Exchange key: CBT Chicago Board of Trade; CME Chicago Mercantile Exchange; CSCE Coffee, Sugar & Cocoa Exchange, New York; CTN New York Cotton Exchange; EUREX European Exchange, Zurich & Frankfurt; IMM International Monetary Market at CME, Chicago; KC Kansas City Board of Trade; LIFFE London International Financial Futures and Options Exchange; MATIF Marché à Terme International de France; MCE MidAmerica Commodity Exchange, Chicago; MPLS Minneapolis Grain Exchange; NYFE New York Futures Exchange; NYM New York Mercantile Exchange; WPG Winnipeg Commodity Exchange

Margin source: jackcarl.com/margins.html and various exchanges
0002

Trading Liquidity: Futures is a reference chart for speculators. It compares markets according to their per-contract potential for profit and how easily contracts can be bought or sold (i.e., trading liquidity). Each is a proportional measure and is meaningful only when compared to others in the same column.

The number in the "Contracts to Trade for Equal Dollar Profit" column shows how many contracts of one commodity must be traded to obtain the same potential return as another commodity. Contracts to Trade = (Tick $ value) × (3-year Maximum Price Excursion).

"Relative Contract Liquidity" places commodities in descending order according to how easily all of their contracts can be traded. Commodities at the top of the list are easiest to buy and sell; commodities at the bottom of the list are the most difficult. "Relative Contract Liquidity" is the number of contracts to trade times total open interest times a volume factor, which is the greater of:

$$1 \; or \; \exp\left[\frac{\ln(volume)}{\ln(5000)}\right] - 2$$

Figure 9.2 Futures liquidity table. From 'Futures Liquidity', *Technical Analysis of Stocks & Commodities*, Vol. 18, No. 2 (Feb. 2000), p. 35. Copyright © 2000, Technical Analysis, Inc. Used with permission.

---

[12]For a review of earlier empirical research on exchange-traded derivative pricing, see Section 19.9 of Hull (1997).
[13]Available at http://www.nyse.com.

differences of opinion among participants regarding the valuation model. In the case of futures trading, one can avoid many problems encountered if a 'fair' price of non-linear derivatives, such as options, is targeted. In particular, the volatility of the underlying asset, the most troublesome of the external parameters in the option pricing, does not play any role here and does not have to be estimated. This makes the forward and futures contracts especially convenient for empirical studies of time dynamics of arbitrage returns.

Let us consider a forward contract in the frictionless market, with zero transaction costs and fixed interest rate r_0. Selling at time t a forward contract at forward price $F(t, T)$ with delivery time T means that the party is obliged to sell at time T an agreed amount of the underlying asset at price $F(t, T)$. For forward or futures contracts, there is no upfront payment. Thus, in contrast to futures, whose profits or losses are realized on an everyday marking-to-market basis, profits and losses on forward contracts are not realized until the delivery date. In what follows, we will be interested in the contracts on an index of stocks where the index represents a capitalization-weighted basket of stocks paying a continuous dividend rate d. It is absolutely straightforward to find the forward price from the no-arbitrage assumption. Consider the portfolio constructed at time t from the following:

1. The basket of stocks bought at the spot price $S(t)$ and held until the delivery date reinvesting the dividends continuously at the riskless rate till time T;

2. A debt of $S(t)$ dollars that were borrowed to finance the acquisition;

3. The forward contract sold at the forward price $F(t, T)$.

The value of this portfolio at time t is equal to zero. At time T, the stocks are delivered and an amount $F(t, T)$ is received. To avoid certain losses or gains, this latter has to offset the debt accumulated on the bank account, which is equal to $S(t, T)e^{(r_0-d)(T-t)}$. Therefore, in the no-arbitrage world, the forward price is given by the equation

$$F_{\text{no-arbitrage}}(t, T) = S(t)e^{(r_0-d)(T-t)}. \tag{4}$$

In the case where the forward price at the market, $F(t, T)$, is greater than the right-hand-side of (4), a strategy that buys the index and sells the forward contract will earn riskless profit in excess of the risk-free rate r_0. This lifts the spot price of the basket and pushes the forward price down, thus moving prices closer to the no-arbitrage bound. If there is enough money available for the arbitrage, this strategy will lead to complete elimination of the arbitrage. A similar consideration holds for the opposite case where the forward contracts are cheaper than they have to be from (4).

With deterministic interest rates, forward prices coincide with futures prices[14] (Cox et al, 1981). As a result, we can use the same formula (4) to detect mispricing between the futures and the index. As a quantitative measure of mispricing, it is convenient to use the difference between the market futures price and its theoretical value given by (4), normalized by the price of the underlying asset, which in our case is the index value (Lo and Mackinlay, 1999):

$$\kappa_{t,T} = \frac{F(t, T) - S(t)e^{(r_0-d)(T-t)}}{S(t)}.$$

---

[14]Here we have neglected the possibility of default and therefore higher credit risk associated with forward contracts.

This quantity is particularly convenient for discussing arbitrage in the presence of transaction costs, which often can be expressed as a percentage of the price of the underlying asset. The costs include the sum of commission costs in both stocks and futures markets and the corresponding market impact of the trades. The relative transaction costs t_c of most of arbitrageurs create effective limits for $\kappa_{t,T}$ to be profitable, and only breaking the limits can be considered as an arbitrage opportunity.

For reasons listed above, futures arbitrage has attracted the active interest of many researchers (for some early results see Cornell and French, 1983; Modest and Sundaresan, 1983; Figlewski, 1984, 1985; Arditti et al, 1986). It was realized that, in a real market, futures contracts are not always traded at the price predicted by the simple no-arbitrage relation (4) and there are significant arbitrage deviations. Several explanations for the variability of $\kappa_{t,T}$ were proposed, such as differential tax treatment for spot and futures (Cornell, 1985), and marking-to-market requirements for futures, but it was argued that 'noise' is the main source of the mispricing (Figlewski, 1984). It was also noted that there are certain factors that influence the arbitrage strategies and slow down the market reaction on the arbitrage. The factors include constrained capital requirements (Stoll and Whaley, 1987), position limits, and transaction costs (Brennan and Schwarts, 1988, 1990).

Below we primarily follow Lo and MacKinlay (1990) who describe analysis of the arbitrage on the futures on the S&P500 index using transaction data from April 1982 to June 1987. In computing the mispricing series, they used quotes that were approximately 15 minutes apart, and each contract was followed from the expiration date of the previous contract until its expiration.[15] Owing to the non-synchronous nature of the data, the error in the mispricing lifetime is of the order of 30 seconds and the typical time to take an arbitrage position could vary from 60 seconds to several minutes.[16] Further details on the data set and its properties as well as the estimated dividend and interest rates can be found in Lo and MacKinlay (1999).

Variance Test

The first test of the presence of arbitrage can be carried out using the variance of the change of the log futures price divided by the variance of the change of the log index price. As is easy to check from (4), in the case of a no-arbitrage market, this ratio has to be equal to 1 (since the contribution from the dividends and interest rates can be safely ignored at 15-minute, intervals). However, it turns out that the ratio differs considerably from 1 (see Table 9.1) and the difference survives for intervals up to one trading day. This therefore signals the violation of the no-arbitrage relation (4). In this context, the variance test plays the same role that volatility tests play in empirical studies on market efficiency (Shiller, 1981; Cuthbertson, 1996). The costs of trade are lower for the futures market. This makes the futures market more suitable for speculations that bring higher volatility. The futures price is defined by both speculators and arbitrageurs, in contrast to what we assumed in the derivation of (4). This leads to two possible conclusions: (i) one has *to include speculators in pricing models*; (ii) one might expect to find *a correlation between the arbitrage return and the return on the underlying asset.*

---

[15]The contracts followed a March – June – September – December cycle. All together, 16 contracts were studied.
[16]Automated trading systems later reduced this time considerably.

Table 9.1 Statistics for the changes of the logarithm of the futures price for the S&P500 futures, and the index for 15- and 30-minute intervals.[a]

	Futures		Index		
Contract	Standard deviation	First-order autocorrelation	Standard deviation	First-order autocorrelation	Variance ratio
Panel A: Data at 15-minute invervals					
Sep 83	0.163	0.022	0.128	0.408	1.634
Dec 83	0.125	−0.001	0.095	0.409	1.739
Mar 84	0.147	−0.005	0.119	0.313	1.536
June 84	0.150	−0.010	0.114	0.369	0.715
Sep 84	0.176	−0.011	0.149	0.289	1.410
Dec 84	0.155	−0.055	0.114	0.213	1.858
Mar 85	0.145	−0.078	0.112	0.156	1.664
Jun 85	0.115	−0.079	0.093	0.178	1.506
Sep 85	0.108	−0.020	0.083	0.249	1.683
Dec 85	0.128	−0.065	0.102	0.184	1.575
Mar 86	0.172	−0.029	0.137	0.140	1.576
Jun 86	0.171	−0.005	0.142	0.103	1.460
Sep 86	0.202	−0.018	0.173	0.045	1.362
Dec 86	0.182	−0.021	0.147	0.079	1.520
Mar 87	0.219	−0.136	0.168	0.038	1.703
Jun 87	0.219	0.048	0.214	0.086	1.049
Panel B: Data at 30-minute intervals					
Sep 83	0.233	−0.085	0.214	0.093	1.186
Dec 83	0.177	0.036	0.159	0.170	1.233
Mar 84	0.208	−0.035	0.193	0.121	1.164
Jun 84	0.210	0.010	0.189	0.152	1.240
Sep 84	0.248	0.007	0.239	0.093	1.081
Dec 84	0.213	−0.027	0.177	0.062	1.448
Mar 85	0.197	0.021	0.171	0.063	1.327
Jun 85	0.156	−0.018	0.143	0.055	1.178
Sep 85	0.151	0.052	0.131	0.137	1.321
Dec 85	0.175	0.103	0.157	0.096	1.244
Mar 86	0.239	0.019	0.207	0.067	1.342
Jun 86	0.242	0.002	0.211	0.020	1.318
Sep 86	0.283	0.014	0.251	0.074	1.280
Dec 86	0.254	−0.004	0.216	0.038	1.380
Mar 87	0.287	−0.143	0.241	0.012	1.417
Jun 87	0.318	0.028	0.316	0.039	1.013

[a]From Lo, A.W. and MacKinlay, A.C.: *A Non-Random Walk Down Wall Street.* Copyright © 1999 by PUP. Reprinted by permission of Princeton University Press.

Statistics of the Mispricing

Table 9.2 shows the summary statistics for the level and first differences in mispricing. One can see that the autocorrelation for the mispricing is generally quite high. This indicates that the series tends to persist above or below zero and fluctuate randomly around zero. This can

Table 9.2 Summary statistics on the level and first differences in mispricing in the S&P500 futures contracts[a]

Contract	Mean (%)	Standard deviation (%)	Autocorrelations lag								Number of observations
			1	2	3	4	5	6	7	8	
Panel A: Statistics on the levels											
Sep 83	0.01	0.29	0.83	0.73	0.70	0.70	0.70	0.71	0.69	0.67	1575
Dec 83	0.37	0.29	0.86	0.75	0.65	0.56	0.45	0.33	0.21	0.07	1575
Mar 84	0.50	0.36	0.85	0.73	0.62	0.52	0.41	0.28	0.12	−0.04	1550
Jun 84	0.96	0.23	0.81	0.71	0.67	0.66	0.65	0.64	0.63	0.62	1500
Sep 84	0.11	0.32	0.84	0.79	0.76	0.74	0.73	0.71	0.71	0.68	1700
Dec 84	0.78	0.48	0.84	0.71	0.58	0.44	0.27	0.10	−0.11	−0.33	1600
Mar 85	0.64	0.60	0.93	0.87	0.82	0.75	0.69	0.61	0.53	0.44	1425
Jun 85	0.28	0.34	0 91	0.87	0.83	0.79	0.74	0.69	0.64	0.58	1700
Sep 85	0.04	0.28	0.94	0.92	0.90	0.89	0.87	0.85	0.84	0.83	1575
Dec 85	−0.17	0.30	0.91	0.87	0.85	0.83	0.80	0.78	0.76	0.73	1718
Mar 86	0.01	0.30	0.86	0.82	0.81	0.79	0.78	0.78	0.77	0.77	1674
Jun 86	−0.03	0.29	0.85	0.81	0.81	0.80	0.78	0.77	0.77	0.76	1701
Sep 86	−0.16	0.27	0.74	0.66	0.63	0.59	0.56	0.54	0.52	0.48	1701
Dec 86	−0.20	0.34	0.85	0.82	0.80	0.78	0.76	0.74	0.71	0.67	1728
Mar 87	−0.02	0.21	0.65	0.58	0.60	0.59	0.56	0.53	0.52	0.51	1674
Jun 87	−0.11	0.22	0.46	0.34	0.31	0.27	0.25	0.23	0.20	0.17	1674
Overall	0.12	0.44	0.93	0.91	0.90	0.89	0.88	0.87	0.86	0.85	26 070
Panel B: Statistics on the first differences											
Sep 83	0.00	0.15	−0.08	−0.14	−0.12	−0.05	−0.02	0.01	0.05	−0.01	1512
Dec 83	0.00	0.11	−0.16	−0.14	−0.06	0.00	−0.01	−0.02	0.03	0.01	1512
Mar 84	0.00	0.14	−0.15	−0.10	−0.11	−0.03	0.00	0.03	−0.06	0.04	1488
Jun 84	0.00	0.13	−0.17	−0.08	−0.10	−0.02	−0.03	−0.01	0.00	−0.03	1440
Sep 84	0.00	0.16	−0.19	−0.06	−0.06	−0.05	0.03	−0.04	0.05	−0.06	1632
Dec 84	0.00	0.13	−0.27	−0.08	0.01	0.04	−0.05	0.04	0.00	−0.06	1536
Mar 85	0.00	0.12	−0.27	−0.08	0.04	−0.01	−0.04	−0.02	0.00	0.03	1368
Jun 85	0.00	0.11	−0.25	−0.06	0.00	0.00	0.00	−0.03	0.02	−0.03	1632
Sep 85	0.00	0.09	−0.26	−0.03	0.00	−0.03	0.02	−0.02	−0.04	0.02	1512
Dec 85	0.00	0.11	−0.26	−0.09	0.01	0.00	−0.01	0.01	−0.02	0.01	1654
Mar 86	0.00	0.14	−0.30	−0.01	0.00	−0.02	−0.03	0.03	−0.03	0.02	1612
Jun 86	0.00	0.14	−0.30	−0.08	0.02	0.01	−0.04	0.01	0.02	−0.06	1638
Sep 86	0.00	0.16	−0.26	−0.05	−0.01	−0.03	0.01	0.04	−0.01	−0.01	1638
Dec 86	0.00	0.15	−0.24	−0.06	−0.03	0.01	−0.01	0.02	0.00	0.00	1664
Mar 87	0.00	0.16	−0.34	−0.10	0.04	0.03	−0.02	0.01	−0.02	0.00	1612
Jun 87	0.00	0.18	−0.20	−0.05	0.04	−0.03	0.02	−0.01	0.03	−0.04	1612
Overall	0.00	0.14	−0.23	−0.07	0.02	−0.01	−0.01	0.01	0.00	−0.02	25 062

[a]From Lo, A.W. and MacKinlay, A.C.: *A Non-Random Walk Down Wall Street*. Copyright © 1999 by PUP. Reprinted by permission of Princeton University Press.
Mispricing = futures − theoretical forward price.

be seen from Fig. 9.3 which shows a typical mispricing chart for December 1984 futures contract (transaction bounds are estimated as 0.6%). In contrast, the autocorrelations of the first differences of the mispricing are smaller and negative, and disappear quickly. The negative sign of the latter autocorrelation means that there exist forces in the market that react

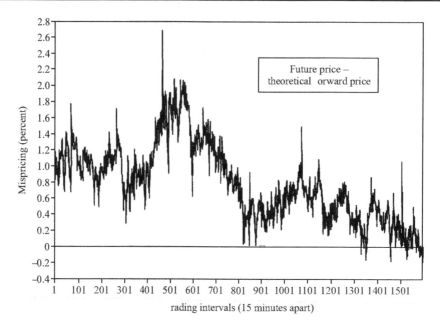

Figure 9.3 Mispricing (futures price – theoretical forward price) for December 1984 S&P500 futures contract. From Lo, A.W. and MacKinlay, A.C.: *A Non-Random Walk Down Wall Street.* Copyright © 1999 by PUP. Reprinted by permission of Princeton University Press.

to eliminate the mispricing. Figures 9.4 and 9.5 illustrate the autocorrelation of the mispricing and its first differences. They demonstrate that the stochastic process for the arbitrage return can be, to a certain extent, approximated by the Ornstein – Uhlenbeck process with an exponentially decreasing correlation function.

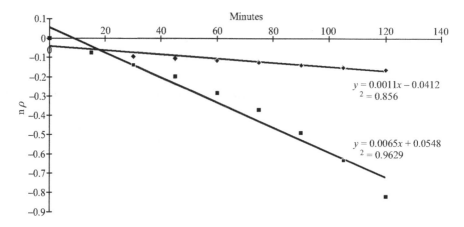

Figure 9.4 Logarithm of the autocorrelator ρ of the mispricing (15-minute intervals) for the S&P500 March 1985 futures contract and the overall average over the September 1983 – June 1987 period (using data from Lo and MacKinlay, 1999). Best linear fits are shown.

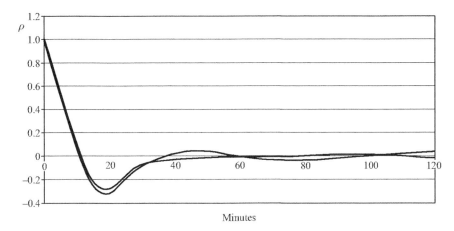

Minutes

Figure 9.5 Plot of the autocorrelator ρ of first differences of mispricing (15-minute intervals) for the S&P500 March 1985 futures contract (dashed line) and the overall average over the September 1983 – June 87 period (solid line) (using data from Lo and MacKinlay, 1999).

Correlation Between the Mispricing and the Underlying Asset

Consider the following chain of equalities:

$$\log F(t, T) = \log[S(t) - S(t) + F(t, T)] = \log S(t) + \log\left(1 + \frac{F(t, T) - S(t)}{S(t)}\right),$$

which leads to the the equation

$$\log F(t, T) \simeq \log S(t) + \frac{F(t, T) - S(t)}{S(t)} \simeq \log S(t) + \kappa_{t,T}. \tag{5}$$

This equation connects the difference between logarithms of the futures price and the index and the mispricing. Using this equation, we find that

$$\langle \log F(t, T) \rangle \simeq \langle \log S(t) \rangle + \langle \kappa_{t,T} \rangle$$

and

$$\langle [\log F(t, T)]^2 \rangle \simeq \langle [\log S(t)]^2 \rangle + \langle \kappa_{t,T}^2 \rangle + 2\langle \kappa_{t,T} \log S(t) \rangle.$$

The last two equalities allow us to express the variance of $\log F(t, T)$ through the variance of $\log S(t)$:

$$
\begin{aligned}
\mathrm{var}[\log F(t, T)] &= \langle [\log F(t, T)]^2 \rangle - \langle \log F(t, T) \rangle^2 \\
&\simeq \langle [\log S(t)]^2 \rangle - \langle \log S(t) \rangle^2 \\
&\quad + \langle \kappa_{t,T}^2 \rangle - \langle \kappa_{t,T} \rangle^2 + 2\langle \kappa_{t,T} \log S(t) \rangle - 2\langle \kappa_{t,T} \rangle \langle \log S(t) \rangle,
\end{aligned}
$$

which in compact form looks like

$$\mathrm{var}(\log F(t, T)) = \mathrm{var}[\log S(t, T)) + \mathrm{var}(\kappa_{t,T}) + 2\sqrt{\mathrm{var}(\log S(t))\mathrm{var}(\kappa_{t,T})}\rho\big(\kappa_{t,T} \log S(t)\big), \tag{6}$$

Table 9.3 Correlation coefficients for the mispricing and the logarithm of the index for 15-minute intervals. SD = standard deviation. Data are taken from Tables 9.1 and 9.2. The value − 1 is substituted when (6) gives values less than − 1. The correlation is clearly overestimated owing to neglect of the factor $e^{(R_0 - d)(T - t)}$

Contract	SD of log F (%)	SD of log S (%)	SD of mispricing (%)	Correlation coefficient (%)
Sep 83	0.163	0.128	0.29	− 0.995622306
Dec 83	0.125	0.095	0.29	− 1
Mar 84	0.147	0.119	0.36	− 1
Jun 84	0.15	0.114	0.23	− 0.827536232
Sep 84	0.176	0.149	0.32	− 0.981805789
Dec 84	0.155	0.114	0.48	− 1
Mar 85	0.145	0.112	0.6	− 1
Jun 85	0.115	0.093	0.34	− 1
Sep 85	0.108	0.083	0.28	− 1
Dec 85	0.128	0.102	0.3	− 1
Mar 86	0.172	0.137	0.3	− 0.963321168
Jun 86	0.171	0.142	0.29	− 0.910915493
Sep 86	0.202	0.173	0.27	− 0.663937058
Dec 86	0.182	0.147	0.34	− 1
Mar 87	0.219	0.168	0.21	− 0.345280612
Jun 87	0.219	0.214	0.22	− 0.491025913

where $\rho(\kappa_{t,T} \log S(t))$ is the correlation coefficient of κ and $\log S$. Using Tables 9.1 and 9.2 and (6), we can find the corresponding correlation coefficients. From Table 9.3, the reader can see that there is a strong negative correlation between the mispricing and the logarithm of the index, which is also clear from the definition of $\kappa_{t,T}$. As we have mentioned before, the larger variance for the futures contracts is brought about by comparatively low transaction costs and higher speculative activity. The speculators compete with the arbitrageurs in the price formation, and effectively create arbitrage opportunities. This is reflected in the non-zero correlation coefficient $\rho(\kappa_{t,T} \log S(t))$. In the course of the modelling of the virtual arbitrage return, it might be important to account for these types of correlations.

Path Dependence of the Mispricing

The formula (4) was obtained under the assumption that arbitrageurs keep their positions until the expiration of the contract. However, arbitrageurs have the option of reversing their positions prior to the expiration in the case of reverse arbitrage movement. This strategy will lead to a greater profit than indicated by the current mispricing level, $\kappa_{t,T}$. Once an arbitrage position has been taken, it will be optimal to close that position prior to putting on a new arbitrage programme in the reverse direction. This action will affect the mispricing process, and, in fact, will cause a path dependence. Let us consider, for example, a situation where the historical trajectory of the mispricing, $k_{t,T}$, has been positive and large. Arbitrageurs who had undertaken positions long in index stocks and short in futures will undo them when the mispricing has fallen to some negative value.[17] This will push up the future prices and pull

---

[17]This level depends on the transaction costs in the markets. See Section 7 for the calculation of optimal arbitrage strategies.

down the index, thus increasing the mispricing κ. Therefore, conditional on the mispricing having crossed one arbitrage bound, it is less likely to cross the opposite bound, which implies a path dependence for the mispricing process. Table 9.4 documents this type of behaviour for the S&P500 futures contracts for the period September 1983–June 1987. From 16 contracts, 15 are dominated by either upper-bound or lower-bound violations. To quantify the path dependence, MacKinlay and Ramaswamy introduced the conditional probabilities P_{uu} of κ hitting the upper-bound condition and crossing zero. They also considered its counterpart, P_{ll}, and found that in the data set the conditional probabilities differ from 0.5:

$$P_{uu} = 0.73, \qquad P_{lu} = 0.27,$$

and

$$P_{uu} = 0.64, \qquad P_{lu} = 0.36.$$

The fact that the probabilities differ substantially from 0.5 demonstrates the path dependence.

Time to Maturity

One might expect the mispricing to be larger and to appear more often for longer times until expiration $T - t$. There are several reasons for this. First of all, for longer times until expiration, there is an increasing risk of wrong prognosis for the model parameters such as the dividend rate and the interest rate. Secondly, an attempt to use the arbitrage opportunities trading in a less than full basket of stocks is riskier for longer times until expiration and requires higher arbitrage return to stimulate the arbitrageurs to take the arbitrage position. Thirdly, for long times until expiration, the difference between forward and futures prices is more important, because of interest earnings and costs associated with the marking-to-market. All of these factors increase the return required by the arbitrageurs to step in and thus increase the magnitudes of allowed mispricing fluctuations. Figure 9.6 shows a plot of the mean absolute value of the mispricing as a function of time until expiration. It is obtained by assuming a linear dependence of $|\kappa_{t,T}|$ as a function of $T - t$ based on the data for S&P500 futures contracts for the September 1983–June 1987 period. It is consistent with the previous discussion of the impact of other factors in addition to the transaction costs, which would otherwise generate a flat corridor.

Time Lag

The last feature of the arbitrage that we want to mention here is the time lag between futures prices and the index. From the general scenario of arbitrage trading, one might expect that the mispricing will be removed by simultaneous movements of stocks and futures prices rather than one of the prices tuning to another one. Stoll and Whaley (1990) found that the latter is, in fact, the case, when they analysed 5-minute data for S&P500 futures during the period April 1982–March 1987. They reported that most of the time the returns in the futures lead those in the stock market, even after adjusting for the infrequent trading of stocks. Occasionally returns in futures are led by the stocks, but the futures have significantly greater tendency to lead. The lead (lag) time was in average around 5 minutes, but sometimes reached 10 minutes and longer.

The development of computer trading has stimulated a faster market reaction on arbitrage opportunities and has further reduced the time of arbitrage fluctuations. Sofianos (1993)

Table 9.4 Path dependence for S&P500 futures contracts[a]

Contract	Number of upper-bound violations[b]	Number of upper-bound crossings	Average time above upper bound[c]	Number of lower-bound violations[b]	Number of lower-bound crossings	Average time below lower bound[c]	Number of observations[d]
Sep 83	30	20	23	29	14	31	1575
Dec 83	371	66	84	0	0	NA	1575
Mar 84	631	64	148	0	0	NA	1550
Jun 84	17	9	28	4	4	15	1500
Sep 84	92	44	31	21	15	21	1700
Dec 84	974	61	240	0	0	NA	1600
Mar 85	625	28	335	0	0	NA	1425
Jun 85	271	29	140	0	0	NA	1700
Sep 85	64	24	40	0	0	NA	1575
Dec 85	4	4	15	143	41	52	1718
Mar 86	7	4	26	36	31	17	1674
Jun 86	46	23	30	19	17	17	1701
Sep 86	1	1	15	83	44	28	1701
Dec 86	2	2	15	233	62	56	1728
Mar 87	5	5	15	16	9	27	1674
Jun 87	9	9	15	18	12	23	1674
Overall	3149	393	120	602	249	36	26070

[a]From Lo, A.W. and MacKinlay, A.C.: *A Non-Random Walk Down Wall Street*. Copyright © 1999 by PUP. Reprinted by permission of Princeton University Press.
[b]The upper bound is set at +0.6% and the lower bound at −0.6%.
[c]The average time outside the bounds is in trading minutes.
[d]The observations are recorded at 15-minute intervals.
NA, not applicable.

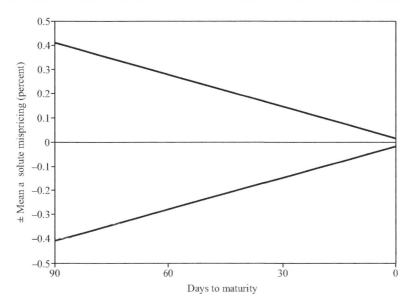

Figure 9.6   Mean absolute value of mispricing as a function of time to expiration. From Lo, A.W. and MacKinlay, A.C.: *A Non-Random Walk Down Wall Street*. Copyright © 1999 by PUP. Reprinted by permission of Princeton University Press.

reported for S&P500 futures that over the six month sample period between 15 January and 13 July, 1990, profitable mispricings were narrow and short-lived, lasting on average about three minutes, i.e. at least three times shorter than reported by MacKinlay and Ramaswamy for the period of September 1983 – June 1987 (see Table 9.4). Despite this short arbitrage lifetime, the average early-closing return was approximately five percentage points above the return on alternative investments.[18] During this period, the average number of stocks in the arbitrage stock basket was only 280, and 8% of the arbitrage dollar volume consisted of trades with fewer than 70 stocks. This reduced the transaction costs, making the 'arbitrage' more profitable but at the same time making the strategy riskier because of the imperfect hedging. Notwithstanding the quantitative changes in the arbitrage statistical characteristics with time, one might assume that the principle qualitative features of the arbitrage stochastic process remain the same, since the technology has not changed the underlying economic behaviour of the market participants.

2.2   Arbitrage and Extreme Market Events

We saw in the previous subsection that usually an arbitrage is quite small and short-lived. If any profitable opportunities appear, arbitrageurs can spot them, react, make an arbitrage profit, and return a market to the no-arbitrage state. The scheme works, however, only if the arbitrageurs step into the game believing that the market will return to the equilibrium no-arbitrage state. The latter will happen if the arbitrageurs as a group are powerful enough to

---

[18]During this period, 70% of the arbitrage positions were closed before expiration following profitable mispricing reversals.

reverse the prices. Therefore in the cases where the mispricing is created by large movements of speculative money flows that have a tendency to persist, the arbitrageurs can be reluctant to take arbitrage positions and damp the mispricing. As a matter of fact, the speculators play a double role in the arbitrage. First of all, they create the opportunities for the arbitrageurs. At the same time, they increase uncertainty and increase the risk faced by the arbitrageurs, thus inhibiting their activity (Shleifer and Vishny, 1997). If the speculative flows are too large for the arbitrageurs to reverse, they simply stay aside and allow the arbitrage to persist. In these cases, the arbitrage can reach huge proportions and survive for a comparatively long time until the speculators reduce their trading and the market calm down, reaching its new quasi-equilibrium state. Therefore one can consider the arbitrage as an indicator of the market instability of the market, which grows high if the market is in unrest.[19] Indeed, as we will see below, all large market movements are accompanied by large arbitrage mispricings. For example, Taylor (1987, 1989) studied covered arbitrage in FOREX market and found that while in the 'tranquil' phase the arbitrage is small and short-lived, during the turbulent phase, the arbitrage return was an order of magnitude larger and comparatively long-lived.

Since the coming of exchange-traded index derivatives, there have been five major market events that can be considered as large market movements:[20]

1. Black Monday (19 October 1987), followed by Roller Coaster Tuesday (20 October 1987). The Dow Jones Industrial Average (DJIA) plunged almost 23% on 19 October and rose 6% on the next day. See Figures 9.7 and 9.8, which come from the 1988 Report of the US Presidential Task Force on Market Mechanisms (the Brady Commisson).

2. Friday 13 October 1989, when the DJIA went down 6.9%, regaining half of this loss on the next Monday 16 October.

3. Friday 15 November 1991, when the DJIA fell 3.9%.

4. Monday 27 October 1997, when the DJIA dropped 7%, with a 4.7% rise on the next day.

5. Monday 31 August 1998, with a massive fall in the DJIA of 6.4% preceded by a decrease of 4.2% on 27 August.

Let us see now how all these events were characterized by large long-lived mispricings.

Black Monday

In his excellent 1999 book *Capital Ideas and Market Realities*, Bruce Jacobs argues that the portfolio insurers were primarily responsible for the crash of 1987 and played the central role in the 'cascade scenario' driven by the confluence of index arbitrage and synthetic portfolio insurance. During the two weeks prior to the crash, the market declined substantially. This prompted a sale of futures by portfolio insurers who used futures contracts as a main hedging instrument, thus driving down the futures prices and causing a futures discount. It only enhanced the futures discount that was reported in the market for a few weeks prior to the crash, indicating a downturn. The futures discount triggered the index arbitrage when the arbitrageurs were selling stocks and buying futures, pushing the stocks prices low. This

---

[19]This note is the basis for the model of Section 8 for derivative pricing for non-equilibrium markets.

[20]A very interesting account of the history of financial crashes can be found in Kindleberger (1996).

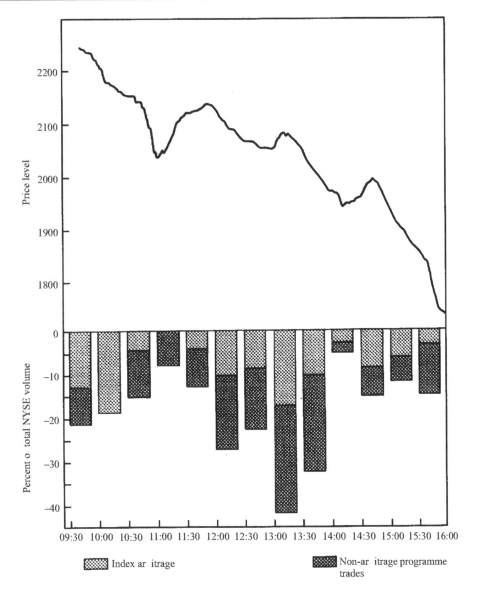

Figure 9.7 This figure from the Brady Commission Report shows DJIA price levels and programme trading on 19 October 1987. Taken from Jacobs (1999).

narrowed the mispricing, but gave a signal to the portfolio insurance programmes to reduce their stock positions further and sell futures. The result would be an even wider futures discount, which would cause further stock sales by the arbitrageurs. As long as the portfolio insurance sales had a greater impact than arbitrageurs' purchases of futures, the prices of both futures and stocks would continue to fall.

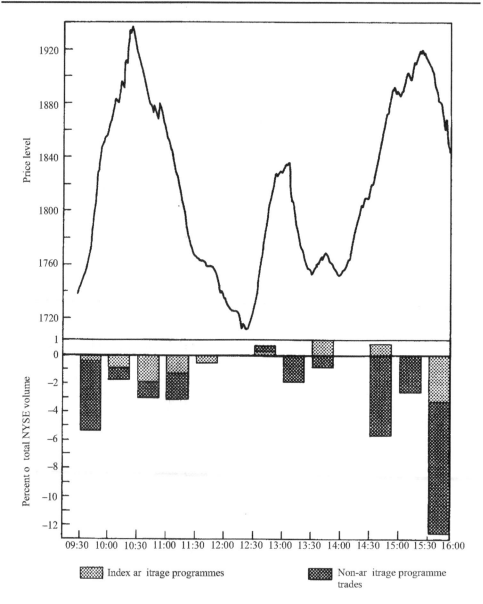

Figure 9.8 This figure from the Brady Commission Report shows DJIA price levels and programme trading on 20 October 1987. Taken from Jacobs (1999).

The scheme could be stopped by drying out the arbitrage and leaving large futures discounts. At the opening on Monday 19 October, insurers sold futures equivalent to about $400 million in stocks, and their direct sell programmes in stocks amounted to $250 million. At the same time, arbitrage programmes brought another $250 million in stock onto the market (Jacobs, 1999). During the day, the programme selling by the portfolio insurers and the arbitrageurs was high, sometimes reaching 60% of the total NYSE volume. However, later in the day the market illiquidity stopped the arbitrageurs and created huge mispricing.

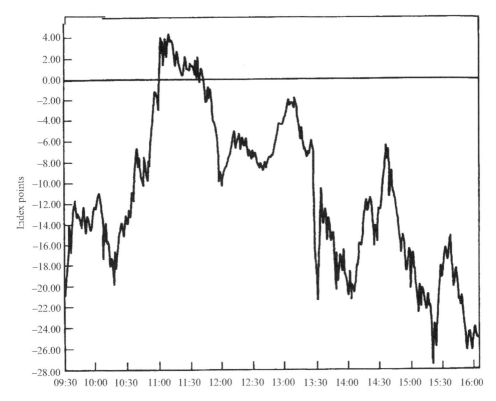

Figure 9.9 This figure from the Brady Commission Report shows the S&P500 futures discount on 19 October 1987. Taken from Jacobs (1999).

Figure 9.9 shows S&P500 index futures mispricing on 19 October. The discount stayed as high as 15% on average,[21] and occasionally reached 26%. The discount proceeded on Tuesday, reaching an unprecedented 40% in the morning (Fig. 9.10).

Mini-Crashes of 1989, 1991, and 1997

All the mini-crashes were accompanied by futures discounts. On 13 October, 1989, selling pressure pushed S&P500 futures prices to a discounted level and created arbitrage opportunities. These were used by the arbitrage trading programmes, which caused a bulk of programme trading, accounting for 11% of NYSE trading volume on 13 October. The arbitrage reappeared later on 16 October, and led the morning sale of stocks and the corresponding price plunge. On Friday 15 November 1991, much of the decline came in the afternoon and, as before, futures contracts started gapping down relative to the underlying stock market, and were traded at considerable discount. A similar picture was detected for the 27 October 1997 crash. Bruce Jacobs argues that there are certain similarities between the intrinsic dynamics of these mini-crashes and Black Monday, with the the portfolio insurers substituted by OTC put writers (Jacobs, 1999).

---

[21] Part of this mispricing can be explained by non-synchronous trading and stale quotes for stocks that were not in fact traded.

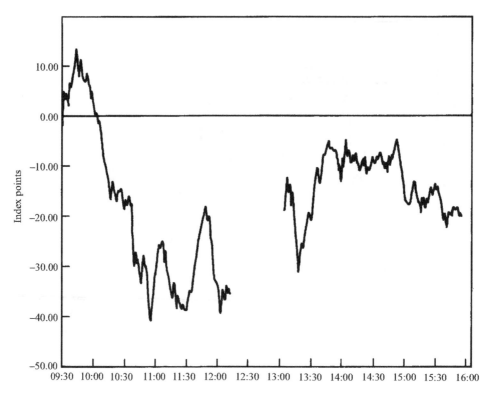

Figure 9.10   This figure from the Brady Commission Report shows the S&P500 futures discount on 20 October 1987. Taken from Jacobs (1999).

August 1998 and Hedge Funds

After hitting its peak value 9337.97 in July 1998, the DJIA started to slide down. Investor's confidence was low, exchange-listed put options became expensive, Federal Reserve Board Chairman Alan Greenspan warned that the stock market was overpriced, and the Russian government announced devaluation of the rouble and effective default on Russian debts. After the Asian market crisis of 1997 and turmoil in the currency market, the Russian default added pressure on investors, and caused a shift from risky markets to save government bonds. Many hedge funds were selling off their liquid assets, including index futures, stocks, and high-yield bonds, to cover losses on leveraged stakes in Russia and other emerging markets. The first shock hit the US market on 27 August, when the DJIA fell 4.2%, accompanied by 3% slides in Tokyo and London. After this fall, investors demanded better hedging, which increased the demand for put options, pushed their prices higher, and forced option market makers and other sellers of protective options to hedge themselves dynamically by selling futures and stocks. On 31 August, heavy selling of futures by put writers and hedge funds caused a futures discount. This discount prompted index arbitrageurs to sell in the underlying equity market, contributing to the overall market plunge of 6.4% on that day.

Much of the blame for the August fall lies with hedge funds who were heavily involved in highly leveraged 'arbitrage' operations. Being very profitable in winning deals, the leverage multiplies losses in the case of adverse market moves. Hedge funds enter arbitrage deals betting, in fact, on their model of equilibrium 'fair' pricing and expecting the mispricing to disappear. If, however, as a result of non-equilibrium changes in the market state, the mispricings grow, the losses mount and additional capital is required to meet margin calls. If the capital cannot be found, the hedge fund needs to unwind its positions (usually the most liquid ones) to provide it. When the participants in the same situation constitute a large fraction of a market, this might cause a liquidity crisis and amplify the original mispricing, running the hedge fund even deeper into the problems.[22]

Usually the operations of hedge funds are not totally risk-free. Buying Russian government bonds or mortgage-backed securities and selling US, British, or German government bonds is not an arbitrage, because the funds make profit (or losses), taking the risk of default. So-called risk arbitrage when one wants to profit from betting on mergers and acquisitions is not risk-free either. Theoretically, these operations are less risky than direct speculation, because adverse market movements for a long position are partially compensated by the short position and vice versa. However, if market preferences are changed dramatically, the equilibrium connection between the more risky and less risky assets will break down, and losses from the long positions will be exacerbated by losses from the short positions. It has been argued that the 'flight to safety' in August 1998 was such an event, with the equilibrium relations being broken. Investors withdrew from risky assets, pushing the prices down, and transferred money to safe government bonds, contributing to the rise in their prices. This widened the mispricing gaps and forced hedge funds to liquidate some of their positions, making the gaps even larger. Figure 9.11 shows the time dynamics of spread between high-yield bonds and Treasury bonds, which depicts the growing mispricing. Figure 9.12 demonstrates similar mispricing dynamics for the spread in yields calculated from the Treasury bonds and interest rate swaps. Both figures are, in fact, analogues of Figures 9.9 and 9.10 with a very different time scale but the same origin—breaking of the equilibrium market structure in cases of large market events, with consecutive growth of the (defined from an equilibrium theory) mispricing.

3 GAUGE MODEL FOR DERIVATIVE PRICING

In this section, we construct a gauge model for a share – cash – derivative system essentially following the paper of Ilinski and Kalinin (1997). To simplify the model, we consider only one type of shares and assume perfect capital market conditions. The consideration is not restricted by any type of concrete derivative contracts. However, for simplicity, we will illustrate the application of the model by analysing European and American call options.

The logic of this construction is very similar to those of Section 2 of Chapter 8. Once again, one has to analyse portfolios consisting of two risky assets and one leading parameter: this time, they are the derivative and the underlying shares, with the share price as the single factor. We also assume the existence of a single riskless asset – the bank deposit with the

---

[22]The most notorious hedge fund that suffered severe losses and nearly collapsed in August 1998 was Long Term Capital Management (LTCM). It was headed by one-time bond trading star John Meriwether and had among its partners Myron Scholes and Robert Merton. High returns and big names attracted billions of dollars and led to a fantastic level of leverage. From about 25 at the beginning of 1998, it climbed to 150 in mid-September. After the fund faced collapse, it was bailed out by 14 major investment institutions, which invested in the fund. An interesting account of the LTCM story can be found in Jacobs (1999) and Dunbar (1999).

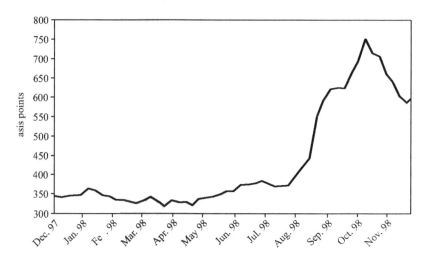

Figure 9.11 Bear Stearns Global High Yield Research date on the time dynamics of spread between high-yield bonds and Treasury bonds. From B.I. Jacobs, *Capital Ideas and Market Realities*. Oxford: Blackwell, 1999. Reproduced by permission of Bruce I. Jacobs.

corresponding interest rate r_b. Shares or derivatives can be exchanged for cash, and vice versa. The corresponding exchange rates are S_i and C_i, i.e. one share or derivative contract is exchanged for S_i or C_i units of cash at some moment t_i, and the rates for the reverse exchange are S_i^{-1} and C_i^{-1}. We consider the period from a starting point $t = 0$ up to time $t = T$. It is convenient to choose the time T as the expiration time of the derivative contract. We assume that there exists a shortest time horizon $\Delta = T/N$, and this Δ is taken as a time unit. This means that the exchange rates S_i and C_i are quoted on the set of equidistant times $\{t_i\}_{i=0}^{N}$, $t_i = i\Delta$, and represent parallel transport along the legs of a double-ladder base

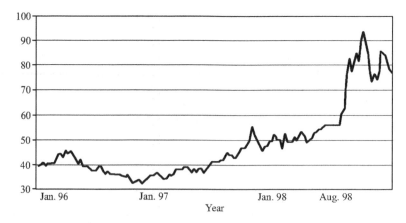

Figure 9.12 Time dynamics for the spread in yields calculated from the Treasury bonds and interest rate swaps. Taken from D. Kestenbaum *Science* **283**, 1246 (1999).

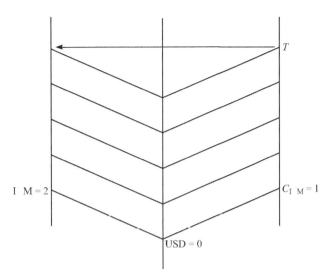

Figure 9.13 Double-ladder base space for cash–share–derivative system. The additional link at the final time corresponds to a European contract.

graph[23] (see Fig. 9.13). The interest rate for cash is r_b, so that between two subsequent times t_i and t_{i+1} the volume of cash increases by factor $e^{r_b \Delta}$. The shares and derivatives are characterized by rates r_1 and r_2 respectively. These rates are responsible for parallel transport in the time direction.

As was discussed in Chapters 3 and 5, to construct a gauge field action, one has to use curvature tensor elements associated with elementary plaquette operations. For example, the cash–shares plaquette operation comprises the following course of actions: a trader borrows one share at time t_i, sells it for S_i units of cash, puts the cash in the bank until time t_{i+1}, and closes his short position at time t_{i+1}, borrowing $e^{r_1 \Delta} S_{i+1}$ units of cash and buying shares. The result of the operation for the trader will be $e^{r_b \Delta} S_i - e^{r_1 \Delta} S_{i+1}$ units of cash. The excess return on this operation is

$$Q_i^{(1)} = S_i e^{r_b \Delta} S_{i+1}^{-1} e^{-r_1 \Delta} - 1. \tag{7}$$

To get this expression, we have discounted the amount and converted it into shares, since the operation was started in the shares. Equation (7) has the form of the curvature tensor element corresponding to drawing assets through the cycle. If $Q_i^{(1)} \neq 0$, a trader can get an excess return performing this or the reverse operation. The quantity

$$R_i^{(1)} = (S_i^{-1} e^{r_1 \Delta} S_{i+1} e^{-r_b \Delta} + S_i e^{r_b \Delta} S_{i+1}^{-1} e^{-r_1 \Delta} - 2)/\Delta \tag{8}$$

is used to measure the mispricing (excess rate of return) on local cash–share operations. Absence of mispricing is equivalent to the equality

$$S_i^{-1} e^{r_1 \Delta} S_{i+1} e^{-r_b \Delta} = S_i e^{r_b \Delta} S_{i+1}^{-1} e^{-r_1 \Delta} = 1.$$

---

[23] As was shown in Section 4 of Chapter 5, lattice and continuous bases give essentially the same gauge field theory, but the money flow actions can differ substantially.

The same can be done for other possible plaquette operations. For example, the curvature tensor element for the cash–derivative plaquette is given by

$$Q_i^{(2)} = C_i e^{r_b \Delta} C_{i+1}^{-1} e^{-r_2 \Delta} - 1. \tag{9}$$

The plaquette quantities are gauge-invariant, i.e. they do not change under local rescaling gauge transformations.

In this section, as in Chapter 8, we work with the simplest gauge action choice that accommodates asset correlations, namely the local-in-time quadratic action of Section 3.2 of Chapter 5:

$$A_g = \frac{1}{2} \int_{-\infty}^{\infty} d\tau \left[\alpha_{11} \left(\frac{S'}{S} + r_1 - r_0 \right)^2 \right.$$
$$\left. + \alpha_{22} \left(\frac{C'}{C} + r_2 - r_0 \right)^2 + 2\alpha_{12} \left(\frac{C'}{C} + r_2 - r_0 \right) \left(\frac{S'}{S} + r_1 - r_0 \right) \right]. \tag{10}$$

Here the matrix $||\alpha||$ is the inverse of the correlation matrix of the plaquette quantities. The correlation is important, since the derivative, by its very definition, depends on the underlying price that causes the correlation.

The action (10) dictates the character of the underlying price motion. Namely, the price in the above model follows geometrical Brownian motion in the absence of money flow fields. These money flows can significantly change the form of the distribution function and other properties of the price random walk. Indeed, in the presence of money flows, more complicated random processes for price motion emerge, which resemble real data observations, as we saw in Chapter 6.

Let us now turn to gauge fixing. Since the action A_g is gauge-invariant, it is possible to perform a gauge transformation that will not change the dynamics but will simplify further calculations. In lattice gauge theory (Creutz, 1983) there are several standard choices of gauge one of which is the axial gauge. In the axial gauge, elements of the structural group are taken as being fixed on links in the time direction and along one link in the 'space' direction at some particular time. This kind of gauge fixing is convenient for the model in question.

We choose r_b to be the riskfree interest rate, and $r_b - r_1$ and $r_b - r_2$ to be the average rates of return on the share, and the derivative. This means that in the situation of the double-ladder base (Fig. 9.13), the only dynamical variables are the prices $S(t)$ and $C(t)$ as functions of time. The corresponding measure of integration in the functional integral for the transition probability is the invariant measure

$$\mathcal{D}C \, \mathcal{D}S = \prod_t \frac{dS(t)}{S(t)} \frac{dC(t)}{C(t)}. \tag{11}$$

Below we fix the price of the shares at time $t = 0$, taking $S_0 = S(0)$. We also fix the exchange rate of the derivative with the share at the moment of the derivative exercise.

To summarize, the probability weight of the price trajectories in the absence of money flows is given by the action (10) and the measure (11). To proceed, we need to calculate the correlation matrix $||C_{ij}||$ and its inverse $||\alpha_{ij}||$ to substitute into (10). Before doing this, it is appropriate to add the following note. As we said above, since it is a derivative instrument from the share price, the price of the derivative has to be correlated with, or even defined by, the share price. That is why it is natural and more convenient for our purposes to write the function $C(t)$ as some unknown function of $S(t)$. Since we integrate over all $C(t)$ (or over all functions $C(t, S(t))$), this does not mean any loss of generality. This trick allows us to get explicit expressions for the correlation coefficients.

First of all, the correlation coefficient C_{11} is, by definition, the share price volatility:

$$C_{11} = \left\langle \left(\frac{1}{S} dS\left(t\right) + \left(r_1 - r_0\right) dt \right), \left(\frac{1}{S} dS(t) + \left(r_1 - r_0\right)dt \right) \right\rangle \Big/ dt = \frac{1}{\beta_1}.$$

We denote the second correlator C_{12} by $\alpha(t)/2\beta_1$, introducing

$$\alpha\left(t\right) \equiv \frac{\left\langle \left(\frac{1}{C(t)} dC(t) + \left(r_2 - r_0\right) dt \right), \left(\frac{1}{S(t)} dS(t) + \left(r_1 - r_0\right) dt \right) \right\rangle}{\left\langle \left(\frac{1}{S(t)} dS(t) + \left(r_1 - r_0\right) dt \right), \left(\frac{1}{S(t)} dS(t) + \left(r_1 - r_0\right) dt \right) \right\rangle}. \tag{12}$$

Using the expansion

$$dC(S, t) = \frac{\partial C}{\partial S} dS + \frac{\partial C}{\partial t} dt + \cdots$$

and arguing that only the first term depends on dS, we find an expression for α:[24]

$$\alpha = \frac{S}{C} \frac{\partial C}{\partial S}. \tag{13}$$

Therefore the correlation coefficient C_{12} can be rewritten as

$$C_{12} = \frac{S}{C} \frac{\partial C}{\partial S} \Big/ 2\beta_1.$$

The last coefficient, C_{22}, can be calculated in a similar manner. One can say that the correlation in changes of derivative prices results from the mentioned S dependence and from the stochastic nature of the function $C(S)$ itself. This means that it can be expressed as a sum of correlations $\alpha^2(t)/2\beta_1$ due to S and some residual correlation:

$$C_{22} = \left\langle \left(\frac{1}{C(t)} dC(t) + \left(r_2 - r_b\right) dt \right), \left(\frac{1}{C(t)} dC(t) + \left(r_2 - r_b\right) dt \right) \right\rangle \Big/ dt$$

$$= \frac{\alpha^2(t)}{2\beta_1} + \frac{(1 - \alpha)^2}{2\beta_2}.$$

The last term disappears if the derivative is, in fact, the share, so that $\alpha = 1$ and $C_{22} = C_{11} = C_{12}$. The resulting correlation matrix has the form:

$$\|C_{ij}\| = \begin{pmatrix} \dfrac{1}{2\beta_1} & \dfrac{\alpha}{2\beta_1} \\ \dfrac{\alpha}{2\beta_1} & \dfrac{\alpha^2(t)}{2\beta_1} + \dfrac{(1 - \alpha)^2}{2\beta_2} \end{pmatrix},$$

---

[24]Up to terms that are $o(dt)$ and are neglected.

and its inverse $||\alpha_{ij}||$ can be found immediately as

$$
||\alpha_{ij}|| = \begin{pmatrix} 2\beta_1 + \dfrac{2\alpha^2}{(1-\alpha)^2}\beta_2 & \dfrac{2\alpha}{(1-\alpha)^2}\beta_2 \\[3mm] \dfrac{2\alpha}{(1-\alpha)^2}\beta_2 & \dfrac{2}{(1-\alpha)^2}\beta_2 \end{pmatrix}.
$$

(14)

Substituting (14) into (10), we find that the action functional can be rewritten in the form

$$
\mathcal{A}_g = \int_{-\infty}^{\infty} \beta_1\, dt \left(\frac{1}{S(t)}\frac{dS(t)}{dt} + (r_1 - r_b) \right)^2
$$

$$
+ \int_{-\infty}^{\infty} \frac{\beta_2\, dt}{(1-\alpha)^2} \left[\left(\frac{1}{C(t)}\frac{dC(t)}{dt} + (r_2 - r_b) \right) - \alpha(t)\left(\frac{1}{S(t)}\frac{dS(t)}{dt} + (r_1 - r_b) \right) \right]^2.
$$

(15)

It is interesting to note that this expression gives the leading order (with respect to Δ of the lattice action

$$
\mathcal{A}_g = \sum_i \left(\beta_1 R_i^{(1)} + \frac{\beta_2}{(1-\alpha)^2} R_i^{(2,1)} \right).
$$

(16)

where $R^{(1)}$ and $R^{(2,1)}$ are defined as

$$
R^{(1)} = \frac{(Q^{(1)})^2}{\Delta}, \qquad R_i^{(2,1)} = \frac{(Q_i^{(2)} - \alpha_i Q_i^{(1)})^2}{\Delta}
$$

(17)

and

$$
\alpha_i = \frac{\left\langle Q_i^{(2)}, Q_i^{(1)} \right\rangle}{\left\langle Q_i^{(1)}, Q_i^{(1)} \right\rangle}.
$$

(18)

This is the action with which one has to deal when lattice systems are considered; we use the action (15) in the continuous-time limit.

3.1 Derivation of the Black–Scholes Equation

In this subsection, we obtain the Black–Scholes equation as the equation of the saddle-point in the quasiclassical limit of the gauge theory in absence of money flows. Equation (15) for the action in the continuous-time limit provides a basis for the derivation. The first term on the right-hand side of this equation corresponds to geometrical random walks for the underlying asset price, and it allows us to use the Itô lemma[25] in the derivation.

---

[25]The reader might be disappointed with the fact that the Itô lemma is used again. As is explained in Section 6 of the Appendix on quantum field-theoretical methods, the Itô lemma can be derived in the functional integral framework. Therefore by using the Itô lemma here we save time – instead of keeping all terms in the Taylor expansion of dC and analysing them in perturbation theory, as is done in Section 6 of the Appendix. Whichever method is used the result will be the same.

Let us turn our attention to the second term in (15):

$$\int_{-\infty}^{\infty} dt \left[\left(\frac{1}{C(t)} \frac{dC(t)}{dt} + (r_2 - r_b) \right) - \alpha(t) \left(\frac{1}{S(t)} \frac{dS(t)}{dt} + (r_1 - r_b) \right) \right]^2.$$

Since the process $S(t)$ follows geometrical Brownian motion, we can use the Itô lemma to expand dC:

$$dC = \frac{\partial C}{\partial t} \, dt + \frac{\sigma^2}{2} S^2 \frac{\partial^2 C}{\partial S^2} \, dt + \frac{\partial C}{\partial S} \, dS.$$

This expansion and (13) allow us to rewrite the above action term as

$$\int \beta_2 \, dt \, \frac{C^2}{\left(C - \frac{\partial C}{\partial S} S \right)^2} \left[\frac{1}{C} \frac{\partial C}{\partial t} + \frac{1}{C} \frac{\sigma^2}{2} S^2 \frac{\partial^2 C}{\partial S^2} - r_b \left(1 - \frac{S}{C} \frac{\partial C}{\partial S} \right) + \left(r_2 - \frac{S}{C} \frac{\partial C}{\partial S} r_1 \right) \right]^2. \qquad (19)$$

This last expression can be simplified if the time component of the connection (which is fixed in the axial gauge that we use here) is fixed so that

$$r_2 = r_1 \frac{S}{C} \frac{\partial C}{\partial S}. \qquad (20)$$

In fact, both r_1 and r_2 can be fixed as arbitrary functions of C and S. But in the general case, the values S and C will not be the market prices of a fixed number of shares and derivatives. In the case where the average rate of return on shares obeys the relation

$$r_1 = r_b - \mu,$$

the gauge is chosen so that S corresponds to a fixed number of shares. In the same way, the gauge fixing (20) corresponds to a choice of C as the price of a fixed number of the derivative contracts.[26] This finally allows us to obtain expression for the arbitrage term in the action:

$$\int \beta_2 \, dt \left(\frac{\frac{\partial C}{\partial t} + \frac{\sigma^2}{2} S^2 \frac{\partial^2 C}{\partial S^2} - r_b \left(C - S \frac{\partial C}{\partial S} \right)}{C - \frac{\partial C}{\partial S} S} \right)^2. \qquad (21)$$

It is easy to see that this term describes Gaussian fluctuations of the arbitrage return on a riskless portfolio consisting of one unit of the derivative contracts and $-\partial C/\partial S$ shares, in full analogy with the general consideration of Chapter 8. This is exactly the portfolio that we analysed in Section 1 in the derivation of the Black–Scholes equation.

In the classical limit,[27] i.e. $\beta_2 \to \infty$, which corresponds to the absence of arbitrage, the action reduces the functional integration over functions $C(t, S)$ to the contribution from the

---

[26]If, say, the choice of derivative units is a non-constant function of time – one contract today, two contracts tomorrow and so on – then $r_2 - r_1(S/C)\partial C/\partial S$ will be non-zero and the price of the derivative unit will not obey the Black–Scholes equation.

[27]See Section 5.2 of the Appendix.

classical trajectory only, and this trajectory is defined by the Black–Scholes equation for the price of the financial derivative:

$$\frac{\partial C}{\partial t} + \frac{\sigma^2}{2} S^2 \frac{\partial^2 C}{\partial S^2} - r_b \left(C - S \frac{\partial C}{\partial S} \right) = 0. \tag{22}$$

This equation does not depend on the particular type of derivative that is encoded in the boundary conditions. We proceed with the derivation of the boundary conditions, which are discussed in the next subsection.

3.2 Boundary Conditions

The previous analysis is valid for any type of derivative contracts. A particular type of derivative is defined by the details of its exercise, which are reflected in the construction of the base of the corresponding fibre bundle. For example, the European contract can be exchanged on shares only at the expiration time, and this causes a single boundary link additional to the double-ladder base. This link is directed (see Section 1 of Chapter 5), and connects the derivative and the shares points at the final time. More numerous additional links correspond to more complicated types of contracts, such as American or Bermudan. The base graph for the American option and the underlying share contains the same double ladder and the directed links from option and cash to share at any intermediate times before the expiration time T. These links are the same as that for the European option. In this subsection, we show how to construct boundary plaquettes[28] for European and American options using the call options as an example. We will see that the standard boundary conditions for these contracts reappear in the zero-arbitrage limit.

The links that are responsible for the swap of the derivative to the share, i.e. for the exercising of the option, generate new plaquettes on the 'space'–time graph. The corresponding plaquette quantities R'_b have to be taken into account when the full action for a particular type of derivative is analysed. We keep these terms separate from the general action (21), so that the full action has the form

$$\mathcal{A}_{g,b} = \mathcal{A}_{g,b} + \sum_i \beta'_i R'_{b,i}, \tag{23}$$

where i labels the boundary plaquettes. The primed plaquettes contain the directed links, and contribute to the boundary conditions only. Everywhere else in this chapter, we will neglect arbitrage fluctuations at the expiration time, thus neglecting the primed plaquettes and using the no-arbitrage boundary conditions. However, to make the analytical and numerical analysis complete, they have to be retained.

Let us turn to the derivation of the boundary plaquette quantities. We first consider in more detail the European call option. At the expiration time T, the option can be sold or bought for $C(T)$ units of cash, but it can also be exchanged (together with E units of cash) for a share. If the price of the share S is less than E, this leads to a scrap of the call.

---

[28]The construction of boundary terms in the action looks more natural in the continuous-base case because, in fact, shares are exchanged on portfolios containing the derivative and the cash. However, we proceed with the lattice formulation to show that it is possible to analyse the boundary terms in the lattice formulation as well.

The new link creates new arbitrage opportunities, which we take into account by introducing the $\beta' R'_N$ term in the action (23). There exists a new arbitrage operation that is available at the expiration time T: one can borrow the portfolio consisting of the option and E currency units, exchange it for the share if $S(T) > E$ (directed link on the base graph), sell the share for $S(T)$ units of cash, and buy the portfolio again. This gives us the plaquette excess return

$$Q'_N = [S(T)\theta(S(T) - E) + E\theta(E - S(T))][C(T) + E]^{-1} - 1,$$

and for the plaquette quantity R'_N we get

$$R'_N = \frac{E\theta(E - S(T)) + S(T)\theta(S(T) - E)}{C(T) + E} + \frac{C(T) + E}{E\theta(E - S(T)) + S(T)\theta(S(T) - E)} - 2. \qquad (24)$$

In the quasiclassical (no-arbitrage) limit, we have $\beta' \to \infty$, which reproduces the well-known boundary condition for the European call option from (24):

$$C(T) = [S(T) - E]\theta(S(T) - E). \qquad (25)$$

If we neglect this arbitrage possibility at time T, we can use this equation as a gauge-fixing condition, and we do not need to consider additional links and boundary plaquettes. This approximation is quite realistic, and clearly simplifies the scheme.

Let us examine the American call option case. It can be exchanged for the share at any time up to T by paying an additional E units of cash. In this case, the base graph contains links from the option to the share (but not backwards) at all time points. It presents two possible arbitrage operations. The first operation is similar to the above operation with the European option at exercise time T. This operation is available at any moment $t \leq T$. One can borrow the portfolio consisting of an option and E currency units, exchange it for the share, sell the share for $S(t)$ units of money, and buy the portfolio again. The excess return on this operation is

$$Q'_t = S(t)[C_A(t) + E]^{-1} - 1,$$

and for the boundary plaquette quantity we get

$$R'_t = \frac{S(t)}{C_A(t) + E} + \frac{C_A(t) + E}{S(t)} - 2. \qquad (26)$$

Exactly as for the case of the European option in the quasiclassical limit (the absence of arbitrage), we get the first boundary condition for the American call option:

$$C_A(t) = S(t) - E. \qquad (27)$$

Now we have to determine the moment when the American option has to be exercised. To this end, we consider another available arbitrage operation. Suppose an arbitrageur has the portfolio of the option and E units of cash at some time t. He can exchange the portfolio for a share that he keeps up to time $t + dt$, or hold the portfolio and exchange it for a share at time $t + dt$. The expected return on the portfolio is $[C_A(t)(r_b - r_2) + Er_b]/[C_A(t) + E]$ so that, at time $t + dt$, an arbitrageur will have

$$\left(1 + \frac{C_A(t)(r_b - r_2) + Er_b}{C_A(t) + E} dt\right) \frac{C_A(t) + E}{C_A(t + dt) + E}$$

portfolios of the option and E units of cash, which he can exchange for an equal number of shares. The expected return on the share is $r_b - r_1$. Therefore the excess return on this operation is

$$Q''_t = \left(1 + \frac{C_A(t)(r_b - r_2) + Er_b}{C_A(t) + E} dt\right) \frac{C_A(t) + E}{C_A(t + dt) + E} \left([1 + (r_b - r_1) dt] \frac{S(t)}{S(t + dt)}\right)^{-1} - 1,$$

and for the boundary plaquette quantity we obtain the expression

$$R''_t = (Q''_t + 1) + (Q''_t + 1)^{-1} - 2. \tag{28}$$

In the no-arbitrage limit, it satisfies the equation

$$Q''_t = 0$$

at the exercise time. This gives us the second boundary condition for the American call:

$$\frac{\partial C_A(t, S)}{\partial S} = 1. \tag{29}$$

To derive this expression, one has to use the no-arbitrage condition $Q''_t = 0$ and the expression (20) for r_2, and take into account the first boundary condition (27).

So, finally, we obtain the set of well-known boundary conditions for the American call option:

$$\frac{\partial C_A(t, S)}{\partial S} = 1, \qquad C_A(t, S) = S(t) - E. \tag{30}$$

These equations determine the time when the option is exchanged for the share and the corresponding payoff. It is easy to show from the plaquette analysis that, in the absence of dividends, the American call is never exercised early, and hence is equivalent to the European call – but we do not stop to do this.

To summarize, we have shown that in the absence of money flows and in the quasiclassical limit, which corresponds to a no-arbitrage world, the Black – Scholes equation emerges as the equation for the saddle point and is provided with the appropriate boundary conditions.

3.3   Connection with Black–Scholes Analysis

In this short subsection, we clarify the connection with the original Black – Scholes analysis from Section 1. Let us return to the formula for (17) $R^{(2,1)}$:

$$R_i^{(2,1)} = (Q_i^{(2,1)})^2 / \Delta,$$

with $Q_i^{(2,1)}$ defined as

$$Q_i^{(2,1)} \equiv Q_i^{(2)} - Q_i^{(1)} \alpha_i.$$

To first order in Δ, the last expression can be rewritten as

$$Q_i^{(2,1)} = C_i S_i^{-\alpha_i} e^{\alpha_i r_1 \Delta} e^{(1-\alpha_i) r_b \Delta} e^{-r_2 \Delta} S_{i+1}^{\alpha_i} C_{i+1}^{-1} - 1.$$

It is easy to give a simple interpretation of the last expression. Indeed, it is obvious that it describes the following transaction circle:

$$C \rightarrow USD \rightarrow (1 - \alpha)USD \oplus \alpha S \rightarrow USD \rightarrow C.$$

The portfolio comprising shares and cash (in proportions α and $1 - \alpha$) emerging at the intermediate state is the Black–Scholes hedging portfolio and the condition (18) is exactly the hedging relation. From this point of view, the plaquette quantity $Q_i^{(2,1)}$ represents the arbitrage fluctuations in the hedging portfolio–derivative plaquette. This takes us back to the treatment of the expression

$$\left[\frac{\partial C}{\partial t} + \frac{\sigma^2}{2}S^2\frac{\partial^2 C}{\partial S^2} - r_b\left(C - S\frac{\partial C}{\partial S}\right)\right]\bigg/\left(C - S\frac{\partial C}{\partial S}\right)$$

as the arbitrage excess return on the infinitesimal arbitrage operation.

3.4 Arbitrage Money Flows

Arbitrage money flows can be introduced here in exactly the same way as was done in Section 2 of Chapter 8 for the case of general asset pricing. To construct the action for the arbitrage money flows, it is convenient to use the continuous-base fibre bundle (see Section 4 of Chapter 5). In the case of the derivative–cash–share system, the coordinates in the base are (t, x_C, x_S), where t is time, x_S is the fraction of a portfolio stored in the shares, and x_C is the corresponding fraction stored in the derivatives. This implies that the remaining part the portfolio is positioned in cash.

The arbitrageurs, by their very definition, exploit the riskless arbitrage opportunities. This is why their configuration space is restricted to the riskless portfolios. To this end, one has to introduce an external potential

$$-\lambda \int \left(x_C \frac{dC}{C} + x_S \frac{dS}{S}\right)^2 \tag{31}$$

into the arbitrageurs' action (see Section 4 of Chapter 6 for a discussion of risk aversion and external potentials). The action itself can be constructed using the same set of first principles examined in Chapter 6. Essentially, these are gauge invariance and profit maximization (for more details, see Section 3 of Chapter 6).

In the case of absolute risk aversion, $\lambda \to \infty$, the trajectories of the money flows with non-zero probabilities are confined to the reduced subspace defined by the equation

$$x_S + x_C \frac{S}{C}\frac{\partial C}{\partial S} = 0,$$

which eliminates the potential term (31). This means that the coordinates of the arbitrageurs' portfolios are parametrized by a single parameter k:

$$x_C = k\frac{C}{C - S\dfrac{\partial C}{\partial S}}, \qquad x_S = -k\frac{S\dfrac{\partial C}{\partial S}}{C - S\dfrac{\partial C}{\partial S}}. \tag{32}$$

Therefore the action for the arbitrageurs defines a one-dimensional field theory with the line (32) as the configuration space. Further simplification will be achieved if we assume that the arbitrageurs keep portfolios with a maximum possible absolute value of k, thus maximizing their profit from mispricing. The maximum value k_0 is dictated by position limits for an average arbitrageur, since the meaning of the parameter k is the fraction of the arbitrageur's full portfolio invested in risky assets. This assumption allows us to reduce the set of arbitrage portfolios to two points only:

$$\left(k_0 \frac{C}{C - S\frac{\partial C}{\partial S}}, \; -k_0 \frac{S\frac{\partial C}{\partial S}}{C - S\frac{\partial C}{\partial S}} \right)$$

and

$$\left(-k_0 \frac{C}{C - S\frac{\partial C}{\partial S}}, \; +k_0 \frac{S\frac{\partial C}{\partial S}}{C - S\frac{\partial C}{\partial S}} \right).$$

In this form, the arbitrageurs' money flows are described by the simple ladder model already studied in Chapters 6 and 7. This allows us later to use the results of these chapters in the analysis of the market reaction to virtual arbitrage fluctuations.

It was explained in Section 4 of Chapter 5 that in the case of a continuous fibre bundle, it is convenient to fix the gauge so that the price of basis portfolios at each point of the base is equal to one and the corresponding components of the connexion at point (t, x_C, x_S) are:

$$A_0 = (1 - x_S - x_C)r_b + x_S\left(r_1 + \frac{dS(t)}{S(t)} \right) + x_C\left(r_2 + \frac{dC(t)}{C(t)} \right),$$

$$A_1 = A_2 = 0.$$

For the case of the ladder base, the single-investor unnormalized transition matrix for time step Δ in this gauge has the form

$$P(t_i, t_{i-1}) = \begin{pmatrix} e^{\tilde{\beta}\Delta A_0(-k_0)} & 1 \\ 1 & e^{\tilde{\beta}\Delta A_0(+k_0)} \end{pmatrix},$$

which follows directly from equation (10) of Chapter 6. We substitute into this the portfolio fractions (32) and the corresponding expression for $A_0(\pm k_0)$,

$$A_0(\pm k_0) = r_b(1 \mp k_0) \mp \frac{k_0}{C - S\frac{\partial C}{\partial S}} S\frac{\partial C}{\partial S}\left(r_1 + \frac{dS}{S(t)} \right)$$

$$\pm \frac{k_0 C}{C - S\frac{\partial C}{\partial S}}\left(r_2 + \frac{dC}{C(t)} \right)$$

$$= r_b(1 \mp k_0) \pm \frac{k_0}{C - S\frac{\partial C}{\partial S}}\left(\frac{\partial C}{\partial t} + \frac{S^2\sigma^2}{2}\frac{\partial^2 C}{\partial S^2} \right)$$

$$\pm \frac{k_0 C}{C - S\frac{\partial C}{\partial S}}\left(r_2 - \frac{S}{C}\frac{\partial C}{\partial S} \right)$$

$$= r_b \pm k_0\left(\frac{\partial C}{\partial t} + \frac{S^2\sigma^2}{2}\frac{\partial^2 C}{\partial S^2} + r_b S\frac{\partial C}{\partial S} - r_b C \right)\Big/\left(C - S\frac{\partial C}{\partial S} \right),$$

and we rewrite the transition matrix as

$$P(t_i, t_{i-1}) =$$

$$\begin{pmatrix} \exp\left[\tilde{\beta}r_b\Delta - k_0\tilde{\beta}\Delta \dfrac{\frac{\partial C}{\partial t}+\frac{S^2\sigma^2}{2}\frac{\partial^2 C}{\partial S^2}+r_bS\frac{\partial C}{\partial S}-r_bC}{C-S\frac{\partial C}{\partial S}}\right] & 1 \\[4mm] 1 & \exp\left[\tilde{\beta}r_0\Delta + k_0\tilde{\beta}\Delta \dfrac{\frac{\partial C}{\partial t}+\frac{S^2\sigma^2}{2}\frac{\partial^2 C}{\partial S^2}+r_bS\frac{\partial C}{\partial S}-r_bC}{C-S\frac{\partial C}{\partial S}}\right] \end{pmatrix}.$$

In practice, one can safely neglect the riskless interest rate r_b in comparison with the arbitrage return. Normalizing $P(t_i, t_{i-1})$ and introducing the notation

$$\mathcal{L}_{BS}C = \frac{\partial C}{\partial t} + \frac{S^2\sigma^2}{2}\frac{\partial^2 C}{\partial S^2} + r_bS\frac{\partial C}{\partial S} - r_bC,$$

we obtain the normalized transition matrix:

$$P(t_i, t_{i-1}) = \frac{1}{2}\,\text{sech}^{-1}\left[\frac{1}{2}k_0\tilde{\beta}\Delta\mathcal{L}_{BS}C \Big/ \left(C - S\frac{\partial C}{\partial S}\right)\right]$$

$$\times \begin{pmatrix} e^{-\frac{1}{2}k_0\tilde{\beta}\Delta\mathcal{L}_{BS}C/(C-S\frac{\partial C}{\partial S})} & e^{-\frac{1}{2}k_0\tilde{\beta}\Delta\mathcal{L}_{BS}C/(C-S\frac{\partial C}{\partial S})} \\[2mm] e^{\frac{1}{2}k_0\tilde{\beta}\Delta\mathcal{L}_{BS}C/(C-S\frac{\partial C}{\partial S})} & e^{\frac{1}{2}k_0\tilde{\beta}\Delta\mathcal{L}_{BS}C/(C-S\frac{\partial C}{\partial S})} \end{pmatrix}. \tag{33}$$

This expression for the normalized transition matrix has the same form as the transition probability in equation (28) of Chapter 6. Together with the arbitrage action term (21), they constitute the part that describes the arbitrage fluctuations and the corresponding market reaction. This subsystem is equivalent to the simple gauge model of Chapters 6 and 7. It means that the characteristics of the arbitrage return in this model will be exactly the same as for the gauge single-asset model. In particular, there will be mean reversion for the arbitrage returns and an exponentially decaying correlation function with some characteristic lifetime λ. We infer therefore that, like the gauge model of Chapter 8, to the first non-trivial order, the gauge model with the arbitrage money flows is equivalent to the much simpler model where the arbitrage return $\mathcal{R}$ on the portfolio of k derivatives and $-k\partial C/\partial S$ shares follows the Ornstein–Uhlenbeck process

$$\frac{d\mathcal{R}}{dt} + \lambda\mathcal{R} = v(t), \qquad \langle v(t)\rangle_v = 0, \qquad \langle v(t)v(t')\rangle_v = \Sigma^2\delta(t - t'), \tag{34}$$

with the parameter Σ^2 equal to $1/\beta_2$ (see (21)). This is the model that we derive below from a phenomenological point of view, and which will be central to the pricing of derivatives in quasi-equilibrium situations.

3.5 Other Money Flows

The arbitrageurs are not the only participants in the trading of derivatives and shares. There are two other groups of market participants who influence market dynamics. These are hedgers and speculators.

Hedgers

One source of money flows is the existence of transactions caused by hedging strategies. It was already mentioned in Section 2 that it is important to take into account the hedging strategies for relatively illiquid markets or for liquid markets in cases of temporary illiquidity associated with large market events. As was shown by Platen and Schweizer (1994),[29] the dynamic feedback from the hedging strategies leads to the implied volatility 'smile' and the 'skewness,' and thus can be one of the factors responsible for the effects. Another important aspect of the feedback is its destabilizing nature (see De Long et al, 1990b), which is sometimes blamed for market crashes (see also the discussion of crashes in Section 2).

It is easy to account for the hedgers and their impact on the market in the gauge model. First of all, they are absolutely risk-aversive, and therefore their action contains the same potential term (31) with $\lambda \to \infty$. Secondly, they have a fixed number of derivative contracts that they are hedging, and the only changes in their portfolios are dictated by the requirement of the absence of risk for the portfolios. Thirdly, their only objective is to be hedged, and they do not maximize their profit. Therefore their action does not contain any hopping terms and the only contribution from the hedgers enters the share price term as a technical demand dictated by the hedging strategies in the form of Farmer's term (see Section 5 of Chapter 5). Effectively, one has to change the share price term in (10)

$$\beta_1 \int dt \left(\frac{S'}{S} - \mu\right)^2,$$

to a term that includes the technical demand from the hedgers,

$$\beta_1 \int dt \left(\frac{1}{S}\frac{dS}{dt} - \mu - \lambda'\frac{d\Delta_h(S, t)}{dt}\right)^2. \tag{35}$$

Here N is the number of hedged derivatives contracts, λ' is Farmer's liquidity, and $\Delta_h(S, t)$ is the hedging strategy.[30] Using the expression (35) in the previous derivation of the gauge action for the shares – cash – derivative system gives a consecutive account of the hedgers' impact on the system description. In the quasiclassical (no-arbitrage) limit, the pricing equation derived from the theory coincides with the Black – Scholes equation in the presence of the hedgers' feedback (for an introduction to the feedback effects and the corresponding derivative pricing, see Chapter 29 in Wilmott, 1998).

Speculative Money Flows

Speculators create mispricing opportunities and play against arbitrageurs. We saw in Chapter 6 that it is vital to introduce speculative money flows to produce a realistic statistical description of price time series.

Moreover, in some cases, the speculative money flows simply cannot be ignored because of the nature of the derivative to be priced. For example, the passport option[31] has a payoff

---

[29]Originating from Föllmer (1991), Föllmer and Schweizer (1993), and Frey and Strerine (1993).
[30]This expression can easily be generalized to the case of many different hedging strategies.
[31]The passport option gives a client a right to trade on a certain notional in the underlying asset and walk away if her account turns negative at the expiration date. In reality, passport options are traded well above their theoretical values.

which depends directly on the speculative strategy used by a client. The standard method to price the option is to assume that the client's trading strategy is such that the value of the option that she bought is maximal (Andersen et al, 1998). Although it is convenient (and probably safe) to ignore the problem as long as one's competitors do the same, the assumption that an agent's objective is to maximize her insurance is hardly realistic: we definitely do not want to become terminally ill just to maximize our life insurance. Instead, we want to live our full life and have some 'safety net' in case things go wrong. The same is true for buyers of the passport option: it is a 'safety net' for an agressive speculator. To ignore the speculative nature of the option is to create a model that overprices the option and will not sustain a fair competition. The speculative nature of passport options and the corresponding pricing was considered in Ilinski (2000b). There is no doubt that the further development of exotic derivatives with an active client's role will lead to the necessity to fully incorporate speculative money flows in their pricing.

Speculative money flows have already been discussed extensively in Chapters 6 and 7. The only difference from the previous consideration is the nature of the base graph – instead of the ladder graph for the single-asset model, we have to analyse the theory on the double-ladder base. We formulate the dynamics for the speculative cash-debt flows based on several assumptions, such as the gauge invariance of the dynamics, profit maximization, and bounded rationality. This leaves us with the following functional integral representation for the matrix elements of an evolution operator in the coherent-state representation (see Section 4 of Chapter 6) of money flows in the case of our double-ladder base graph ($r_0 \equiv r_b$):

$$\langle \{\bar{\psi}^h(T), \bar{\chi}^h(T)\} | \hat{U}(T, t) | \{\psi^h(0), \chi^h(0)\} \rangle$$

$$= \int \prod_h \prod_{k=0}^{2} \prod_{i_h: t \leq i_h \leq T} d\bar{\psi}^h_{k,i_h} \, d\psi^h_{k,i_h} \, d\bar{\chi}^h_{k,i_h} \, d\chi^h_{k,i_h} \, e^{s1+s1'},$$

with the following actions for the multi-horizon cash and debt flows:[32]

$$s1 = \sum_h \sum_{k=0}^{2} \sum_{i_h} (\bar{\psi}^h_{k,i_h+1} e^{\beta r_k h} \psi^h_{k,i_h} - \bar{\psi}^h_{k,i_h} \psi^h_{k,i_h}) + \sum_{i_h} [(1 - t_c)^\beta C^\beta_{i_h} \bar{\psi}^h_{0,i_h+1} \psi^h_{2,i_h}$$

$$+ (1 - t_c)^\beta C^{-\beta}_{i_h} \bar{\psi}^h_{2,i_h+1} \psi^h_{0,i_h} + (1 - t_c)^\beta S^\beta_{i_h} \bar{\psi}^h_{0,i_h+1} \psi^h_{1,i_h}$$

$$+ (1 - t_c)^\beta S^{-\beta}_{i_h} \bar{\psi}^h_{1,i_h+1} \psi^h_{0,i_h}],$$

$$s1' = \sum_h \sum_{k=0}^{2} \sum_{i_h} (\bar{\chi}^h_{k,i_h+1} e^{-\beta r_k h} \chi^h_{k,i_h} - \bar{\chi}^h_{k,i_h} \chi^h_{k,i_h}) + \sum_h \sum_{i_h} [(1 + t_c)^{-\beta} C^{-\beta}_{i_h} \bar{\chi}^h_{0,i_h+1} \chi^h_{2,i_h}$$

$$+ (1 + t_c)^{-\beta} C^\beta_{i_h} \bar{\chi}^h_{2,i_h+1} \chi^h_{0,i_h} + (1 + t_c)^{-\beta} S^{-\beta}_{i_h} \bar{\chi}^h_{0,i_h+1} \chi^h_{1,i_h}$$

$$+ (1 + t_c)^{-\beta} S^\beta_{i_h} \bar{\chi}^h_{1,i_h+1} \chi^h_{0,i_h}].$$

Here t_c is the relative transaction cost and h is the investment horizon. The action has a clear meaning: when a portion of wealth flows in time or 'space,' it transforms from one asset to another, and the number of asset units changes according to the rules of parallel transport dictated by the rates r_i and the prices (exchange rates). Using the above expressions, it is easy to obtain the unnormalized transition probability in the occupation number representation simply by integrating over the variables $\bar{\psi}$, ψ, $\bar{\chi}$ and χ following formula (17) of Chapter 6.

---

[32] For the sake of simplicity, we have omitted interaction terms.

4 PHENOMENOLOGICAL MODEL OF DERIVATIVE PRICING WITH VIRTUAL ARBITRAGE

From the previous section, the reader can see that the complete gauge model for derivative pricing is quite complicated and requires computer simulations rather than an analytical study. This is why we will concentrate below on corrections to the no-arbitrage picture caused by only the arbitrage money flows, keeping in mind that other factors can be added later.

In this section, we develop a phenomenological model for derivative pricing with virtual arbitrage, and show that it is in agreement with the gauge model of Section 3.4. We also derive the corresponding pricing equation, which generalizes the Black–Scholes equation to the case of virtual arbitrage. The logic behind this approach is very similar to that of Section 3 of Chapter 8.

In the Black–Scholes world the portfolio comprising the derivative and and $\partial C/\partial S$ shares is riskless. Its price $\Pi = C - (\partial C/\partial S)S$ is defined by the equation

$$d\Pi = r\Pi \, dt. \tag{36}$$

This leads to the Black–Scholes equation

$$\mathcal{L}_{BS}C = 0, \qquad \mathcal{L}_{BS} = \frac{\partial}{\partial t} + \frac{\sigma^2 S^2}{2} \frac{\partial^2}{\partial S^2} + rS \frac{\partial}{\partial S} - r.$$

Let us imagine that at some moment of time $\tau < t$, a fluctuation of the return (an arbitrage opportunity) appeared in the market. It happened when the price of the underlying stock was $S' \equiv S(\tau)$. We then denote this instantaneous arbitrage return by $v(\tau, S')$. Arbitrageurs would react to this circumstance and act in such a way that the arbitrage gradually disappears and the market returns to its equilibrium state, i.e. the absence of arbitrage. The relaxation process can therefore be described by an evolution equation

$$\frac{d\mathcal{R}}{dt} = F(\mathcal{R}), \qquad \mathcal{R}(\tau) = v(\tau, \Pi).$$

The market reaction function $F(\mathcal{R})$ is expanded as

$$F(\mathcal{R}) = -\lambda \mathcal{R} - \lambda_2 \mathcal{R}^2 - \lambda_3 \mathcal{R}^3 - \cdots. \tag{37}$$

with, in general, time- and S-dependent coefficients $\{\lambda_i\}$. If one neglects the influence of short selling restrictions, the market reaction to the arbitrage is antisymmetric with respect to the sign of $\mathcal{R}$ which leaves us with only odd terms in the expansion (37):

$$F(\mathcal{R}) = -\lambda \mathcal{R} - \lambda_3 \mathcal{R}^3 - \lambda_5 \mathcal{R}^5 - \cdots. \tag{38}$$

For small enough fluctuations, it is natural to keep only the first term on the right-hand side and rewrite (38) in the form

$$\frac{d\mathcal{R}}{dt} = -\lambda \mathcal{R}, \qquad \mathcal{R}(\tau) = v(\tau, S'), \tag{39}$$

with the single characteristic parameter λ. The parameter itself can be either estimated from the micro-theory of Section 3 or found from the market using an analogue of the fluctuation–

dissipation theorem (Callen, 1960). In the latter case, λ can be estimated from the market data as

$$\lambda = -\frac{1}{t-t'}\log\left[\left\langle\frac{\mathcal{L}_{BS}C}{C-S\frac{\partial C}{\partial S}}(t)\frac{\mathcal{L}_{BS}C}{C-S\frac{\partial C}{\partial S}}(t')\right\rangle_{market}\middle/\left\langle\left(\frac{\mathcal{L}_{BS}C}{C-S\frac{\partial C}{\partial S}}\right)^2(t)\right\rangle_{market}\right],$$

and can be a function of time and the price of the underlying asset. In what follows, however, we consider λ to be a constant to get tractable analytical formulae for the derivative prices.

The solution of (39) gives us $\mathcal{R}(t, S) = v(\tau, S)e^{-\lambda(t-\tau)}$, which, after summing over all possible fluctuations with the corresponding frequencies, leads us to the following expression for the arbitrage return at time t:

$$\mathcal{R}(t, S) = \int_0^t d\tau \int_0^\infty dS' \, e^{-\lambda(t-\tau)}P(t, S|\tau, S')v(\tau, S'), \qquad t < T, \tag{40}$$

where T is the expiration date for the derivative contract started at time $t = 0$. The function $P(t, S|\tau, S')$ is the frequency with which the arbitrage fluctuations appear at time τ when the underlying price was S' and at time t the underlying price is S. The appearance of this function is due to the presence of speculators in the market, whose price-sensitive activities effectively create the arbitrage opportunities. To specify the stochastic process $v(t, S)$ we assume that the fluctuations at different times and underlying prices are independent and form white noise with variance $\Sigma^2 f(t)$:

$$\langle v(t, S)\rangle = 0, \qquad \langle v(t, S)v(t', S')\rangle = \Sigma^2\theta(T-t)f(t)\delta(t-t')\delta(S-S'). \tag{41}$$

The function $f(t)$ is introduced here to model the empirical time dependence of the arbitrage returns (see Section 2.1) and to smooth out the transition to the zero virtual arbitrage at the expiration date. The quantity $\Sigma^2 f(t)$ can be estimated from the market data as

$$\frac{\Sigma^2}{2\lambda}f(t) = \left\langle\left(\frac{\mathcal{L}_{BS}C}{C-S\frac{\partial C}{\partial S}}\right)^2(t)\right\rangle_{market}, \tag{42}$$

and has to vanish as time approaches the expiration date.

As soon as we introduce the stochastic arbitrage return $\mathcal{R}(t, S)$, (36) has to be replaced by the equation

$$d\Pi = [r + \mathcal{R}(t, S)]\Pi \, dt, \tag{43}$$

which can then be rewritten as

$$\mathcal{L}_{BS}C = \mathcal{R}(t, S)\left(C - S\frac{\partial C}{\partial S}\right), \tag{44}$$

using the operator $\mathcal{L}_{BS}$. Equations (44), (40), and (41) complete the formulation of the phenomenological model. In Section 3.4, a model of this structure was derived from the gauge model for the derivative – cash – share system. It is worth noting that the model reduces to the pure Black – Scholes analysis in the case of infinitely fast market reaction, i.e. $\lambda \to \infty$. It also returns to the Black – Scholes model when there are no arbitrage opportunities at all, i.e. when $\Sigma = 0$.

In the presence of the random arbitrage fluctuations $\mathcal{R}(t, S)$, the only objects that can be calculated are the average value and other higher moments of the derivative price. Below we examine the average price and derive the pricing equation for it.

4.1 Effective Equation for Derivative Price

We start by noting that the probability distribution of $\mathcal{R}(t, S)$ is Gaussian. Moreover, it can be shown that the probability weight (up to a normalization constant) of the trajectory $\mathcal{R}(\cdot, \cdot)$ has the form

$$P[\mathcal{R}(\cdot, \cdot)] \sim \exp\left(-\frac{1}{2\Sigma^2} \int_0^\infty dt\, dt'\, dS\, dS'\, \mathcal{R}(t, S) K^{-1}(t, S|t', S') \mathcal{R}(t', S')\right), \qquad (45)$$

where the kernel of the operator K is defined as

$$K(t, S|t', S') = \theta(T - t)\theta(T - t') \int_0^\infty d\tau\, ds\, f(\tau)\theta(t - \tau)\theta(t' - \tau)e^{-\lambda(t + t' - 2\tau)}$$
$$\times P(t, S|\tau, s)P(t', S'|\tau, s). \qquad (46)$$

It is easy to see that the kernel is of order $1/\lambda$ and vanishes as $\lambda \to \infty$. Equation (45), in particular, results in the following equation for the correlation function:

$$\langle \mathcal{R}(t, S)\mathcal{R}(t', S')\rangle = \Sigma^2 K(t, S|t', S'), \qquad (47)$$

which we use below.

Now let us return to the dynamical equation for the derivative price,

$$\mathcal{L}_{BS} C(t, S) = \mathcal{R}(t, S)\left(C(t, S) - S\frac{\partial C(t, S)}{\partial S}\right),$$

and note that, since Σ^2/λ plays the role of the small parameter in the problem, the noise $\mathcal{R}$ can be considered as weak and we can find a formal iterative $\mathcal{R}$-dependent solution of the last equation. At the lowest non-trivial order, one has the equation

$$\mathcal{L}_{BS} C = \mathcal{R}\left(C - S\frac{\partial C}{\partial S}\right)$$
$$= \mathcal{R}\left(1 - S\frac{\partial}{\partial S}\right)\mathcal{L}_{BS}^{-1}\mathcal{R}\left(C - S\frac{\partial C}{\partial S}\right),$$

which, after averaging (using (47)) over all possible realizations of the fluctuations $\mathcal{R}$, give the equation for the average derivative price $\bar{C} \equiv \langle C\rangle_{\mathcal{R}}$ up to and including terms proportional to Σ^2/λ:

$$\mathcal{L}_{BS}\bar{C}(t, S) = \Sigma^2 \int_0^\infty dt'\, dS'\, \left[\left(1 - S\frac{\partial}{\partial S}\right)\mathcal{L}_{BS}^{-1}\right](t, S|t', S')$$
$$\times K(t, S|t', S')\left[\left(1 - S\frac{\partial}{\partial S}\right)\bar{C}\right](t', S'), \qquad (48)$$

together with the payoff condition

$$\bar{C}(T, S) = C_{\mathrm{payoff}}(S).$$

Equation (48) is the central result of this section. This is an integro-differential equation that, in the limit $\lambda \to \infty$ or $\Sigma \to 0$, reduces to the Black–Scholes equation and accounts for local arbitrage opportunities and the corresponding market reaction to them. Equations of this type are very familiar in physics, where they are called one-loop Dyson equations. A similar derivation can be carried out for various correlation functions of the derivative price. They also have a direct analogue in physics in the form of the Bethe-Salpeter equation.

To conclude this subsection, it is interesting to add that, owing to the properties of the integrand on the right-hand side of (48), the integration is effectively limited to the interval from time t to the expiration date. This means that any mispricings that happened in the past do not influence the derivative price, as one would expect, and the only relevant contribution comes from future mispricings. The explicit perturbative solutions of (48) for European vanilla options are obtained in Ilinski and Stepanenko (1998).

4.2 Discussion of the Model

Finally we want to discuss some obvious drawbacks of the model and ways to improve it.

First of all, all critical comments regarding Black–Scholes analysis can be applied to this model, except for the no-arbitrage constraint. Indeed, if there are transaction costs or if the price process for the underlying asset is not quasi-Brownian motion, then it is impossible to create a riskless portfolio and, hence, to derive the model. This is not a new problem, and many efforts to overcome this difficulty have been undertaken. It is possible to demonstrate that these methods improve the virtual arbitrage model in the same manner as they improve the no-arbitrage Black–Scholes analysis. This, in principle, allows one to include the transaction costs, the 'fat' tails of the underlying assets probability distribution function, and the stochastic volatility in the present model by redefinition of the operator $\mathcal{L}_{\mathrm{BS}}$.

The second point concerns the market reaction to the arbitrage opportunity, or, qualitatively the form of $\mathcal{R}(t, S)$ in (43). It may be argued that the market reaction is not exponential, as assumed in (40), but has another functional dependence. This dependence can be extracted from the statistical analysis of the stock and the derivative prices and then included in the equation for $\mathcal{R}(t, S)$. This certainly complicates the model, but leaves the general framework intact.

Another point to consider is the absence of correlations between virtual arbitrage opportunities that we have assumed, i.e. the white noise character of the process $v(t, S)$. It is clear that some correlations can be included in the model by replacing the relations in (41) by the equations

$$\langle v(t, S) \rangle = 0, \qquad \langle v(t, S)v(t', S') \rangle = \Sigma^2 G(t, S|t', S'),$$

with some correlation function $G(t, S|t', S')$. Such generalizations, although making the analytical study almost impossible, allow one to proceed with numerical analysis of the model.

Finally, the model contains the new parameters Σ and λ. Although the parameters can be estimated from the statistical data as we mentioned above, they still have to be considered as fitting parameters. If we follow this line, to define their values, some kind of test of the final formulae on real market data should be carried out. This can include profit maximization from the trading strategies based on the virtual arbitrage model. The values of the parameters found in this way can be interpreted as the market's expectations of their future values and therefore can be treated as implied, similarly to the implied volatility.

5   PARTIAL DIFFERENTIAL EQUATIONS FRAMEWORK

Let us return to (46). In the limit of sufficiently fast market relaxation ($\lambda \gg \sigma^2, \mu$) and far from the expiration date (so that one can ignore the smoothing function $f(t)$), the kernel takes the form

$$K(t, y | t', y') = \delta(S - S')\theta(T - t)\theta(T - t')K(t, t'),$$

where the following notation has been introduced:

$$K(t, t') = \frac{1}{2\lambda}\theta(t - t')e^{-\lambda(t-t')} + \frac{1}{2\lambda}\theta(t' - t)e^{-\lambda(t'-t)}.$$

This kernel corresponds to the Ornstein-Uhlenbeck process for the variable $x(t)$:

$$\frac{dx}{dt} + \lambda x = \eta(t), \tag{49}$$

where $\eta(t)$ is the white-noise stochastic process:

$$\langle \eta(t) \rangle = 0, \qquad \langle \eta(t)\eta(t') \rangle = \Sigma^2 \delta(t - t').$$

Therefore, in this limit, the model replaces the constant interest rate r_0 as the rate of return on a riskless portfolio with some stochastic process $r_0 + x(t)$.[33] In this form the connection between the phenomenological model of Section 4 and the gauge model of Section 3.4 is obvious.

This new stochastic framework allows us to look at the problem of derivative pricing under virtual arbitrage from a new angle. In the previous section, we found an effective pricing equation at first order with respect to the parameter $\Sigma^2/2\lambda$. However, it is clear that in the case $\Sigma^2/2\lambda \geq 1$, this expansion does not make much sense, and we have to find a way to sum over all relevant terms. But how real is this possibility? Let us assume that the arbitrage on the riskless portfolio $C - S\partial C/\partial S$ appears every day and is on average about 1% (in absolute value). We assume also that the arbitrage is washed out during the day and there is no interference between different arbitrage opportunities. Then, according to (42), the arbitrage produces the annual return of about 250% and the parameter $\Sigma^2/2\lambda$ is about $6.25 = (2.5)^2 \gg 1$. In this case, the no-arbitrage Black–Scholes pricing formulae are too crude an approximation. If, however, the arbitrage appears only once a week then $\Sigma^2/2\lambda \simeq 0.25$ and the parameter can be used as an expansion parameter. These examples show that accounting for the virtual arbitrage can sometimes be very appropriate. It is worth mentioning that here we have neglected for illustrative purposes the bid–ask spread and transaction costs. In reality, both effects have to be included, and we consider them later in this chapter.

---

[33] For interest rate derivatives, this corresponds to the introduction of an additional factor in multifactor models.

Before going further, we replace the relaxation parameter λ by $\lambda' \equiv \lambda/g(T-t)$ where g is a decreasing function of the time until expiration $T-t$, such that

$$g(T-t) \rightarrow 0 \quad \text{as} \quad T-t \rightarrow 0.$$

In this form, the process ensures that the arbitrage disappear at the expiration time T even in the absence of the smoothing function $f(t)$ in (41).

Let us now tackle the problem of finding a partial differential equation for the average price using the Ornstein–Uhlenbeck process for the virtual arbitrage return. First of all, we introduce the function $C(x, S, t)$, which gives the price of the derivative as a function of time t, the underlying price S, and the arbitrage return x. Secondly, we derive for the function $C(x, S, t)$ a partial differential equation in a similar way to those we used in Section 1. Using the Itô lemma (1) for $C(x, S, t)$ with respect to both $S(t)$ and $x(t)$ processes, we get

$$dC(x, S, t) = \frac{\partial C}{\partial t} dt + \frac{\partial C}{\partial S} dS + \frac{\partial C}{\partial x} dx + \frac{\sigma^2 S^2}{2} \frac{\partial^2 C}{\partial S^2} dt + \frac{\Sigma^2}{2} \frac{\partial^2 C}{\partial x^2} dt.$$

This means that the portfolio Π consisting of the derivative and $-\partial C/\partial S$ shares grows during the time interval dt on average as

$$d\Pi = \frac{\partial C}{\partial t} dt - \lambda' x \frac{\partial C}{\partial x} dt + \frac{\sigma^2 S^2}{2} \frac{\partial^2 C}{\partial S^2} dt + \frac{\Sigma^2}{2} \frac{\partial^2 C}{\partial x^2} dt$$

which has to coincide with the riskless plus arbitrage growth

$$d\Pi = (r_0 + x)\Pi \, dt.$$

The last two relations lead to the following equation for the average derivative price $\bar{C}(x, S, t)$ (Otto, 1999):

$$\frac{\partial \bar{C}}{\partial t} - \lambda' x \frac{\partial \bar{C}}{\partial x} + \frac{\sigma^2 S^2}{2} \frac{\partial^2 \bar{C}}{\partial S^2} + \frac{\Sigma^2}{2} \frac{\partial^2 \bar{C}}{\partial x^2} + (r_0 + x)S \frac{\partial \bar{C}}{\partial S} - (r_0 + x)C = 0, \qquad (50)$$

with the final payoff

$$\bar{C}(x, S, t)|_{t=T} = \delta(x) \, \text{Payoff}(S).$$

A concise informal derivation of the equation without reference to the Itô lemma is given in Section 3.3 of the Appendix, where we demonstrate the advantages of working with functional integrals. Equation (50) has to be used for both pricing and hedging; it allows standard numerical methods to be used in its calculation, and can serve as a basis for further generalizations.

Two such generalizations are immediately obvious:

1. It is possible to use another form of the stabilizing *market reaction*, if it better fits the observable data. In this case, the process will be defined as

$$\frac{dx}{dt} + f(x, t) = \eta(t), \qquad (51)$$

with the same white noise $\eta(t)$

$$\langle \eta(t) \rangle = 0, \qquad \langle \eta(t)\eta(t') \rangle = \Sigma^2 \delta(t-t'),$$

which leads to the following problem for the function $\bar{C}(x, S, t)$:

$$\frac{\partial \bar{C}}{\partial t} + \frac{\sigma^2 S^2}{2} \frac{\partial^2 \bar{C}}{\partial S^2} + (r_0 + x)S \frac{\partial \bar{C}}{\partial S} - (r_0 + x)\bar{C} + \frac{\Sigma^2}{2} \frac{\partial^2 \bar{C}}{\partial x^2} - f(x, t)\frac{\partial \bar{C}}{\partial x} = 0,$$

$$\bar{C}(x, S, t)|_{t=T} = \delta(x) \, \text{Payoff}(S).$$

2. In a similar manner, it is possible to improve the *stochastic volatility* models (Merton, 1973; Wang, 1998; Hull and White, 1987), the jump diffusion model (Merton, 1976), and others. For example, in the case of a price process S with stochastic volatility σ,

$$dS = \mu S \, dt + \sigma S \, dW, \qquad V \equiv \sigma^2, \qquad dV = \phi V \, dt + \xi V \, dZ,$$

such that the Wiener processes W and Z have correlation ρ and the volatility process has zero systematic risk (Hull and White, 1987), the pricing equation takes the form

$$\frac{\partial \bar{C}}{\partial t} + \frac{1}{2}\left(\sigma^2 S^2 \frac{\partial^2 \bar{C}}{\partial S^2} + 2\rho\sigma^3 \xi S \frac{\partial^2 \bar{C}}{\partial S \partial V} + \xi^2 V^2 \frac{\partial^2 \bar{C}}{\partial V^2}\right) + (r_0 + x)S \frac{\partial \bar{C}}{\partial S} + \phi\sigma^2 \frac{\partial \bar{C}}{\partial V}$$

$$- (r_0 + x)\bar{C} + \frac{\Sigma^2}{2} \frac{\partial^2 \bar{C}}{\partial x^2} - \lambda'x \frac{\partial \bar{C}}{\partial x} = 0, \tag{52}$$

with the corresponding final condition

$$\bar{C}(x, S, t)|_{t=T} = \delta(x) \, \text{Payoff}(S).$$

3. The *transaction costs and the bid−ask spread* can be included as well. To this end, we specify the form of the function $f(x)$ in (51) as

$$f_{\text{tr}}(x) = \lambda[(x - a)\theta(x - a) + (x + a)\theta(-a - x)], \tag{53}$$

where a is a percentage of the bid−ask spread and the transaction costs. If the virtual arbitrage return is less than a then there is no practical possibility to benefit from the arbitrage, and hence it does not trigger any market reaction. Combining this with an effect of transaction costs on the hedging strategy according to Leland (1985), we find the following pricing equation for the function $\bar{C}(x, S, t)$:

$$\frac{\partial \bar{C}}{\partial t} + \frac{\sigma^2 S^2}{2} \frac{\partial^2 \bar{C}}{\partial S^2} - \frac{a\sigma S^2}{\sqrt{\pi \delta t/2}}\left|\frac{\partial^2 \bar{C}}{\partial S^2}\right| + (r_0 + x)S \frac{\partial \bar{C}}{\partial S} - (r_0 + x)\bar{C} + \frac{\Sigma^2}{2} \frac{\partial^2 \bar{C}}{\partial x^2} + \frac{\partial[f_{\text{tr}}(x)\bar{C}]}{\partial x} = 0,$$

where δt is a characteristic rehedging time. The derivation of the last equation assumes that the virtual arbitrage does not change the sign of $\Gamma = \partial^2 C/\partial S^2$.

It is possible to combine these generalizations or expand the treatment to other Black−Scholes-like equations. In any case, the choice of one or another variant should involve extensive empirical validation. It is important to emphasize, however, that as soon as we accept the derivative price averaged over the arbitrage fluctuations as the object of interest[34] all the pricing ideology, technology of calculations, and numerical methods remain essentially the same. This means that the corresponding software can be easily adapted to the presence of the virtual arbitrage.

---

[34]Which is, of course an approximation, because of the ignored price of model risk.

We have already mentioned an apparent analogy between the virtual arbitrage return and a stochastic interest rate with mean reversion. However, the typical time scale of changes of the interest rate is much longer while the characteristic fluctuation size is considerably smaller than their virtual arbitrage counterparts. This makes the corrections valuable even for short-living derivatives when the stochasticity of the interest rate is negligible. Another difference is more theoretically important. In models with stochastic interest rate, the risk can be hedged using bonds with various maturities. In the case of virtual arbitrage, this risk is intrinsic and cannot be hedged. In other words, there is no tradeable instrument involving the same risk that can be used for pricing and hedging. Even the concept of pricing and hedging using duplication becomes somewhat obscure.

6 EXPLICIT SOLUTIONS

In this section, we derive several explicit formulae for the average derivatives prices

$$\bar{V}(t, S) = \langle V(t, S, x) \rangle,$$

with the virtual arbitrage $x(\cdot)$.[35] More precisely, we will look for the average solutions of the equation

$$\frac{\partial V}{\partial t} + \frac{\sigma^2 S^2}{2} \frac{\partial^2 V}{\partial S^2} + r(t) S \frac{\partial V}{\partial S} - r(t)V = 0, \tag{54}$$

with the boundary conditions[36]

$$V(t, S)|_{t=T} = \text{Payoff}(S)$$

and the stochastic process $r(t)$. We assume that $r(t)$ is a stochastic function owing to the presence of arbitrage, transaction costs and other reasons. In what follows we assume that this process is independent of the share price process. It is convenient to decompose it as

$$r(t) = r_0 + x(t),$$

where $x(t)$ is the stochastic part of the return and r_0 is the constant riskless interest rate. The generalization for r_0 a non-stochastic function of time is straightforward.

To move forward, we need the following well-known fact concerning the solution of (54) (Merton, 1973): the solution of this equation is given by the solution of the standard Black–Scholes equation with fixed interest rate r if one changes[37] r for $\int_t^T r(\tau)\, d\tau/(T - t)$. This means that to find an average solution of (54), one has to average the configuration-dependent

---

[35]The results of this section are mainly due to Gleb Kalinin (St Petersburg Technological Institute).
[36]For the sake of simplicity we consider only the European boundary conditions.
[37]To see this, one has to change variables in (54) as

$$V \to V e^{\int_t^T r(\tau)\, d\tau}, \quad S \to S e^{\int_t^T r(\tau)\, d\tau},$$

to get the equation

$$\frac{\partial V}{\partial t} + \frac{\sigma^2 S^2}{2} \frac{\partial^2 V}{\partial S^2} = 0,$$

which does not know about the interest rates at all.

solution of (54) for an arbitrary function $r(t)$. For the European vanilla call and put options, this gives the formulae

$$C(t, S) = SN(d_1(t, S)) - Ee^{-\int_t^T r(\tau)\,d\tau} N(d_2(t, S)) \tag{55}$$

$$P(t, S) = Ee^{-\int_t^T r(\tau)d\tau} N(-d_2(t, S)) - SN(-d_1(t, S)) \tag{56}$$

with the notation

$$d_{1(2)}(t, S) = \frac{\log(S/E) + \int_t^T r(\tau)\,d\tau \pm \sigma^2(T - t)/2}{\sigma\sqrt{T - t}}$$

and

$$N(x) \equiv \frac{1}{\sqrt{2\pi}} \int_{-\infty}^x e^{-y^2/2}\,dy.$$

To average (55) and (56) over the random process $r(t)$, we use the relations

$$N(x) = \frac{1}{\sqrt{2\pi}} \int_{-\infty}^\infty \theta(x - y) e^{-y^2/2}\,dy, \qquad \theta(x - y) = \int_{-\infty}^\infty \frac{e^{i\omega(x-y)}\,d\omega}{\omega - i0\ 2\pi i},$$

which results in the integral representation for the error function:

$$N(x) = \int\int_{-\infty}^\infty e^{-y^2/2} \frac{e^{i\omega(x-y)}}{\omega - i0} \frac{dy}{\sqrt{2\pi}} \frac{d\omega}{2\pi i} = \int_{-\infty}^\infty \frac{e^{i\omega x - \omega^2/2}}{\omega - i0} \frac{d\omega}{2\pi i}. \tag{57}$$

After rescaling of ω, this last equation transforms to the equality

$$\frac{1}{2\pi i} \int_{-\infty}^\infty \frac{dw}{w - i0} e^{-\gamma w^2/2 + iw\beta} = N(\beta/\sqrt{\gamma}), \tag{58}$$

which we also use below.

Substituting the representation (57) into (55) and averaging over the random process $r(t)$, one obtains expressions for the call and put prices through the generating function

$$\Phi(\alpha, T, t) = \left\langle e^{\alpha \int_t^T x(\tau)\,d\tau} \right\rangle \tag{59}$$

only. This gives the average call price as

$$\bar{C}(t, S) = S \int_{-\infty}^\infty \frac{dw}{2\pi i} \frac{e^{-\omega^2/2} e^{iw\hat{d}_1(t,S)}}{w - i0} \left\langle e^{iw \int_t^T x(\tau)\,d\tau \left(\frac{1}{\sigma\sqrt{T-t}}\right)} \right\rangle$$

$$- Ee^{-r_0(T-t)} \int_{-\infty}^\infty \frac{dw}{2\pi i} \frac{e^{-\omega^2/2} e^{iw\hat{d}_2(t,S)}}{w - i0} \left\langle e^{\int_t^T x(\tau)\,d\tau \left[\frac{iw}{\sigma\sqrt{T-t}} - 1\right]} \right\rangle, \tag{60}$$

where $\hat{d}_{1(2)}(t, S)$ are the no-arbitrage expressions

$$\hat{d}_{1(2)}(t, S) = \frac{\log(S/E) + r_0(T - t) \pm \sigma^2(T - t)/2}{\sigma\sqrt{T - t}}.$$

A similar expression can be derived for the European put option:

$$\bar{P}(t, S) = Ee^{-r_0(T-t)} \int_{-\infty}^\infty \frac{dw}{2\pi i} \frac{e^{-\omega^2/2} e^{-iw\hat{d}_2(t,S)}}{w - i0} \left\langle e^{-\int_t^T x(\tau)\,d\tau \left(\frac{iw}{\sigma\sqrt{T-t}} + 1\right)} \right\rangle$$

$$- S \int_{-\infty}^\infty \frac{dw\,e^{-\omega^2/2} e^{-iw\hat{d}_1(t,S)}}{2\pi i} \frac{}{w - i0} \left\langle e^{-iw \int_t^T x(\tau)\,d\tau \left(\frac{1}{\sigma\sqrt{T-t}}\right)} \right\rangle. \tag{61}$$

One can see that the virtual arbitrage corrections are clearly factorized and can be found as soon as the generating function $\Phi(\alpha, T, t)$ for the random process $r(t)$ is calculated. Below, we will find the exact expression for generating functions for the pure Ornstein–Uhlenbeck process that describes the virtual arbitrage fluctuations in the absence of transaction costs. We also derive explicit approximate expressions for the restricted Brownian motion that models the uncertainty in the return due to the presence of the transaction costs in the absence of virtual arbitrage, and the compound process that takes into account both virtual arbitrage and transaction costs.

6.1 Pure Ornstein–Uhlenbeck Process

If the process $x(\cdot)$ with the boundary conditions $x(t) = x$ and $x(T) = x'$ is the Ornstein–Uhlenbeck process

$$\frac{dx(\tau)}{d\tau} = -\lambda x(\tau) + \Sigma \eta(\tau), \tag{62}$$

it is possible to find an exact expression for the generating function using the path integral method for stochastic processes as described in Section 6 of the Appendix on quantum field theory methods. In the path integral representation, the generating function is equal to

$$\langle e^{\alpha \int_t^T x(\tau)d\tau} | x(t) = x, x(T) = x' \rangle = \frac{\int_{x(t)=x}^{x(T)=x'} Dx \exp\left[-\frac{1}{2\Sigma^2} \int_t^T d\tau \left(\frac{dx(\tau)}{d\tau} + \lambda x \right)^2 + \alpha \int_t^T ds\, x(\tau) \right]}{\int_{x(t)=x}^{x(T)=x'} Dx \exp\left[-\frac{1}{2\Sigma^2} \int_t^T d\tau \left(\frac{dx(\tau)}{d\tau} + \lambda x \right)^2 \right]}.$$

Calculating the path integral following Section 3.2 of the Appendix, we find that

$$\langle e^{\alpha \int_t^T x(\tau)d\tau} \rangle = \frac{1}{\text{norm}} \exp\left[\frac{\alpha^2 \Sigma^2}{2\lambda^2}[T - t - B(T - t)] - \frac{\lambda}{2\Sigma^2 \sinh[\lambda(T-t)]} \right.$$

$$\times \left(\cosh[\lambda(T-t)] (x^2 + x'^2) - 2xx' - \alpha \Sigma^2 B^2 (T-t) e^{\lambda(T-t)}(x+x') \right.$$

$$\left. + \frac{\alpha^2 \Sigma^4}{2\lambda} B^3 (T-t) e^{\lambda(T-t)} \right) + \frac{\lambda}{2\Sigma^2}(x^2 - x'^2) \right]$$

$$= \frac{1}{\text{norm}} \exp\left[\frac{\alpha^2 \Sigma^2}{2\lambda^2}\left(T - t - \frac{2}{\lambda}\frac{\cosh[\lambda(T-t)]-1}{\sinh[\lambda(T-t)]} \right) - \frac{\lambda}{2\Sigma^2 \sinh[\lambda(T-t)]} \right.$$

$$\times \left\{ \cosh[\lambda(T-t)] (x^2 + x'^2) - 2xx' - \alpha \Sigma^2 B^2 (T-t) e^{\lambda(T-t)}(x+x') \right\}$$

$$\left. + \frac{\lambda}{2\Sigma^2}(x^2 - x'^2) \right], \tag{63}$$

where we have introduced the notation

$$B(T) = (1 - e^{-\lambda T})/\lambda$$

and 'norm' is a normalization constant, which is equal to the exponent in (63) with $\alpha = 0$.

As we discussed earlier, for times close to the expiration date, one has to correct the Ornstein–Uhlenbeck process to account for the fact that the arbitrage fluctuations dry out. If the expiration date is sufficiently far away and we are not concerned with boundary effects, the disappearance of arbitrage should be ignored, and the last expression has to be integrated over x' without restrictions.[38] Furthermore, to find an expression that does not depend on the arbitrage return at time t, we have to average the generating function over $x(t) = x$ with the weight given by the stationary distribution of the Ornstein–Uhlenbeck process, $\exp(-x^2\lambda/\Sigma^2)$, and get

$$\left\langle e^{\alpha \int_t^T x(\tau)d\tau} \right\rangle = \exp\left(\frac{\alpha^2\Sigma^2}{2\lambda^2}[T - t - B(T - t)] \right). \tag{64}$$

This expression gives the final result for the generating function of the Ornstein–Uhlenbeck process for the arbitrage return.

6.2 Generating Function for Restricted Brownian Motion

Here we find an approximation for the generating function (59) when the process $x(t)$ is restricted Brownian motion ($x \in [-a, a]$). This corresponds to the situation of finite transaction costs dictating the interval for the arbitrage return, which does not attract arbitrageurs and therefore is not eliminated. Similar to the previous subsection, we average over $x(0)$ with the stationary distribution of restricted Brownian motion, which is the homogeneous distribution on the interval $[-a, a]$.

The transition probability function $\psi(t, x, x_0)$ obeys the Fokker–Planck equation

$$\frac{\partial\psi}{\partial t} = \frac{\Sigma^2}{2}\frac{\partial^2\psi}{\partial t^2},$$

with the boundary conditions

$$\frac{\partial\psi}{\partial x}\Big|_{x=\pm a} = 0.$$

The solution for the initial condition

$$\psi(0, x', x) = \delta(x' - x)$$

can be found as the series

$$\psi(t, x', x) = \frac{1}{2a} + \frac{1}{a}\sum_{k=1}^{\infty} e^{-\frac{\Sigma^2}{2}(kv)^2 t}\cos[vk(x' + a)]\cos[vk(x + a)], \qquad v \equiv \frac{\pi}{2a}. \tag{65}$$

This allows us to look for the generating function in the form of a Taylor series

$$\langle e^{\alpha \int_t^T x(\tau)\,d\tau}\rangle = 1 + \alpha\left\langle \int_t^T x(\tau)\,d\tau \right\rangle + \frac{\alpha^2}{2}\left\langle \int_t^T x(\tau)\,d\tau \int_t^T x(s)\,ds \right\rangle + \cdots,$$

---

[38] Otto (1999), instead of integrating over x', put it equal to zero, thus forcing the Ornstein-Uhlenbeck process to end-up at the zero point. Since the use the pure Ornstein–Uhlenbeck process until the expiration date is equivalent to disregarding boundary effects, the decision to constrain $x(T)$ does not seem to be logical, in contrast to what we had in Section 5.

evaluating the averages using the function (65). The second term is equal to zero because of the symmetry $x \to -x$, which leaves us with the first non-trivial contribution:

$$\frac{\alpha^2}{2}\left\langle \int_t^T x(\tau)d\tau \int_t^T x(s)\,ds \right\rangle = \alpha^2 \int_t^T d\tau \int_t^\tau ds \int_{-a}^a dx_T\,dx_\tau\,dx_s\,\frac{dx_0}{2a}$$
$$\times \psi(T-\tau, x_T, x_\tau)x(\tau)\psi(\tau-s, x_\tau, x_s)x(s)\psi(s-t, x_s, x_0).$$

The last integrals can be evaluated straightforwardly, and give the result

$$\frac{2\alpha^2}{2a^2}\sum_{k=1}^{\infty}\int_t^T d\tau \int_t^\tau ds\, e^{-\frac{\Sigma^2}{2}(kv)^2(\tau-s)}\left(\int_0^{2a} dx\,(x-a)\cos(vkx)\right)^2$$

$$= \frac{\alpha^2 8(T-t)}{2a^2\Sigma^2}\sum_{m=1}^{\infty}\left(\frac{2a}{\pi(2m-1)}\right)^6\left(1 - \frac{1-e^{-\frac{\Sigma^2}{2}\left(\frac{\pi(2m-1)}{2a}\right)^2(T-t)}}{\frac{\Sigma^2}{2}\left(\frac{\pi(2m-1)}{2a}\right)^2(T-t)}\right). \qquad (66)$$

If $(\Sigma^2/a^2)(T-t) \to \infty$, the last factor on the right-hand side of (66) is approximately equal to 1. Therefore the second term in the Taylor expansion can be written as[39]

$$\frac{\alpha^2}{2}\left\langle \int_t^T x(\tau)\,d\tau \int_t^T x(s)\,ds \right\rangle \approx \alpha^2 a^4 \frac{4(T-t)}{15\Sigma^2}. \qquad (67)$$

For $(\Sigma^2/a^2)(T-t) \to 0$, it is possible to approximate the last factor on the right-hand side of (66) as

$$1 - \frac{1-e^{-\frac{\Sigma^2}{2}\left(\frac{\pi(2m-1)}{2a}\right)^2(T-t)}}{\frac{\Sigma^2}{2}\left(\frac{\pi(2m-1)}{2a}\right)^2(T-t)} \approx \frac{\Sigma^2}{4}\left(\frac{\pi(2m-1)}{2a}\right)^2(T-t),$$

which gives[40]

$$\frac{\alpha^2}{2}\left\langle \int_t^T x(\tau)\,d\tau \int_t^T x(s)\,ds \right\rangle \approx \frac{1}{6}\alpha^2 a^2(T-t)^2. \qquad (68)$$

Interpolating between (67) and (68), we arrive at the approximate formula for the generating function that describes the both limiting cases:

$$\left\langle e^{\alpha \int_t^T x(\tau)\,d\tau} \right\rangle \approx \exp\left(\alpha^2 a^4 \frac{4(T-t)}{15\Sigma^2}\left(1 - e^{-\frac{5\Sigma^2(T-t)}{8a^2}}\right)\right).$$

---

[39]Here we use the equality

$$\sum_{m=1}^{\infty}\left(\frac{1}{\pi(2m-1)}\right)^6 = \frac{1}{960}.$$

[40]Evaluating the series

$$\sum_{m=1}^{\infty}\left(\frac{1}{\pi(2m-1)}\right)^4 = \frac{1}{96}.$$

6.3 Compound Process

To model both the virtual arbitrage and the transaction costs, we consider the process

$$\frac{dx(t)}{dt} = -\lambda x\left(1 - \frac{a}{\sqrt{x^2 + a^2}}\right) + \Sigma\eta(t), \qquad (69)$$

which is a smoothed version of the process with the reaction function (53). The graph of the function $-\lambda x(1 - a/\sqrt{x^2 + a^2})$ is shown in Fig. 9.14. From Section 6 of the Appendix, we have the path integral representation for the generating function:

$$\left\langle e^{\alpha \int_t^T x(\tau) d\tau} \right\rangle = \frac{1}{\text{norm}} \int_{x(t)=x}^{x(T)=x'} Dx(\tau) \exp\left\{ -\int_t^T \frac{d\tau}{2\Sigma^2}(\dot{x}^2 + \lambda^2 x^2) + \alpha \int_t^T x(\tau)\, d\tau \right.$$

$$\left. -\int_t^T \frac{\lambda^2 x^2}{2\Sigma^2}\left[\left(1 - \frac{a}{\sqrt{x^2+a^2}}\right)^2 - 1\right] d\tau - \frac{\lambda}{2\Sigma^2}(x^2 - 2a\sqrt{x^2+a^2})\Big|_t^T \right\}, \qquad (70)$$

which has to be averaged over x with the stationary distribution for the process (69),

$$\text{Weight}(a, x) = \text{norm} \times \exp\left(-\frac{\lambda}{\Sigma^2}(x^2 - 2a\sqrt{x^2 + a^2}) \right),$$

and integrated over x' without any weight.

It is impossible to calculate the path integral (70) exactly. Instead, we use perturbation theory and expand the integral in a series with respect to the parameter a, which is assumed to be small. At zeroth order, this gives us the generating functional for the Ornstein–Uhlenbeck

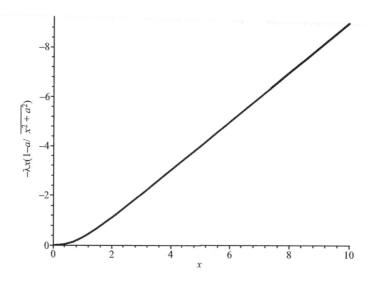

Figure 9.14 Graph of the market reaction function. The reaction to the fluctuations of the return is suppressed inside the spread and is linear outside it. The parameters are: $a = 1$ and $\lambda = 1$.

process calculated in Section 6.1. After a long but, in principle, straightforward calculation, one can find at first order the generating function

$$\left\langle e^{\alpha \int_t^T x(\tau) d\tau} \right\rangle \approx \exp\left(a\sqrt{\frac{\Sigma^2}{\pi\lambda}\frac{\alpha^2(T-t)}{\lambda}}\right) \exp\left(\frac{\alpha^2\Sigma^2}{2\lambda^2}[T-t-B(T-t)]\right).$$

The first factor reflects the presence of transaction costs with characteristic size a, while the second factor describes the market reaction to the arbitrage opportunities and coincides with the generating function for the pure Ornstein–Uhlenbeck process found in Section 6.1. We rearrange the last expression as

$$\langle e^{\alpha \int_t^T x(\tau) d\tau} \rangle \approx \exp\left(\frac{\alpha^2\Sigma^2}{2\lambda^2}[(T-t)(1+a\xi) - B(T-t)]\right), \quad \xi \equiv 2\sqrt{\frac{\lambda}{\pi\Sigma^2}}. \tag{71}$$

In this form, it will be used below to calculate derivative prices.

6.4   Particular Derivatives

The formulae (60) and (71) give the price for the vanilla call option:

$$\bar{C}(t, S) = \frac{S}{2\pi i} \int_{-\infty}^{\infty} \frac{dw}{w - i0} \exp\left[iw\hat{d}_1(t, S) - \frac{w^2}{2} - \frac{w^2}{2}\frac{\Sigma^2}{\lambda^2\sigma^2}\left(1 + a\xi - \frac{B(T-t)}{T-t}\right)\right]$$

$$- \frac{Ee^{-r_0(T-t)}}{2\pi i} \int_{-\infty}^{\infty} \frac{dw}{w - i0} \exp\left[iw\hat{d}_2(t, S) - \frac{w^2}{2}\right.$$

$$\left. + \left(\frac{iw}{\sigma\sqrt{T-t}} - 1\right)^2 \frac{\Sigma^2}{2\lambda^2}[(1+a\xi)(T-t) - B(T-t)]\right].$$

Applying (58), we finally get

$$\bar{C}(t, S) = SN\left(\frac{\hat{d}_1(t, S)}{\sqrt{1 + \frac{\Sigma^2}{\lambda^2\sigma^2}\left(1 + a\xi - \frac{B(T-t)}{T-t}\right)}}\right)$$

$$- Ee^{-r_0(T-t) + \frac{\Sigma^2}{2\lambda^2}[(1+a\xi)(T-t) - B(T-t)]}$$

$$\times N\left(\frac{\hat{d}_2(t, S) - \frac{\Sigma^2}{\lambda^2\sigma\sqrt{T-t}}[(1+a\xi)(T-t) - B(T-t)]}{\sqrt{1 + \frac{\Sigma^2}{\lambda^2\sigma^2}\left(1 + a\xi - \frac{B(T-t)}{T-t}\right)}}\right). \tag{72}$$

A similar expression can be found for the put option. In this case, we substitute (71) into (61),

$$\bar{P}(t, S) = \frac{Ee^{-r_0(T-t)}}{2\pi i} \int_{-\infty}^{\infty} \frac{dw}{w - i0} \exp\left[- iw\hat{d}_2(t, S) - \frac{w^2}{2} \right.$$

$$+ \left(\frac{iw}{\sigma\sqrt{T - t}} + 1 \right)^2 \frac{\Sigma^2}{2\lambda^2} [(1 + a\xi)(T - t) - B(T - t)] \right]$$

$$- \frac{S}{2\pi i} \int_{-\infty}^{\infty} \frac{dw}{w - i0} \exp\left[-iw\hat{d}_1(t, S) - \frac{w^2}{2} - \frac{w^2}{2} \frac{\Sigma^2}{\lambda^2\sigma^2} \left(1 + a\xi - \frac{B(T - t)}{T - t} \right) \right] \qquad (73)$$

and get, again using (58), the pricing formula

$$\bar{P}(t, S) = Ee^{-r_0(T-t)+\frac{\Sigma^2}{2\lambda^2}[(1+a\xi)(T-t)-B(T-t)]}$$

$$\times N\left(\frac{-\hat{d}_2(t, S) + \frac{\Sigma^2}{\lambda^2\sigma\sqrt{T - t}}[(1 + a\xi)(T - t) - B(T - t)]}{\sqrt{1 + \frac{\Sigma^2}{\lambda^2\sigma^2}\left(1 + a\xi - \frac{B(T - t)}{T - t}\right)}} \right)$$

$$- SN\left(\frac{-\hat{d}_1(t, S)}{\sqrt{1 + \frac{\Sigma^2}{\lambda^2\sigma^2}\left(1 + a\xi - \frac{B(T - t)}{T - t}\right)}} \right). \qquad (74)$$

The reader can check that (72) and (74) imply the call–put parity theorem

$$\bar{C}(t, S) - \bar{P}(t, S) = \bar{V}(t, S),$$

where the average price $\bar{V}(t, S)$ of the forward contract is equal to

$$\bar{V}(t, S) = S - Ee^{-r_0(T-t)}e^{\frac{\Sigma^2}{2\lambda^2}(1+a\xi)(T-t)-B(T-t)]}.$$

Figures 9.15 and 9.16 show comparisons of the derived prices (72) and (74) and the Black–Scholes formulae. The figures demonstrate that the contribution from the fluctuating rate of return on the riskless portfolio deforms the solutions, with the effect being particulary profound for prices close to the strike. This shows that virtual arbitrage has to be accounted for together with other market imperfections such as discrete hedging with finite transaction costs.

7 TRANSACTION COSTS AND ARBITRAGE STRATEGIES

In Section 2, we pointed out that the simple arbitrage strategy[41] does not provide an impressive arbitrage return. However, if one closes or reverts positions before the expiration the return can be considerably higher and hence more attractive. Sofianos (1990) reported that

---

[41]Where, in the case of mispricing, an arbitrageur buys a 'cheap' portfolio, sells its 'expensive' equivalent, and keeps the positions until the expiration.

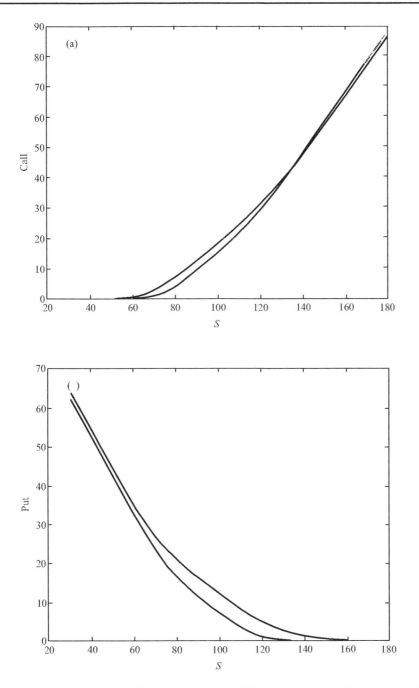

Figure 9.15 (a)   Call price (solid line) calculated from (72) in comparison with the Black–Scholes solution (dashed line). The correction to the Black–Scholes solution reaches up to 100%. (b) Put price (solid line) calculated from (74) in comparison with the Black–Scholes solution (dashed line). The corrction is quantitatively significant. The parameters values in both (a) and (b) are $a = 0.005$, $\lambda = 250$, $\Sigma^2/\lambda = 9$, $r_0 = 0.08$, $T - t = 1$, and $E = 100$.

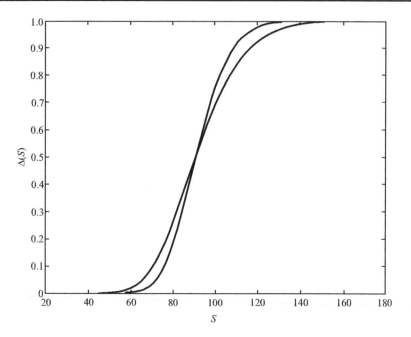

Figure 9.16 The delta-hedging ratio $\Delta(S)$ (solid line) for the European call option calculated from (72). The dashed line is the corresponding Black–Scholes ratio. The parameter values are the same as in Fig. 9.15.

for the period 15 January – 13 July 1990, about 70% of arbitrage positions in S&P500 futures were closed before expiration following profitable arbitrage reversals. Assuming that the positions remain open on average 24 hours,[42] Sofianos found that 'the average early-closing return was five percentage points above the return on alternative investments'. In the same sample, the average arbitrage return to expiration was 0.4 percentage points below this line.

It is clear that reversals in the arbitrage positions following the reversals in the mispricings will enhance the performance of the arbitrage strategies. However, in the presence of transaction costs, the reversals will cost, and one has to find optimal conditions for the opening or the closing of the arbitrage positions. We will do it here for the case of the futures arbitrage following the paper by Brennan and Schwartz (1990). Similar considerations can be developed for other types of derivatives.

Brennan and Schwartz defined the mispricing ϵ as the difference between the present value of the futures price and dividends, G, and the underlying asset price S:

$$\epsilon = G - S.$$

If ϵ is positive, an arbitrageur buys the underlying asset, hedging it with a short position in futures, and holds the arbitrage position until maturity of the futures contracts. This strategy yields an immediate cash inflow ϵ and no further net cash flows. In the case of negative ϵ, the arbitrageur reverts the position and gains the arbitrage profit $-\epsilon$.

---

[42]This was the average time between profitable reversals.

The described arbitrage scheme did not take the transaction costs into account. As shown in Stoll and Whaley (1987), the transaction costs for the reverting position and opening of a new position are different. Indeed, arbitrage involves transactions in both the stock and futures markets and account must be taken of commissions and bid–ask spread in both markets. To open an arbitrage position involves futures commissions, stock commissions, and the market impact associated with the underlying asset transaction and due to the bid–ask spread. If the arbitrage position is held until expiration, the only additional cost is the commission to close out the future position and the stock commission associated with the reversal in the stock position. There is no market impact cost, since the stock can be sold at the market closing price, which is the same as the terminal futures price. We denote by C_1 the transaction costs incurred in the simple arbitrage strategy with the position being kept until expiration. If the arbitrage position is closed early, there is an additional market impact cost on the stock position, C_2. Thus, in comparison with the simple arbitrage strategy with cost C_1, the early closing strategy has higher costs $C_1 + C_2$, and one faces the problem of finding optimal conditions for the position reverting and the position closing.

Let $V(\epsilon, \tau)$ (respectively $V^*(\epsilon, \tau)$) be the value of the right to close a long (respectively short) arbitrage position prior to maturity when the simple arbitrage profit before the transaction costs is ϵ and the time to maturity is τ. In the presence of position limits,[43] closing an outstanding arbitrage position not only yields an immediate arbitrage profit but also gives the arbitrageurs the right to initiate a new arbitrage position in the future. Denoting this right by $W(\epsilon, \tau)$ we can put down the inequalities that the functions $V(\epsilon, \tau)$ and $V^*(\epsilon, \tau)$ must obey:

$$V(\epsilon, \tau) \geq \max[W(\epsilon, \tau) - \epsilon - C_2, 0], \qquad V^*(\epsilon, \tau) \geq \max[W(\epsilon, \tau) + \epsilon - C_2, 0]. \qquad (75)$$

On the other hand, the right to initiate a new position itself has to satisfy the inequality

$$W(\epsilon, \tau) \geq \max[\epsilon + V(\epsilon, \tau) - C_1, V^*(\epsilon, \tau) - \epsilon - C_1, 0], \qquad (76)$$

because initiating an arbitrage position gives not only immediate arbitrage profit but also the right to close it early. It is also clear that, at expiration, the values of all three quantities $W(\epsilon, \tau)$, $V(\epsilon, \tau)$, and $V^*(\epsilon, \tau)$ are equal to zero.

In what follows, we assume that the mispricing ϵ follows the Ornstein–Uhlenbeck process (49) derived earlier from the gauge model:

$$\frac{d\epsilon}{dt} + \lambda\epsilon = \eta(t),$$

where $\eta(t)$ is the white noise stochastic process

$$\langle \eta(t) \rangle = 0, \qquad \langle \eta(t)\eta(t') \rangle = \Sigma^2 \delta(t - t'),$$

and $\lambda = \lambda'/\tau$. As usual, the values of the options $W(\epsilon, \tau)$, $V(\epsilon, \tau)$, and $V^*(\epsilon, \tau)$ satisfy the Black–Scholes-type partial differential equation

$$\frac{\Sigma^2}{2} \frac{\partial V}{\partial \epsilon^2} - \frac{\lambda'}{\tau}\epsilon \frac{\partial V}{\partial \epsilon} - \frac{\partial V}{\partial \tau} - r_0 V = 0. \qquad (77)$$

---

[43]The corresponding solution in the situation without position limits gives an infinite arbitrage profit (Brennan and Schwartz, 1990). The position limit is a realistic feature because of the existence of capital requirements and self-imposed exposure limits. We assume here that an arbitrageur is restricted to a single open position only.

In contrast to this simple equation, the boundary conditions corresponding to (75) and (76) are trickier. For the option $V(\epsilon, \tau)$, the American-style boundary condition derived from the first inequality (75) are

$$V(\epsilon_c, \tau) = W(\epsilon_c, \tau) - \epsilon_c - C_2, \qquad \frac{\partial V}{\partial \epsilon}(\epsilon_c, \tau) = \frac{\partial W}{\partial \epsilon}(\epsilon_c, \tau) - 1, \tag{78}$$

where ϵ_c is the optimal value of ϵ to close a long arbitrage position. Similar equations can be written for $V^*(\epsilon, \tau)$, with $\epsilon_c^* = -\epsilon_c$ being the optimal value to close a short arbitrage position. In the same way, the right to open a position satisfies the following boundary conditions:

$$W(\epsilon_o, \tau) = V(\epsilon_o, \tau) + \epsilon_o - C_1, \qquad \frac{\partial W}{\partial \epsilon}(\epsilon_o, \tau) = \frac{\partial V}{\partial \epsilon}(\epsilon_o, \tau) + 1,$$

$$W(-\epsilon_o, \tau) = V^*(\epsilon_o, \tau) - \epsilon_o - C_1, \qquad \frac{\partial W}{\partial \epsilon}(\epsilon_o, \tau) = \frac{\partial V^*}{\partial \epsilon}(\epsilon_o, \tau) - 1. \tag{79}$$

Figure 9.17 shows the solution of the system of (77) for V, V^*, and W with boundary conditions (78) and (79). One can see that

$$V(\epsilon, \tau) = V^*(-\epsilon_o, \tau),$$

and $W(\epsilon, \tau)$ is an even function of ϵ. It is interesting to note that the solutions allows an apparently paradoxical situation where *it may be optimal to open a new arbitrage position even when the simple arbitrage return is less than the cost of executing the simple arbitrage.*

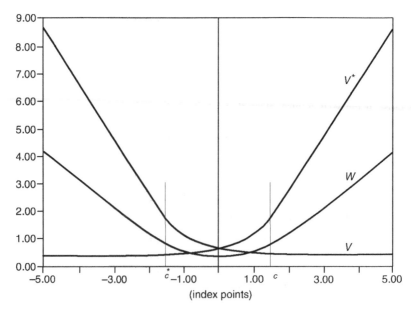

Figure 9.17 Values of the options to open an arbitrage position, $W(\epsilon, \tau)$, and to close a position early, $V(\epsilon, \tau)$ and $V^*(\epsilon, \tau)$. The values of the parameters in the model are $\lambda' = 2.28$, $\Sigma = 0.3$, $r_0 = 0.07$, $C_1 = 1.2$, and $C_2 = 0.5$. The dashed lines correspond to ϵ_c and ϵ_c^*. Reprinted from M. J. Brennan and E. S. Schwartz, *Journal of Business* **63**, s7–s31 (1990). Copyright © 1990 University of Chicago Press. Reproduced by permission of University of Chicago Press.

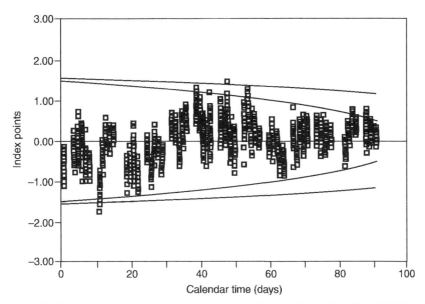

Figure 9.18   Evolution of ϵ as a function of calendar time for the September 1984 S&P500 futures contract. Observations on the same day form vertical lines, and the gaps between the lines represent non-trading days. Two inner lines give optimal closing mispricings ϵ_c. The outer lines correspond to the optimal position initiation ϵ_o. Reprinted from M. J. Brennan and E. S. Schwartz, *Journal of Business* **63**, s7–s31 (1990). Copyright © 1990 University of Chicago Press. Reproduced by permission of University of Chicago Press.

The reason for this is that the opening of a new position carries with it an option to close the position, which may bring an additional arbitrage profit.

Brennan and Schwartz tested the model on the data set described in Section 2.1. They estimated a profitability of the developed arbitrage strategy for each of 16 contracts for the period between September 1983 and June 1987, and found that profitability increased in 1986 and 1987. Figure 9.18 shows the empirical mispricings for the September 1984 S&P500 contract and the theoretical optimal boundaries.

8   DERIVATIVE PRICING FAR FROM EQUILIBRIUM

In this section, we construct a new model for non-equilibrium derivative pricing, and this time we do it without referring to the quasi-equilibrium assumptions. The consideration is carried for the case of the vanilla put option, but it will be clear that the put can be replaced with any other derivative.

All the models that we considered before implied that the state of the market is a quasi-equilibrium one i.e. fluctuations are small and the system tends to evolve towards its equilibrium state. However, as we have already discussed, if the fluctuations are sufficiently large, market participants can change their beliefs about the future outcomes. This will drive the market further from equilibrium instead of stabilizing the market. In this case, the system leaves its previous quasi-equilibrium region in phase space, so that the pricing procedures based on the quasi-equilibrium assumptions cease to be valid. This means that, besides the variables already introduced in the standard pricing models, one needs to add a variable that signals that a system is out of the quasistable state and the market goes through a large market event. We call this variable the *signal variable*[44] to emphasize its economic meaning.

We saw in Section 2 that empirical studies of large market events also prompt the introduction of such a variable. Indeed, the arbitrage return or discount, which is assumed to be zero for an equilibrium market, grows to huge proportions during large directed market movements (see Section 2.2 and Figs. 9.9 and 9.10). Moreover, it essentially characterizes the state of the market and signals the break down of stable market mechanisms. If speculators and hedgers drive the market out of equilibrium, arbitrageurs are reluctant to participate in the arbitrage clearing. They tend to stay out until the stampede slows down and the system reaches its new quasistable region in phase space, which is essential in the identification of arbitrage opportunities. Following this line, we construct a pricing model for the non-equilibrium market that uses the mispricing as the signal variable.

An interesting thing to note about mispricing is that in this context it plays a double role, appearing naturally in pricing relations and also being the signal variable. This makes the use of mispricing in non-equilibrium pricing both unique and convenient. Indeed, as we mentioned earlier in this chapter and in Chapter 8, the mispricing reveals itself by entering pricing equations for a riskless portfolio, indicating a deviation of its return from the risk-free one. Thus, in a sense, the mispricing is an observable quantity, in contrast to many other options for introducing a signal variable that one can imagine. On the other hand, the very feature of the mispricing being a deviation from predictions of the equilibrium theory emphasizes its importance in the non-equilibrium framework.

8.1 Underlying Price Stochastic Dynamics

We start with the formulation of the underlying price process, and proceed with the construction of the pricing theory construction afterwards. We choose to use the Hull and White stochastic volatility equilibrium model as the basis for our non-equilibrium generalization. According to this model, at equilibrium, the underlying price process S with stochastic volatility σ is given by the equations

$$dS = \mu S \, dt + \sigma S \, dX, \qquad V \equiv \sigma^2, \qquad dV = \phi(V_0 - V) \, dt + \xi V \, dY, \qquad (80)$$

where X and Y are Wiener processes with correlation $\rho_{XY} = \langle dX \, dY \rangle / dt$, which might be a function of time, price S, and volatility σ. The freedom in the choice of ρ_{XY} can be used to fit the corresponding implied volatility curve. The term $\phi(V_0 - V)$ describes the mean reversion for the volatility process. We now update the model to quasi-equilibrium status by adding a new (signal) variable to the system, the arbitrage return η. In the quasi-equilibrium setting, this obeys the equation

$$d\eta = -\lambda \eta \, dt + \Sigma \, dZ, \qquad (81)$$

---

[44]'Dummy variable' according to Kindleberger (1996). Recently, Zumbach et al (2000) suggested a volatility-related quantity to distinguish stable and unstable markets. A similar idea (but with a technically different realization based on real-time high-frequency analysis) was implemented by Kiselev and Ilinski in proprietary software for a last-minute crash warning system.

where Z is yet another Wiener process and the parameter λ gives the inverse semi-life time of the arbitrage fluctuations. Let us assume that

$$\langle dY\, dZ \rangle = 0, \qquad \langle dX\, dZ \rangle = \rho_{XZ},$$

so that the coefficient ρ_{XZ} describes the correlation between the mispricing and the underlying price found in empirical studies, as illustrated in Section 2.1. Equations (80) and (81) comprise the stochastic equations for the market variables in the case of a quasi-equilibrium market.

We now turn to the non-equilibrium case, and assume that absolute values of the signal variable η below a certain threshold[45] η_t correspond to a quasi-equilibrium state, while values beyond the threshold characterize highly non-equilibrium market behaviour and breakdown of the stable market relations.

As soon as the signal variable has passed the threshold, the dynamics of the mispricing changes. The first signature of this change is a decrease in the mean reversion for the mispricing, because arbitrageurs are reluctant to take the arbitrage positions calculated from their quasi-equilibrium models in the face of the speculators' driven transition. One can model this effect by the relation[46]

$$\lambda \rightarrow \lambda e^{-(\eta/\eta_t)^2}, \tag{82}$$

which describes the dying out of the arbitrage market mechanism. However, this is not the only change that we have to make in (81). If the arbitrage trade dries out at the beginning and in the course of large market events, it returns back when speculators 'lose their nerve' and relax their pressure on the price as a result of changes in their beliefs. This happens as soon as the underlying price reaches its upper (S_u) or lower (S_l) bounds defined by the 'worst case' expectations of most of the market participants. Therefore we can model this revival of the arbitrage trading by an additional term on the right-hand side of (82):

$$\lambda \rightarrow \lambda e^{-(\eta/\eta_t)^2} + \kappa\left(1 - e^{-\frac{(2S/S_d - S_u/S_d - 1)^2}{(S_u/S_d - 1)^2}}\right).$$

with some parameter κ. The last term is small inside the strip (S_d, S_u), but grows to κ as the price leaves the strip. This last expression allows us to write down an equation that generalizes (81) to the case of large mispricings:

$$d\eta = -\eta\left[\lambda e^{-(\eta/\eta_t)^2} + \kappa\left(1 - e^{-\frac{(2S/S_d - S_u/S_d - 1)^2}{(S_u/S_d - 1)^2}}\right)\right]dt + \Sigma\, dZ. \tag{83}$$

When the mispricing is much smaller than η_t and the underlying price stays inside the strip, this last equation reduces to the quasi-equilibrium equation (81) used before in this chapter.

The next step is to update (80) to the case of breakdown of the quasi-equilibrium dynamics. We start with the stochastic equation for the underlying price, and then turn to the volatility. First of all, we note that in the unstable phase, the mispricing indicates the direction of the price movements. For example, it was described in Section 2 that, during crashes, futures are

---

[45]Whose numerical value depends on the liquidity of the market, and can be estimated as $2\sqrt{\langle \eta^2 \rangle}$.
[46]The particular form of the fitting functions in this section is motivated by reasons of convenience only. The reader might find other fitting functions more applicable if empirical research prompts her to.

traded at discount while put option prices rocket up. The simplest way to include this in the non-equilibrium picture is to replace the first equation in (80) by the following one:

$$dS = \mu\left(1 - \frac{\alpha\eta}{\eta_t}\right)S \, dt + \sigma S \, dX, \tag{84}$$

with some parameter α, which can be estimated from historical peak values of the underlying price and the mispricing. In this form, a large positive mispricing prompts a decrease in the average price changes. Indeed, this is what one might expect in the case of expensive put options (see Section 2.2), which reflects overall downturn expectations. Equation (84) reduces to the quasi-equilibrium case (80) when η/η_t is small, there is no considerable speculative pressure, and the disbalance between 'buy' and 'sell' sites is small and approximately random. However, the large mispricings signal break down of this stable balance and the start of large speculative movements. In the latter case, the direction of the price moves is directly dictated by the speculative pressure, which in turn is characterized by the value of the signal variable, the mispricing. This is exactly what is encoded in (84).

Let us now return to the volatility process. Similar to the underlying price process, it is affected by the presence of large mispricings. It is common knowledge that the volatility increases in the vicinity of a crash. However, it is important to remember that this volatility is calculated using deviations of the price increments from the long-term average μ. It has large values because the losses in returns are compared with the long-term average. Since we have already directly accounted for the change in the average price increments, this source of the boosts of the volatility disappears. In fact, one can think that this instant volatility *decreases* during the crash because the corresponding large speculative pressure pushes the price in a certain direction, thus making the situation more predictable. This is why we model the volatility process by the stochastic equation

$$dV = \phi(V_0 e^{-(\eta/\eta_t)^2} - V) \, dt + \xi e^{-(\eta/\eta_t)^2} V \, dY, \tag{85}$$

which effectively says that when the speculative pressure is strong and the mispricing is large, the instant volatility is small and less volatile however paradoxical this may sound. When the mispricing is small compared with η_t, one can neglect the exponential factors in (85) and return back to the quasi-equilibrium equation (80).

Collecting together (84), (85), and (83), we obtain the system of stochastic equations that model the underlying price, the instant volatility, and the mispricing for the case of a non-equilibrium market[47]

$$dS = \mu(1 - \alpha\eta/\eta_t)S \, dt + \sigma S \, dX,$$

$$dV = \phi(V_0 e^{-(\eta/\eta_t)^2} - V) \, dt + \xi e^{-(\eta/\eta_t)^2} V \, dY, \tag{86}$$

$$d\eta = -\eta\left[\lambda e^{-(\eta/\eta_t)^2} + \kappa\left(1 - e^{-\frac{(2S/S_d - S_u/S_d - 1)^2}{(S_u/S_d - 1)^2}}\right)\right]dt + \Sigma \, dZ.$$

---

[47]One might think that Σ, the volatility of the arbitrage return, has to be a function of η/η_t too. As far as I know, there is no empirical study on this matter, and for now we leave Σ as a constant.

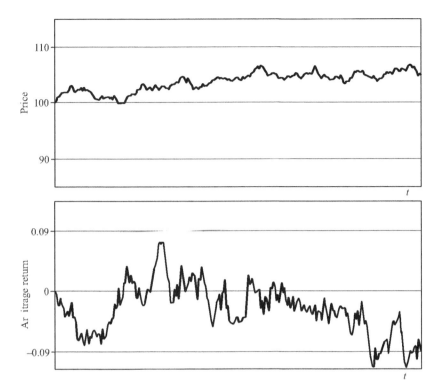

Figure 9.19   Typical chart of the price and the arbitrage in the quasi-equilibrium phase. The threshold $\eta_t = 0.09$ and the fundamental price bounds $S_u = 110$ and $S_d = 90$ are shown.

This is the system that has to be used to derive the put pricing equation or to perform Monte Carlo calculations. The price S and the arbitrage return η are shown in Figs. 9.19 and 9.20. The reader can compare them with the corresponding figures in Section 2 to see that they demonstrate similar behaviour.

8.2   Pricing Equation

The derivation below will be very similar to what we have done to get (52) in Section 5. The change in the put price $C(S, V, \eta)$ is given by

$$dC = \frac{\partial C}{\partial t}\, dt + \frac{VS^2}{2} \frac{\partial^2 C}{\partial S^2}\, dt + \frac{\xi^2 e^{-2(\eta/\eta_t)} V^2}{2} \frac{\partial^2 C}{\partial V^2}\, dt + \frac{\Sigma^2}{2} \frac{\partial^2 C}{\partial \eta^2}\, dt + \rho_{XY}\xi e^{-(\eta/\eta_t)} VS\sigma \frac{\partial^2 C}{\partial V\, \partial S}\, dt$$
$$+ \rho_{XZ}\Sigma S\sigma \frac{\partial^2 C}{\partial \eta\, \partial S}\, dt + \frac{\partial C}{\partial S}\, dS + \frac{\partial C}{\partial \eta}\, d\eta + \frac{\partial C}{\partial V}\, dV.$$

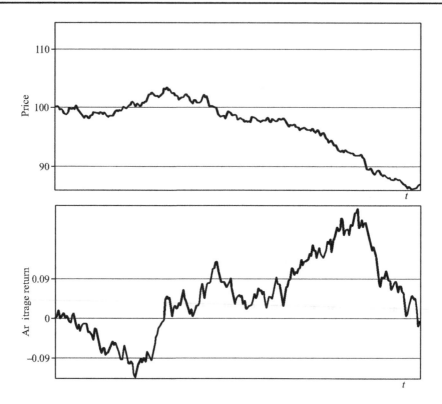

Figure 9.20 Typical chart of the price and the arbitrage in the non-equilibrium (crash) phase. The threshold $\eta_t = 0.09$ and the fundamental price bounds $S_u = 110$ and $S_d = 90$ are shown.

Following the standard steps and assuming zero systematic risk to avoid unnecessary complications here (see Hull and White, 1987), we arrive at the pricing equation

$$\frac{\partial C}{\partial t} + \frac{VS^2}{2}\frac{\partial^2 C}{\partial S^2} + \frac{\xi^2 e^{-2(\eta/\eta_t)} V^2}{2}\frac{\partial^2 C}{\partial V^2} + \frac{\Sigma^2}{2}\frac{\partial^2 C}{\partial \eta^2}$$

$$+ \rho_{XY}\xi e^{-(\eta/\eta_t)} VS\sigma \frac{\partial^2 C}{\partial V \partial S} + \rho_{XZ}\Sigma S\sigma \frac{\partial^2 C}{\partial \eta \partial S}$$

$$+ S\frac{\partial C}{\partial S}(r_0 + \eta) - \frac{\partial C}{\partial \eta}\left[\lambda e^{-(\eta/\eta_t)^2} + \kappa\left(1 - e^{-\frac{(2S/S_d - S_u/S_d - 1)^2}{(S_u/S_d - 1)^2}}\right)\right]$$

$$+ \frac{\partial C}{\partial V}\phi(V_0 e^{-(\eta/\eta_t)^2} - V) - (r_0 + \eta)C = 0, \qquad V \equiv \sigma^2. \qquad (87)$$

The reader can see that the mispricing η enters the equation in a dual role: as the signal variable and as the additional arbitrage return on the riskless portfolio. The solution of (87) provided with an appropriate final payoff gives the put option price for the non-equilibrium pricing model.

To conclude this section, we note that there is another important issue that has to be addressed here. We mentioned in Section 2 that sometimes hedging strategies are blamed for the deterioration of market instability. Indeed, according to the standard view, a large decrease in the underlying price requires hedgers to sell the underlying assets in the hedging portfolio to maintain its risklessness. This facilitates further price decreases, and creates a 'chain reaction'. Most of the time, the price movements are small and the hedging impact on the underlying price is barely noticeable. However, during extreme market events, this factor becomes more pronounced and has to be taken into account. In fact, there are two sources that enhance the hedging impact in the case of large events compared with the situation of a stable market. First of all, large underlying price moves cause large hedging sales. Secondly, and more importantly, it is common that large market movements are accompanied by a liquidity crisis, which makes it difficult for traders to sell[48] and increases the corresponding market impact. These two effects can be also easily accommodated in the model presented above.

To this end, we have to introduce an additional term in the first equation of the system (86) to reflect changes in price due to hedging money flows (see the discussion in Section 3.5). If $\Delta_h(S, \sigma, \eta, t)$ is the market hedging strategy and $\epsilon(\eta)$ is the inverse Farmer's liquidity multiplied by the number of hedged contracts, then the first equation of (86) will be rewritten as

$$dS = \mu(1 - \alpha\eta/\eta_t)S\,dt + \sigma S\,dX + S\epsilon(\eta)\,d\Delta_h. \tag{88}$$

When the mispricing η is small, we expect the effect to be negligible.[49] However, if the mispricing is large and the market is destabilized, one often faces a liquidity crisis, which means a considerable increase in ϵ. It is possible to model this effect in the same way as we advocated above, and take

$$\epsilon(\eta) = \epsilon_0 e^{(\eta/\eta_t)^2}.$$

To proceed further, we have to apply the Itô lemma to the hedging strategy Δ_h:

$$d\Delta_h = A_{\Delta_h}(t)\,dt + \frac{\partial\Delta_h}{\partial S}\,dS + \frac{\partial\Delta_h}{\partial\eta}\,d\eta + \frac{\partial\Delta_h}{\partial V}\,dV, \tag{89}$$

where the following notation has been used:

$$A_{\Delta_h}(t) = \frac{\partial\Delta_h}{\partial t} + \frac{VS^2}{2}\frac{\partial^2\Delta_h}{\partial S^2} + \frac{\xi^2 e^{-2(\eta/\eta_t)}V^2}{2}\frac{\partial^2\Delta_h}{\partial V^2} + \frac{\Sigma^2}{2}\frac{\partial^2\Delta_h}{\partial\eta^2}$$
$$+ \rho_{XY}\xi e^{-(\eta/\eta_t)}VS\sigma\frac{\partial^2\Delta_h}{\partial V\partial S} + \rho_{XZ}\Sigma S\sigma\frac{\partial^2\Delta_h}{\partial\eta\partial S}.$$

Substituting (89) into (88), we find that

$$dS = \mu(1 - \alpha\eta/\eta_t + \epsilon_0 e^{(\eta/\eta_t)^2}A_{\Delta_h})S\,dt + \sigma S\,dX$$
$$+ \epsilon_0 e^{(\eta/\eta_t)^2}S\frac{\partial\Delta_h}{\partial S}\,dS + \epsilon_0 e^{(\eta/\eta_t)^2}S\frac{\partial\Delta_h}{\partial\eta}\,d\eta + \epsilon_0 e^{(\eta/\eta_t)^2}S\frac{\partial\Delta_h}{\partial V}\,dV,$$

---

[48]For example, to unwind arbitrage positions.
[49]Except, perhaps, for expiration dates.

which results in the final stochastic equation for the price S:

$$dS = \frac{\mu(1 - \alpha\eta/\eta_t + \epsilon_0 e^{(\eta/\eta_t)^2} A_{\Delta_h})}{1 - \epsilon_0 e^{(\eta/\eta_t)^2} S \frac{\partial \Delta_h}{\partial S}} S\, dt + \frac{\sigma}{1 - \epsilon_0 e^{(\eta/\eta_t)^2} S \frac{\partial \Delta_h}{\partial S}} S\, dX$$

$$+ \frac{\epsilon_0 e^{(\eta/\eta_t)^2}}{1 - \epsilon_0 e^{(\eta/\eta_t)^2} S \frac{\partial \Delta_h}{\partial S}} S \frac{\partial \Delta_h}{\partial \eta}\, d\eta + \frac{\epsilon_0 e^{(\eta/\eta_t)^2}}{1 - \epsilon_0 e^{(\eta/\eta_t)^2} S \frac{\partial \Delta_h}{\partial S}} S \frac{\partial \Delta_h}{\partial V}\, dV. \qquad (90)$$

This last equation replaces the first equation of the system (86). In the case of dynamical hedging strategies such as delta-hedging,

$$\Delta_h = \frac{\partial C}{\partial S}.$$

This causes the pricing problem and the corresponding analogue of the pricing equation (87) to be highly nonlinear. However, it is perfectly straightforward to rewrite (87) for the new underlying price dynamics, so we leave it for the reader as an exercise.

8.3 Final Remarks

Throughout this section, we have used a very simple mispricing-dependent factor $e^{-(\eta/\eta_t)^2}$ for all relevant entities to avoid the introduction of many parameters into the model. However, one might expect that the law of how the liquidity decreases is different from the law of how the arbitrage trades dry out. This is why the approach can be further refined by using more elaborate fitting for the η-dependence of the principal quantities.

It is not difficult to include the possibility of large market events and developed non-equilibrium market dynamics into the gauge model of Section 3 constructed for the case of a quasi-equilibrium market. To accomplish this task, one has to update the action terms for the money flows to accommodate the behavioural aspects that we have discussed in this section. It will make the model more complicated as well as more realistic. The gauge framework and the language of creation – annihilation operators will be particularly convenient for the task of detailed agent-based non-equilibrium modelling, because the signal variable, the mispricing, and the agents' money flows are intrinsic objects of the gauge theory.

In this chapter, we have discussed non-equilibrium derivative pricing for both quasi-equilibrium and strongly non-equilibrium markets. We have shown how to adapt a general prescription of gauge modelling to derivative pricing. This can be done by constructing base graphs for the theory that describe an exchange of the derivatives and the underlying shares not only for cash but also for each other at some prespecified moments of time. The framework is general enough to describe both European and American derivatives with various payoffs. We have demonstrated that in the quasiclassical limit in the absence of money flows, the treatment reproduces the Black – Scholes equation with the appropriate boundary conditions. The reader has been shown how to introduce various types of money flows, among which the arbitrage money flows have been considered in more detail. The phenomenological model for the arbitrage fluctuations and the corresponding market reaction has been discussed and it has been shown how this type of model can be derived within the gauge framework. Based on this model various aspects of derivative pricing with the virtual arbitrage assumptions have been studied, and some explicit and exact results for derivative prices have been obtained. Finally, we have formulated a model for non-equilibrium option pricing that accounts for ineffective markets and large market events. All the above results are obtained analytically.

9 SUMMARY

- Equilibrium pricing and the no-arbitrage assumptions are popular in financial modelling. However, empirical studies show that they do not always hold true, and one has to model the corresponding deviations, especially when one wants to take large market events into account.

- It is possible to construct a gauge model for derivative pricing and to include in it various types of money flows, such as arbitrage money flows, hedging money flows, and speculative money flows. It is also clear how to include in the gauge model any other types of money flows as soon as their importance is recognized.

- For many applications, it is sufficient to analyse simpler phenomenological models of virtual arbitrage pricing. The simplest model describes the arbitrage return as an Ornstein–Uhlenbeck process, and allows one to obtain explicit analytical expressions for the derivative prices.

- The same type of models can be used to account for various market imperfections such as the bid–ask spread and transaction costs, with or without virtual arbitrage contributions.

- Virtual arbitrage is particularly important if one wants to construct pricing models for markets that are far from equilibrium. In this case, the arbitrage return plays the role of the signalling variable and characterizes the measure of market efficiency. The corresponding pricing models generalize the standard derivative pricing theory to include non-equilibrium market dynamics in cases of large market events.

10

Conclusions

'We know all models are false.'

Eugene F. Fama (Fama, 1991)

Very good – it is almost over! What would I like the reader to get from this book? First of all, that the financial market, like any exchange economy system, has a very interesting and powerful symmetry: a local symmetry with respect to rescaling of asset units and the corresponding change of the exchange factors. This symmetry is called a gauge symmetry, and is, in fact, very similar to the symmetries in physics responsible for all known fundamental interactions. In a financial setting, this symmetry is something very natural, and people have been using it for years to simplify cumbersome financial calculations.

The most natural language to describe this symmetry is the language of fibre bundle geometry. This allows us to deal with prices and money flows on the same geometrical basis, and provides us with corresponding well-developed mathematical methods.

The gauge symmetry of financial markets is only approximate owing to the presence of some market imperfections such as bid–ask spread, transaction costs, and traders' psychological price levels. Strictly speaking, these imperfections break the ideal gauge symmetry, but quantitatively the violations are usually comparatively small, so that one can safely ignore them at first and treat them later as perturbations.

If we accept the presence of gauge symmetry in financial markets, any dynamical model of a market has to be gauge-invariant, i.e. all dynamical equations describing prices and money flows have to obey the gauge symmetry. This does not sound very restrictive, but, in fact, reduces the possible structures of theories to those dictated by the corresponding fibre bundle mathematics. However, gauge symmetry does not fix a theory completely, so there is still space for other important economic principles.

It is very tempting to formulate a theory in its most general form, because the more general a theory and the fewer the assumptions, the more applicable the theory is. On the other hand, the more general a theory, the more difficult it is to extract something practical from it. This is not something particular to economics, but is rather a ubiquitous fact in science. This is why one has to find a compromise between generality and applicability. This is the art of modelling phenomena: extracting the important factors while ignoring the unimportant ones, and then formulating the theory.

The reader might find this very disappointing: we have looked for a fundamental theory and ended up with a modeller's choice. But, in fact, it is not that bad. The system itself is extremely complicated, it has many complex features, such as inductive reasoning and self-organization, and it deals with the results of human behaviour. Reducing all of this to a simple mathematical statement would be very suspicious. The choice of factors is the choice of the additional assumptions of a theory, and it is fortunate that the gauge framework has a place for them. On the other hand, in using observable and robust gauge invariance, we have definitely taken a step forward, narrowing the set of possible general theories to the set of gauge theories and finding appropriate mathematical tools. It is not the end of the road, but we are definitely better off than we were before.

In this book, we have discussed several basic economic assumptions to be put into the gauge models. From a practical point of view, they mean that without introducing money flows, the theory is essentially equivalent to standard economic constructions, i.e. the gauge theory is not 'instead of' but rather 'as well as'. The money flows introduce corrections that are not necessarily small and whose quantitative impact depends on the parameters dictated by the particular market in question. The money flows are the bridge between the behavioural agent-based finance that is currently mainly computer modelling, technical analysis, and the familiar pricing theory employed by most practitioners. From this perspective, gauge theory is the way to ask relevant questions, and to say what to simulate on a computer and where to plug the result into the pricing theory.

Appendix
Methods of Quantum Field Theory and Their Financial Applications

1 PRIMER ON CREATION–ANNIHILATION OPERATORS

In this section, the language of creation–annihilation operators[1] will be introduced. This language is very popular among many-body physicists[2] for two reasons. First of all, it allows one to deal with systems containing a variable number of elementary components. Secondly, it makes formal many-body expressions look like single-particle or two-particle analogues, thus sparing the scientist from the need to write equations with a huge number of variables. Both these advantages are very important indeed not only in theoretical physics but virtually in any type of modelling, in particular in the modelling of financial markets. Clearly a number of investors[3] playing at a certain time is not a constant number, and changes with time. Thus it would be useful to have machinery that does not require all its equations to be changed all the time as the number of investors increases or decreases. The second property is very much connected with the first. It is very convenient to have equations with only a few variables instead of labeling all investors with indices and explicitly managing terms corresponding to each particular investor. Instead, we can reduce the description to a single-investor level, study this case, and then use creation–annihilation operators to generalize the equations to the multi-investor case. This is exactly what we did in chapter 6 when the money flows for the single-asset gauge model were considered.

1.1 Occupation Number Representation in a Simple Case

Let us now see how it works. Imagine a simple system where money units (say pence) can be either in a bank deposit or in a stock. Putting aside the stock for the moment, we will first examine the money in the bank deposit. Thus, the only coordinate to characterize the residual

---

[1]They are also commonly called creation and destruction operators.
[2]For a perfect first-time physical introduction to the subject, see Mattuck (1967).
[3]Or money invested in a market.

system is the number n of pence in the bank. Let us make a correspondence between the state when n pence are placed in the deposit and a vector $|n\rangle$ in some vector space $\mathcal{H}$. The space itself will consist of the linear combinations of the vectors $\{|n\rangle\}_{n=0}^{\infty}$ with complex coefficients $\{c_n\}_{n=0}^{\infty}$ such that the following condition is obeyed:[4]

$$\sum_{n=0}^{\infty} \frac{1}{n!} |c_n|^2 < \infty.$$

This allows us to provide the space $\mathcal{H}$ with the scalar product $\langle \cdot | \cdot \rangle$ (we reserve the notation $(\cdot | \cdot)$ for the standard Euclidean scalar product). For arbitrary vectors $|\phi\rangle$ and $|\psi\rangle$ in $\mathcal{H}$

$$|\phi\rangle = \sum_{n}^{\infty} c_n(\phi)|n\rangle, \quad |\psi\rangle = \sum_{n}^{\infty} c_n(\psi)|n\rangle,$$

the scalar product is defined as

$$\langle \psi | \phi \rangle \equiv |\psi\rangle \cdot |\phi\rangle = (\psi | G | \phi) = \sum_{n=0}^{\infty} \bar{c}_n(\psi) \frac{1}{n!} c_n(\phi), \tag{1}$$

with the metric matrix

$$G = \mathrm{diag}\left(\frac{1}{0!}, \frac{1}{1!}, \frac{1}{2!}, \frac{1}{3!}, \ldots, \frac{1}{n!}, \ldots\right) = \begin{pmatrix} \frac{1}{0!} & 0 & 0 & 0 & \cdots \\ 0 & \frac{1}{1!} & 0 & 0 & \cdots \\ 0 & 0 & \frac{1}{2!} & 0 & \cdots \\ 0 & 0 & 0 & \frac{1}{3!} & \cdots \\ \cdot & \cdot & \cdot & \cdot & \cdot \\ \cdot & \cdot & \cdot & \cdot & \cdot \end{pmatrix}. \tag{2}$$

The space $\mathcal{H}$ with the scalar product defined above is called the *Hilbert state space* and the vectors $\{|n\rangle\}_{n=0}^{\infty}$ are the basis in the *occupation number representation*.

We are now ready to introduce linear operators in this space. As far as linear operators are concerned, it is sufficient to define their action on the basis vectors only. The two simplest operators to look at are operators A and B such that

$$A|n\rangle = |n+1\rangle, \qquad B|n+1\rangle = |n\rangle, \qquad B|0\rangle = 0,$$

for any $n = 0, \ldots, \infty$. The operator A transforms a state vector with n pence to a state vector with $n + 1$ pence, thus effectively *creating* an additional penny in the bank account. Similarly, the operator B transforms a vector that corresponds to a state with $n + 1$ pence in the bank deposit to a vector with only n pence in it. The operator B therefore effectively *annihilates* or *destroys* a penny. One can call the operators A and B the operator for the creation of a penny and the operator for the annihilation of a penny in the deposit. However, as it will be clear in the following, it is more convenient to modify the last expressions by inserting some numerical coefficients in them:

$$A|n\rangle = |n+1\rangle, \qquad B|n+1\rangle = (n+1)|n\rangle, \qquad B|0\rangle = 0.$$

---

[4]The convention that we use in this appendix is different from the standard quantum-mechanical one $\sum_{n=0}^{\infty} |c_n|^2 < \infty$, but it is better suited for the consideration of classical systems.

It is easy to check now that the matrix of the operator A in the basis $\{|n\rangle\}_{n=0}^{\infty}$,

$$||A_{kl}|| \equiv ||\langle k|A|l\rangle|| = \begin{pmatrix} 0 & 0 & 0 & 0 & \cdots \\ 1 & 0 & 0 & 0 & \cdots \\ 0 & 1 & 0 & 0 & \cdots \\ 0 & 0 & 1 & 0 & \cdots \\ \cdot & \cdot & \cdot & \cdot & \cdots \\ \cdot & \cdot & \cdot & \cdot & \cdots \end{pmatrix},$$

is connected with the matrix of the operator B,

$$||B_{kl}|| \equiv ||\langle k|B|l\rangle|| = \begin{pmatrix} 0 & 1 & 0 & 0 & \cdots \\ 0 & 0 & 2 & 0 & \cdots \\ 0 & 0 & 0 & 3 & \cdots \\ 0 & 0 & 0 & 0 & \cdots \\ \cdot & \cdot & \cdot & \cdot & \cdots \\ \cdot & \cdot & \cdot & \cdot & \cdots \end{pmatrix},$$

by the relation

$$A = (GB^{\text{tr}}G^{-1}).$$

Since all the matrix elements are real, the latter relation means that the operators A and B are adjoint to each other with respect to the scalar product (1), and A can be formally written as B^{+}. In what follows, we use the notations B^{+} and B for the operators and call them *creation and annihilation operators*.

The reason for introducing the additional multipliers is that they simplify the commutation relations for the operators. Indeed, the reader can check that the operators B^{+} and B obey the following commutation relation:

$$[B, B^{+}] \equiv BB^{+} - B^{+}B = 1 \tag{3}$$

which is easy to derive from the matrix representation of the operators. Without the numerical factors, the operators do not have any simple commutation relations, which considerably complicates manipulations with them. Another pleasant consequence of the presence of the factors is the following relation:

$$B^{+}B|n\rangle = n|n\rangle. \tag{4}$$

This says that the product of the operators B^{+} and B acting on the basis vectors transforms them to themselves up to a factor n, which is the number of pence in the corresponding state. The operator $B^{+}B$ thus can be called the *number-of-pence operator*.

It is possible to look at the relation (4) from a different point of view: we can say that we have found an expression for an operator for the number of pence! Following this line one can prove that *any* linear operator $\hat{O}$ in the space $\mathcal{H}$ can be expressed as a sum of monomials $(B^{+})^{k}B^{l}$:

$$\hat{O} = \sum_{k,l=0}^{\infty} \alpha_{kl}(B^{+})^{k}B^{l},$$

with some complex coefficients α_{kl}. Indeed, if P is a projection operator onto the state $|0\rangle$, the operator

$$\sum_{k,l=0}^{\infty} \frac{1}{l!} \hat{O}_{kl} (B^+)^k P B^l$$

has exactly the same matrix elements as the operator O. The projection itself can be written as

$$P = \sum_{m=0}^{\infty} \frac{(-1)^m}{m!} (B^+)^m B^m.$$

This results in the final expression for the operator $\hat{O}$ in terms of the creation and annihilation operators.[5]

$$\hat{O} = \sum_{k,l,m=0}^{\infty} \frac{(-1)^m}{m!l!} \hat{O}_{kl} (B^+)^{k+m} B^{l+m}.$$

It means that any object of interest, like a dynamical evolution operator, can be written in terms of the creation-annihilation operators with the simple algebra (3) which is definitely quite convenient.

1.2 Multicoordinate Generalization

Let us now return to the original system with the bank deposit and the stock. Once again, we can characterize the system by n_1, the number of pence in the deposit, and n_2, the number of pence in the stock. Repeating the above consideration with the only difference being that the basis vectors $|n_1, n_2\rangle$ now have two labels rather than one, we arrive at the operators for creation and annihilation of a penny in the deposit, B_1^+ and B_1, and in the stock, B_2^+ and B_2. They act on a basis vector as

$$B_1^+ |n_1, n_2\rangle = |n_1 + 1, n_2\rangle, \qquad B_1 |n_1 + 1, n_2\rangle = (n_1 + 1)|n_1, n_2\rangle, \qquad B_1 |0, k\rangle = 0$$

and

$$B_2^+ |n_1, n_2\rangle = |n_1, n_2 + 1\rangle, \qquad B_2 |n_1, n_2 + 1\rangle = (n_2 + 1)|n_1, n_2\rangle, \qquad B_2 |k, 0\rangle = 0,$$

for all k. Again any linear operator in the Hilbert space can be represented as a sum of the monomials

$$(B_1^+)^{k_1} (B_2^+)^{k_2} B_1^{l_1} B_1^{l_2}.$$

But what is particularly important for our goals is that the operators still satisfy the simple *algebra*

$$[B_i, B_k^+] = \delta_{ik}, \qquad [B_i, B_k] = [B_i^+, B_k^+] = 0, \tag{5}$$

which is a direct generalization of the relation (3). In this form, it is valid for any M, the number of coordinates (places to put pence), if we allow the indices i and k to vary from 1 to M.

---

[5] More details on this sort of trick and the corresponding functional integral representations can be found in Ilinskaia and Ilinski (1996).

The algebra of the creation–annihilation operators would look like the algebra of the complex numbers if one could drop the δ_{ik} on the right-hand side of the first equation in (5) but unfortunately (or, indeed, fortunately) the delta symbol is the very source of the complexity and the non-trivial behaviour of the system. However, the analogy with the complex numbers will come back in Section 2.2 when we formulate the dynamics of the operators in terms of functional integrals over the complex-valued functions.

1.3   Why Do We Need Creation–Annihilation Operators?

Imagine a dynamical system whose states are characterized by vectors ψ in some vector space. Suppose that the time evolution of this state vector is defined by a differential equation

$$\frac{d\psi}{dt} = O\psi, \tag{6}$$

with some linear operator O. To find the time-dependent state vector, one has to solve the equation with some initial condition $\psi(0) = \psi_0$. The problem just described is a very common setting in quantum physics, where the corresponding equation is called the Schrödinger equation and the state vector is the wave function. We derived the same type of equation in Section 4 of Chapter 6 for a non-normalized probability. In the last example, the vector was two-dimensional, $\psi^{(1)} = (\psi_1^{(1)}, \psi_2^{(1)})$, and the components represented the non-normalized probability for a typical amount of money (e.g. one penny) either in cash or in shares.

Let us now add a second penny to the system. Since the money amounts do not affect each other, the dynamics of the second lot will be also defined by the equation (6) with the state vector $\psi^{(2)}$. Therefore the joint probability $\Psi' = \psi^{(1)} \otimes \psi^{(2)}$ to find both lots obeys the equation

$$\frac{d\Psi'}{dt} = (O \otimes I + I \otimes O)\Psi'.$$

The first penny and the second penny are identical, and we should identify the state $|1, 0\rangle \otimes |0, 1\rangle$ with the state $|0, 1\rangle \otimes |1, 0\rangle$, which leaves us with a three-dimensional state vector $\Psi = (\psi_{20}, \psi_{11}, \psi_{02})$. The dynamical equation will then take the form

$$\frac{d\Psi}{dt} = O^{(2)}\Psi,$$

with the 3×3 matrix

$$O^{(2)} = \begin{pmatrix} 2O_{11} & 2O_{12} & 0 \\ 2O_{21} & O_{11} + O_{22} & 2O_{12} \\ 0 & 2O_{21} & 2O_{11} \end{pmatrix}. \tag{7}$$

Similarly, in the case of M pence, the state vector Ψ obeys the equation

$$\frac{d\Psi}{dt} = O^{(M)}\Psi, \tag{8}$$

with the matrix $O^{(M)}$ constructed from

$$O \otimes I \otimes \cdots \otimes I + I \otimes O \otimes \cdots \otimes I + \ldots I \otimes I \otimes \cdots \otimes O$$

by identifying all states that can be transformed into each other by permutations of pence. The latter identification of states corresponds to the fact that all pence are identical. One can see that as soon as the number of units increases, the equations start to become complicated and the matrices become huge. This is when the creation–annihilation operators are useful. First of all, we introduce the operator

$$\hat{O} = \sum_{i,k=1}^{2} O_{ik} B_i^+ B_k.$$

Since the operator $\hat{O}$ commutes with the number-of-pence operator $N = B_1^+ B_1 + B_2^+ B_2$, a property that is easy to check from the relations (5),

$$[\hat{O}, N] = \hat{O}N - N\hat{O} = 0,$$

the operator $\hat{O}$ has a block structure and each of the blocks is labelled by the number of pence in the game. This means that $\hat{O}$ does not mix states with different numbers of pence. The first block corresponds to the first eigenvalue of the operator N, which is equal to zero: no pence are invested in stocks or put in the bank. Owing to the property $B_i|0, 0\rangle = 0$, the operator $\hat{O}$ acts on this vector as

$$\hat{O}|0, \ldots, 0\rangle = 0.$$

The second block corresponds to a single penny invested in stock or placed in a deposit. The basis vectors in this block are $|1, 0\rangle = B_1^+|0, 0\rangle$ and $|0, 1\rangle = B_2^+|0, 0\rangle$, so that

$$N|1, 0\rangle = |1, 0\rangle, \quad N|0, 1\rangle = |0, 1\rangle.$$

Now we use the commutation relations (5) and the annihilation property $B_i|0, 0\rangle = 0$ to find the result of the action of $\hat{O}$ on the vectors:

$$\hat{O}|1, 0\rangle = \sum_{i,k=1}^{2} O_{ik} B_i^+ B_k B_1^+ |0, 0\rangle = (O_{11} B_1^+ B_1 + O_{21} B_2^+ B_1) B_1^+ |0, 0\rangle$$

$$= O_{11} B_1^+ [B_1, B_1^+]|0, 0\rangle + O_{11} B_1^+ B_1^+ B_1 |0, 0\rangle$$

$$+ O_{21} B_2^+ [B_1, B_1^+]|0, 0\rangle + O_{21} B_2^+ B_1^+ B_1 |0, 0\rangle$$

$$= O_{11} B_1^+ |0, 0\rangle + O_{21} B_2^+ |0, 0\rangle = O_{11}|1, 0\rangle + O_{21}|0, 1\rangle.$$

Repeating the calculation, we find

$$\hat{O}|0, 1\rangle = O_{12}|1, 0\rangle + O_{22}|0, 1\rangle.$$

The last two equations imply that in the single-lot sector, the operator $\hat{O}$ acts like the *matrix O*:

$$\hat{O}|_{\{|1,0\rangle, |0,1\rangle\}} = \begin{pmatrix} O_{11} & O_{21} \\ O_{21} & O_{22} \end{pmatrix}.$$

The reader can already appreciate what is coming next. Indeed, we look at the two-pence sector with the basis vectors

$$|2, 0\rangle = (B_1^+)^2|0, 0\rangle, \quad |1, 1\rangle = B_1^+ B_2^+|0, 0\rangle, \quad |0, 2\rangle = (B_2^+)^2|0, 0\rangle,$$

and find that the operator $\hat{O}$ acts on them as the matrix $O^{(2)}$ defined in (7). For example,

$$
\begin{aligned}
\hat{O}|2,0\rangle &= \sum_{i,k=1}^{2} O_{ik}B_i^+ B_k (B_1^+)^2|0,0\rangle = (O_{11}B_1^+ B_1 + O_{21}B_2^+ B_1)(B_1^+)^2|0,0\rangle \\
&= O_{11}B_1^+[B_1,B_1^+]B_1^+|0,0\rangle + O_{11}B_1^+ B_1^+ B_1 B_1^+|0,0\rangle \\
&\quad + O_{21}B_2^+[B_1,B_1^+]B_1^+|0,0\rangle + O_{21}B_2^+ B_1^+ B_1 B_1^+|0,0\rangle \\
&= O_{11}(B_1^+)^2|0,0\rangle + O_{11}B_1^+ B_1^+[B_1 B_1^+]|0,0\rangle + O_{11}B_1^+ B_1^+ B_1^+ B_1|0,0\rangle \\
&\quad + O_{21}B_2^+ B_1^+|0,0\rangle + O_{21}B_2^+ B_1^+[B_1 B_1^+]|0,0\rangle + O_{21}B_2^+ B_1^+ B_1^+ B_1|0,0\rangle \\
&= 2O_{11}|2,0\rangle + 2O_{21}|1,1\rangle,
\end{aligned}
$$

which gives the first row of the matrix $O^{(2)}$. In exactly the same way, one can derive the transformations

$$
\begin{aligned}
\hat{O}|1,1\rangle &= \sum_{i,k=1}^{2} O_{ik}B_i^+ B_k B_1^+ B_2^+|0,0\rangle \\
&= 2O_{12}|2,0\rangle + (O_{11}+O_{22})|1,1\rangle + 2O_{21}|0,2\rangle,
\end{aligned}
$$

$$
\hat{O}|0,2\rangle = \sum_{i,k=1}^{2} O_{ik}B_i^+ B_k(B_2^+)^2|0,0\rangle = 2O_{12}|1,1\rangle + 2O_{22}|0,2\rangle.
$$

One can check this directly from the definition of $\hat{O}$ and the commutation relations (5). In fact, $\hat{O}$ will act on the M-pence subspace of the state space exactly as we expect it to do, and will precisely reproduce matrix $O^{(M)}$ from (8). In other words, the single operator $\hat{O}$, which looks like a way to present a matrix, indeed comprises all possible related operators for any number of pence in the game! So, as promised, the language of creation–annihilation operators allows to consider any number of pence on the same ground and the same measure of difficulty, sparing us the pain of dealing with multidimensional matrices and a host of indices.

I.4 Famous Example: the Harmonic Oscillator

The first and de facto most famous appearance of creation-annihilation operators is the eigenvalue problem for the quantum-mechanical harmonic oscillator:

$$
-\frac{1}{2}\frac{d^2\psi_n(x)}{dx^2} + \frac{1}{2}x^2\psi_n(x) - \frac{1}{2}\psi_n(x) = E_n\psi_n(x), \quad \int_{-\infty}^{\infty}|\psi_n(x)|^2 dx < \infty. \tag{9}
$$

One way to treat the problem is to analyze the differential equation and deal with special functions. Instead, we choose another path and represent the differential operator in the form

$$
-\frac{1}{2}\frac{d^2}{dx^2} + \frac{1}{2}x^2 - \frac{1}{2} = B^+ B,
$$

where we have introduced the notation

$$
B^+ = \frac{1}{\sqrt{2}}\left(-\frac{d}{dx}+x\right), \qquad B = \frac{1}{\sqrt{2}}\left(\frac{d}{dx}+x\right).
$$

This notation itself prompts us to check the commutation relation for the operators:

$$[B, B^+] = \frac{1}{2}\left[\frac{d}{dx}, x\right] - \frac{1}{2}\left[x, \frac{d}{dx}\right] = 1,$$

which coincides exactly with the relation (3). The factorization found here is not just a beautiful detail. It helps to solve the problem. Indeed, since the differential operator on the right-hand side of (6) is the number of 'pence', its eigenvalues E_n are simply given by the number of 'pence' n:

$$E_n = n,$$

while the corresponding eigenstates are the states with n 'pence'. To find the eigenstate with zero pence, we have to solve the equation

$$B\psi_0(x) \equiv \left(\frac{d}{dx} + x\right)\psi_0(x) = 0,$$

which has the normalized solution

$$\psi_0(x) = \frac{1}{\sqrt{2\pi}}e^{-x^2/2}.$$

All other normalized states can be constructed by consecutively adding a new 'penny' to the system:

$$\psi_n(x) = \frac{1}{\sqrt{n!}}(B^+)^n\psi_0(x) = \frac{1}{\sqrt{2\pi n! 2^n}}\left(-\frac{d}{dx} + x\right)^n e^{-x^2/2}. \tag{10}$$

The latter relation is, in fact, what we would find from (9) using special functions: (10) is the well-know recurrence relation for Hermite polynomials, which enter in the solutions of the differential equation (9).

The idea presented above of factorizing a differential operator into differential operators of lower order found a very interesting sequel in supersymmetric quantum mechanics, which, surprisingly, has helped to prove many interesting results in the differential geometry of fibre bundles (for further references see e.g. Junker, 1996; Green et al, 1987).

2   FUNCTIONAL INTEGRALS

Despite their threatening name, functional integrals are very natural and useful objects, which are based on a very simple idea. Suppose that we want to solve a first-order differential equation

$$\frac{d\Psi}{dt} = H\Psi, \qquad \Psi|_{t=0} = \Psi_0,$$

where H is a linear operator in some space $\mathcal{H}$ and Ψ is a vector field in this space. The solution of the problem (as well as other problems differing by initial conditions Ψ_0) can be represented as

$$\Psi(t) = U(t, 0)\Psi_0,$$

employing the evolution operator U defined by the dynamical equation

$$\frac{dU}{dt} = HU, \qquad U(0,0) = I. \tag{11}$$

The great thing about the evolution operator $U(t,0)$ is that it can be represented as a product of evolution operators on small times:

$$U(t,0) = U(t, t - \Delta t)U(t - \Delta t, t - 2\Delta t) \ldots U(\Delta t, 0), \tag{12}$$

which is extremely useful, keeping in mind the fact that, for sufficiently small Δt, each of the factors can approximated as

$$U(t' + \Delta t, t') = I + H(t')\Delta t. \tag{13}$$

If now we have a vector set $\{|x\rangle\}$ parametrized by some continuous variable x so that there exists a decomposition of the identity operator

$$I = \int dx \, |x\rangle\langle x|,$$

we can rewrite (12) in terms of matrix elements as

$$
\begin{aligned}
\langle x_N|U(t,0)|x_0\rangle =& \int dx_{N-1} \int dx_{N-2} \ldots \int dx_1 \\
& \times \langle x_N|U(t, t - \Delta t)|x_{N-1}\rangle\langle x_{N-1}|U(t - \Delta t, t - 2\Delta t)|x_{N-2}\rangle \ldots \\
& \times \langle x_1|U(\Delta t, 0)|x_0\rangle, \\
& N = t/\Delta t.
\end{aligned}
\tag{14}
$$

Substituting (13) into the last equation, we find

$$
\begin{aligned}
\langle x_N|U(t,0)|x_0\rangle =& \int dx_{N-1} \int dx_{N-2} \ldots \int dx_1 \\
& \times \langle x_N|I + H(t - \Delta t)\Delta t|x_{N-1}\rangle\langle x_{N-1}|I + H(t - 2\Delta t)\Delta t|x_{N-2}\rangle \ldots \\
& \times \langle x_1|I + H(0)\Delta t|x_0\rangle,
\end{aligned}
\tag{15}
$$

which, with the same measure of accuracy, can be written as

$$
\begin{aligned}
\langle x_N|U(t,0)|x_0\rangle =& \int dx_{N-1} \int dx_{N-2} \ldots \int dx_1 \langle x_N|x_{N-1}\rangle\langle x_{N-1}|x_{N-2}\rangle \ldots \langle x_1|x_0\rangle \\
& \times e^{\frac{\langle x_N|H(t-\Delta t)\Delta t|x_{N-1}\rangle}{\langle x_N|x_{N-1}\rangle}} e^{\frac{\langle x_{N-1}|H(t-2\Delta t)\Delta t|x_{N-2}\rangle}{\langle x_{N-1}|x_{N-2}\rangle}} \ldots e^{\frac{\langle x_1|H(0)\Delta t|x_0\rangle}{\langle x_1|x_0\rangle}}.
\end{aligned}
\tag{16}
$$

If the interval Δt tends to zero, the representation (13) becomes exact. The number N tends to infinity, which means that the number of integrations in (16) also becomes infinite. Instead of thinking of infinite number of simple integrations over $x_1, x_2, \ldots, x_{N-1}$, we can think of an integration over *functions* $x(\cdot)$ on the interval $(t, 0)$ with fixed boundary conditions

$$x(t) = x_N, \qquad x(0) = x_0,$$

identifying $x(i\Delta t)$ with x_i. Equation (16) thus becomes a *functional integral* where the integration is carried over all possible dynamic trajectories of the system. To proceed, we have to choose a particular vector set $\{|x\rangle\}$ that best suits our objectives. In what follows we will consider two such choices: the coordinate representation, which leads to the famous Feynman path integral, and the coherent state representation, which is most convenient for dealing with creation–annihilation operators. The latter is the one the reader met in Chapter 6.

2.1 Feynman Path Integral

Let us consider a one-dimensional system with coordinate x, $-\infty < x < \infty$. The system is characterized by a function $\phi(x)$, which has, for example, the meaning of a non-normalized probability to find the system in a state with coordinate x. Assume that the dynamics of the function ϕ is governed by the equation

$$\frac{\partial \phi}{\partial t} = \frac{\partial^2 \phi}{\partial x^2} + V(x)\phi,$$

which we will solve using the functional integral method. First of all, we have to find a convenient basis set to use in the identity operator decomposition. One of the simplest choices is the set of eigenfunctions of the coordinate operator $\hat{x}$, which we denote by $\{|x)\}$:

$$\hat{x}|x) = x|x).$$

The state $|x)$ is a state with a definite position of the system, the position given by the coordinate x. It is clear that

$$I = \int dx \, |x)(x|,$$

since the system should be somewhere. Moreover, the scalar product of the vectors has the particular simple form

$$(x'|x) = \delta(x - x'),$$

which considerably simplifies the functional integral derivation. Let us return to (15). The matrix elements $(x_k|I + H((k-1)\Delta t)\Delta t|x_{k-1})$ can be represented as

$$(x_k|I + H((k-1)\Delta t)\Delta t|x_{k-1}) = \delta(x_k - x_{k-1})\big[1 + V(x_{k-1})\Delta t\big] + \Delta t\left(x_k\left|\frac{\partial^2}{\partial x^2}\right|x_{k-1}\right).$$

The last term on the right-hand side is equal to

$$\Delta t\left(x_k\left|\frac{\partial^2}{\partial x^2}\right|x_{k-1}\right) = -\Delta t \int_{-\infty}^{\infty} \frac{dp}{2\pi} e^{ip(x_k - x_{k-1})} p^2,$$

which, together with the well-known representation for the delta function

$$\delta(x_k - x_{k-1}) = \int_{-\infty}^{\infty} \frac{dp}{2\pi} e^{ip(x_k - x_{k-1})},$$

results in the following expression for the matrix element:

$$(x_k|I + H((k-1)\Delta t)\Delta t|x_{k-1}) = \int \frac{dp_{k-1}}{2\pi}[1 - \Delta t p_{k-1}^2 + \Delta t V(x_k)]e^{ip_{k-1}(x_k - x_{k-1})}$$

$$\simeq \int \frac{dp_{k-1}}{2\pi} e^{ip_{k-1}(x_k - x_{k-1}) - \Delta t p_{k-1}^2 + \Delta t V(x_k)}. \tag{17}$$

Substituting (17) for all k in the expression (15), we finally get

$$\langle x_N | U(t,0) | x_0 \rangle = \int dx_{N-1} \int dx_{N-2} \cdots \int dx_1 \int \frac{dp_{N-1}}{2\pi} \int \frac{dp_{N-2}}{2\pi} \cdots \int \frac{dp_1}{2\pi} \int \frac{dp_0}{2\pi}$$
$$\times \exp\left\{ \sum_{k=1}^{N-1} [ip_{k-1}(x_k - x_{k-1}) - \Delta t p_{k-1}^2 + \Delta t V(x_k)] \right\}. \tag{18}$$

Taking the final step by denoting

$$Dx \equiv \int dx_{N-1} \int dx_{N-2} \cdots \int dx_1, \qquad Dp = \int \frac{dp_{N-1}}{2\pi} \int \frac{dp_{N-2}}{2\pi} \cdots \int \frac{dp_1}{2\pi} \int \frac{dp_0}{2\pi},$$

and considering $\Delta t \to 0$, we arrive at the functional integral representation for the matrix elements of the evolution operator $U(t,0)$:

$$\langle x | U(t,0) | x' \rangle = \int Dx \int Dp \; e^{\int_0^t d\tau [ip(\tau)\frac{dx}{d\tau} - p(\tau)^2 + V(x(\tau))]}. \tag{19}$$

In the last equation, the integration is over all functions $p(\tau)$ on the interval[6] $[t, 0]$ and all functions $x(\tau)$ with the boundary conditions

$$x(t) = x, \qquad x(0) = x'. \tag{20}$$

The representation (18) is commonly known as the *Feynman path integral*. In the next sections we will see how it can be calculated and used in financial applications.

2.2 Coherent State Representation and Functional Integrals

Let us consider now the case when the operator H governing the dynamics

$$\frac{\partial \phi}{\partial t} = H\psi$$

is expressed in terms of creation–annihilation operators:[7]

$$H = \sum_{i,k=1}^{M} H_{ik} B_i^+ B_k. \tag{21}$$

Of course, the first thing that comes to mind is to use the basis vectors $\{|n_1, \ldots, n_M\rangle\}$ as a set of vectors for the decomposition of the identity operator:

$$I = \sum_{n_1,\ldots,n_M=0}^{\infty} |n_1, \ldots, n_M\rangle\langle n_1, \ldots, n_M|. \tag{22}$$

---

[6]The reader has probably noticed that there was no integration over p_N, although in the continuous limit we still treat the expression as if there was one. Strictly speaking, we have to be cautious about this. In reality, it does not matter – compared with the infinite number of integrations, this last one is negligible.

[7]For the sake of simplicity, we examine here the case of quadratic operators, but this is just to make the expressions compact, and nothing changes in the general construction.

However, the final expressions will look much nicer if we employ a different but closely related set of states, the *coherent states:*

$$|b_1, \ldots, b_M\rangle \equiv \sum_{n_1,\ldots,n_M=0}^{\infty} \frac{1}{n_1! n_2! \ldots n_M!} (b_1 B_1^+)^{n_1} (b_2 B_2^+)^{n_2} \ldots (b_M B_M^+)^{n_M} |0, \ldots, 0\rangle, \qquad (23)$$

where $b_1, b_2, \ldots, b_M$ are complex numbers labelling the state. The whole set of vectors comprises the vectors (23) with all possible choices of the numbers $b_1, b_2, \ldots, b_M$ on the complex plane. At first sight, the coherent states seem to be more complicated than our original choice. However, they have several remarkable properties that greatly facilitate the construction of functional integrals.

1. The coherent states are the eigenvectors of the annihilation operators:

$$B_k |b_1, \ldots, b_M\rangle = b_k |b_1, \ldots, b_M\rangle \qquad k = 1, \ldots, M.$$

This relation can be checked directly from the definition of the coherent states and the action of the annihilation operators.

2. For the coherent co-vectors defined as[8]

$$\langle \bar{b}_1, \ldots, \bar{b}_M | \equiv \sum_{n_1,\ldots,n_M=0}^{\infty} \frac{1}{n_1! n_2! \ldots n_M!} \langle 0, \ldots, 0 | (\bar{b}_1 B_1)^{n_1} (\bar{b}_2 B_2)^{n_2} \ldots (\bar{b}_M B_M)^{n_M}, \qquad (24)$$

there exists an analogous relation

$$\langle \bar{b}_1, \ldots, \bar{b}_M | B_k^+ = \bar{b}_k \langle \bar{b}_1, \ldots, \bar{b}_M |, \qquad k = 1, \ldots, M.$$

3. The coherent states have the scalar product

$$\langle \bar{b}_1, \ldots, \bar{b}_M | b_1', \ldots, b_M' \rangle = e^{\sum_{k=1}^{M} \bar{b}_k b_k'}.$$

4. There exists an integral representation for the identity operator

$$I = \int \prod_{k=1}^{M} \frac{db_k \, d\bar{b}_k}{2i\pi} e^{-\sum_{k=1}^{M} \bar{b}_k b_k} |b_1, \ldots, b_M\rangle \langle \bar{b}_1, \ldots, \bar{b}_M |. \qquad (25)$$

To prove this property one has to rewrite the integrals over b and $\bar{b}$ as

$$\int \frac{db \, d\bar{b}}{2i\pi} = \int_0^{\infty} |b| \frac{d|b|}{\pi} \int_0^{2\pi} d\alpha, \qquad b = |b| e^{i\alpha},$$

---

[8] The operators B^+, B act on co-vectors as $\langle n|B^+ = \langle n-1|$ and $\langle n|B = \langle n+1|(n+1)$. This action can be deduced from the equalities

$$\delta_{n,k+1} = \langle n|B^+|k\rangle, \qquad k\delta_{n,k-1} = \langle n|B|k\rangle,$$

which are valid for any k and n.

and perform first the integration over the phase α. This leaves us with the expression

$$\prod_{k=1}^{M} \sum_{n_k=0}^{\infty} (B_k^+)^{n_k} |0, \ldots, 0\rangle \int dr_k e^{-r_k} r_k^{n_k} \frac{1}{n_k! n_k!} \langle 0, \ldots, 0|(B_k)^{n_k}$$

$$= \sum_{n_1, \ldots, n_M=0}^{\infty} |n_1, \ldots, n_M\rangle \langle n_1, \ldots, n_M|,$$

which, owing to (22), gives the identity operator.

Now everything is ready for us to derive a functional integral representation for the matrix element evolution operator $U(t, 0)$ in the coherent state representation. As before, the evolution operator is defined by (11), but the Hamiltonian is expressed in terms of the creation–annihilation operators (21). The matrix elements of the Hamiltonian can be easily calculated using Properties 1 and 2 of the coherent states:

$$\langle \bar{b}_1, \ldots, \bar{b}_M | H(t) | b_1', \ldots, b_M' \rangle = \sum_{i,k=1}^{M} H_{ik} \langle \bar{b}_1, \ldots, \bar{b}_M | B_i^+ B_k | b_1', \ldots, b_M' \rangle$$

$$= \langle \bar{b}_1, \ldots, \bar{b}_M | b_1', \ldots, b_M' \rangle \sum_{i,k=1}^{M} H_{ik} \bar{b}_i b_k'.$$

If we substitute this expression into (16) and take into account Property 3 of the coherent states, the matrix element of the evolution operator will take the form

$$\langle \bar{b}_1^{(N)}, \ldots, \bar{b}_M^{(N)} | U(t, 0) | b_1^{(0)}, \ldots, b_M^0 \rangle = \int \prod_{k=1}^{M} \frac{db_k^{N-1} d\bar{b}_k^{N-1}}{2i\pi} \cdots \int \prod_{k=1}^{M} \frac{db_k^1 d\bar{b}_k^1}{2i\pi} e^{-\sum_{j=1}^{N-1} \sum_{k=1}^{M} \bar{b}_k^j b_k^j}$$

$$\times \left(e^{\sum_{k=1}^{M} \bar{b}_k^N b_k^{N-1}} \cdots e^{\sum_{k=1}^{M} \bar{b}_k^1 b_k^0} \right) \left(e^{\Delta t \sum_{i,k=1}^{M} H_{ik} \bar{b}_i^N b_k^{N-1}} \cdots e^{\Delta t \sum_{i,k=1}^{M} H_{ik} \bar{b}_i^1 b_k^0} \right). \quad (26)$$

The first term in the integrand arises from the integration measure in the identity decomposition (Property 4 of the coherent states). The second term is due to the scalar products of the intermediate states, while the last one comes from the matrix elements of the Hamiltonian H. In the continuous-time limit $\Delta t \to 0$, the number of integrations tends to infinity, and the last term on the right-hand side of (26) converges to

$$e^{\int d\tau \sum_{i,k=1}^{M} H_{ik}(\tau) \bar{b}_i(\tau) b_k(\tau)}.$$

Using the notation

$$D\bar{b} \, Db = \prod_{j=1}^{N-1} \prod_{k=1}^{M} \frac{db_k^j \, d\bar{b}_k^j}{2i\pi},$$

and noticing that

$$-\sum_{j=1}^{N-1} \sum_{k=1}^{M} \bar{b}_k^j b_k^j + \sum_{j=0}^{N-1} \sum_{k=1}^{M} \bar{b}_k^{j+1} b_k^j = \sum_{k=1}^{M} \bar{b}_k^0 b_k^0 + \sum_{k=1}^{M} \sum_{j=0}^{N-1} \left(\bar{b}_k^{j+1} - \bar{b}_k^j \right) b_k^j,$$

we transform (26) into its final form:

$$\langle \bar{b}_1, \ldots, \bar{b}_M | U(t, 0) | b_1^{(0)}, \ldots, b_M^0 \rangle = e^{\sum_{k=1}^{M} \bar{b}_k^0 b_k^0} \int D\bar{b}\, Db$$

$$\times \exp\left[\int_0^t d\tau \left(\sum_{k=1}^{M} \frac{\partial \bar{b}_k(\tau)}{\partial \tau} b_k(\tau) + \sum_{i,k=1}^{M} H_{ik}(\tau)\bar{b}_i(\tau)b_k(\tau)\right)\right]. \quad (27)$$

This is the *functional integral* representation that we wanted to derive. The matrix elements of the evolution operator are represented in the form of a functional integral over complex functions $\bar{b}(\cdot)$ and $b(\cdot)$, which are defined on the segment $[0, t]$ and satisfy the boundary conditions

$$\bar{b}_k(t) = \bar{b}_k, \qquad b_k(0) = b_k^0.$$

The reader can see that once again the labels of the matrix elements appear in the boundary conditions of the functional integral. However, this time they are also present in the prefactor $e^{\sum_{k=1}^{M} \bar{b}_k^0 b_k^0}$.

The functional integral (27) is the one that we used in Chapter 6 to find an expression for the non-normalized transition probability when developing a model with many money lots in the simple cash – stock system. The lattice formulation does not complicate things – one just has to approximate $\partial \bar{b}_k(\tau)/\partial \tau$ by a finite difference $[\bar{b}_k(t + \Delta t) - \bar{b}_k(t)]/\Delta t$. With this modification, all functional integrals of Chapter 6 can be derived from the expression (27).

We end this subsection with two remarks. First of all, the particular form of the Hamiltonian was not important. The only fact that we used is that the Hamiltonian can be represented in terms of creation – annihilation operators in such a way that all the B^+ operators stand to the left of the B operators. The result of this subsection, (27), holds for any Hamiltonian of this form, with the only difference being that the expression $\sum_{i,k=1}^{M} H_{ik}(\tau)\bar{b}_i(\tau)b_k^0(\tau)$ will be substituted by the expression for any new Hamiltonian where all operators B^+ are replaced by numbers $\bar{b}$ and the operators B by numbers b.

This leads us to the second point to be mentioned here. Let us have another look at (27). If we drop the prefactor, the sign of the functional integral, and the term $[\partial \bar{b}(\tau)/\partial \tau]b(\tau)$, the only term left will be

$$\exp\left(\int d\tau \sum_{i,k=1}^{M} H_{ik}(\tau)\bar{b}_i(\tau)b_k(\tau)\right).$$

This expression would be the correct answer for the evolution operator if all operators B^+ and B were replaced by complex numbers $\bar{b}$ and b, which is, in fact, equivalent to ignoring the non-zero right-hand side of the commutation relations (5):

$$B_i B_k^+ - B_k^+ B_i = \delta_{ik}.$$

The non-commutative nature of the operators is what led to the need for a functional integration. If the operators do not commute, i.e. the right-hand side of the commutation relations is not zero, the correct expression for the evolution operator is an integral of the evolution operator[9] in the commutative case over all possible trajectories of the evolution. The

---

[9]Note the presence of the term $[\partial \bar{b}(\tau)/\partial \tau]b(\tau)$ in the non-commutative case. In general, the D-dimensional non-commutative case can be cast into the $D + 1$ commutative case, and vice versa.

non-commutativity leads to the virtual existence of trajectories that would otherwise be forbidden. Since this is a common properties of quantum systems (see Chapter 4), functional integrals fit very naturally into quantum theory.[10]

2.3   Proof of the Relation (18) from Chapter 6

In this subsection, we show why the non-symmetric normalization of vectors and non-trivial scalar product should be used to calculate the transition probability for many-particle states. To this end, we note that a general form of a matrix element of the evolution operator can be written as:

$$U(t, t') \equiv \langle \bar{\psi}(t) | \hat{U}(t, t') | \psi(t') \rangle = \exp\left(\sum_{l,m=1,2} \bar{\psi}_l(t) A_{lm}(t, t') \psi_m(t') \right).$$

It is not difficult to show that the matrix elements $A_{lm}(t, t')$ coincides with the single particle transition probability. Indeed, by definition,

$$P_{\alpha\beta} = \int \prod_{i,k} \frac{1}{2\pi i} d\bar{\psi}_{i,k} \, d\psi_{i,k} \, e^{-\bar{\psi}_{i,k}\psi_{i,k}} \langle 0 | \hat{\psi}_\alpha | \psi_{1,k} \rangle e^{\sum_{lm} \bar{\psi}_{1,l} A_{lm} \psi_{2,m}} \langle \bar{\psi}_{2,k} | \hat{\psi}_\alpha^+ | 0 \rangle,$$

which gives the relation

$$P_{\alpha\beta} = A_{\alpha\beta}(t, t').$$

It is possible to check now that in the case of non-interacting particles, the many-particle transition probability can be expressed through the single-particle ones:

$$P_{(n_1,n_2)(m_1,m_2)} = \delta_{m_1+m_2,n_1+n_2} \sum_{i,k=0}^{m_1,m_2} C_{m_1}^i C_{m_2}^k P_{2,1}^i P_{1,1}^{m_1-i} P_{1,2}^k P_{2,2}^k \delta_{m_1-i+k,n_1}, \tag{28}$$

which results for simple combinatorial reasons. If we introduce non-symmetric vector states

$$\langle n_1, n_2 | = \langle 0 | (\hat{\psi}_1)^{n_1} (\hat{\psi}_2)^{n_2} \frac{1}{n_1! n_2!}, \qquad |m_1, m_2\rangle = (\hat{\psi}_1^+)^{m_1} (\hat{\psi}_2^+)^{m_2} |0\rangle,$$

it is straightforward to evaluate the matrix element of the evolution operator in these states:

$$\int \prod_{i,k} \frac{1}{2\pi i} d\bar{\psi}_{i,k} \, d\psi_{i,k} \, e^{-\bar{\psi}_{i,k}\psi_{i,k}} \langle n_1, n_2 | \psi_{1,k} \rangle e^{\sum_{lm} \bar{\psi}_{1,l} A_{lm} \psi_{2,m}} \langle \bar{\psi}_{2,k} | m_1, m_2 \rangle.$$

Simple calculation shows that the last expression is precisely equal to the right-hand side of (28). This proves that the non-symmetric normalization of the vectors should be used to calculate the transition probability for many-particle states.

---

[10]There are a huge number of books covering functional integrals. Almost any textbook on quantum field theory contains a section or a chapter on functional integrals, although some of them are quite difficult to read. For further reading, I would advise one to see first the classic book by Feynman and Hibbs (1965) to get the idea, and then Popov (1983) and Kleinert (1990) to learn many useful tricks in applications of functional integrals to many-body interacting systems.

3   EXACT RESULTS FOR FUNCTIONAL INTEGRALS

In the previous section, we defined functional integrals as a result of a limiting procedure. Unless we can find some other way to calculate the integrals, they will remain a shorthand notation only, and to calculate them one will have to return to the final product and to work with it. Fortunately, there is a way to deal with functional integrals without reference to their finite-step approximations. This way either gives an exact result for a problem or gives a prescription how to calculate the integral in the form of a series. We cover some of the exact results in this section, and leave the series and approximations until Section 4.

If a functional integral is calculated exactly, it produces a complete solution of a problem, full stop. This means that the calculation of the integral should be as worthwhile as the exact solution obtained by other methods. In a certain sense, this connection can be used as a method for the indirect evaluation of functional integrals as well as a method of solution of a problem with functional integrals. For example, the Feynman–Kac lemma is a statement about the direct connection between evaluations of functional integrals of a particular type and the solution of Schrödinger-like partial differential equations. In general, it is important to remember that there are always indirect ways to evaluate functional integrals as well as direct ones, and the choice of a method is a matter of simplicity and convenience.

At this point, the reader can ask, very legitimately, why we bother at all about functional integrals if there is always another way to the answer,[11] i.e. the functional integrals are equivalent to conventional methods. There are two answers to this criticism. First, if the problem cannot be solved exactly, the functional integrals are a handier and shorter way to develop a theory that gives a perturbative solution. Secondly, functional integrals allow one to consider non-perturbative effects naturally and develop some successful approximations, which are very difficult to produce otherwise. Although further discussion of this matter is outside of the scope of this book, we want to add that the latter is especially important in applications of functional integrals to many-body interacting systems, which, as shown in Chapter 6, include financial markets.

3.1   Gaussian integrals

Frankly speaking, all functional integrals that can be evaluated exactly and explicitly are Gaussian or can be transformed to this class by some change of variables. We examine now why the Gaussian functional integrals are so special.

Let us start with the one-dimensional case and increase the dimension step by step. The integral

$$I_1(A) \equiv \int_{-\infty}^{\infty} \frac{dx}{\sqrt{2\pi}}\, e^{-\frac{1}{2}Ax^2 + bx}, \qquad A > 0,$$

---

[11]Physics folklore says that for any problem that is exactly solvable with functional integrals there is a conventional way to find the solution, and vice versa.

can be calculated directly and is equal to $\dfrac{1}{\sqrt{A}}e^{\frac{1}{2}b^2/A}$. The two-dimensional analogue of this result would be

$$I_2(A) \equiv \int_{-\infty}^{\infty} \prod_{k=1}^{2} \frac{dx_k}{\sqrt{2\pi}}\ e^{-\frac{1}{2}\sum_{k=1}^{2} A_{kk}x_k^2 + \sum_{k=1}^{2} b_k x_k}$$

$$= \prod_{k=1}^{2} \frac{1}{\sqrt{A_{kk}}} e^{\frac{1}{2}b_k^2/A_{kk}}, \qquad A_{kk} > 0.$$

Generalizing this procedure to the case of M dimensions, we obtain

$$I_M(A) \equiv \int_{-\infty}^{\infty} \prod_{k=1}^{M} \frac{dx_k}{\sqrt{2\pi}}\ e^{-\frac{1}{2}\sum_{k=1}^{M} A_{kk}x_k^2 + \sum_{k=1}^{M} b_k x_k}$$

$$= \prod_{k=1}^{M} \frac{1}{\sqrt{A_{kk}}} e^{\frac{1}{2}b_k^2/A_{kk}}, \qquad A_{kk} > 0,$$

or, introducing a matrix $A = \mathrm{diag}(A_{11}, \ldots, A_{MM})$ and vectors $x = (x_1, \ldots, x_M)$ and $b = (b_1, \ldots, b_M)$,

$$I_M(A) = \int \prod_{k=1}^{M} \frac{dx_k}{\sqrt{2\pi}}\ e^{-\frac{1}{2}xAx + bx} = \frac{1}{\sqrt{\det(A)}} e^{\frac{1}{2}bA^{-1}b}, \qquad A > 0. \tag{29}$$

It is possible to prove that in the final form the result holds not only for diagonal matrices A but for any positive symmetric matrix.[12] Moreover, in this form the right-hand side already does not depend explicitly on the dimension of the integration and can be generalized to the case of infinite M. Let us, for example, consider the functional integral

$$\int Dx\ \exp\left(-\frac{1}{2}\int d\tau\, d\tau'\ x(\tau)A(\tau,\tau')x(\tau') + \int d\tau\ b(\tau)x(\tau)\right), \qquad Dx \equiv \prod_\tau \frac{dx(\tau)}{\sqrt{2\pi}}.$$

The formula (29) implies that this is equal to

$$\frac{1}{\sqrt{\det(A)}}\ \exp\left(\frac{1}{2}\int d\tau\, d\tau'\ b(\tau)A^{-1}(\tau,\tau')b(\tau')\right), \tag{30}$$

where $A^{-1}(\tau,\tau')$ is the kernel of the operator inverse to the operator A with kernel $A(\tau,\tau')$. Therefore we have reduced the problem of calculation of the Gaussian functional integral to the problem of finding an inverse operator and its determinant.

For our first example of a functional integral calculation, we return to (19):

$$(x|U(t,0)|x') = \int Dx \int Dp\ e^{\int_0^t d\tau\left[ip(\tau)\frac{dx}{d\tau} - p(\tau)^2 + V(x(\tau))\right]}, \qquad Dx\ Dp = \prod_\tau dx(\tau)\frac{dp(\tau)}{2\pi}. \tag{31}$$

One can see that although the integral over x looks quite complicated, the integral over p is Gaussian and, luckily, the operator A is proportional to the identity operator I:

$$A = 2I.$$

---

[12]If the matrix is not symmetric, it is always possible to find a symmetric matrix with the same integrand in (29). To prove (29) for a general real symmetric matrix, it should be first transformed to its diagonal form.

The latter fact simplifies our task, because

$$A^{-1} = \frac{1}{2} \cdot I \quad \text{and} \quad \det(A) = \prod_\tau 2.$$

Applying the formula (30), we find

$$(x|U(t,0)|x') = \int Dx \ e^{\int_0^t d\tau \left[-\frac{1}{4}\left(\frac{dx}{dt}\right)^2 + V(x(\tau)) \right]}, \qquad Dx = \prod_\tau \frac{dx(\tau)}{\sqrt{4\pi}},$$

or, changing $x(\tau)$ to $x(\tau)/\sqrt{2}$ for every τ,

$$(x|U(t,0)|x') = \int Dx \ e^{\int_0^t d\tau \left[-\frac{1}{2}\left(\frac{dx}{dt}\right)^2 + V(\sqrt{2}x(\tau)) \right]}, \qquad Dx = \prod_\tau \frac{dx(\tau)}{\sqrt{2\pi}}. \tag{32}$$

The boundary conditions stay the same (see (20)).

The path integral (32) is remarkable in itself. What we need to note here is that if we put $V(x) = 0$, it becomes Gaussian again and can be calculated. The reader can work out the result himself, once again using the formula (30):

$$(x|U(t,0)|x') = \frac{1}{\sqrt{2\pi t}} e^{-\frac{(x-x')^2}{2t}}. \tag{33}$$

The answer has the very familiar form of the Gaussian distribution. This means that the conditional probability to find a Brownian particle at point x at time t if it was at point x' at zero time is given by the path integral (32) with $V = 0$. From this point of view, the meaning of the path integral becomes especially clear: since the Brownian path is stochastic, to find the conditional probability, one has to sum other all paths that start at x and end at x' the corresponding probabilities that the particle follows the paths. The probabilistic weight of each trajectory is equal to $e^{-\int_0^t d\tau \frac{1}{2}\left(\frac{dx}{d\tau}\right)^2}$. Similarly, the conditional probability for the Ornstein–Uhlenbeck process is represented by the path integral

$$(x|U(t,0)|x') = \int Dx \ e^{-\int_0^t d\tau \frac{1}{2}\left(\frac{dx}{dt} + \lambda x\right)^2}, \qquad Dx = \prod_\tau \frac{dx(\tau)}{\sqrt{2\pi}}. \tag{34}$$

We will need this path integral representation when the Vasicek model is studied in the next section.

3.2 Path Integral for the Harmonic Oscillator

For a general non-zero potential V, it is impossible to evaluate the functional integral (32) exactly. However, there are some practically interesting potentials that allow explicit evaluation of the path integral. One of them is the harmonic potential in the presence of an external force $f(\tau)$:

$$V(x) = -\frac{1}{2}\omega^2 x^2 - f(\tau)x(\tau).$$

Such a potential leaves the path integral Gaussian, which once again can be evaluated explicitly. So, the path integral we calculate in this subsection has the form:

$$(x|U(t, 0)|x') = \int_{x(0)=x'}^{x(t)=x} Dx \ e^{-\int_0^t d\tau\left[\frac{1}{2}\left(\frac{dx}{d\tau}\right)^2 + \frac{1}{2}\omega^2 x(\tau)^2 + f(\tau)x(\tau)\right]}, \qquad Dx = \prod_\tau \frac{dx(\tau)}{\sqrt{2\pi}}. \qquad (35)$$

To this end, we could apply the formula (30). Instead, we use another trick, which sheds new light on the relation (30) itself. Let us shift the functional variable $x(\cdot)$ by some (fixed) function $y(\cdot)$ with the boundary conditions $y(0) = x'$ and $y(t) = x$:

$$x(\cdot) \to z(\cdot) + y(\cdot).$$

After the shift, the functional variable $z(\cdot)$ has zero boundary conditions. This allows us to rewrite the functional

$$A = \int_0^t d\tau \left[\frac{1}{2}\left(\frac{dx}{d\tau}\right)^2 + \frac{1}{2}\omega^2 x(\tau)^2 + f(\tau)x(\tau)\right], \qquad (36)$$

which we call the *action*, as

$$A = z(\tau)\left(\frac{1}{2}\frac{dz}{d\tau} + \frac{dy}{d\tau}\right)\Big|_{\tau=0}^{\tau=t} + \int_0^t d\tau \left[-\frac{1}{2}z(\tau)\frac{d^2z}{d\tau^2} + \frac{1}{2}\omega^2 z(\tau)^2\right.$$

$$+ \frac{1}{2}\left(\frac{dy}{d\tau}\right)^2 + \frac{1}{2}\omega^2 y(\tau)^2 + f(\tau)y(\tau)$$

$$\left. + z(\tau)\left(-\frac{d^2y}{d\tau^2} + \omega^2 y(\tau) + f(\tau)\right)\right].$$

After the change, the action seems to become more complicated, but, in fact, it has not. First, the boundary terms are all equal to zero, since the functions $z(\cdot)$ have zero boundary conditions. Secondly, if we fix the function $y(\cdot)$ so that

$$-\frac{d^2y}{d\tau^2} + \omega^2 y(\tau) + f(\tau) = 0, \qquad y(0) = x', \qquad y(t) = x, \qquad (37)$$

the last term on the right-hand side also vanishes, and the path integral takes the form

$$(x|U(t, 0)|x') = e^{-\int_0^t d\tau\left[\frac{1}{2}\left(\frac{dy}{d\tau}\right)^2 + \frac{1}{2}\omega^2 y(\tau)^2 + f(\tau)y(\tau)\right]} \int_{z(0)=0'}^{z(t)=0} Dz \ e^{-\int_0^t d\tau\left(-\frac{1}{2}z\frac{d^2z}{d\tau^2} + \frac{1}{2}\omega^2 z(\tau)^2\right)},$$

$$Dz = \prod_\tau \frac{dz(\tau)}{\sqrt{2\pi}}.$$

We know already that the last path integral is simply unity divided by the square root of the determinant of the operator

$$A = -\frac{d^2}{d\tau^2} + \omega^2,$$

defined on the Sobolev space[13] $W_2^2[0, t]$ of functions with Dirichlet boundary conditions.

---

[13] If the reader is not familiar with functional analysis, he can safely ignore these words.

For non-zero ω, this is a positive self-adjoint operator, so that we can apply the results of the previous section:

$$\int_{z(0)=0'}^{z(t)=0} Dz\ e^{-\int_0^t d\tau\left(-\frac{1}{2}z\frac{d^2z}{d\tau^2}+\frac{1}{2}\omega^2 z(\tau)^2\right)} = \frac{1}{\sqrt{\det(A)}}.$$

Therefore the path integral of interest is equal to

$$\int_{x(0)=x'}^{x(t)=x} Dx\ e^{-\int_0^t d\tau\left[\frac{1}{2}\left(\frac{dx}{d\tau}\right)^2+\frac{1}{2}\omega^2 x(\tau)^2+f(\tau)x(\tau)\right]} = \frac{1}{\sqrt{\det(A)}} e^{-\int_0^t d\tau\left[\frac{1}{2}\left(\frac{dy}{d\tau}\right)^2+\frac{1}{2}\omega^2 y(\tau)^2+f(\tau)y(\tau)\right]}. \tag{38}$$

The right-hand side of (38) does not contain any functional integrals, and is already completely determined, since the function $y(\cdot)$ is completely defined by the solution of the ordinary differential equation (37).

The interesting feature of (37) is that it is the Euler–Lagrange equation for extremal trajectories of the action (36) with fixed endpoints. One can say therefore that the only thing one has to do to calculate Gaussian path integrals is to find the extremal trajectories and calculate the actions on them. The path integral will be equal (up to a factor) to the exponent of the corresponding extremal value of the action. This is exactly how physicists calculate most of their functional integrals!

Another point to make is that (38) is consistent with the general formula (30). Since the presence of the factor $1/\sqrt{\det(A)}$ is made clear already, to prove the statement, one has to show that

$$e^{-\int_0^t d\tau\left(\frac{1}{2}\left(\frac{dy}{d\tau}\right)^2+\frac{1}{2}\omega^2 y(\tau)^2+f(\tau)y(\tau)\right)} = e^{\frac{1}{2}\int_0^t d\tau f(\tau)A^{-1}(\tau,\tau')f(\tau')}.$$

This is not difficult, because the function $y(\cdot)$ is defined by the equation

$$Ay = -f$$

and

$$e^{-\int_0^t d\tau\left[\frac{1}{2}\left(\frac{dy}{d\tau}\right)^2+\frac{1}{2}\omega^2 y(\tau)^2+f(\tau)y(\tau)\right]} = e^{-fy-\frac{1}{2}yAy} = e^{fA^{-1}f-\frac{1}{2}AfAA^{-1}f} = e^{\frac{1}{2}fA^{-1}f}.$$

This concludes the proof.[14] Thus the calculation of Gaussian path integrals using extremal trajectories is equivalent to the general method referring to the limiting procedure and matrix operators.

It is possible to go one step further and give an explicit expression for the path integral (38). The solution of the Euler–Lagrange problem (37) is easy to find:

$$y(\tau) = x'\cosh(\omega\tau) + \frac{x - x'\cosh(\omega t) - \int_0^t d\xi\, e^{\omega(2\xi-\eta-t)}\int_0^\xi d\eta\, f(\eta)}{\sinh(\omega t)}\sinh(\omega\tau)$$

$$+ \int_0^\tau d\xi\, e^{\omega(2\xi-\eta-\tau)}\int_0^\xi d\eta\, f(\eta).$$

---

[14]To make the proof really strict, one has to deal carefully with the boundary terms. However, the final result is the same.

Substituting this function into (38), we find

$$\int_{x(0)=x'}^{x(t)=x} Dx \ e^{-\int_0^t d\tau \left[\frac{1}{2}\left(\frac{dx}{d\tau}\right)^2 + \frac{1}{2}\omega^2 x(\tau)^2 + f(\tau)x(\tau)\right]} = \frac{1}{\sqrt{\det(A)}} e^{-\Phi},$$

$$\Phi = -\frac{1}{4\omega} \int_0^t d\tau \int_0^t d\tau' \ e^{-\omega|\tau - \tau'|} f(\tau)f(\tau') + \frac{\omega}{2\sinh(\omega t)} \{[(x^2 + (x')^2]\cosh(\omega t) - 2x'x$$
$$+ 2a(xe^{\omega t} - x') + 2b(x'e^{\omega t} - x) + (a^2 + b^2)e^{\omega t} - 2ab\}, \tag{39}$$

where

$$a = \frac{1}{2\omega} \int_0^t d\tau e^{-\omega\tau} f(\tau), \qquad b = \frac{1}{2\omega} \int_0^t d\tau \ e^{-\omega(t-\tau)} f(\tau).$$

This is the answer that we used in Section 6 of Chapter 9 and it is sufficient for all our needs. We have not bothered to calculate the factor $1/\sqrt{\det(A)}$, because it usually does not enter final expressions. The reader can find a description of its calculation in (Kleinert, 1990), while we give here only the final result:

$$1/\sqrt{\det(A)} = \sqrt{\omega/2\pi \sinh(\omega t)}.$$

3.3 Derivation of Equation (50) of Chapter 9 Using Path Integrals

Let us derive equation (50) of Chapter 9 using the functional integral method rather than the Itô lemma for the derivative price as a function of the mispricing.

We start with the Black–Scholes equation with the rate of return on the riskless portfolio $C - S \ \partial C/\partial S$ given by $r_0 + x$:

$$\frac{\partial C}{\partial t} + \frac{\sigma^2 S^2}{2} \frac{\partial^2 C}{\partial S^2} + (r_0 + x)S \frac{\partial C}{\partial S} - (r_0 + x)C = 0,$$

$$C(S, t)|_{t=T} = \delta(S - S').$$

It is convenient to change variables to $\tau = T - t$ and $y = \ln S$, which casts the previous equations into the form

$$\frac{\partial C}{\partial \tau} = \frac{\sigma^2}{2} \frac{\partial^2 C}{\partial y^2} + \left(r_0 + x - \frac{\sigma^2}{2}\right) \frac{\partial C}{\partial y} - (r_0 + x)C,$$

$$C(y, \tau)|_{\tau=0} = \frac{1}{S'} \delta(y - y').$$

The solution of the problem can be expressed as the following path integral:[15]

$$C(y, \tau) = \frac{1}{S'} \int_{q(T-t)=y}^{q(0)=y'} Dq \ D\left(\frac{p}{2\pi}\right) \ e^{\int_0^\tau \left[ip\dot{q} - \frac{\sigma^2}{2}p^2 - [r_0 + x(\tau)] + i\left(r_0 + x(\tau) - \frac{\sigma^2}{2}\right)p\right]d\tau}.$$

This path integral form of the solution is extremely convenient for the purpose of averaging over trajectories $x(\tau)$, since it presents the dependence in explicit form. We, however, will use

---

[15]This can be derived following step by step the consideration of Section 2.1.

another trick. Let us first of all average the previous expression over realisations of the stochastic process $x(\tau)$ with fixed ends, i.e. when $x(\tau) = x$ and $x(0) = 0$ (there is no arbitrage at the expiration date of the contract and later). For the Ornstein–Uhlenbeck process

$$\frac{dx}{dt} + \lambda x = v(t), \qquad \langle v(t) \rangle_v = 0, \qquad \langle v(t)v(t') \rangle_v = \Sigma^2 \delta(t - t').$$

the conditional probability $P(0, t|x, 0)$ is defined by the Kolmogorov equation

$$\frac{\partial P}{\partial t} = \frac{\Sigma^2}{2} \frac{\partial^2 P}{\partial x^2} + \lambda x \frac{\partial P}{\partial x},$$

and allows the following path integral representation:[16]

$$\int_{x(t)=x}^{x(T)=0} Dx \int D\left(\frac{\xi}{2\pi}\right) e^{\int_0^\tau \left(i\xi\dot{x} - \frac{\Sigma^2}{2}\xi^2 + i\lambda x\xi\right)d\tau'}.$$

After changing t to $\tau = T - t$ and $\xi(\cdot)$ to $-\xi(\cdot)$, the integral will have the form

$$P(0, t|x, 0) = \int_{x(t)=x}^{x(T)=0} Dx \int D\left(\frac{\xi}{2\pi}\right) e^{\int_t^T \left(i\xi\dot{x} - \frac{\Sigma^2}{2}\xi^2 - i\lambda\xi x\right)d\tau}.$$

This leads to the following expression for the conditional average value of the contract:

$$\bar{C}(x, y, \tau) = \frac{1}{S'} \int Dq\, D\left(\frac{p}{2\pi}\right) Dx\, D\left(\frac{\xi}{2\pi}\right) e^{\int_0^\tau \left[i\xi\dot{x} + ip\dot{q} - \frac{\sigma^2}{2}p^2 - [r_0 + x(\tau)] + i\left(r_0 + x(\tau) - \frac{\sigma^2}{2}\right)p - \frac{\Sigma^2}{2}\xi^2 - i\lambda\xi x\right]d\tau'},$$

$$q(0) = y', \quad q(\tau) = y, \quad x(0) = 0, \quad x(\tau) = x.$$

Now, instead of evaluating these integrals, we find a partial differential equation for $\bar{V}(x, y, \tau)$ that has the same path integral representation:

$$\frac{\partial \bar{C}}{\partial \tau} = \frac{\sigma^2}{2} \frac{\partial^2 \bar{C}}{\partial y^2} + \left(r_0 + x - \frac{\sigma^2}{2}\right) \frac{\partial \bar{C}}{\partial y} - (r_0 + x)\bar{C} + \frac{\Sigma^2}{2} \frac{\partial^2 \bar{C}}{\partial x^2} - \lambda x \frac{\partial \bar{C}}{\partial x},$$

with the initial conditions

$$\bar{C}(x, y, \tau)|_{\tau=0} = \frac{1}{S'} \delta(y - y')\delta(x).$$

Returning the initial variables t and S, we obtain the problem

$$\frac{\partial \bar{C}}{\partial t} + \frac{\sigma^2 S^2}{2} \frac{\partial^2 \bar{C}}{\partial S^2} + (r_0 + x)S \frac{\partial \bar{C}(x, S, t)}{\partial S} - (r_0 + x)\bar{C} + \frac{\Sigma^2}{2} \frac{\partial^2 \bar{C}}{\partial x^2} - \lambda x \frac{\partial \bar{C}}{\partial x} = 0,$$

$$\bar{C}(x, S, t)|_{t=T} = \delta(x)\delta(S - S').$$

Integration of the solution over x (to get the unconditional average) and the convolution with the final payoff complete the consideration.

In a similar way, various generalizations of the equations can be derived. It is clear that the functional integral is a very convenient tool for such manipulations. We would like to note, however, that the functional integral formalism is full of subtleties that we have not emphasized here. It serves for quick derivations rather than for proving results.[17]

---

[16]After integration over $\xi(\cdot)$, this returns us to (34).

4 FINANCIAL APPLICATIONS

In this section, we consider applications of path integrals to the pricing of interest rate derivatives (for a detailed account of interest rate derivative modelling, see Rebonato, 1996). First we define related objects of interest and then solve two well-know interest rate models exactly using the path integral ideas.

4.1 Short-Term Interest Rate Models

Imagine you are borrowing money, first for three months, then for another three months, and keep doing this for three years. Clearly you know the current (spot) three months interest rate, but you cannot be so sure about following rates. Thus you are facing the interest rate risk, which, as usual, you can reduce or eliminate completely by buying an *interest rate derivative*. There are many different types of interest rate derivatives, but the most popular are bonds, swaps, options on bonds, caps, and floors. For the sake of simplicity, we deal here only with bonds and options on bonds, although the technique is powerful enough to work for the general case.

Since the future interest rates are not known, one has to model them with a stochastic process and then apply the same general pricing approaches as for commodity derivatives or FOREX derivatives. Most of the interest rate models that are in use today are defined through the stochastic differential equation[18]

$$dr(t) = \mu(r(t), t)\, dt + \sigma(r(t), t)\, dW(t),$$

where $r(t)$ is a short-term interest rate at time t, μ and σ are some functions of r and t, and dW is the Wiener process. One might want to consider the latter functions as stochastic, but we do not do this here in order to keep things as simple as possible. The interest rate model and the no-arbitrage assumption are sufficient to find prices of any derivative product. For example, a price of any derivative with a payoff X at time T is valued at time t according to

$$V(t, r, T) = E_Q\left[e^{-\int_t^T ds\, r(s)} X \big| r(t) = r \right]. \tag{40}$$

Here E_Q is an expectation with respect to the martingale measure Q defined by the interest rate process.[19] For a zero-bond, which is a promise to pay 1 unit of cash at the maturity time T, (40) results in the following expression for the bond price $P(t, T)$ at time $t < T$:

$$P(t, r, T) = E_Q\left[e^{-\int_t^T ds\, r(s)} X \big| r(t) = r \right]. \tag{41}$$

---

[17]The rule of thumb for manipulations with functional integrals is always to check how reasonable the final result is. If limiting cases and other trivial checks are correct then, most probably, anything is OK. If not, then one has to scrutinize the functional integral in more detail.

[18]An alternative way is to write a stochastic model for bonds prices or forward rates. Under the no-arbitrage assumption, all these approaches are equivalent.

The price of a European call at time 0 with strike K expiring at time t on zero bond with maturity T, with $t < T$ is again given by the same Eqn (40) but with a different payoff:

$$C(0, r) = E_Q\left[e^{-\int_t^T ds\, r(s)} \max(P(t, T) - K; 0)\big| r(0) = r\right]. \tag{42}$$

Thus the problem of interest rate derivative pricing is equivalent to the calculation of the expectations, or, as we will see, to the calculation of path integrals.

Below we consider two well-known interest models.

1. Vasicek model, originating from Vasicek (1977):

$$dr(t) = a[b - r(t)]\, dt + \sigma\, dW(t). \tag{43}$$

The parameters a and b model the mean reversion, which seems to be a well-observed feature of interest rates; σ is the volatility of the short rate. a, b, and σ are all constant in time.

2. The Salomon Brothers model (Kopprasch et al, 1987; Tuckman, 1995):

$$\frac{dr}{r} = \mu\, dt + \sigma\, dW. \tag{44}$$

The model simply states that the short interest rate follows geometrical Brownian motion and thus is the direct analogue of the corresponding underlying price model in the Black–Scholes model. The parameters μ and σ are assumed to be constant in time.

Below we derive explicit exact results for the bond and call options for the models, and comment on generalization of the methods to other interesting cases.

4.2 Exact Results for the Vasicek Model from Path Integrals

We derive the zero-bond price and the price of call on the bond using the path integral method.[20] The reader has surely already realized that the Vasicek model is nothing other than the Ornstein–Uhlenbeck process. Therefore we can use the results of Section 3.1, where it was found that the probability density functional (one can consider it as the 'probability' of a trajectory) is equal to

$$N \exp\left[-\frac{1}{2\sigma^2}\int_t^T ds\left(\frac{dr(s)}{ds} - a[b - r(s)]\right)^2\right], \tag{45}$$

---

[19]Strictly speaking, the martingale measure should be for a price of an underlying tradable. The interest rate itself is not tradable. In this case, the tradables are bonds and the martingale process is the price process for the discounted bond price. This all implies that we have to average not over the interest rate process but rather over a process where the price of risk is already taken into account. This merely changes parameters in the process. Since we do not fix parameters anyway, we do not pay attention to the difference between processes. For a clear introduction to this stuff, see Baxter et al (1998). For an easy way to see things, read Wilmott (1998).
[20]In this subsection, we closely follow Otto (1998).

where N is some normalization constant. This and (41) together result in the following path integral representation for the zero-coupon bond price:

$$P(t, T) = \frac{\int_{-\infty}^{\infty} dr(T) \int_{r(t)=r}^{r(T)} Dr \exp\left[-\frac{1}{2\sigma^2} \int_t^T ds \left[\frac{dr(s)}{ds} - a[b - r(s)]\right]^2 - \int_t^T ds \, r(s)\right]}{\int_{-\infty}^{\infty} dr(T) \int_{r(t)=r}^{r(T)} Dr \exp\left[-\frac{1}{2\sigma^2} \int_t^T ds \left(\frac{dr(s)}{ds} - a[b - r(s)]\right)^2\right]}$$ (46)

The argument of the expectation value in (41) enters the numerator of the last equation as the second term inside the exponential function. The first term stems from the probability density functional (45). The denominator gives the proper normalization. The functional integrations in the numerator are due to the fact that the expectation is conditional on the value of the interest rate at time t: $r(t) = r$.

Let us first of all change $r(s)$ to $x(s) = b - r(s)$. Then, after carrying out integrations involving boundary terms, (46) reads as

$$P(t, T) = \frac{X}{Y},$$ (47)

with

$$X = \int_{-\infty}^{\infty} dx(T) \int_{x(t)}^{x(T)} Dx \, \exp\left\{ -\frac{1}{2\sigma^2} \int_t^T ds \left[\left(\frac{dx(s)}{ds}\right)^2 + a^2 x^2(s)\right]\right.$$
$$\left. -\frac{a}{2\sigma^2}[x^2(T) - x^2(t)] - b(T - t) + \int_t^T ds \, x(s)\right\}$$

and

$$Y = \int_{-\infty}^{\infty} dx(T) \int_{x(t)}^{x(T)} Dx \, \exp\left\{ -\frac{1}{2\sigma^2} \int_t^T ds \left[\left(\frac{dx(s)}{ds}\right)^2 + a^2 x^2(s)\right] - \frac{a}{2\sigma^2}[x^2(T) - x^2(t)]\right\}.$$

Luckily, the path integrals over $x(s)$ in both X and Y coincide exactly with the path integral for the harmonic oscillator that we calculated in Section 3.2. Using (39), we find the numerator to be

$$X = \sqrt{\frac{a}{2\pi\sigma^2 \sinh[a(T - t)]}} \int_{-\infty}^{\infty} dx(T) \exp\left[\frac{\sigma^2}{2a^3}\left[e^{-a(T-t)} - 1 + a(T - t)\right]\right.$$
$$-\frac{a}{2\sigma^2 \sinh(a[T - t])}\left([x^2(T) + x^2(t)] \cosh[a(T - t)] - 2x(T)x(t)\right.$$
$$+ 2\left(e^{a(T-t)} - 1\right)\{c[x(T) + x(t)] + c^2\}$$
$$\left.-\frac{a}{2\sigma^2}[x^2(T) - x^2(t)] - b(T - t)\right],$$ (48)

where

$$c = \frac{\sigma^2}{2a^2}(e^{-a(T-t)} - 1) \equiv -\frac{\sigma^2}{2a}B(t, T), \qquad B(t, T) = \frac{1 - e^{-a(T-t)}}{a}.$$

Likewise, the expression for the denominator is calculated as

$$Y = \sqrt{\frac{a}{2\pi\sigma^2 \sinh[a(T-t)]}} \int_{-\infty}^{\infty} dx(T) \exp\left[-\frac{a}{2\sigma^2}[x^2(T) - x^2(t)] \right.$$

$$\left. -\frac{a}{2\sigma^2 \sinh[a(T-t)]} \left\{ [x^2(T) + x^2(t)] \cosh[a(T-t)] - 2x(T)x(t) \right\} \right].$$

It remains to perform the (Gaussian) integration with respect to $x(T)$. Collecting terms from the Gaussian integration in (48) and (49) substituting the results for X and Y in (47), one finally obtains:

$$P(t, T) = A(t, T)\exp[-B(t, T)r],$$

with

$$A(t, T) = \exp\left[[-B(t, T) + T - t]\left(\frac{\sigma^2}{2a^2} - b\right) - \frac{\sigma^2}{4a}B^2(t, T) \right].$$

This result is in full agreement with a well-known result by Vasicek, who first found this expression from partial differential equation method.

Let us now turn to the call option on the zero-bond and find its price from (42). The right-hand side of (42) vanishes unless $P(t, T) > K$. The zero-bond price has the form right-hand side

$$P(t, T) = A(t, T)e^{-B(t,T)r},$$

and the condition is equivalent to the inequality

$$r(t) < \frac{1}{B(t, T)} \ln\left(\frac{A(t, T)}{K}\right) = \tilde{k}.$$

The call price formula is then given by

$$c(0) = A(t, T)E_Q\left[e^{-\int_0^t ds\, r(s) - B(t,T)r} \middle| r(t) < \tilde{k} \right] - KE_Q\left[e^{-\int_0^t ds\, r(s)} \middle| r(t) < \tilde{k} \right]. \qquad (51)$$

Again, we first change $r(s)$ to $x(s) = b - r(s)$. The condition $r(t) < \tilde{k}$ then translates into $x(t) > b - \tilde{k}$. The first expectation value on the right-hand side (51) is equal to

$$E_Q\left[e^{-\int_0^t ds\, r(s) - B(t,T)r} \middle| r(t) < \tilde{k} \right] = \frac{X}{Y},$$

with

$$X = \int_{b-\tilde{k}}^{\infty} dx(t) \int_{x(0)}^{x(t)} Dx\, \exp\left\{ -\frac{1}{2\sigma^2} \int_0^t ds \left[\left(\frac{dx(s)}{ds}\right)^2 + a^2x^2(s) \right] \right.$$

$$\left. -\frac{a}{2\sigma^2}[x^2(t) - x^2(0)] - b(T - t) + \int_0^t ds\, x(s) - B(t, T)[b - x(t)] \right\} \qquad (52)$$

and

$$Y = \int_{-\infty}^{\infty} dx(t) \int_{x(0)}^{x(t)} Dx \, \exp\left\{ -\frac{1}{2\sigma^2} \int_0^t ds \left[\left(\frac{dx(s)}{ds}\right)^2 + a^2 x^2(s) \right] - \frac{a}{2\sigma^2} [x^2(t) - x^2(0)] \right\}. \quad (53)$$

The condition $x(t) > b - \tilde{k}$ enters into the numerator X as a lower bound of integration with respect to $x(t)$. The next steps of integration are straightforward, and follow along the lines of (48)–(50). Using the no-arbitrage relations

$$P(0, T) = E_Q\left[e^{-\int_0^t ds \, r(s)} P(t, T) \middle| r(0) = r \right]$$

and

$$P(0, t) = E_Q\left[e^{-\int_0^t ds \, r(s)} \middle| r(0) = r \right],$$

the bond prices $P(0, T)$ and $P(0, t)$ make up the two terms on the right-hand side od (51) up to factors $N(h)$ and $KN(h - \sigma_P)$ that result from the bounded integrations with respect to $x(t)$. This produces Jamshidian's formula for a European call on a zero bond (Jamshidian, 1989):

$$c(0) = P(0, T)N(h) - KP(0, t)N(h - \sigma_P),$$

where $N(x)$ is a cumulative normal distribution and

$$h = \frac{1}{\sigma_P} \ln\left(\frac{P(0, T)}{KP(0, t)}\right) + \frac{\sigma_P}{2},$$

with

$$\sigma_P = \frac{\sigma}{a}(1 - e^{-a(T-t)})\sqrt{\frac{1 - e^{-2at}}{2a}}.$$

The price of the corresponding put option can be immediately derived from the put–call parity relation.

4.3   Salomon Brothers Model

Let us now return to the Salomon Brothers model and find an exact solution for a zero-bond price following Kalinin and Ilinski (1999). After the change of variable

$$x = \log r, \qquad dx = \frac{dr}{r} - \frac{\sigma^2}{2} \, dt,$$

the equation for the process takes the form

$$dx = \left(\mu - \frac{\sigma^2}{2}\right) dt + \sigma \, dW.$$

Therefore, similar to (46), the bond price can be represented as a ratio of two path integrals:

$$P(t, T) = \frac{\int_{-\infty}^{\infty} dx(T) \int_{x(t)}^{x(T)} Dx \exp\left\{-\int_{t}^{T} ds \left[\frac{1}{2\sigma^2}\left(\dot{x} - \mu + \frac{\sigma^2}{2}\right)^2 + \alpha e^x\right]\right\}}{\int_{-\infty}^{\infty} dx(T) \int_{x(t)}^{x(T)} Dx \exp\left[-\frac{1}{2\sigma^2}\int_{t}^{T} ds\left(\dot{x} - \mu + \frac{\sigma^2}{2}\right)^2\right]},$$

$$\alpha = 1.$$

The path integral in the denominator is Gaussian, and is not difficult to calculate. The real problem is to calculate the path integral in the numerator:

$$\int_{x(t)}^{x(T)} Dx \exp\left\{-\int_{t}^{T} ds \left[\frac{1}{2\sigma^2}\left(\dot{x} - \mu + \frac{\sigma^2}{2}\right)^2 + \alpha e^x\right]\right\}.$$

To tackle this integral, we first rearrange it as

$$\int_{x(t)}^{x(T)} Dx \exp\left\{-\int_{t}^{T}\left(\frac{\dot{x}^2}{2\sigma^2} + \alpha e^x\right)ds + \left(\frac{\mu}{\sigma^2} - \frac{1}{2}\right)[x(T) - x(t)] - \frac{T-t}{2\sigma^2}\left(\mu - \frac{\sigma^2}{2}\right)^2\right\},$$

and consider the first term in more detail. It follows from the results of Section 3 that this corresponds to the non-normalized transition probability defined by the equation

$$\frac{d\psi}{ds} = \frac{\sigma^2}{2}\frac{d^2\psi}{dx^2} - \alpha e^x \psi, \quad \psi(s, x)|_{s=0} = \delta(x - x_0), \quad x_0 \equiv x(t).$$

This means that if we can find the solution of this equation, we can effectively calculate the path integral. After Laplace transformation, the equation takes the form

$$pF(p, x) - \psi(0, x) = \left(\frac{\sigma^2}{2}\frac{d^2}{dx^2} - \alpha e^x\right)F(p, x),$$

and we get the following differential equation:[21]

$$F'' - \frac{2}{\sigma^2}(\alpha e^x + p)F = -\frac{2}{\sigma^2}\delta(x - x_0).$$

After the substitution

$$v \equiv iu = i\sqrt{\frac{8\alpha}{\sigma^2}}e^{\frac{x}{2}}, \quad F(p, x) = \hat{F}(p, v) = \hat{F}(p, iu), \quad v \equiv \sqrt{\frac{8p}{\sigma^2}},$$

the latter equation turns into a Bessel-type one:

$$\hat{F}''v^2 + \hat{F}'v + (v^2 - v^2)\hat{F} = -\frac{4iu_0}{\sigma^2}\delta(v - iu_0), \quad u_0 \equiv \sqrt{\frac{8\alpha}{\sigma^2}}e^{\frac{x_0}{2}}$$

This equation has the solution

$$\hat{F}(p, iu) = \begin{cases} C_1 I_v(u) & (u < u_0), \\ C_2 K_v(u) & (u > u_0), \end{cases}$$

---

[21] A prime denotes the partial derivative with respect to the second argument.

expressed in terms of the Infeld function[22]

$$I_v(u) = i^{-v}J_v(iu) = \sum_{k=0}^{\infty} \frac{1}{\Gamma(k+1)\Gamma(k+1+v)} \left(\frac{u}{2}\right)^{2k+v}$$

and the McDonald function[23]

$$K_v(u) = \frac{\pi}{2}i^{v+1}H_v^{(1)}(iu).$$

The solution decreases as $u \to \infty$ and $u \to 0$, as it should. The constants C_1 and C_2 are defined by the system

$$C_1 I_v(u_0) = C_2 K_v(u_0),$$

$$C_1 I_v'(u_0) = C_2 K_v'(u_0) + \frac{4}{\sigma^2 u_0},$$

which has the solution

$$C_1 = \frac{-K_v(u_0)}{I_v(u_0)K_v'(u_0) - K_v(u_0)I_v'(u_0)} \frac{4}{\sigma^2 u_0},$$

$$C_2 = \frac{-I_v(u_0)}{I_v(u_0)K_v'(u_0) - K_v(u_0)I_v'(u_0)} \frac{4}{\sigma^2 u_0}.$$

The denominator of the latter expression is the Wronskian of the two special functions,

$$I_v(u_0)K_v'(u_0) - K_v(u_0)I_v'(u_0) = W[I_v(u_0), K_v(u_0)] = \frac{i\pi}{2}W[J_v, H_v^{(1)}](iu_0),$$

and is known to be equal to

$$\frac{-1}{u_0}.$$

Therefore the function $\hat{F}(p, iu)$ simplifies to

$$\hat{F}(p, iu) = \begin{cases} \dfrac{4}{\sigma^2} K_v(u_0)I_v(u) & (u < u_0) \\ \dfrac{4}{\sigma^2} I_v(u_0)K_v(u) & (u > u_0). \end{cases}$$

Further simplification comes from the relation:[24]

$$\int_0^\infty \frac{dt}{t} \exp\left(-\frac{t}{2} - \frac{x^2 + X^2}{2t}\right) I_v\left(\frac{xX}{t}\right) = \begin{cases} 2I_v(x)K_v(X) & (X > x), \\ 2K_v(x)I_v(X) & (X < x). \end{cases}$$

---

[22] J_v is the Bessel function with index v.
[23] $H_v^{(1)}$ is the Hankel function of the first kind with index v.
[24] Formula (37), Section 7.7.6 in Erdelyi et al (1953).

Collecting all together, we arrive at the expression for the zero-bond price:

$$P(t, T) = \frac{\displaystyle\int_{-\infty}^{\infty} dx(T)\, \psi(T - t, x(T), r)e^{(\frac{\mu}{\sigma^2} - \frac{1}{2})x(T)}}{\displaystyle\int_{-\infty}^{\infty} dx(T)\, \frac{1}{\sqrt{2\pi\sigma^2(T - t)}}\, e^{-\frac{[x(T)-\log r]^2}{2\sigma^2(T-t)} + (\frac{\mu}{\sigma^2} - \frac{1}{2})x(T)}}$$

$$= e^{-\frac{1}{2}\sigma^2(T-t)(\frac{\mu}{\sigma^2} - \frac{1}{2})^2} \int_{-\infty}^{\infty} dx(T)\psi(T - t, x(T), r)e^{(\frac{\mu}{\sigma^2} - \frac{1}{2})[x(T)-\log r]},$$

with the function $\psi(T - t, x(T), r)$ given by the expression

$$\psi(t, x, r) = \frac{1}{\pi i \sigma^2} \int_{\gamma - i\infty}^{\gamma + i\infty} dp\, e^{pt} \int_0^{\infty} \frac{ds}{s} \exp\left(-\frac{s}{2} - \frac{4(r + e^x)}{s\sigma^2}\right) I_{\sqrt{8p/\sigma^2}}\left(\frac{8e^{x/2}\sqrt{r}}{s\sigma^2}\right).$$

This concludes the calculation of the zero-coupon bond price.

It is possible to proceed with the calculation of the option on bond price as was done in the previous section for the Vasicek model. Indeed, the principal difficulty in this calculation lies in the calculation of the path integral, which has already been done above, and the only contract dependence is in the integration over $x(T)$ with the final payoff. However, the explicit result is quite cumbersome, and we do not discuss it here. Instead, we would like to highlight the following two points:

1. The technique developed above can be successfully implemented to minimize numerical calculations of derivative prices (in practice, it is almost always the Monte Carlo calculations that are comparatively slow).

2. It allows one to approach analytically more complicated (but, at the same time, more realistic) models for the interest rates. For example, a very popular model, the Black–Karasinski model

$$d \log r = (\theta - a \log r)\, dt + \sigma\, dW$$

has the mean-reversion of the Vasicek model and the geometrical Brownian motion feature of the Salomon Brothers model, and (at least for some values of parameters) can be treated perturbatively around these models. Time dependence of the parameters can also be accommodated using the monodromy method for evolution equations.

5   CALCULATION OF FUNCTIONAL INTEGRALS

As we said before, only a few functional integrals can be calculated exactly. Therefore one needs a perturbative procedure to develop regular controlled approximations and working numerical algorithms. Without going into details, we describe some of these methods in this section.

5.1 Perturbation Theory and Feynman Diagrams

The essence of the diagram technique can be demonstrated with the very simple example of a one-dimensional integral

$$I_1 = \int_{-\infty}^{\infty} \frac{dx}{\sqrt{2\pi\alpha}}\, e^{-\frac{1}{2}\alpha x^2} e^{f(x)}.$$

The first trick is to use the identity

$$e^{x\frac{d}{db}} F(b)|_{b=0} = F(x),$$

which can be checked for any smooth function $F(x)$ by expanding it in a Taylor series. This allows us to rewrite the integral I_1 as

$$I_1 = \int_{-\infty}^{\infty} dx\, e^{-\frac{1}{2}\alpha x^2 + x\frac{d}{db}} e^{f(b)}|_{b=0},$$

and further evaluating the Gaussian integral over x, we find

$$I_1 = e^{\frac{1}{2}\frac{d}{db}\alpha^{-1}\frac{d}{db}} e^{f(b)}|_{b=0} \tag{54}$$

This formula is the basis for the diagram representation. Suppose that $f(x) = cx^4/4!$; then (54) can be rewritten as

$$I_1 = e^{\frac{1}{2}\frac{d}{db}\alpha^{-1}\frac{d}{db}} \sum_{k=0}^{\infty} \frac{c^k b^{4k}}{(4!)^k k!}\Big|_{b=0}.$$

Now, each term in the sum on the right-hand side can be calculated exactly,

$$e^{\frac{1}{2}\frac{d}{db}\alpha^{-1}\frac{d}{db}} \frac{c^n b^{4n}}{(4!)^n n!}\Big|_{b=0} = \frac{(4n)!}{(2n)!n!2^{2n}(4!)^n} c^n (\alpha^{-1})^{2n}, \tag{55}$$

but – more importantly here – it can be represented by a series of diagrams (see Fig. A.1). A diagram consists of n points (each carrying a factor c) with four 'tails'. These 'tails' are connected by lines, each of which carries a factor α^{-1}. It is clear that each differentiation is accompanied by fixing a line to the point 'tail' that represents the differentiated monomial. Each of the diagrams is provided with a combinatorial multiplier, which is proportional to the number of ways to construct the graph starting with n *equivalent* points and adding $2n$ *equivalent* lines. The factor $\frac{(4n)!}{(2n)!n!2^{2n}(4!)}$ is already a sum of all the combinatorial factors. The diagrams in Fig. A.1 are the *Feynman diagrams* for the integral I_1.

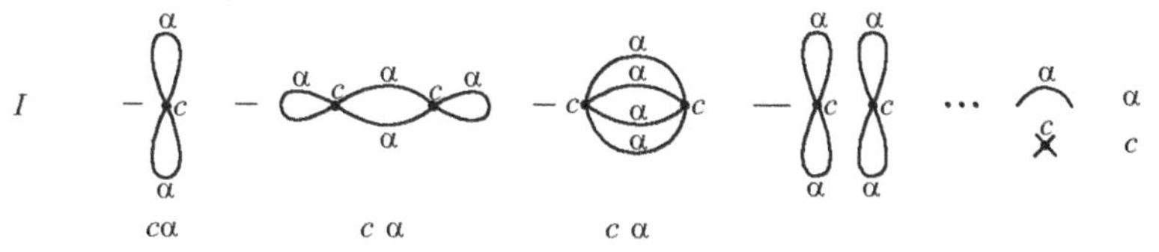

Figure A.1 Feynman diagrams for the one-dimensional integral I_1 to the first three orders in c.

One can treat functional integrals similarly to what we have just done in the case of the one-dimensional integral. Following the previous example step by step, we arrive at the representation

$$\int Dx\, e^{\int d\tau d\tau' x(\tau)A(\tau,\tau')x(\tau')} e^{\int d\tau\, V(x(\tau))} = e^{\frac{1}{2}\frac{\delta}{\delta b(\tau')}A^{-1}(\tau,\tau')\frac{\delta}{\delta b(\tau)}} e^{\int d\tau\, V(b(\tau))}\Bigg|_{b=0}. \tag{56}$$

The only difference between (54) and (56) is the change from b to $b(\tau)$ and from d/db to the variational derivative $\delta/\delta b(\tau)$. Expanding the functional $e^{\int d\tau V(b(\tau))}$ in a Taylor series, one gets the perturbation theory expansion

$$Dx\, e^{-\int d\tau\, d\tau' x(\tau)A(\tau,\tau')x(\tau')} e^{\int d\tau\, V(x(\tau))}$$

$$= e^{\frac{1}{2}\int d\tau\, d\tau'\frac{\delta}{\delta b(\tau')}A^{-1}(\tau,\tau')\frac{\delta}{\delta b(\tau)}} \sum_{k=0}^{\infty}\frac{1}{k!}\int d\tau_1 \ldots \int d\tau_k\, V(b(\tau))\ldots V(b(\tau_k))|_{b=0}.$$

Differentiation on the right-hand side will produce a sum of terms for each order k in the sum. Some of these terms will be equal, thus accumulating a combinatorial factor. However, in contrast to the previous one-dimensional example, there will be terms with distinctively different structures. Each of the terms can be represented by a Feynman diagram. The perturbation theory expansion will then consist of the terms corresponding to the diagrams, accompanied with the corresponding combinatorial factors. Figure A.2 shows the first few diagrams for the x^4 theory with the interaction term $V(x) = cx^4/4!$.

This ends our superficial introduction to the perturbation theory and Feynman diagrams.[25] The real business of diagrams calculating is many-sided and complicated. Some diagram series or even some individual diagrams may diverge; such cases require special treatment, using, for example, renormalization group or non-perturbative methods. A complete account

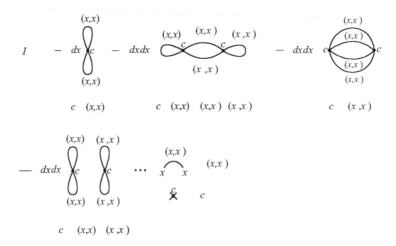

Figure A.2 Feynman diagrams for x^4 theory to the first three orders in c.

---

[25]Mattuck (1967) is the best ever introductory text on Feynman diagrams.

of functional methods in quantum field theory can be found in Vasiliev (1998) and Zinn-Justin (1993).

5.2 Quasiclassical Approach and Effective Action

Let us start again with a one-dimensional integral

$$I_1 = \int_{-\infty}^{\infty} dx \sqrt{\frac{h}{2\pi\alpha}} \, e^{-\frac{1}{2h}\alpha x^2} e^{\frac{c}{h}f(x)}.$$

What was done in the previous subsection is essentially perturbation theory with respect to the perturbation $\frac{c}{h}f(x)$ characterized by the constant c. Thus the corresponding Feynman diagram expansion is the power series

$$I_1 = \sum_{k=0}^{\infty} C_k c^k,$$

with some coefficients $\{C_k\}$. However, there is another parameter in I_1, which also can be used for the power series expansion. This is the parameter h, which in quantum physics is called the *Planck constant*. If the Planck constant is small and $1/h \to \infty$, the integral is dominated by regions where

$$S(x) = \frac{1}{2}\alpha x^2 - cf(x)$$

is minimal, *i.e.* regions around points $x_0^{(i)}$ solving the equation

$$\frac{d}{dx}S(x) = \frac{d}{dx}\left(\frac{1}{2}\alpha x^2 - cf(x)\right) = 0.$$

Then the function $S(x)$ can be expanded around these points so that

$$I_1 = \sum_i e^{-\frac{1}{2h}\alpha(x_0^{(i)})^2 + \frac{c}{h}f(x_0^{(i)})} \int_{-\infty}^{\infty} dx \sqrt{\frac{h}{2\pi\alpha}} \, e^{-\frac{1}{h}[\alpha - cf''(x_0^{(i)})](x - x_0^{(i)})^2 + \cdots]}.$$

This results in the following series for the integral:

$$I_1 = \sum_i e^{-\frac{1}{2h}\alpha(x_0^{(i)})^2 + \frac{c}{h}f(x_0^{(i)})} \sum_{k=0}^{\infty} H_k h^k. \tag{57}$$

The expansion (57) is called the *quasi-classical expansion*, because the case of small Planck constant and $1/h \to \infty$ corresponds to the almost-classical model defined by the functional integral. Therefore it is mainly governed by the classical equation

$$\frac{d}{dx}S(x) = 0.$$

The solutions of the equation define the terms in the sum over k in (57), while the main contribution comes from factors

$$e^{-\frac{1}{2h}\alpha(x_0^{(i)})^2 + \frac{c}{h}f(x_0^{(i)})},$$

the exponentials of the classical action at the classical solutions. It can be used as a first approximation for the integral I_1 as $h \to 0$. This is exactly what was done in Chapter 7 in the analysis of fast market dynamics.

Let us turn to functional integrals. The classical dynamics is described by the classical equations of motion

$$\frac{\delta S}{\delta \varphi(x)} = 0, \tag{58}$$

derived from the classical action functional

$$S(\varphi) = \int dx \, \mathcal{L}(\varphi(x), \partial_x \varphi(x)). \tag{59}$$

Suppose we are interested in the Feynman path integral

$$Z(J) = \int D\varphi \, \exp\left[\frac{1}{h}\left(S(\varphi) + \int dx \, J(x)\varphi(x)\right)\right] \tag{60}$$

constructed with the classical action $S(\phi)$ and some classical sources, J which are usually introduced to investigate the linear reaction of the system on the external perturbation. All the content of the theory defined by the functional integral (60), with all quantum or stochastic effects, is contained in the following objects, which are known as the *Green functions*:

$$\langle \varphi(x_1) \cdots \varphi(x_n) \rangle$$
$$= \frac{1}{Z(J)} \int D\varphi \, \varphi(x_1) \dots \varphi(x_n) \, \exp\left[\frac{1}{h}\left(S(\varphi) + \int dx J(x)\varphi(x)\right)\right]\Bigg|_{J=0}. \tag{61}$$

It is easy to show that all of these Green functions can be obtained by functional differentiation of the functional $Z(J)$, which is therefore called the generating functional. Moreover, factorizing the unconnected diagrammatic contributions,[26] one comes to the generating functional for connected Green functions $W(J) = h \log Z(J)$:

$$\langle \varphi(x_1) \dots \varphi(x_n) \rangle = (h)^n \exp\left(-\frac{1}{h}W\right) \frac{\delta^n}{\delta J(x_1) \dots \delta J(x_n)} \exp\left(\frac{1}{h}W\right). \tag{62}$$

The simplest connected Green functions have special names: the *mean field*

$$\langle \varphi(x) \rangle \equiv \phi(J, x) = \frac{\delta W}{\delta J(x)} \tag{63}$$

and the *propagator*

$$\langle [\varphi(x) - \phi(x)][\varphi(x') - \phi(x')] \rangle \equiv -hG(J, x, x') = h\frac{\delta^2 W}{\delta J(x)\delta J(x')}. \tag{64}$$

Further, the connected Green functions are expressed in terms of vertex functions. The generating functional for vertex functions is defined by the Legendre functional transform

$$\Gamma(\phi) = W(J(\phi)) - \int dx \, J(\phi(x))\phi(x). \tag{65}$$

---

[26]Whose Feynman diagrams contain unconnected parts like the final diagrams in Figs A.1 and A.2.

This is the most important object in quantum field theory. It contains all the information about the quantized fields.

1. First, one can show that it satisfies the equation

$$\frac{\delta\Gamma}{\delta\phi(x)} + J(\phi(x)) = 0. \tag{66}$$

This equation replaces the classical equation of motion (58) and describes the effective dynamics of fluctuating fields, taking into account all quantum corrections. That is why $\Gamma(\phi)$ is usually called the *effective action*.

2. Secondly, it determines the exact propagator of quantized fields:

$$-\frac{\delta^2\Gamma}{\delta\phi(x)\delta\phi(x')} G(x, x') = 1. \tag{67}$$

3. Finally, when the external sources J vanish, the effective action is just equal to $-\text{Log}\, Z(J)|_{J=0}$.

So, the effective action is defined to satisfy the equation

$$\exp\left(\frac{1}{h}\Gamma(\phi)\right) = \int D\varphi\, \exp\left[\frac{1}{h}\left(S(\varphi) - \int dx\, [\varphi(x) - \phi(x)]\frac{\delta\Gamma}{\delta\phi(x)}(\phi)\right)\right]. \tag{68}$$

At this stage, we can adopt the quasiclassical approach and decompose the fields into the classical and quantum parts,

$$\varphi = \phi + \sqrt{h}\tilde{\phi}, \tag{69}$$

and look for a solution of the equation for the effective action in form of an asymptotic series in powers of the Planck constant:

$$\Gamma(\phi) = S(\phi) + \sum_{n \geq 1} h^n \Gamma_{(n)}(\phi). \tag{70}$$

All the coefficients of this expansion can be found. They are expressed in terms of Feynman diagrams. The number of loops in these diagrams correspond to the power of the Planck constant in (70). The most frequently used approximation is the so-called *one-loop effective action*

$$\Gamma(\phi) = S(\phi) - \frac{h}{2}\log\det(F), \tag{71}$$

where the operator F has the kernel $\delta^2 S/\delta\phi(x)\delta\phi(x')$. The effective action contains the classical piece $S(\phi)$ and the first non-trivial correction, which is due to the Gaussian fluctuations in the corresponding path integral.

5.3 Numerical Methods

By construction, a functional integral effectively involves an infinite number of simple one-dimensional integrations. Therefore one way to deal with functional integrals is to return to the finite time steps and to perform numerical integrations over a finite, multidimensional space. Standard numerical procedures that work well for one- or two-dimensional integrals are not applicable in the case of a very large number of space variables because of their inefficiency and time requirements. That is why when evaluating functional integrals numerically, one has to apply stochastic integration methods, which are commonly known as *Monte Carlo (MC) methods.*

Suppose that we want to calculate an integral of the function $f(x)$ as depicted in Fig. A.3. One of the ways to do this is to discretize the variable x and find the integral as

$$\int_0^1 dx\, f(x) \simeq \frac{1}{N} \sum_{i=0}^{N-1} f(i/N).$$

The multidimensional analogue of this formula would be

$$\int_0^1 dx_1 \ldots \int_0^1 dx_n\, f(x_1, \ldots, x_n) \simeq \frac{1}{N^n} \sum_{i_1=0}^{N-1} \ldots \sum_{i_1=0}^{N-1} f(i_1/N, \ldots, i_n/N). \tag{72}$$

The reader can see that the number of summations grows exponentially with n, $e^{n \log N}$, and so does the computation time. Therefore this type of naive method is not advised when the number of integrations N tends to be very large.

To find another method, we can look again at the Fig. A.3 and realize that the integral is equal to the ratio of the area under the graph of the function to the area of the whole of the square box (which is equal to 1). Thus, if we 'shoot' points with coordinates (x, y) randomly at the square, the ratio of the number of points below the function graph and the full number of shots will be equal to the ratio of the corresponding areas, and therefore to the integral in question:

$$\int_0^1 dx\, f(x) \simeq \frac{1}{N} \sum_{i=0}^{N-1} \theta(f(x^{(i)}) - y^{(i)}).$$

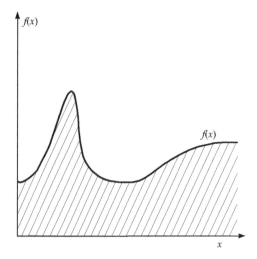

Figure A.3 One-dimensional integral of function $f(x)$.

The corresponding multidimensional analogue of this equation is

$$\int_0^1 dx_1 \ldots \int_0^n dx_1 f(x_1, \ldots, x_n) \simeq \frac{1}{N} \sum_{i=0}^{N-1} \theta(f(x_1^{(i)}, \ldots, x_n^{(i)}) - y^{(i)}), \qquad (73)$$

where $(x_1^{(i)}, \ldots, x_n^{(i)}, y^{(i)})$ are the coordinates of the randomly shot point at the ith step. In (73), the dimensionality of the space of integration already does not enter explicitly, which is very convenient for multidimensional integrations. The only problem is to generate a sufficiently large number of random 'shots' to make the stochastic error small enough. This requires some computer time, but already for the case of three- or four-dimensional integrals, this time is smaller than the computer time needed to get the same result using (72).

There are, however, though several things to worry about. First of all, the random numbers generated by a computer are not precisely random but rather are *quasirandom*, which means that, after some time, the set of random numbers can repeat itself. Since this will affect the precision of the calculation, it is important to use a good random number generator and be careful not to exceed its cycle length in the computer program. For further reading on random number generators, see Press et al (1992).

Secondly, the effectiveness of the computational algorithm might depend on the shape of the function. Indeed, if a function has a very sharp peak at a point x_0 and is nearly zero everywhere else, the algorithm just described will generate an answer close to zero, because only a few points will be close enough to the peak to make a significant contribution. An extreme example of this type is the delta function: with probability 1, all points will generate zero contribution to the numerical value (73) but, at the same time, we definitely know that the integral is equal to 1. To improve the situation, we have to shoot points more densely around important points. This is what is known as *importance sampling* Monte Carlo. In reality, almost any interesting physical problem requires one or another variant of importance sampling MC. For introductory reading on MC simulations in statistical physics with applications to random walks and percolation, see Binder et al (1997). Numerical methods in statistical field theory are covered in Itzykson and Drouffe (1994). A description of the MC method for lattice gauge theories can be found in Creutz (1983).

Importance sampling sounds easy, but, in fact, it is not. One needs a real understanding of the problem to identify classes of important functions to be integrated over in a functional integral. The situation here is more or less similar to the quasiclassical expansion of the previous subsection, where we argued that the regions around classical trajectories make the main contributions to a functional integral. Usually it is not that easy to find the classical solutions. Furthermore, it might happen that there are classes of functions that are not strictly speaking classical solutions but are still important to take into account. One such case may appear if the action functional diverges at a classical solution but stays finite for slightly 'deformed' functions that are not already solutions but generate important contributions to a functional integral *and* describe a certain physics of the problem. We stop here, pointing out that, as always, numerical calculation is an art and the numerical evaluation of functional integrals is a particular tough discipline.

6 FUNCTIONAL INTEGRALS AND ITÔ CALCULUS

We have seen in this chapter that functional integrals are a convenient way to deal with complicated things. One such thing that is particularly easy to deal with in the framework of functional integrals is stochastic calculus. To illustrate this statement, in this section, we give the functional integral representation of expectation values for a general quasi-Brownian process, and derive the corresponding Fokker–Planck equation and the Itô lemma.

6.1 Functional Integrals for Quasi-Brownian Processes

Consider a quasi-Brownian stochastic process

$$dS = \mu(S, t)\, dt + \sigma(S, t)\, dW, \tag{74}$$

with average rate $\mu(S, t)$ and volatility $\sigma(S, t)$. The process $W(t)$ is the standard Wiener process. For a given realization of $W(t)$, we have the conditional probability density functional for all pathwise realizations of the process $S(t)$:

$$p(\{S(t)\}|\{W(t)\}) = N \prod_t \delta(dS - \mu\, dt - \sigma\, dW(t)).$$

The constant N is a normalization factor. Next, we sum over the $W(t)$:

$$p(\{S(t)\}) = N \int DW\; e^{-\frac{1}{2}(dW)^2/dt} \prod_t \delta(dS - \mu\, dt - \sigma\, dW(t))$$

The integration is weighted by a Gaussian, since we have imposed white noise correlations because of the nature of the Wiener process. Now we can carry out the functional integral with respect to $W(t)$. For this purpose, the delta function needs to be rewritten for fixed t as follows:

$$\delta(dS - \mu\, dt - \sigma\, dW(t)) = \frac{1}{\sigma}\delta\left(\frac{1}{\sigma}(dS - \mu\, dt) - dW(t)\right).$$

Finally, one obtains for the probability density functional for the process $S(t)$

$$p(\{S(t)\}) = N \prod_t \frac{1}{\sigma} e^{\frac{-(dS - \mu\, dt)^2}{2\sigma^2 dt}} = N e^{-\int dt\, \frac{1}{2\sigma^2}\left(\frac{dS(t)}{dt} - \mu\right)^2} \prod_t \frac{1}{\sigma}. \tag{75}$$

This is the expression that we use below for the probability weight functional corresponding to the process $S(t)$ in the functional integral framework. It generalizes the expressions for the probability weights for the Brownian process and the Ornstein–Uhlenbeck process that we have already obtained in Section 3. The general procedure for functional weight derivation sketched above is known as the Martin–Siggia–Rose formalism (Martin et al, 1972).

Having derived the probability weight (75), it is possible to express any average quantity of interest in the form of a functional integral. If $F(S(\cdot))$ is a functional of the process $S(t)$ its expectation is equal to

$$\langle F(S(\cdot))\rangle = N \int DS\; F(S(\cdot)) e^{-\int dt\, \frac{1}{2\sigma^2}\left(\frac{dS(t)}{dt} - \mu\right)^2}, \qquad DS = \prod_t \frac{dS(t)}{\sqrt{2\pi\sigma^2}}. \tag{76}$$

For example, the conditional probability to find $S(t) = x$ while $S(0) = x'$ is given by the functional integral

$$p(x, t|x', 0) = \frac{\int_{S(0)=x'}^{S(t)=x} DS \, e^{-\int d\tau \frac{1}{2\sigma^2} \left(\frac{dS(\tau)}{d\tau} - \mu \right)^2}}{\int dx \int_{S(0)=x'}^{S(t)=x} DS \, e^{-\int d\tau \frac{1}{2\sigma^2} \left(\frac{dS(\tau)}{d\tau} - \mu \right)^2}}. \tag{77}$$

Let us derive the Fokker–Planck equation for the function $p(x, t|x', 0)$ from its functional representation (77).

6.2   Fokker–Planck Equation

First of all, since the action functional is additive, the functional integral (77) obeys the equation

$$\int dx \, f(x) p(x, t + dt|x', 0) = \int dx \, f(x) \int dy \, p(x, t + dt|t, y) p(y, t|x', 0),$$

for any function $f(x)$. One can therefore reduce the problem to the study of the infinitesimal transition probability $p(x, t + dt|t, y)$, which can be written as

$$p(x, t + dt|y, t) = \frac{\int_{S(t)=y}^{S(t+dt)=x} DS \, e^{-\int d\tau \frac{1}{2\sigma^2} \left(\frac{dS(\tau)}{d\tau} - \mu \right)^2}}{\int dx \int_{S(t)=y}^{S(t+dt)=x} DS \, e^{-\int d\tau \frac{1}{2\sigma^2} \left(\frac{dS(\tau)}{d\tau} - \mu \right)^2}} \tag{78}$$

$$\underset{dt \to 0}{\simeq} \frac{1}{\sqrt{2\pi \, dt \, \sigma^2}} e^{-\frac{1}{2 \, dt \, \sigma^2} (x - y - \mu \, dt)^2}.$$

This means that

$$\int dx \, f(x) p(x, t + dt|x', 0) = \int dx \, f(x) \int dy \, \frac{1}{\sqrt{2\pi \, dt \, \sigma^2}} e^{-\frac{1}{2 \, dt \, \sigma^2} (x - y - \mu \, dt)^2} p(y, t|x', 0).$$

Expanding the function $f(x)$ around y, one finds

$$\int dx \, f(x) p(x, t + dt|x', 0)$$

$$= \int dx \left(f(y) + \frac{\partial f}{\partial y} (x - y) + \frac{1}{2} \frac{\partial^2 f}{\partial y^2} (x - y)^2 + \frac{1}{6} \frac{\partial^3 f}{\partial y^3} (x - y)^3 + \cdots \right)$$

$$\times \int dy \, \frac{1}{\sqrt{2\pi \, dt \, \sigma^2}} e^{-\frac{1}{2 \, dt \, \sigma^2} (x - y - \mu \, dt)^2} p(y, t|x', 0).$$

In the last expression the integral over x can be now calculated exactly, which results in the following equality:

$$\int dx \, f(x) p(x, t + dt|x', 0) = \int dy \left(f(y) + \frac{\partial f}{\partial y} \mu \, dt + \frac{1}{2} \frac{\partial^2 f}{\partial y^2} \sigma^2 \, dt + o(dt) \right) p(y, t|x', 0).$$

We see that in the integration over x, terms proportional to the third and higher powers of $x - y$ can be omitted, since they are proportional to, at least, $(dt)^{3/2}$ and small compared with the first three terms. This leaves us with the equation

$$\int dy\, f(y) \left(p(y, t|x', 0) + \frac{\partial p(y, t|x', 0)}{\partial t} dt \right)$$

$$= \int dy \left(f(y) + \frac{\partial f}{\partial y} \mu\, dt + \frac{1}{2} \frac{\partial^2 f}{\partial y^2} \sigma^2\, dt \right) p(y, t|x', 0).$$

After integration by parts and taking into account that the function $f(x)$ was not fixed and is therefore arbitrary, we find that the last equation is equivalent to the partial differential equation

$$\frac{\partial}{\partial t} p(x, t|x', 0) = \left(-\frac{\partial}{\partial x} \mu + \frac{1}{2} \frac{\partial^2}{\partial x^2} \sigma^2 \right) p(x, t|x', 0) = 0, \tag{79}$$

which is known as the Fokker–Planck equation. The obvious relation $p(x, t|x', 0)|_{t=0} = \delta(x - x')$ provides (79) with an initial condition.

6.3 Itô Lemma

Suppose that we have a function $C(t, S)$ that depends both on time t and the stochastic process $S(t)$ defined by (74). Let us examine the distribution function of the stochastic variable

$$x(t) = C(t + dt, S(t + dt)) - C(t, S(t))$$

for infinitesimally small dt. By definition, the distribution function $f(x)$ is equal to

$$f(x) = \langle \delta(x(t) - x) \rangle_S,$$

which, according to (76) is equal to

$$\langle \delta(x(t) - x) \rangle_S = N \int_{S(t)} DS\, \delta(x(t) - x) e^{-\int d\tau \frac{1}{2\sigma^2} \left(\frac{dS(t)}{dt} - \mu \right)^2}.$$

Substituting into the last equation the explicit delta-function representation

$$\delta(x(t) - x) = \frac{1}{2\pi} \int_{-\infty}^{\infty} dk\, e^{ik[x(t) - x]},$$

and using as in (78) the infinitesimal scale of dt, we find

$$f(x) = \frac{1}{2\pi} \int_{-\infty}^{\infty} dk \int dS\, \frac{1}{\sqrt{2\pi\, dt\, \sigma^2}} e^{-\frac{1}{2\, dt\, \sigma^2}(dS - \mu\, dt)^2} e^{ik[C(t+dt, S+dS) - C(t, S(t)) - x]}.$$

Expanding the function $C(t + dt, S + dS)$ in a Taylor series so that

$$C(t + dt, S + dS) - C(t, S) = \frac{\partial C}{\partial t} dt + \frac{\partial C}{\partial S}(dS) + \frac{1}{2} \frac{\partial^2 C}{\partial S^2}(dS)^2 + \cdots,$$

we can rewrite the previous integral as

$$f(x) = \frac{1}{2\pi} \int_{-\infty}^{\infty} dk \int dS\, \frac{1}{\sqrt{2\pi\, dt\, \sigma^2}} e^{-\frac{1}{2\, dt\, \sigma^2}(dS - \mu\, dt)^2} e^{ik\left(\frac{\partial C}{\partial t} dt + \frac{\partial C}{\partial S} dS + \frac{1}{2} \frac{\partial^2 C}{\partial S^2}(dS)^2 - x \right)} e^{ik\left(\frac{1}{6} \frac{\partial^3 C}{\partial S^3}(dS)^3 + \cdots \right)}.$$

Once again, it is possible to check perturbatively (exactly as we did in the derivation of the Fokker–Planck equation) that the last multiplier in the integrand does not contribute for small dt, thus leaving us with the Gaussian integral over dS, which can be calculated exactly:

$$f(x) = \frac{1}{2\pi} \int_{-\infty}^{\infty} dk \; \frac{1}{\sqrt{1 - ik \, dt \, \sigma^2 \frac{\partial^2 C}{\partial S^2}}} e^{ik\left(\frac{\partial C}{\partial t} dt - x\right)} e^{-\frac{\mu^2 dt}{2\sigma^2}} e^{\frac{\left(\frac{\mu}{\sigma^2} + ik\frac{\partial C}{\partial S}\right)^2 \frac{dt \, \sigma^2}{2\left(1 - ik \, dt \, \sigma^2 \frac{\partial^2 C}{\partial S^2}\right)}}}. \tag{80}$$

For small dt, the square-root prefactor can be approximated as

$$\frac{1}{\sqrt{1 - ik \, dt \, \sigma^2 \frac{\partial^2 C}{\partial S^2}}} \simeq 1 + \frac{1}{2} ik \, dt \, \sigma^2 \frac{\partial^2 C}{\partial S^2} \simeq e^{\frac{1}{2} ik \, dt \, \sigma^2 \frac{\partial^2 C}{\partial S^2}},$$

while the last exponent in (80) simplifies to the form

$$e^{\left(\frac{\mu}{\sigma^2} + ik\frac{\partial C}{\partial S}\right)^2 \frac{dt \, \sigma^2}{2}}.$$

This makes the integral over k Gaussian again,

$$f(x) = \frac{1}{2\pi} \int_{-\infty}^{\infty} dk \; e^{ik\left(\frac{\partial C}{\partial t} dt + \frac{\partial C}{\partial S}\mu \, dt - x\right)} e^{\frac{1}{2} ik \, dt \, \sigma^2 \frac{\partial^2 C}{\partial S^2}} e^{-\frac{1}{2} k^2 \left(\frac{\partial C}{\partial S}\right)^2 \sigma^2 \, dt},$$

which allows its exact evaluation:

$$f(x) = \frac{1}{\sqrt{2\pi \, dt \, \sigma^2 \left(\frac{\partial C}{\partial S}\right)^2}} e^{-\frac{1}{2\sigma^2 \left(\frac{\partial C}{\partial S}\right)^2}\left(\frac{\partial C}{\partial t} dt + \frac{\partial C}{\partial S}\mu \, dt + \frac{1}{2} dt \, \sigma^2 \frac{\partial^2 C}{\partial S^2} - x\right)^2}. \tag{81}$$

Equation (81) solves the problem, giving the probability distribution function of the stochastic variable $C(t + dt, S(t + dt)) - C(t, S(t))$. From the discussion in Section 6.1, the reader knows that this probability distribution corresponds to the quasi-Brownian stochastic process defined by the following stochastic differential equation:

$$dC \equiv C(t + dt, S(t + dt)) - C(t, S(t)) = \frac{\partial C}{\partial t} \, dt + \frac{\partial C}{\partial S} \, \mu \, dt + \frac{1}{2} \, dt \, \sigma^2 \frac{\partial^2 C}{\partial S^2} + \sigma \frac{\partial C}{\partial S} \, dW,$$

or, using (74),

$$dC = \frac{\partial C}{\partial t} \, dt + \frac{\partial C}{\partial S} \, dS + \frac{1}{2} \, dt \, \sigma^2 \frac{\partial^2 C}{\partial S^2}. \tag{82}$$

This last equation expresses the statement of the famous Itô lemma, which is part of the basis of financial mathematics in continuous time.

Glossary

Action   A functional that is the logarithm of an integrand in a *functional* integral.

Annihilation operator   An operator that transforms a state with n asset units into a state with $n - 1$ asset units.

Arbitrage   A possibility to get abnormal return on a *riskless* operation.

Arbitrage Pricing Theory (APT)   A pricing theory that derives relations for the average return assuming that (1) the return is driven by several economic factors; (2) there are no *arbitrage* opportunities.

Arbitrageur   An agent who profits from *arbitrage* operations.

ARCH (autoregressive conditional heteroscedasticity) process   A nonlinear stochastic process where the variance is time-varying and conditional upon the past values of the series.

Base   A submanifold of a *fibre bundle space* that is the result of a canonical projection of the fibre bundle. See *fibre bundle*.

Behavioural finance   A financial theory that studies behavioural aspects of financial decision-making.

Black–Scholes equation   An equation for a derivative price derived by F. Black and M. Scholes from the assumptions of: (1) no-arbitrage; (2) geometrical Brownian motion for the underlying price. Black–Scholes analysis is based on the construction of a hedging portfolio for a derivative and pricing the derivative as a price of the portfolio.

Brownian motion   See *Wiener process*.

Call option   A right but not an obligation to buy an asset at some particular time in the future (European call) or before some particular time in the future (American call).

Capital Asset Pricing Model (CAPM)   An equilibrium asset pricing model that, in its simple form, states that assets are priced according to their relationship to the market portfolio of all risky assets, as determined by the security's delta. Generalized models include Zero-Beta CAPM, Post-Tax CAPM and Consumption CAPM.

Central Limit Theorem   The Law of Large Numbers; it states that as a sample of independent identically distributed random numbers approaches infinity, its probability distribution function approaches the normal distribution.

Charting   A way to predict future prices from the charts of historic prices. See also *Technical Analysis*.

Coherent state   An eigenstate of the annihilation operator.

Commutator   The commutator of two operators A and B is equal to $AB - BA \equiv [A, B]$.

Connection   A rule of comparison of elements in *fibres* that correspond to different points in the base. See also *gauge field*.

Covariant derivative   A derivative (in the mathematical sense) defined by the rules of *parallel transport* so that the result of an infinitesimal parallel transport has zero covariant derivative.

Creation operator   An operator that transforms a state with $n - 1$ asset units in to a state with n asset units.

Credit risk   A risk of default on someone's obligations.

Cross-section   A function on a base that maps the base to the corresponding fibres.

Curvature of fibre bundle   A quantity that reflects the non-trivial rules of *parallel transport* on a *fibre bundle*. Technically, the curvature is represented by the curvature tensor, which is the *commutator* of two *covariant derivatives*.

Derivatives   A financial derivative is a financial instrument whose value is defined by values of other (underlying) financial instruments. These underlying variables may be prices of stocks, bonds or other derivatives, interest rates, market indices, and the like. Derivatives can be traded on exchanges (exchange-traded derivatives) or over the counter (OTC derivatives).

Dilatation group   A group of dilatations that change the scale of asset units. These changes can be associated with splits and devaluations. The dilatation group is a group of *gauge transformations* for a financial market.

Directional trader   A trader who bets on the direction of market movements.

Efficient frontier   In mean/variance analysis, the curve formed by the set of efficient portfolios which have highest level of expected return for their level of risk (variance).

Efficient Market Hypothesis (EMH)   A hypothesis according to which (1) there exists a perfect pricing model and agents know this model; (2) agents have all relevant information to incorporate into the model; (3) agents are rational; (4) real returns are randomly distributed around the model prediction.

Efficient Market Theory   A theory based on the *Efficient Market Hypothesis*.

Electrodynamics   A classical theory that describes the electromagnetic interaction of moving charged particles.

Equilibrium market   A time-independent state of the market.

Equilibrium pricing model   A model that assumes the existence of an *equilibrium market*.

Expiration date   A time in the future that bounds the life of a *derivative* contract.

Farmer's term   An approximate expression for the price change in response to a disbalance in buy/sell orders in a market supported by market-makers.

Feynman path integral   A *functional integral* in the coordinate/momentum representation.

Feynman diagrams   A graphical way to represent perturbation expansions of *functional integrals*.

Fibre   A subspace of a *fibre bundle space* that projects onto the same point of the base under a canonical projection of the fibre bundle. See *fibre bundle*.

Fibre bundle   A fibre bundle is a space consisting of identical subspaces (fibres) that are 'glued' together to give the whole space and are labelled by points of another subspace, the base. Under a canonical projection, the fibres collapse into the labelling points of the base. Examples of fibre bundles are shown in Chapter 2.

Fluctuation–dissipation theorem   This theorem relates a measure of internal fluctuations or a measure of response of the system to a small external perturbation.

Forward (forward contract)   An obligation to exchange assets at some moment of time in the future. The exchange will be performed according to the forward price, which was set in advance.

Fractal   An object with fractional dimension. Self-similar fractals have parts that in some way are related to the whole. An example of a self-similar fractal is given by Fig. 1.6 in Chapter 1.

Fractal Market Hypothesis (FMH)   A hypothesis according to which the market consists of agents with many different investment horizons with the same type of financial dynamics. The latter dynamics differ from each other only by the value of parameters and information sets, but not the functional dependence. In this form, markets resemble self-similar *fractals*.

Functional integrals   Integrals over functions in some function space. A handy tool for quick solutions of evolution problems. See also *path integrals*.

Futures (futures contract)   A contract similar to a *forward contract*, with profit and loss accounted an everyday basis (marking-to-market procedure).

GARCH (generalized ARCH) process A generalized *ARCH process* with additional flexibility in the definition of the variance process, which includes conditional dependence on previous variances.

Gauge field Another name for the *connection field*.

Gauge fixing The act of choosing particular asset units and the corresponding rules of *parallel transport*.

Gauge invariants Quantities that do not change under *gauge transformations*.

Gauge symmetry (invariance) A symmetry with respect to *gauge transformations*.

Gauge theory A dynamical theory whose dynamical variables include the *connection* field and that can be formulated in *gauge-invariant* terms.

Gauge transformations A change in co-ordinate system by means of acting by an element of the *structure group*. In the financial setting, gauge transformations correspond to changes in the scale of asset units. These changes can be associated with splits and devaluations.

Gaussian functional (path) integral A *functional integral* whose *action* is a quadratic functional of the functions.

Geometrical Brownian motion The continuous-time process whose logarithm follows *Brownian motion*.

Hedging A reduction of risk on a portfolio by taking positions in other financial assets with opposite sensitivities with respect to price movements.

Implied volatility A volatility of the underlying asset estimated from derivative prices using the Black–Scholes formulae. Usually one plots the implied volatility as a function of the corresponding *strike*. If the plot is not flat one says that the implied volatility has a 'smile' or a 'skew'.

Itô lemma A mathematical statement that expresses an (Itô) time derivative of a function of the Brownian motion.

Kurtosis A measure of non-Gaussian behaviour of a probability distribution function. It is calculated as a shifted ratio of the fourth moment and the square of the second moment, and is equal to zero for a Gaussian distribution function.

Lagrangian When an *action* can be represented by an integral, the integrand is called the Lagrangian.

Lattice gauge theory A dynamical theory that describes an interaction mediated by *gauge fields* in a *fibre bundle* whose *base* is a lattice.

Leptokurtotic distribution   A probability distribution with positive *kurtosis*.

Levy flight   A continuous-time stochastic process whose increments are drawn from the *Levy stable distribution*.

Levy stable distribution   A probability distribution with infinite second moment whose convolution with itself reproduces the same functional form.

Manifold   A geometrical space that can be considered as a set of local neighbourhoods and a rule of how to 'glue' them together.

Martingale   A stochastic process $X(\cdot)$ whose expectation at any future time T calculated at time t coincides with $X(t)$.

Martingale measure   A measure under which a process is a *martingale*. If one assumes the *no-arbitrage* condition, all prices of tradeable assets are martingales wtih respect to some measure. If the market is complete, this measure will be unique.

Model risk   A risk due to limited validity of the pricing model.

No-Arbitrage   The assumption that there are no *arbitrage* opportunities.

Non-equilibrium market   A market whose state variables are time-dependent and have non-trivial dynamics.

Parallel transport   A rule of 'pulling' an element in a fibre along some curve in the base such that the difference defined by the *connecton* is zero.

Path integrals   See *functional integrals*.

Price adjustment   A dynamical process leading a price to some intrinsic value.

Put option   A right but not an obligation to sell an asset at some particular time in the future (European call) or before some particular time in the future (American call).

Quantum Electrodynamics (QED)   A theory that generalizes *electrodynamics* to the case of particles obeying quantum laws.

Quasi-efficient market   A generalization of the *efficient market* where agents are *quasi-rational*.

Quasi-equilibrium market   A non-equilibrium market whose dynamics tends to return it to its equilibrium.

Quasirational agents   Agents whose decisions are drawn from an identical random distribution that substitutes for the perfect prediction model in the formulation of the *Efficient Market Hypothesis*. The stochastic decision-making model involves bounded rationality, incomplete or expensive information, and multiparameter decision rules.

Random walk   See *Brownian motion*.

Risk-aversion   A characteristic of an agent when she demands to be paid above the corresponding average rate of return (the risk premium) for taking a risk.

Risk-neutrality   A characteristic of an agent when she does not demand to be paid above the corresponding average rate of return for taking a risk.

Riskless (risk-free) asset   An asset that does not bear any risk associated with it.

Speculator   See *directional trader*.

Strike   A price according to which assets will be exchanged under an option contract. See *call option* and *put option*.

Structure group   A group whose elements act in 'gluing' local neighbourhoods of a *fibre bundle*.

Swap   A financial contract that allows one to swap fixed interest payments with flexible-rate payments.

Technical analysis   A theory according to which future prices can be predicted by studying charts of historical prices and applying phenomenological rules – technical indicators.

Utility function   A function that defines the preferences of an agent.

Virtual arbitrage pricing   A pricing model that allows for the existence of virtual (stochastic) *arbitrage* opportunities (in contrast to *Arbitrage Pricing Theory*).

Volatility   The standard deviation of a return on a security. In derivative pricing, one usually considers an *implied volatility* in contrast to the historic volatility calculated from the previous prices.

Wiener process   A continuous-time random process X such that (1) dX is a random variable drawn from a normal distribution; (2) the mean of dX is zero; (3) The variance of dX is dt.

References

Achelis S.B. (1995) *Technical Analysis from A to Z*. Irwin Professional Publishing.

Akgiray V. (1989) *J. Business* **62**, 55–80.

Amihud Y. and Mendelson H. (1987) *J. Finance* **42**, 533–553.

Andersen L., Andreasen J. and Brotherton-Ratcliffe R. (1998) *J. Comput. Finance* **1**(3), 15–35.

Aparicio F. and Estrada J. (2000) *Eur. J. Finance* **6**(3), to appear.

Appel G. and Hitschler F. (1980) *Stock Market Trading Systems*. Homewood, IL: Dow Jones–Irwin.

Arditti F., Ayadin S., Mattu R. and Rigsbee S. (1986) *Financial Anal. J.* **42**, 63–66.

Arifovich J. (1996) *J. Polit. Econ.* **104**, 504–541.

Bachelier L. J. B. (1900) *Theorie de la Speculation*. Paris: Gauthier-Villars.

Baille R. T. (1996) *J. Econometr.* **73**, 5–59.

Baillie R.T. and Bollerslev T. (1989) *J. Business Econ. Statist.* **7**, 297–305.

Baille R. T. and Bollerslev T. (1991) *Rev. Econ. Stud.* **58**, 565–585.

Bak P, Paczuski M. and Shubik M. (1997) *Physica* **A246**, 430–453.

Banz R. W. (1981) *J. Financial Econ.* **9**, 3–18.

Barnett W. A. and Serletis A. (2000) *J. Econ. Dyn. Control* **24**, 703–724.

Bar-Yosef B. and Brown L. D. (1977) *J. Finance* **32**, 1074.

Baxter M. and Reny A. (1996) *Financial Calculus*. Cambridge University Press.

Benford F. (1938) *Proc. Am. Philos. Soc.* **78**, 551–572.

Bensoussan A., Crouhy M. and Galai D. (1994) *Philos. Trans. R. Soc. Lond.* **A347**, 449–598.

Bertoin J. (1996) *Levy Processes*. Cambridge University Press.

Bergmann P. G. (1979) Unitary field theories. *Phys. Today* March 1979, 44–51.

Bernstein P. L. (1992) *Capital Ideas*. The Free Press.

Binder K. and Heermann D. W. (1997) *Monte Carlo Simulation in Statistical Physics*. Berlin: Springer–Verlag.

Black F. (1986) *J. Finance* **41**, 526–543.

Black F. and Scholes M. (1973) *J. Polit. Econ.* **81**, 637–654.

Black F. and Scholes M. (1972) *J. Finance* **27**, 399–418.

Black F., Jensen M. C. and Scholes M. (1972) The capital asset pricing model: some empirical tests. In: M. C. Jensen (ed.), *Studies in the Theory of Capital Markets*. New York: Praeger.

Blake D. (1990) *Financial Market Analysis*. New York: McGraw–Hill.

Blattberg R. and Gonedes N. (1974) *J. Business* **47**, 244–280.

Bollerslev T. (1986) *J. Econometr.* **31**, 307–327.

Bollerslev T., Chou R. Y. and Kroner K. F. (1992) *J. Econometr.* **52**, 5–59.

Bouchaud J.-P. (1999) *Physica* **A263**, 415–426.

Bouchaud J.-P. and Cont R. (1998). *Eur. Phys. J.* **B6**, 543–550.

Bouchaud J.-P. and Potter M.(1998) *Theorie des Risques Financieres*. Alea–Saclay: Eyrolles.

Bouchaud J-P. and Sornette D. (1994) *J. Phys. I (Paris)* **4**, 863–899.

Bouchaud J.-P., Potters M. and Meyer M. (2000) *Eur. Phys. J.* **B13**, 595–599.

Brennan M. J. and Schwartz E. S. (1988) Optimal arbitrage strategies under basis variability. In: M. Sarnat (ed.) *Essays in Financial Economics*. New York: North-Holland.

Brennan M. J. and Schwartz E. S. (1990) *J. Business* **63**(1), Part 2, 7–32.

Breymann W., Ghashghaie S. and Talkner P. (2000) A stochastic cascade model for FX dynamics. Preprint cond-mat/0004179; available at http://xxx.lanl.gov/labs/cond–mat/0004179.

Brian A. W. (1992) On learning and adaptation in the economy. Santa Fe Institute Working Paper 92-07-038.

Brian A. W. (1994) *Am. Econ. Rev.* **84**, 406–411.

Brian A. W., Holland J., LeBaron B., Palmer R. and Taylor P. (1996) Asset pricing under inductive reasoning in an artificial stock market. Santa Fe Institute Working Paper.

Brock W. A., Lakonishok J. and LeBaron B. (1992) *J. Finance* **47**, 1731–1764.

Buckley H. (1927) *A Short History of Physics*. London: Methuen.

Cajori F. (1935) *A History of Physics*. London: Macmillan.

Callen H. B. (1960) *Thermodynamics*. New York: Wiley.

Caldarelli G., Marsili M. and Zhang Y.-C. (1997) *Eur. Phys. Lett.* **40**, 479–484.

Campbell J. Y. (1987) *J. Financial Econ.* **18**, 373–399.

Campbell J. Y. and Shiller R. (1988) *Rev. Financial Stud.* **1**, 195–228.

Campbell J.Y., Lo A. W. and MacKinlay A. C. (1997) *Econometrics of Financial Markets*. Princeton University Press.

Chan K. C. and Chen N. (1988) *J. Finance* **43**, 309–325.

Chan K. C., Chen N. and Hsieh D. A. (1985) *J. Financial Econ.* **14**, 451–471.

Chande T. S. and Kroll S. (1994) *The New Technical Trader*. New York: Wiley.

Charest G. (1978) *J. Financial Econ.* **6**, 265–296.

Chen N. (1983) *J. Finance* **38**, 1393–1414.

Chen N., Roll R. and Ross S. A. (1986) *J. Business* **56**, 383–403.

Cizeau P., Liu Y., Meyer M., Peng C.-K. and Stanley H. E. (1997) *Physica* **A245**, 441–445;

Clare A. D. and Thomas S. H. (1994) *J. Business Finance Accounting* **21**, 309–330.

Clark P. K. (1973) *Econometrica* **41**, 135–155.

Cohen K., Maier S., Schwartz R. and Whitcomb D. (1986) *Microstructure of Securities Market*. Englewood Cliffs, NJ: Prentice-Hall.

Conlisk J. (1996) *J. Econ. Lit.* **34**, 669–700.

Conroy R. M., Harris R. S. and Benet B. A. (1990) *J. Finance* **45**, 1285–1295.

Cont R. (1997) Scaling and correlation in financial data. Preprint cond-mat/9705075; available at http://xxx.lanl.gov/abs/cond-mat/9705075.

Cont R. and Bouchaud J. P. (1997) Herd behaviour and aggregate fluctuations in financial market. Preprint cond–mat/9712318; available at http://xxx.lanl/gov/abs/cond-mat/9712318.

Copeland T. (1979) *J. Finance* **34**, 115–141.

Cornell B. (1985) *J. Futures Markets* **5**, 89–101.

Cornell B. and French K. (1983) *J. Finance* **38**, 675–694.

Cox J. C. and Ross S. A. (1976) *J. Financial Econ.* **3**, 145–166.

Cox J. C., Ingersoll J. E. and Ross S. A. (1981) *J. Financial Econ.* **9**, 321–346.

Creutz M. (1983) *Quarks, Gluons and Lattices*. Cambridge University Press.

Cuthbertson K. (1996) *Quantitative Financial Economics*. Chichester: Wiley.

Damodaran A. (1993) *J. Finance* **48**, 387–399.

DeBondt W. F. M. and Thaler R. H. (1985) *J. Finance* **40**, 793–805.

De Grauwe P., Dewachter H. and Embrechts M. (1993) *Exchange Rate Theory: Chaotic Models of Foreign Exchange Markets*. Oxford: Blackwell.

De Long J. B., Shleifer A., Summers L. H. and Waldmann R. J. (1990a) *J. Polit. Econ.* **98**, 703–738;

De Long J. B., Shleifer A., Summers L. H. and Waldmann R. J. (1990b) *J. Finance* **45**, 379–395.

De Long J. B., Shleifer A., Summers L. H. and Waldmann R. J. (1991) *J. Business* **64**, 1–20.

Dimson E. (1979) *J. Financial Econ.* **7**, 197–226.

Ding Z., Granger C. W. and Engle R. F. (1993) *J. Empir. Finance* **1**, 83–106.

Dubofsky D. A. (1992) *Options and Financial Futures. Valuation and Uses*. New York: McGraw-Hill.

Dubrovin B. A., Fomenko A. T. and Novikov S. P. (1985) *Modern Geometry – Methods and Applications*. Part II. The Geometry and Toplogy of Manifolds. New York: Springer-Verlag.

Duffie D. (1992) *Dynamic Asset Pricing Theory*. Princeton University Press.

Dunbar N. (1999) *Inventing Money*. Chichester: Wiley.

Dunis C. and Zhou B. (eds) (1998) *Nonlinear Modelling of High Frequency Financial Time Series*. Chichester: Wiley.

Eguchi T., Gilkey P. B. and Hanson A. J. (1980) *Phys. Rep.* **66**, 213–393.

Elton E. J. and Gruber M. J. (1995) *Modern Portfolio Theory and Investment Analysis*. New York: Wiley.

Engle R. F., (1982) *Econometrica* **50**, 987–1007.

Epps T. W. and Epps M. L. (1976) *Econometrica* **44**, 305–321.

Erdelyi A. et al (1953) *Higher Transcedental Functions*, Vol. 2. New York: McGraw-Hill.

Faddeev L. D. and Slavnov A. A. (1980) *Gauge Fields: Introduction to Quantum Theory*. Reading, MA: Benjaminn/Cummings.

Fama E. F. (1965) *J. Business* **38**, 34–105.

Fama E. F. (1970) *J. Finance* **25**, 383–423.

Fama E. F. (1991) *J. Finance* **46**, 1575–1617.

Fama E. F. and French K. R. (1988) *J. Polit. Econ.* **96**, 246–273.

Fama E. F. and French K. R. (1992) *J. Finance* **47**, 427–465.

Fama E. F. and French K. R. (1996) *J. Finance* **51**, 55–84.

Fama E. F. and MacBeth J. D. (1974) *J. Financial Econ.* **1**, 43–66.

Fama E. F., Fisher L., Jensen M. C. and Roll R. (1969) *Int. Econ. Rev.* **10**, 1–21.

Farmer D. (1998) Market force, ecology and evolution. Preprint adap-org/9812005; available at http://xxx.lanl.gov/abs/adap-org/9812005.

Feynman R. P. (1985) *QED: The Strange Theory of Light and Matter*. Princeton University Press.

Feynman R. P. and Hibbs A. P. (1965) *Quantum Mechanics and Path Integrals*, New York: McGraw-Hill.

Figlewski S. (1984) *J. Finance* **39**, 657–670.

Figlewski S. (1985) *J. Futures Markets* **5**, 183–200.

Föllmer H. (1991) Probabilistic aspects of options. SFB 303 Discussion Paper B-202, University of Bonn.

Föllmer H. and Schweizer M. (1993) *Math. Finance* **3**, 1–23.

Frey R. and Stremme A. (1993) Portfolio insurance and volatility. On robustness of the Black–Scholes pricing model, SFB-303 Discussion Paper B-256, University of Bonn.

Galai D.(1977) *J. Business* **50** 167–197.

Galluccio S., Galdarelli G., Marsili M. and Zhang Y.-C. (1997) *Physica* **A245**, 423–436.

Garman M. B. (1976) *J. Financial Econ.* **3**, 403–427.

Geske R. (1979) *J. Financial Econ.* **7**, 63–81.

Glashghaie S., Breymann W., Peinke J., Talkner P., and Dodge Y. (1996) *Nature* **381**, 767–770.

Goetzman Y. N. (1993) *J. Business* **66**, 249–270.

Gopikrishnan P., Meyer M., Amaral L. A. N. and Stanley H. E. (1998) *Eur. Phys. J* **B3**, 139–140.

Gopikrishnan P., Plerou V., Amaral L. A. N., Meyer M. and Stanley H. E. (1999) *Phys. Rev.* **E60**, 5305–5316.

Granger C. W. and Ding Z. (1996) *J. Econometr.* **73**, 61–77.

Gray B. and French D. (1990) *J. Business, Finance Accounting* **17**, 451–459.

Green M. B., Schwarz J. H. and Witten E. (1987) *Superstring Theory*, 2 Vols. Cambridge University Press.

Grinblatt M. S., Masulis W. W. and Titman S. (1984) *J. Financial Econ.* **13**, 461–490.

Guillaume D. M., Dacorogna M. M., Dave R. D., Muller U. A., Olsen R. B. and Pictet O.V. (1997) *Finance Stochastics* **1**, 95–129.

Harrison J. M. and Pliska S. R. (1981) *Stochast. Process. Applics.* **11**, 215–260.

Hartle T. (1998) *Techn. Anal. Stocks Commodities* **16**(3), 6.

Hausch D. B. and Ziemba W. T. (1990) *J. Business* **63**, 61–78.

Heston S. L. (1993) *Rev. Financial Stud.* **6**, 327–343.

Hill T. P. (1998) *Am. Scientist* **86**, 358–363.

Huang R. and Stoll H. (1997) *Rev. Financial Stud.* **10**, 995–1034.

Hull J. C. and White A. (1987) *J. Finance* **42** 281–299;

Hull J. C. and White A. (1988) *Adv. Futures Options Res.* **3**, 27–61.

Hull J. C. (1997) *Options, Futures and Other Derivatives*. Englewood Cliffs, NJ: Prentice Hall.

Husemoller D. (1994) *Fibre Bundles*, 3rd edn. New York: Springer-Verlag.

Ilinskaia A. and Ilinski K. (1996) *J. Phys* **A29**, L23–L29.

Ilinskaia A. and Ilinski K. (1997) *Russ. Securities Market J.* **21**, 94–98.

Ilinskaia A. and Ilinski K. (1998) How to reconcile technical analysis and market efficiency. IPHYS Group Working Paper.

Ilinski K. (1997) Physics of finance. Preprint hep-th/9710148; available at http://xxx.lanl.gov/abs/hep–th/9710148; see also Ilinski 1998.

Ilinski K. (1998) Physics of finance. In: J. Kertesz and I. Kondor (eds), *Econophysics: An Emerging Science*, Dordrecht: Kluwer.

Ilinski K. (1999) Virtual arbitrage pricing theory, IPHYS Group Working Paper; available at http://xxx.lanl.gov/abs/cond-mat/9902045.

Ilinski K. (2000a) *J. Phys.* **A33**, L5–L14.

Ilinski K. (2000b) Pricing speculations in passport options: theoretical models and business aspects. IPhys Group Working Paper Iphys-1-00.

Ilinski K. and Kalinin G. (1997) Black–Scholes equation from gauge theory of arbitrage. IPhys Group Working Paper IPhys–4–97, 1997; Preprint hep–th/9712034; available at http://xxx.lanl.gov/abs/hep-th/9712034.

Ilinski K. and Stepanenko A. (1998) *Adv. Complex Syst.* **1**, N2–3, 143–148.

Ilinski K. and Stepanenko A. (1999) Derivative pricing with virtual arbitrage. Preprint cond-mat/9902046; available at http://xxx.lanl.gov/abs/cond-mat/9902046.

Itzykson C. and Drouffe J.-M. (1994) *Statistical Field Theory*, Vol. 2. Cambridge University Press.

Jackson J. D. (1975) *Classical Electrodynamics*, 2nd edn. New York: Wiley.

Jacobs B. I. (1999) *Capital Ideas and Market Realities*. Oxford: Blackwell.

James J. (1999) Modelling the money market. *Phys. World* **12**(9), 13–15.

Jamshidian F. (1989) *J. Finance* **44**, 205–209.

Junker G. (1996) *Supersymmetric Methods in Quantum and Statistical Physics*. Berlin: Springer-Verlag.

Kalinin G. and Ilinski K. (1999) Exact results for the Salomon brothers model. IPHYS Group Working Paper.

Kestenbaum D. (1999) Death by the numbers. *Science* **283**, 1244–1247.

Kindleberger C. P. (1996) *Manias, Panics and Crashes*, 3rd edn. London: Macmillan.

Kleinert H. (1990) *Path Integrals in Quantum Mechanics, Statistics and Polymer Physics*, Singapore: World Scientific.

Kon S. J. (1984) *J. Finance*, **39**, 147–165.

Kopprasch R., Boyce W., Koenigsberg H., Tatevossian A. and Yampol M. (1987) *Effective Duration and the Pricing of Callable Bonds*. Salomon Brothers.

Kornilovitch P. E. (1998) *Inertia in Brownian motion and the short-time dynamics of an economic index*. Unpublished.

Lakonishok J. and Maberly E. (1990) *J. Finance*, **45**, 231–243.

Lakonishok J. and Shapiro A. C. (1986) *J. Banking Finance*, **10**, 115–132.

LeBaron B., (2000) *J. Econ. Dyn. Control* **24**, 679–702.

Lehmann B. N. and Modest D. M. (1983) *J. Financial Econ.* **21**, 213–254.

LeBaron B., Arthur A. W. and Palmer R. (1999) *J. Econ. Dyn.Control* **23**, 1487–1516.

Leland H. E. (1985) *J. Finance* **40**, 1283–1301.

LeRoy S. F. (1989) *J. Econ. Lit.* **27**, 1583–1621.

Levich R. M. and Thomas L. R. (1993) *J. Int. Money Finance* **12**, 451–474.

Levy M. and Solomon S. (1996a) *Int. J. Mod. Phys.* **C7**, 595–601.

Levy M. and Solomon S. (1996b) *Int. J. Mod. Phys.* **C7**, 745–751.

Levy M., Levy H. and Solomon S. (1994) *Econ. Lett.* **45** 103–111.

Levy M., Levy H. and Solomon S. (1995) *J. Phys. I (Paris)* **5**, 1087–1107.

Levy M., Solomon S. and Ram G. (1996a) *Int. J. Mod. Phys.* **C7**, 65–72.

Levy M., Persky N. and Solomon S. (1996b) *Int. J. High Speed Comput.* **8**, 93–113.

Ley E.(1996) *Am. Statist.* **50**, 311–313.

Lintner J.(1965) *Rev. of Econ. Statist.* **41**, 13–37.

Lo A. W. (1991) *Econometrica* **59**, 1279–1313.

Lo A. W. and MacKinlay A. C. (1988) *Rev. Financial Stud.* **1**, 41–66.

Lo A. W. and MacKinlay A. C. (1999) *A Non–Random Walk Down Wall Street*, Chap. 11. Princeton University Press. Based on MacKinlay A. C. and Ramaswamy K. (1988) *Rev. Financial Stud.* **1**, 137–158.

Loeb T. F. (1983) *Financial Anal. J.* **39**, 41–42.

Luce D. (1959) *Individual Choice Behaviour*. New York: Wesley.

Lumby S. (1994) *Investment Appraisal and Financial Decisions*. London: Chapman & Hall.

Lux T. (1996) *Appl. Econ. Lett.* **3**, 701–706.

Lux T. and Marchesi M. (1999) *Nature* **397**, 498–500.

McFadden D. (1973) Conditional logit analysis of qualitative choice behavior. In: P. Zarembka (ed.) *Frontiers of Econometrics*, New York: Academic Press.

McFadden D. (1976) *Ann. Econ. Soc. Meas.* **5**, 363–390.

McKelvey R. D. and Palfrey T. R., (1995) *Games Econ. Behav.* **10**, 6.

Mack G. (1994) Gauge theory of things alive and universal dynamics. Preprint DESY 94–184; available at http://xxx.lanl.gov/abs/hep-lat/9411059.

Mack G. (1997) Pushing Einstein's Principles to the extreme. In: G. t'Hooft et al (eds), *Quantum Fields and Quantum Time, Cargèse Lectures, 1996*. Plenum Press; also available at http://xxx. lanl.gov/abs/gr-qc/9704034.

Mandelbrot B. (1963) *J. Business*, **36**, 394–419.

Mandelbrot B. (1982) *The Fract. Geometry of Nature*. New York: W. H. Freeman.

Mandelbrot B., van Ness J. W. (1968) *SIAM Rev.* **10**, 422–437.

Mantegna R. N. (1991) *Physica* **A179**, 232–242.

Mantegna R. N. (1998) *Eur. Phys. J.* **B11**, 193–197.

Mantegna R. N. and Stanley H. E. (1994) *Phys. Rev. Lett.* **73**, 2946–2949.

Mantegna R. N. and Stanley H. E. (1995) *Nature* **376**, 46–49.

Mantegna R. N. and Stanley H. E. (1996) *Nature* **383**, 587–588.

Mantegna R. N. and Stanley H. E., (1998) *Physica* **A254**, N 1–2, 77–84.

Marsili M. (1999) *Physica* **A269**, 9–15.

Martin P. C., Siggia E. D. and Rose H. A. (1973) *Phys. Rev.* **A8**, 423–437.

Matacz A. (1997) Financial modelling and option theory with the truncated Levy process. Preprint cond-mat/9710197; available at http://xxx.lanl.gov/abs/cond-mat/9710197.

Mattuck R. D. (1967) *A Guide to Feynman Diagrams in the Many-Body Problem*. New York: McGraw-Hill (reprinted New York: Dover).

Merton R. C. (1973) *Bell J. Econ. Mgmt. Sci.* **4**, 141–183.

Merton R. C. (1976) *J. Financial Econ.* **3**, 124–144.

Mills T. C. (1993) *Appl. Financial Econ.* **3**, 303–306

Miller M., Muthuswame J. and Whaley R. (1994) *J. Finance* **49**, 479–514.

Modest D. M. and Sundaresan M. (1983) *J. Futures Markets* **3**, 15–42.

Moriyasu K. (1983) *An Elementary Primer For Gauge Theory*. Singapore: World Scientific.

Morris G. L. (1995) *Candlestick Charting Explained*. Irwin Professional Publishing.

Mossin J. (1966) *Econometrica* **34**, 768–783.

Müller U. A., Dacorogna M. M., Olsen R. B., Pictet O. V., Schwarz M. and Morgenegg C. C. (1990) *J. Banking Finance* **14**, 1189–1208.

Müller U. A., Dacorogna M. M., Dave R. D., Olsen R. B., Pictet O. V. and von Weizsäcker J. E. (1997) *J. Empir. Finance* **4**, 213–239.

Nakao H., (2000) Multi–scaling properties of truncated Levy flights. Preprint cond-mat/0002027; available at http://xxx.lanl.gov/abs/cond-mat/0002027.

Nison S. (1994) *Beyond Candlesticks*. New York: Wiley.

Osborn M. F. M. (1959) *Oper. Res.* **7**, 145–173.

Otto M. (1998) Using path integrals to price interest rate derivatives. Preprint cond-mat/9812318; available at http://xxx.lanl.gov/abs/cond-mat/9812318; *Eur. Phys. J.* **B14**, 383–394 (2000).

Otto M. (1999) Towards non–equilibrium option pricing theory. Preprint cond-mat/9906196; available at http://xxx.lanl.gov/abs/cond-mat/9906196.

Palmer R. G., Arthur W. B., Holland J. H., LeBaron B. and Tayler P. (1994) *Physica* **D75**, 264–274.

Peters E. E. (1994) *Fractal Market Analysis: Applying Chaos Theory to Investment and Economics*. New York: Wiley.

Piero A. (1994) *Appl. Financial Econ.* **4**, 431–439.

Pietronero L., Tosatti E., Tossati V. and Vespignani A. (1998) Explaining the uneven distribution of numbers in nature. Preprint cond-mat/9808305; available at http://xxx.lanl. gov/abs/cond-mat/9808305.

Platen E. and Schweizer M. (1994) On smile and skewness. Statistics Research Report SRR 027–94; *Math. Finance* **8**, 67–84 (1998).

Plender J. (1999) Out of sight, not out of mind. *Financial Times*, September 20.

Popov V. N. (1983) *Functional Integrals in Quantum Field Theory and Statistical Physics.* Dordrecht: Reidel.

Praetz P. (1972) *J. Business* **45**, 49–55.

Prechter, R. R. Jr. and Frost A. J. (1995) *Elliott Wave Principle Key to Market Behavior.* New Classics Library.

Press W. H., Teukolsky S. A., Vetterling W. T. and Flannery B. P. (1992) *Numerical Recipes in C.* Cambridge University Press.

Pring M. J. (1991) *Technical Analysis Explained.* New York: McGraw-Hill.

Pring M. J. (1993) *Investment Psychology Explained.* New York: Wiley.

Rebonato R. (1996) *Interest-Rate Option Models.* Chichester: Wiley.

Roll R. and Ross S. A. (1980) *J. Finance* **35**, 1073–1103.

Roll R. and Ross S. A. (1984) *J. Finance* **39**, 347–350.

Roosevelt R. B. (1998) *Tech. Anal. Stocks Commodities* **16**(2), 15–17.

Ross S. A. (1976) *J. Econ. Theory* **13**, 334–360.

Rubinstein M. (1983) *J. Finance* **38**, 213–217.

Ryder L. H. (1985) *Quantum Field Theory.* Cambridge University Press.

Samuelson P. A. (1965) *Indust. Mgmt. Rev.* **6**(2), 13–39.

Sargent T. (1993) *Bounded Rationality in Macroeconomics.* Oxford University Press.

Schwarz A. S. (1994) *Topology for Physicists.* Berlin: Springer–Verlag.

Scott L. O. (1987) *J. Financial Quantit. Anal.* **22**, 419–438.

Simon H. (1969) *The Science of the Artificial.* Cambridge, MA: MIT Press.

Shanken J. (1992) *Rev. Financial Stud.* **5**, 1–33.

Sharpe W. F. (1964) *J. Finance* **19**, 425–442.

Sharpe W. F., Alexander G. J. and Baily J. V. (1995) *Investment.* Englewood Cliffs, NJ: Prentice-Hall.

Shiller R. J. (1981) *Am. Econ. Rev.*, **71**, 421–436.

Shiller R. J. (1989) *Market Volatility.* Cambridge: MIT Press.

Shleifer A. and Vishny R. W. (1997) *J. Finance* **52**, 35–55.

Sofianos G. (1990) Index arbitrage profitability. NYSE Working Paper 90–04.

Sofianos G. (1993). *J. Derivatives* **1**.

Sornette D. (1998) *Int. J. Mod. Phys.* **9**, 503–508.

Soros G. (1987) *Alchemy of Finance: Reading the Mind of the Market.* New York: Wiley.

Soros G. (1998) *The Crisis of Global Capitalism: Open Society Endangered.* London: Little, Brown.

Stein E. M. and Stein J. C. (1991) *Rev. Financial Stud.* **4**, 727–752.

Stigler G. J. (1964) *J. Business* **37**, 117–142.

Stix G. (1998) A calculus of risk, *Sci. Am.*, May, 70–75.

Stoll H. R. and Whaley R. E. (1987) *Financial Anal. J.* **43**, 16–28.

Stoll H. R. and Whaley R. E. (1990) *J. Financial Quantit. Anal.* **25**, 441–468.

Stoll H. R. and Whaley R. E. (1990) *J. Financial Quantit. Anal.* **25**, 441–468.

Sundaram R. K. (1997) *J. Derivatives* Fall, 85–98.

Sweeney R. J. (1986) *J. Finance* **41**, 163–182.

Taylor M. (1987) *Economica* **54**, 429–438.

Taylor M. (1989) *Econ. J.* **99**, 376–391.

Taylor M. and Allen H. (1992) *J. Int. Money Finance* **11**, 304–314.

Taylor S. J. (1986) *Modelling Financial Time Series*. Chichester: Wiley.

Theobald M. and Price V. (1984) *J. Finance* **39**, 377–392.

Theobald M. and Yallup P. (1998) *J. Banking Finance* **22**, 221–243.

Theobald M. and Yallup P. (1999) Determining security speed of adjustment coefficients. Birmingham University Business School Working Paper.

Tuckman B. (1995) *Fixed Income Securities: Tools for Today's Markets*. New York: Wiley.

Vasicek O. A. (1977) *J. Financial Econ.* **5**, 177–188.

Vasiliev A. N. (1998) *Functional Methods in Quantum Field Theory and Statistical Physics*. New York: Gordon and Breach Science Publishers.

Wang D. F. (1998) Hedging the risk in the continuous time option pricing model with stochastic volatility. Preprint cond-mat/9807066; available at http://xxx.lanl.gov/abs/cond-mat/9807066.

Weyl H. (1919) *Ann. Physik* **59**, 101–133.

Wiggins J. B. (1987) *J. Financial Econ.* **19**, 351–372.

Wilmott P. (1998) *Derivatives*. Chichester: Wiley.

Yang C.-N. (1977) *Ann. NY Acad. Sci.* **294**, 86.

Yang C.-N. (1980) *Phys. Today*, June, 42–49.

Young K. (1999) *Am. J. Phys.* **67**, 862–868.

Youssefmir M. and Huberman B. A. (1997) *J. Econ. Behaviour Organ.* **32**, 101–118.

Zajdenweber D. (1994) *Rev. d'Econ. Pol.* **104**, 408–434.

Zinn-Justin J. (1993) *Quantum Field Theory and Critical Phenomena*, 2nd edn. Oxford: Clarendon Press.

Zumbach G., Dacorogna M., J. Olsen and R. Olsen (2000) *Risk*, March, 110–114.

Index

Printed and bound by CPI Group (UK) Ltd, Croydon, CR0 4YY

23/04/2025